VIDEOGAMES FOR HUMANS

TWINE AUTHORS IN CONVERSATION

edited by **merritt kopas**

instar books
we publish the darkness
new york • san francisco • new orleans • everywhere

Copyright © 2015 merritt kopas & all respective contributors.

All rights reserved. No part of this publication may be reproduced, distributed, or transmitted in any form or by any means, including photocopying, recording, or other electronic or mechanical methods, without the prior written permission of the publisher, except in the case of brief quotations embodied in critical reviews and certain other noncommercial uses permitted by copyright law.

For permission requests or other ordering information, please contact the publisher through their website:

www.instarbooks.com

Cover and spine art by Michael DeForge
Book design by Jeanne Thornton

Cataloging-in-publication data to be made available through the Library of Congress.

ISBN 978-0-9904528-4-3

Printed by Bookmobile in the United States of America
First Edition
10 9 8 7 6 5 4 3 2 1

TABLE OF CONTENTS

Introduction **by merritt kopas** — 5

How to Read This Book — 20

Rat Chaos **by Winter Lake** — 23
   played by Eva Problems

Fuck That Guy **by Benji Bright** — 33
   played by Riley MacLeod

Anhedonia **by Maddox Pratt** — 45
   played by Emily Short

SABBAT **by Eva Problems** — 57
   played by Imogen Binnie

Horse Master **by Tom McHenry** — 85
   played by Naomi Clark

Nineteen **by Elizabeth Sampat** — 135
   played by Patricia Hernandez

scarfmemory **by Michael Brough** — 143
   played by Anna Anthropy

Removed **by Aevee Bee** — 157
   played by Lydia Neon

for political lovers, a little utopia sketch **by Bryan Reid** — 171
   played by Avery McDaldno

Your Lover Has Turned into a Flock of Birds **by Miranda Simon** — 183
   played by Bryan Reid

Detritus **by Mary Hamilton** — 189
   played by Auriea Harvey

There Ought to Be a Word **by Jeremy Penner** — 217
   played by Austin Walker

Negotiation **by Olivia Vitolo**   235
    played by Katherine Cross

reProgram **by Soha Kareem**   243
    played by Mattie Brice

Mangia **by Nina Freeman**   273
    played by Lana Polansky

Sacrilege **by Cara Ellison**   317
    played by Soha Kareem

And the Robot Horse You Rode In On **by Anna Anthropy**   335
    played by Cat Fitzpatrick

Electro Primitive Girl **by Sloane**   361
    played by Aevee Bee

The Message **by Jeremy Lonien and Dominik Johann**   373
    played by Squinky

Depression Quest **by Zoe Quinn**   383
    played by Toni Pizza

Even Cowgirls Bleed **by Christine Love**   427
    played by Leigh Alexander

3x3x3 **by Kayla Unknown**   443
    played by Cara Ellison

Eden **by Gaming Pixie**   463
    played by Alex Roberts

Eft to Newt **by Michael Joffe**   489
    played by Pippin Barr

Dining Table **by Leon Arnott**   507
    played by Matthew Burns

I'm Fine **by Rokashi Edwards**   517
    played by John Brindle

Player 2 **by Lydia Neon**   553
    played by Elizabeth Sampat

Notes on Contributors   567

Thanks   575

INTRODUCTION
MERRITT KOPAS

1. ME

I've been trying to think of a way to phrase this that won't sound over the top, but I can't. So here it is:

Twine changed my life.

I know, I know. But hear me out.

When I first encountered Twine I was a graduate student in my early twenties. I went into grad school right out of college, which I went into right out of high school. It wasn't totally bad. I liked getting to read so many books, and getting to talk with clever people. But a couple of years in, I was beginning to realize that something wasn't right. Without sitting down and planning on it, I'd been an academic for my entire adult life. I felt trapped, like I'd gotten on a train and drifted off, and now it was speeding along the tracks of my life so fast that I'd never have a chance to disembark.

Listen: I had been dissociating for so much of my life that academia was easy for me, because it let me distance myself from the subjects of my writing. It let me interpose layers of interpretative analysis between myself and my experience. And those layers functioned as protective barriers, keeping me safe from any unfiltered contact with reality. I wrote paper after paper about queerness and bodies, but I wasn't writing about myself, not really—at least, that's what I told myself. I couldn't write about me, because to do that would mean tearing up boarded-off places in memory and really acknowledging what my life had been like up to that point.

And then I discovered Twine.

The first time I ever played a Twine game I was confronted with this text:

> If there's one thing Encyclopedia Fuckme knows - and this is a hypothetical statement, of course, because she's actually got a lot crammed in her big fat brain - it's how to get off! But in addition to her brain, our hero also has a very greedy pussy - one that sometimes leads her into trouble! Such is "the case" today. But if she does what she does best, she just may solve . . .
>
> **THE CASE OF THE VANISHING ENTREE.**

Fuck.

This was 2012, and I hadn't ever seen writing like that in a videogame. I'd grown up with games, but I'd never felt the presence of their authors. Games were, to me, cultural products similar to big-budget films: Obviously there were people involved in their design, but they never came through as individuals. And although by 2012, I was dimly aware of the existence of independent artists who made their presence as individual human beings felt through games, my experience had led me to believe that even those creators were mostly men, telling stories that were maybe interesting but not directly relevant to my life.

And then, this: Anna Anthropy's *Encyclopedia Fuckme*, a game about a clever lesbian with a submissive streak trying to avoid becoming her seductive cannibal date's dinner.

Maybe it's tipping my hand too much to say this game spoke to me, but it did. It was everything I had been led to believe videogames weren't, couldn't be: funny, hot, relevant to my life. And there were more. There were people writing in ways that resonated with me, about things I didn't even know I needed to see written about. I started devouring Twine works wherever I could find them, building up a renewed appreciation for interactive fiction and digital games.

It was a while before I worked up the courage to write my own story in Twine. I was self-conscious, unconfident in my abilities. It was a struggle trying to write something outside of an academic, analytical mode for the first time in years—looking back, even my personal blog posts at the time were intellectualizing. But I fought through it and ended up writing a piece for a partner I was with at the time, a game called *Brace*, meant for two people to play together and about struggle and perseverance against a hostile world. It wouldn't be the last time I used Twine to write a game as a gift for somebody I cared about: Months later, I wrote a game for distant friends on New Year's Eve (*Queer Pirate Plane*) and a short piece mixing personal narrative and sex education for a lover (*Positive Space*).

It was like a floodgate broke. For the next year, Twine was the main outlet through which I processed my emotions, working through personal

Introduction

and political struggles by making something out of them. I made works about family, love, sex, bodies: things I'd never been able to examine directly before. I made a game about difficult talks with my mother; I made a game about childhood abuse; I made a game about consensual sadomasochism.

Hell, I made a game about muffing, an underground sex act popularized through a zine, and it got coverage on mainstream videogame sites.

What was it that made Twine special for me? I think that something in the form of it, its presentation of nodes and links, felt less intimidating than the blank page and blinking cursor of a word processor. Somehow it felt more inviting. It didn't demand, as that blank page seemed to, that I tell a linear story, one that was neat and made sense and contained some kind of resolution. Of course, there's nothing about traditional text that demands any of these things either. But I'd been writing in an analytic mode for so long that I couldn't look at a blank page without my mind struggling to put things in order before I got a single word down. When I opened up Twine, I felt free to just start writing fragments, each in their own passage. The connections could come later.

Most importantly, I was able to share these works with other people like me. Twine brought me into a network of people who made games outside of the mainstream. On Twitter, we made connections, shared techniques, built friendships and informal collaborations.

Late 2012 and early 2013 was an extraordinarily exciting period for me: I started, for the first time, to feel like I was a part of something. The "queer games scene" covered by videogame outlets might not have been as cohesive as some accounts supposed, but for a little under a year, it definitely felt real. We were telling new stories in new ways, stories that were not just unheard of as subjects for videogames—which they certainly were—but rare in any medium. We were writing about messy lives on the economic and social margins of society, about the complexities of embodiment and community, about our grotesque cyberpunk dreams and gay pulp fantasies.

Things fell apart, as they often do in tightly knit, passionate communities of artistic people with few resources—especially when those people are all also friends, lovers, or something in between. But that period was intensely generative, launching a number of authors into visibility and recognition and solidifying the reputations of others. When the burst of activity around Twine during this time ended, it didn't just fizzle out—it left marks on literary and independent videogames communities.

Twine games ended up on college syllabi, technical resources piled up for those wanting to play with variations on the form, and even the relatively small amount of journalistic and critical attention paid to some prominent Twine works raised the profile of the tool to a new level. When Richard Hofmeier—winner of the 2013 Independent Game Festival's grand prize award for his game *Cart Life*—defaced his own booth and replaced his game's demo with Twine author Porpentine's well-received game *Howling Dogs*, it became impossible to ignore the importance of Twine to independent games.

Of course, we shouldn't overstate that importance. A very small number of authors gained visibility during this period, and almost all of them still struggle with material insecurity. Independent videogames is a notoriously competitive field, one in which a very few people do extremely well while everyone else just tries to get by. Twine authors, being on the margins of an already marginal field, struggle to do even that. The mainstream videogame industry prides itself on being on the cutting edge of technology, for better or for worse. And as Twine work generally doesn't involve high-definition graphics or immersive three-dimensional worlds, Twine authors continue to find themselves defined out of videogames and denied coverage or critical attention in favor of more graphically appealing or lucrative works, while mainstream videogames are just beginning to develop richer narrative techniques and are receiving heaps of praise and money for it.

This is what an artistic revolution looks like: some people get a little famous, nobody gets rich, and years later, people who have more resources than you steal your ideas and use them to get richer and more famous than they already were.

But the thing about artistic revolutions is that people keep working long after the mainstream has moved on to its next fascination. It's 2015, years out from the "Twine revolution," and people continue to produce powerful, unique works with the tool.

And ultimately, Twine's importance goes beyond the work produced by the most visible, recognized creators. Twine showed me that people who weren't interested in becoming "game developers" or "game designers" themselves could use games to tell important, personal stories.

Once I started using the tool, it wasn't long before I started running Twine workshops at schools, conferences, and community spaces. Most memorably, I co-ran a Twine workshop with Anna Anthropy at the Allied Media Conference in Detroit in 2013. The participants included an elderly local man and a mother with her toddler daughter, each of them excited to use the medium to tell their stories in a new way. As Ian Bogost describes in his book *How to Do Things with Videogames*, we're approaching a reality in which people like our workshop participants can use videogames in the same way as they might use a digital camera. We're not quite there yet, but it's exciting to see the form enlarging and expanding, shifting away from a specialized media produced by and for a narrow audience and toward a range of new shapes and contexts.

It's been a huge privilege to be a part of that. In 2012, I was a depressed, impoverished academic. Writing this, in early 2015, I'm still not exactly well-off, and I wouldn't say I'm the most mentally or emotionally well person around, but I have work I'm proud of and networks of friends and colleagues I've met through making it. I've ended up in a place I couldn't imagine I might when I sat down and played that first Twine game a little over two years ago.

Introduction

But this book isn't about me, not really.

2. TWINE

Okay. So what is Twine? For most people, the easiest parallel is to Choose Your Own Adventure books. You know, those books that were popular in the 80s and 90s that presented you with some kind of fantastical narrative along with a list of choices. Like, you're confronted with a weird potion: If you'd like to drink it, turn to page 60; if that sounds like a terrible decision, turn to page 251. These branching narratives were a neat mutation of the textual form of the book, though they mostly remained marginal in literature and were generally marketed only to young readers.

Twine is kind of like that, in that it's a tool you can use to create branching narratives. More broadly, it's a tool for creating hypertexts, collections of passages joined by links. A typical Twine story looks like a textual webpage, and the player generally advances through it by clicking textual hyperlinks. This is one of the great attractions of Twine: playing a Twine game draws on familiar skills. Unlike contemporary videogames, which require the player to navigate bewildering fictional three-dimensional spaces and complicated control schemes, anyone who can navigate a webpage can play a Twine game.

Because of that use of familiar skills, the games produced with Twine are at root far more accessible than most contemporary videogames (though I'll have more to say on this later). As a tool, Twine is more accessible than most game design environments too. Interestingly, this accessibility is partly because Twine's development environment isn't strictly textual. Whereas traditional game design requires the designer to be able to write and understand lines of purely textual code and to visualize the in-game results, Twine's development environment presents the prospective designer with only two core elements: passages and links. To create a passage, it's only necessary to write it, and then any text within the passage can be turned into a link. These passages can be dragged and shifted around the screen, with links between passages represented by arrows, creating a kind of flowchart. Thus it's easy to track branching paths as you build by following the trail of arrows through the narrative. You don't really need to understand the logic of code to make something in Twine, but at the same time, Twine's logical flowchart environment makes it easy to pick up the basic principles that make up more complex structures of code.

Finally, since its creation by Chris Klimas in 2009, Twine has been free for anyone to use and modify, whereas many other game development tools require potential designers to purchase licenses running in the hundreds of dollars.

Twine started as a desktop application. In 2014, Chris Klimas and Leon Arnott released Twine 2 as both a desktop and web application. Crucially, though, Twine 2 continues the original's ideals of accessibility and user control. All user work is still saved locally on user computers, so there's no dependence on centralized servers or services. In the context of this period in which tool creators such as Adobe and Google are shifting to subscription-based models with the purpose of getting users invested in their "ecosystems" and thus fostering dependent relations between tool users and developers, Klimas and Arnott's commitment to user control is more important than ever.

Twine's financial and technical accessibility are major reasons for its broad adoption, especially among economically marginalized, nontraditional game designers—i.e., people who are not white men with college-level programming training. As a result, Twine has been the site of an incredible artistic flourishing at the intersections of digital games and fiction: a rebirth of hypertext. People who might never otherwise make a videogame make them with Twine. Some of these people have taken the skills they develop in using Twine and branch out to other forms and media; others have delved deeper into Twine itself and done things with it that nobody expected; and still others use it to make games that tell stories without the intention of becoming a professional artist or designer, just as one might write a poem or take a photo without needing or wanting extensive training in either of those skills. Authors can use Twine to create choose your own adventure stories, or interactive poetry, or nonlinear essays, or anything composed of sections of text and connections between them. Theoretically, authors could also use a word processor or pen and paper to create those texts. But there's a key difference between traditional writing tools and Twine: Twine simplifies the process of creating digital texts rather than analog ones, and it includes tools that allow Twine authors to conceal the rules and structure of their works from the reader. For example: In a choose-your-own-adventure book, the reader can page through to find the various endings or skip ahead to other segments, and the reader often has to keep track of states relevant to the game (how many weird potions she's carrying, for instance.) Twine keeps track of these states as the author directs, and it doesn't necessarily tell the reader it's doing so. Thus Twine games are often opaque, only revealing their full shapes to the player over the course of the narrative and sometimes not entirely at all.

Actually, this is one of the interesting things about digital games versus analog games as a whole. Think about a board game or a physical sport: You and the other players (or referees) are responsible for keeping the rules. But in the case of a digital game, the author dictates the rules through code, and the computer then enforces those rules while you're playing. You don't have to imagine or keep track of how far Pac-Man moves per second or what happens when a line of Tetris pieces forms; the game constantly tracks

Introduction

these things for you and tells you what happens as a result of your actions. And the game can track them without you even knowing it's happening, so there's the potential for surprise.[1]

Thus Twine readers/players can experience a narrative in a way that would be difficult or impossible to reproduce on paper. Twine games can track how long we've lingered on particular decisions, remember the decisions we've made, and shift the later narrative accordingly without our necessarily being able to perceive a direct connection between our actions and the results. Take a game like Gaming Pixie's *Eden*, which mixes random events, player decisions, and tests of reaction time to create a feeling of urgency and risk, or Tom McHenry's *Horse Master*, which openly tracks a number of statistics for the player while also secretly managing others that affect the course of the narrative in the background.

But the possibilities go beyond digital ruleskeeping, allowing Twine works to go beyond a simple emulation of paper-based texts. In Michael Brough's *scarfmemory*, for example, hyperlinks function as parentheticals, unfolding diversions and side notes in the narrator's internal monologue, adding to, revising, and complicating his recollections as the narrative progresses, turning the experience of reading the game into one that spirals inward rather than moves forward.

In Bryan Reid's *for political lovers, a little utopia sketch*, clicking on links cycles the text through a series of possibilities—occupations, places, dreams—that reflect the hopeful tone of the work. Clicking the verbs in certain sentences cycles them through a dreamy set of options: translating, training dogs, becoming an astronomer, growing vegetables, building houses, and on and on.

Finally, in Christine Love's *Even Cowgirls Bleed*, the cursor itself becomes the crosshair of the player character's touchy gun. The player has to carefully navigate the cursor around the screen—learning the first time that she mouses over a link that her gun will go off at the object or person the link names, whether she wants it to or not. This transforms the usually relaxed, almost thoughtless activity of pointing and clicking a mouse into a deliberate, careful physical interaction with the text of the story.

To put it simply: Authors are doing things with Twine that aren't possible with traditional text. And at the same time, they're using interactive media to tell stories that mainstream videogames couldn't dream of telling. Thus far, this double innovation has made Twine hard to classify, which has left it without a home or much support from either literary or videogame communities. This book is an effort to change that.

---

1   For more discussion of this "digital ruleskeeper" concept, see Anna Anthropy's *Rise of the Videogame Zinesters* (Seven Stories Press, 2012).

3. THIS BOOK

Twine is unique because it is at once a medium, form, and community. People use it to do wildly different things, and individual creators may never come in contact with one another. Yet we can still trace connections between their work.

This is a book about that work, as well as the communities, networks, and individual authors that have developed around Twine. It's about putting them into conversation with one another and with more established literary communities, because the works that they're creating are exciting, experimental, and worthy of sustained consideration. By finding stories we can tell about those works and those people, we can provide that consideration.

For example: Many of the figures who have risen to prominence in Twine circles are trans women. That trans women are recognized as the leaders of an artistic scene is a fact worth appreciating in its own right. But these authors' recognition should also be considered in the context of the emergence of new transgender literatures in the early 2010s, as represented by books like Imogen Binnie's *Nevada* and Casey Plett's *A Safe Girl to Love*. These texts are the result of trans people wresting their stories back from non-trans publishers and audiences, telling stories about themselves for other trans people. The work being done by trans women authors in Twine needs to be seen as a part of this movement, and is just one example of how critical work is emerging in Twine communities in parallel with broader literary developments.

What other kinds of stories can we tell about Twine?

There's the story of Twine as the focal point for the "personal games" movement of 2012-2013, catalyzed by Anna Anthropy's critical text *Rise of the Videogame Zinesters*. This story's been told before in different ways, positioning Twine as a truly accessible tool, the focal point for the growth of a community and the rise of a number of nontraditional authors in games. But there are elements of the story that people have left out, including the rapid pushback by traditional gamers and Twine's relegation to marginalized status both because of the intrinsic accessibility traditional gamers saw it as representing and because of its cultural association with nontraditional authors.

We could tell the story of the mostly invisible labor that's gone into the design and modification of the tool, the support work that's enabled the creation of all of the works that appear in this book. That story hasn't really been told yet, but it's an important one. We tend to privilege people who create flashy, visible products over those who do the work that enables that production. Support work is invisibilized, feminized labor, and there's a rich story to be told about the work that's gone into making Twine into what it is today. (Leon Arnott is our fairy godmother.)

Introduction

Finally, we could tell the story of Twine as the rebirth of hypertext after its decline in the 90s, as well as the repopularization of interactive fiction after its relegation to mostly niche status. Interactive fiction has always had rich, dedicated communities, but parser-based interactive fiction shrank in popularity in the 1980s, after it became cheap and easy to generate digital graphics. Twine represents a broader resurgence of interest in interactive fiction, and it's indirectly led to the development of other tools for producing this kind of work.

We could have told any of these singular stories about Twine—as phenomenon, as platform, as medium. But in putting this book together, it didn't feel right to pick any one of them. Instead, we wanted to tell a number of stories by showcasing the actual works people have created with the tool—and the reactions actual people have had to those works.

Here's the thing, though: Twine's been used by a lot of people to make a lot of work. Go to Twinery.org and scroll through the lists of games: There are hundreds, maybe thousands. Some of these are by prolific writers whose names are well known, whereas others are made by people who gave the tool a shot and might never touch it again. The collective output of Twine users represents a bewildering spread of stories, kinds of authors, and approaches.

By necessity, then, any collection of Twine works is going to be partial. So how did I select the works that appear here?

Most of all, I wanted a wide range: of authors, content, and forms. The works in this book include interactive poetry, traditional choose-your-own-adventure games, therapeutic experiences, personal essays, and elaborate jokes. And their authors are similarly varied: Most don't fit into the traditional game designer profile of a straight, white man (though there are some of those, too).

Finally, the subjects of these games cover topics that mainstream games have still, in 2015, hardly touched. Partly, this speaks to the freedom afforded individual artists who aren't working to create a multi-million dollar product in the context of the massive entertainment industry of contemporary videogames. But partly, I think it also speaks to the ways that the medium of interactive fiction is suited to exploring themes that graphical games—for all their high-definition visuals and incredible technology—still have trouble with.

For instance, digital games have a hard time with sexuality. Maybe it's hard for designers to translate physical intimacy into a medium that's historically been mainly concerned with competition, or maybe it's an issue with the technical challenge of graphically depicting living bodies in a way that doesn't look comical or grotesque. Regardless, narrative text-based games are uniquely positioned to explore sex in a way that many larger-scale graphical games can't. Games like Benji Bright's *Fuck That Guy*, Olivia Vitolo's *Negotiation*, Cara Ellison's *Sacrilege*, Soha Kareem's *reProgram*, and Gaming Pixie's *Eden* get into themes of consent, sexual identity, and cruising, whereas mainstream videogames have only recently gotten past the inclusion of monogamous same-sex partnerships.

More generally, a lot of the work in this book challenges digital games' traditional elision of the body and emotions. Whereas in most mainstream games, protagonists have unfailing, untiring machine bodies and exhibit little to no emotional expression, the characters and roles in the games in this book have physical and psychic weight. Twine has occasionally been mocked for the number of games about physical or mental ailments that it's been used to produce. But these works exist in the context of a medium that historically hasn't made any space for explorations of weakness, hurt, or struggle. And far from being simple excursions in empathy tourism, many Twine games use interactivity to explore complex issues around embodiment and affect in wildly divergent ways.

Consider *Depression Quest* and *Anhedonia*, two games about the experience of depression. The former presents the player with a very systemic interface, one familiar to anyone with experience playing any kind of simulation game, in order to show the slow grind of mental illness, the way it keeps so many options just out of reach. *Anhedonia*, on the other hand, has links that behave in erratic and unpredictable ways, keeping the reader off balance. These two works use their interactive elements to tell very different stories about similar experiences of physical and mental distress.

Conversely, some works in Twine embrace the videogame logic of the power fantasy in order to subvert it. In Eva Problems's *SABBAT*, players invoke dark magic to transform themselves into badass demons. This might be the beginning of any typical videogame, except that from there the player goes on to have abortive sex with a witch, smoke magically enhanced weed, and instigate the overthrow of patriarchal capitalism. It's definitely a power fantasy, but an extremely unusual one, a fantasy of escape for those with antagonistic relationships toward their bodies—those who can feel something strange moving within them, waiting to be called into the world by just the right ritual. (To me it's totally a trans narrative too, but in a way that isn't necessarily obvious to non-trans audiences.)

Similarly, Aevee Bee's *Removed* uses imagery associated with conventional roleplaying games—hit points, turn-based combat, and so on—to tell a story about forms of power found in unusual places. In Sloane's *Electro Primitive Girl*, the trappings of the giant robot genre of manga become a vehicle to talk about femininity and strength. And in Winter Lake's *Rat Chaos*, the feeling of control and heroism produced by so many games is both harnessed and undermined in order to invoke a feeling of illusory power that ultimately must give way to uncertainty and the messiness of reality.

Finally, a number of Twine games aren't about dark magic or struggling with catastrophic psychological maladies or hooking up with the sexual partner of your dreams. They're about mundane experiences of daily life, the kinds of issues that have been widely considered "too boring" to be portrayed in mainstream games.

Introduction

In Michael Brough's *scarfmemory*, the quiet English designer best known for his mechanically complex puzzle games expresses his grief over the loss of a treasured, self-knitted scarf. Even working in text, Brough's attention to the mechanics of play comes through to convey an everyday, personal experience of loss.

Similarly, Mary Hamilton's *Detritus* confronts us with the challenge of leaving and thus, leaving behind. Over a successive series of moves, the player has to decide what to keep and what to abandon. What objects do we invest with meaning? How do we pare down our lives again and again?

Finally, Jeremy Penner's *There Ought to Be a Word* explores the experience of dating during a separation from one's partner. As a piece about the complicated snarl of feelings that arise when a long-term relationship ends—even on the best of terms—it's a resonant, generous work about being a father that stands in stark contrast to mainstream games' recent clumsy, patriarchy-steeped attempts to put fathers in protagonist roles.

To be fair, mainstream videogames are more and more often attempting to deal with challenges other than violent ones, pains that aren't physical, goals that aren't acquisitive. But those projects are necessarily beholden to shareholders, making them subject to conservative convention and to the industry's ongoing desire to cater to young white men in the most reductive, shameful ways possible.

To see what's really exciting in videogames, we have to look to the fringes. From personal experiences of mental illness, to contracting with dark powers, to cruising at gay bars, to the adventures of space banditas in the far future and the experience of being a pregnant mermaid, the games in this book should be refreshing to anyone interested in the potential of interactive narrative but tired of games about grim antiheroes and Tolkien-obsessed fantasy settings.

◆

I feel like it's important to note that I don't see this book as a "best of" Twine thus far, or as perfectly "representative" of the work being created with the tool. It felt simultaneously thrilling and overwhelming to build a list of games and then cull it down to a few dozen, and I tried my best to strike a balance between prolific writers and relative unknowns, between works that had touched me personally and those that had made an obvious impact on broader communities. And I tried to avoid too much of a temporal bias by including both older and more recent pieces. Unfortunately, of course, authors rudely continue to write while anthologies are being printed, and so nothing more recent than the fall of 2014 made it in.

Thus, instead of an exemplary or representative sample, I see this book as a dip into a river at a particular moment in time, gathering up some of the strange and unfamiliar things drifting past in hopes of inspiring others to do the same. If this book inspires further critical consideration of Twine, including more anthologies with their own editors who have their own editorial preferences, then I'll be overjoyed.

◆

Choosing which works to include was hard enough. But then there's another question: how do you anthologize interactive fiction? Collecting the works on their own felt unsatisfying, and trying to literally reproduce them as physical choose-your-own-adventure books, while potentially an interesting commentary on the difference between those forms, seemed like a pointless exercise. So what could a book format add?

Jeanne Thornton suggested that we print playthroughs of each work, drawing on the tradition of annotated literature to produce a book that would be comprised of a series of conversations between games and players. Initially, we thought about printing this commentary in the margins, as annotations. But late in the process, we decided on printing single-column, with commentary following each passage. This format means that the book reads less as a linear collection of hypertext works with some added notes and more as a true series of dialogues between the works and their selected readers.

In choosing those readers for the book, I tried to pick people who I thought might have interesting things to say about a particular piece, who might have a personal connection to it, or who I thought might be fruitfully challenged by it. There's significant overlap between the list of authors who contributed games and those who contributed playthroughs, and that's by design. Twine communities are critically as well as creatively vibrant, with many authors generating insightful critique and analysis of each other's work, and although Twine works are certainly worthy of consideration by more traditional literary critics, we didn't want to set up a dynamic by which all the works in this book were up for judgment.

Still, in some cases I wanted to bring in readers who aren't involved in Twine communities themselves, but who I thought might have interesting perspectives. What would it be like to play through Eva Problems's *SABBAT*—a work that approaches themes of trans experience in a totally unexpected way—with Imogen Binnie, an traditional literary fiction author who writes trans stories like *Nevada*? What might Leigh Alexander, one of the most insightful games critics writing today, have to say about Christine Love's *Even Cowgirls Bleed*?

Admittedly, this was kind of an experiment—I wasn't entirely sure what to expect when I assigned readers their works. But what I got back astonished me. The playthroughs recorded in this book not only give Twine games the critical attention they deserve, but share broader insights about interactive fiction, digital games, and storytelling.

Introduction

    For example, in his reading of *Fuck that Guy*, Benji Bright's game about gay casual sex, Riley MacLeod draws out connections between gay men's tech-enabled hookups and the iterative, repeatable nature of interactive fiction. Just as interactive fiction allures with the promise of taking another path to see what might have been, apps like Scruff and Grindr continually present the promise of someone new -- another chance, another possibility.

    Other readers chose to dive deep into the inner workings of their subjects. As Naomi Clark plays Tom McHenry's *Horse Master*, she admits: "I have flayed this game to its bones, I have read the code." In doing so, she shows us the technical workings of the piece, providing a deeper understanding of the game than most players might typically glean. Nontechnical readers might wonder at the value of this kind of exercise, but given the ways in which all videogames are capable of hiding their rules from the player, this kind of deep reading of the code is as valuable as a technical analysis of the prose that makes up the game as the player experiences it, just as understanding the mechanics of syntax and rhythm gives us new ways to examine poetry.

    And other readers still chart out the personal and artistic relationships between themselves and creators. Far from being signs of "corrupt" or insular design circles, as some conspiracy theorists would have it, these relations are critical to the development of any artistic community. In her reading of Aevee Bee's *Removed*, for example, Lydia Neon intertwines conversations about the messiness of memory and authorial intent with notes on her own relationship to the author. At one point, she actually texts Aevee, asking if one of the characters in the work is meant to be her. These kinds of relationships don't jeopardize some fabled notion of "critical distance"—they're evidence of generative links between authors that make up the broader communities this book is about.

    To me, the conversational format of these "readings" suggests the feeling of sitting next to the player and listening to them talk about the work they're engaging with as they move through it. Some of these reflections are deeply personal, while others focus on the technical qualities of the work. (And given the diversity of approaches, some readings will inevitably appeal more to some readers than others.) In each case, though, the conversation between game and player feels greater than the sum of its parts.

4. THE FUTURE

I'm beyond thrilled that this book has come together; I think it's well past due. But I don't want *Videogames for Humans* to be seen as the capstone of the "Twine revolution," a kind of historical record of some interesting work done in the early 2010s. Because really, in so many ways, this is still a beginning.

First, I hope this book kicks off more communication and crossover between fringe game design and literary communities. Above, I gave the example of the need for conversation between the parallel work being done by trans authors in Twine and in traditional fiction, but I think there's a more general need here too. Twine is marginalized within games circles for not fitting into the dominant shape of videogames—which means that Twine needs to build bridges to other creative communities. And literary and artistic circles, too, could benefit from taking a closer look at Twine and the exciting artists and authors who are finding their voice with it.

Second, I want to challenge the notion that the current state of Twine represents some kind of final achievement of diversity in digital games. Yes, it's fantastic that through Twine, we have more and more games by nontraditional game designers. But it would be a mistake to think that the relative success of Twine means that problems of power have been solved. For one, the status of queers, women, people of color, and people with disabilities in games is still tenuous. Few of these authors are accorded the respect, attention, or monetary success of their white male counterparts, even within alternative games communities, and publicly working in digital games is still an intensely precarious position for women, people of color, queers, and people with disabilities.

And while we should rightly celebrate the achievements of women and queers in this hostile space, I want to be real about the fact that we've been not nearly as proactive as we should about attending to issues of white supremacy. The people whose work the community holds up may be women—and often poor, gay, trans women, at that—but those female authors are still overwhelmingly white. There are people of color doing work in Twine, but they're systematically kept out of the spotlight. I've made an attempt to resist that dynamic in this collection, but it would be naive to believe that this book existed outside of the context of systemic racism.

To put it bluntly, this ongoing exclusion is bullshit, and if we're serious about building radical alternatives to mainstream videogames, to building more inclusive spaces, then we absolutely have to pay more attention to the ways that white supremacy manifests even in our supposedly more progressive communities. We need to constantly remind ourselves and others that so long as the women who are successful and visible as authors or designers are mostly white, we're not doing well enough.

Finally, I see this book as a step towards more human forms of digital play. I mean, I did call it "Videogames for Humans."[2] Twine isn't the only or

---

[2] Of course, naming a book *Videogames for Humans* carries with it some dangers. Namely, that we mistake the progress we've made toward democratizing games with the arrival of a perfect, ideally "human" state of affairs. That's obviously not the case.

Introduction

best route there, but it is an especially inviting one.

So what do more human forms of digital play look like?

They look like a move away from "the industry," from modes of production that rely on exploited labor and that perpetuate the technological fetishism of cutting edge, "hyperrealistic" graphics and "immersive" worlds in which we are meant to lose ourselves.

They look like games by and about more kinds of people, games not just about marginalized experiences, but created by and for people who historically haven't seen themselves in games and who have been denied access to them as a creative medium.

They look like games with a wider range of purposes, games that aren't about collecting or shooting or managing or accomplishing, but that are about communicating, interacting, resting, healing, and growing.

They look like experiences that use the unique features of videogames to connect people, rather than to isolate us from one another.

They look like games that are short, small, and generous with the player's time, that don't want to consume the player, but that invite them into playful engagement.

And they look like games that are positive escapes rather than negative ones, experiences that help us to imagine better worlds rather than simply providing temporary reprieve from the one we live in.

This book is one step toward all of that. Other steps are happening all the time, and I hope this anthology sparks many more anthologies in its wake.

This is *a* book about Twine. But let's not let it be *the* book, yeah?

In ways, Twine (and all text-based media) carries with it some exclusions that other forms of digital games don't. You don't really need to be able to read English to play *Super Mario Brothers* or *Pac-Man*, but every one of the works in this book was originally produced in that language. (Some thankless volunteers like David T. Marchand have translated some of the more popular Twine works into other languages, but most remain English-only.) This emphasis on text can also inadvertently exclude people with disorders like dyslexia. An added complication is that while a reader can check the page count of a book or the length of a poem as a gauge on how long the experience will be, many Twine games don't provide any sort of time estimate, or even rely on this unfolding quality, the ability to conceal the full contours of the work. This is definitely one of the interesting features of the form, but it can also cause problems for readers who would like to have some sense of what it is that they're getting into.

Thus in calling this book *Videogames for Humans*, my goal wasn't to imply that we're there, that we're good.

HOW TO READ THIS BOOK

In each playthrough, we indicate the author's path through the work by printing the link that led them to the next passage as such:

> \> take boat

(If you're familiar with interactive fiction, you might recognize this as a convention associated with parser-based works, where the user has to type each of their actions into a blinking command line, and the computer then parses them. The sometimes strained relationship between traditional interactive fiction communities who favor parser-based works and the authors creating hyperlink-based works in Twine makes this adoption of parser convention kind of amusing to me, but I think it works.)

Occasionally the player is asked to click something that isn't a text link, or to repeatedly click the same link. This is shown by this convention:

> \>

Several Twine games require the player to retrace her steps, revisiting the same textual space multiple times. In order to avoid repeating a great deal of game text, we simply show the narrative choices directly without the intervening text, as follows:

> \> Back
> \> Status screen
> \> Got it
> \> Reflect on afternoon

Very occasionally, players will cancel their choices altogether in order to show parallel routes that may be impossible to achieve on one playthrough. We show this as:

> \> Left

How to Read This Book

> Forward
> ~~Forward~~
> ~~Left~~
> Right

Any other variations are hopefully obvious from context.

RAT CHAOS
BY WINTER LAKE
PLAYED BY EVA PROBLEMS

Two years ago, in the summer of 2012, I wasn't even a girl yet. I was living in a nice old apartment with my girlfriend at the time, I had a job, I was in between school semesters, I did things with friends. Life was good just often enough that I could tell myself it was working. Life was bad just often enough that it didn't completely fall apart for a while.

Summer was a good time, though. We would all get together at the apartment for some tabletops every other week or so and shoot the shit when we were done. One of these weeks, while everyone was hanging out, I checked Winter Lake's site to see if maybe *monster killers* was going to come off hiatus. I had followed her work since the start of *demon planet*, ages ago, and I always recommended it to my friends, but it never seemed to grip them like it did me. I couldn't really explain why it was so important and so influential to me.

Well, *monster killers* was dead and wasn't coming back anytime soon, but there was something else there.

"RAT CHAOS"

Rat Chaos by Winter Lake

This hallways looks very clean. Here's the android sweeper does its job polish the white tile. Closer inspection, you seeing it's clear plastic on top the white tile. Well, the red music coming out down the hall with a balmy scent breeze like bath oils, relaxation steam, lotion drinks, jelly pool. How long you been on this space station, long enough lol. Well, you found some good planets today, chicken dinner waiting back in your Quarters.

Return to Quarters.

Unleash Rat Chaos.

The elegant Sugarcane theme, so familiar now, was something strange and exotic. I had never seen a Twine before. But there was her art, seemingly crude, effortless, unconcerned with proper anatomy or perspective, but compelling, dynamic, and surely the product of considerable labor, and there was her writing, purposefully stilted, jarring, distant but charming like a bad translation of some obscure third party RPG for some forgotten console, and it welcomed me into this new format. I started reading, briefly, then stopped, told everyone about it, started over, started reading it out loud.

This isn't that playthrough, but I'll show you what I read. I'll show you *rat chaos.*

> unleash rat chaos

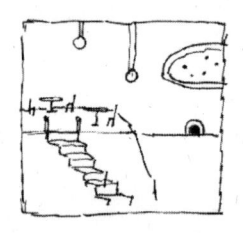

The vast, cold dining hall is filled with chattering species who scrape their forks on metal discs and spread the word of Gossip: that Captain chose to unleash Rat Chaos.

Now they're drinking all their juice up, well, who can blame them.

The way they designed this, you climb up the big trapezoid and the tables are up there. That's where you sit when you eat. Then the big yellow cylinders are the trash, and you have to throw out your trash and put the tray away by yourself.

Enter the White Corridor

Unleash more Rat Chaos

played by Eva Problems

    This is such a good passage. I'm probably gonna be saying that a lot. The fact that she's established the setting as this vague and surreal space station going out and looking for new planets, and you're the captain, and there are countless fantastic species never before imagined under your command, and what Winter chooses to show you out of all of this are the specific dreary mechanics of what you would do in the dining hall when you came in to get a meal. That's such a good joke, and when you're feeling like shit but you don't know why because everything around you is fine and wonderful, that's poignant as hell.

    Let's back off a little from rat chaos for a bit. What happens when you don't unleash rat chaos is just as important and illuminating, in its own way, as what happens when you do.

> Enter the White Corridor

Down the White Corridor in your little golf kart. It suddenly overturns, pinning you under its weight, but wait, the fun balloons burst. The entire cockpit is rapidly filling with water. You remember your training and refuse to breathe it, taking in gulps of air instead, but the air is disappearing because the cockpit is filling with water. The flare gun in your pocket is now damp and useless. The book of matches becomes damp and useless. The revolver is soaked with water (uesless.) Your vintage magazines have been ruined. Your hair and skin have become damp and useless.

I discarded all the useless items for you.

flooded cockpit

    Her jokes are so bleak and so good and I love them. I don't want to focus on the humor too much, though. It's a big part of what makes her stuff so enjoyable, but it's not the only thing that makes it good, and no one should have to be relegated to just "the funny one." That kills you.

    I'll say that the humor is great because of where it comes from and who it's meant for and what it says about things we've gone through when we're feeling crushed and fucked up and like we can't even move. We try to repeat things just because it worked once and it might work again, but it's too different, or you can't get it right, or you've burned out on it. We try to get help but the structure that help comes in is all wrong and does more harm than good before you can even stop it.

> flooded cockpit

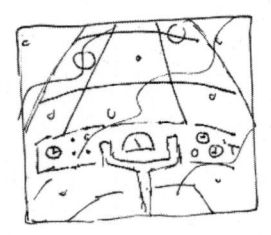

You are drowning. You must exit the cockpit within 2 minutes, but which exit?

Swim North to the Grand Ballroom, its entry doors blocked by collapsed marble statuary.

Swim East to the Kitchen, guarded by Riddling Hydra.

Swim Southwest to Haunted Cemetery.

Swim West to Jungle Chaos.

Well, we fucked up this time. It's a pretty fatalistic Twine sometimes. It gives you plenty of options but they just end up leading to the same place. It's great.

> Jungle Chaos

Buddy, this isn't "Jungle Chaos," this is *Rat Chaos*. If you think Jungle Chaos is gonna save you here, it won't.

YOU DROWNED

However, the fairies have turned you into a water-baby.

GOOD END

played by Eva Problems

RANK: S

Nice.

    For the characters in the Twine, nebulous as they are, it's better to stick to routine, to avoid introspection, to avoid change. It lets them tell themselves they got the good end without actually growing in any way. Where does it leave us as the readers, the players? Well, pretty good in a way because it's still enjoyable, but that's beside the point. Let's go back to when we first unleashed Rat Chaos.

    This time, we're gonna do things differently. This is *Rat Chaos*, and by god, we are going to unleash as much Rat Chaos as physically possible.

    > Unleash more Rat Chaos

"Yes...yes, Captain, can you hear me....but no...you are no Space Ship Captain...Computer User, I know your soul. I know about it. How you managed to unleash this much Rat Chaos...I can not guess. But we get ahead of our selfs. First, the formal introductions. I am New Rat City, Avatar of Rats. And your name? (SAY NAME OUT LOUD)

...aaaah, what an interesting name. Well, [YOUR NAME,] you are ready for more responsibility. Journey with me to Planet of Rat."

O.K.

Sure.

Sounds good.

I want to do it.

Take me to Planet of Rat.

I have always wanted to do this.

O.K.

Only you can take me there.

but you're a rat

Rat Chaos by Winter Lake

O.K.

I love New Rat City. This page was a delight to read out loud to my friends back in that summer.

I'm ready for the Planet of Rat. Are you ready?

> I have always wanted to do this

New Rat City needs a lot of love. Help New Rat City with his needs.

"I'm getting lots of exercise."
"I would like you to construct a large, pink cube."
"I feel fucking miserable."

Feed NRC a pellet
Construct large, pink cube
"Do you need to talk?"

With this adoption of a new layer of video game artifice, we are poised on the precipice of shit getting real. We could tend to NRC's immediate physical needs, certainly, and maybe NRC would think everything was great. Maybe we'd be great. Maybe we could keep grinding away in awful trajectories because they hadn't killed us yet and probably wouldn't for a while if we kept our basic needs met.

We're not going to do that, though. I needed to talk but didn't know how on that summer afternoon in the living room with my friends. I didn't know what I would even talk about. There was still some distance inside me that felt the need to retreat onto my computer in the midst of familiar company, the only difference was that time I found something there I wanted to share.

> "Do you need to talk?"

played by Eva Problems

"I feel like I make everyone uncomfortable. I feel like I'm making you uncomfortable right now. I look at people the wrong way. I react the wrong way. I'm never myself. I get nervous and then I'm being puppeteered by this awful thing. My face freezes up. I can track back to when I was 12? 13? That was a conscious choice, I would try to just stop emoting. If I laughed, if I smiled, it was a sign of weakness. I was used to being attacked. Not physically, after a while, just emotionally. It's almost better the other way, when you're small, when some kid has a problem and they try to beat your ass, so you beat them back, harder. Then you get punished. They punish both of you, because they're cowards. Those kids wise up, they realize they don't have to go through all that. They just call you a faggot, and they watch what happens when that hits you, completes a circuit with the awareness inside that there are people called faggots, and you know who they are, and you know you're one of them, and these guys must be able to tell somehow. No Internet to read, no one to talk to, the entire universe is you and your parents and the TV and the Nintendo."

Ride dune buggy to:

PARTS DEPOT

CATHEDRAL CONSTRUCTION

    I didn't have it this bad. I lucked out in a lot of ways and I continue to luck out, and I try to enjoy that as much as I can and keep the feeling like consequences will catch up to me to a minimum. But even at the time, enough of this page resonated with me that this was hard to read.

    Sometimes when you're writing something and just want to get it all out you realize you're getting too vulnerable. Sometimes you back off, sometimes you keep going, sometimes you throw in a little winking thing for plausible deniability, or like a tether to the distance you're used to. Sometimes you need that.

    > PARTS DEPOT

"So I hated myself, created this second self to exist in my place. He wanted shitty, unhealthy things. He was just trying to execute his cultural program. He was an android. The people who knew him think I'm being too harsh, or that I'm overreacting. They don't know what it was like. This thing with my face trying to live my life for me. My real self like this tiny fetal entity, incapable of growing. It wasn't just because of teasing, you could guess as much. When areas of your mind are radioactive zones you have to stay out of, it's impossible to build an identity."

You have 8000 gold

SOLAR SHIELD : "It didn't help that I was chronically physically ill,"

FUSION PAK : "felt disgusting, hated my body to the point that I didn't want to leave the house,"

GHOST FOOD : "and stayed this way well into my 20s."

I think my voice broke reading this one. That would be a good story, even if it might not be true. The mask was probably a little too secure, but this gave it a good shake. I could tell myself this wasn't about me—and it's not, it's not about me—but all the same it's about someone who's a lot like me in a lot of ways—but I started reading it to my friends because of the jokes, and I knew this wasn't a joke anymore.

I know my voice would break if I read it to someone these days.

> GHOST FOOD

"Creeping forward now, finally, but the god damn regret. All those years. Of course you can't do that to yourself, it's just more shame. Shame on top of shame. Shame for feeling ashamed. Shame for feeling ashamed for feeling ashamed. A life dominated by shame and fear. If fear is ignorance, maybe shame is fear of the self. It always came back to the same idea: 'everyone is thinking the worst possible thing about me, and maybe they're right.' Well of course they fucking weren't, but that's how it feels when the bottom falls out and you start spiraling. The later you interrupt that, the harder you crash."

MENU SELECT

TOOL

GRAPH

DATA PIT

CORRAL CAM

I wasn't. I was floundering, and it was all the worse because I couldn't even see what I was floundering in. I didn't want to think about anything, but *Rat Chaos* forced me to, in a way. It showed me that in some ways, I wasn't alone. That there was a deeper aspect to why Winter Lake's art and writing resonated with me so much.

> DATA PIT

played by Eva Problems

(New Rat City is distracted by text message)

(New Rat City looks up from phone)

"What? Oh. I don't know."

(New Rat City stares out the window, at nothing.)

"Anyway."

It's not a comfortable ending, or a neat one, because we don't get those—and because it *shouldn't* be an ending. It's a way to a new beginning, or a way to keep going if you've already started. We live our lives, we figure out gender shit, we do frivolous little things because we can now. We figure out how we're hurting, we address it, we fix it if it's in our power, and we move on as best we can.

Part of how I did that was through Twine, so that's what Twine means to me. I couldn't have asked for a better or more meaningful or more personally resonant piece to introduce me to Twine than Winter Lake's *Rat Chaos*.

Thanks, Winter.

FUCK THAT GUY
BY BENJI BRIGHT
PLAYED BY RILEY MACLEOD

A round midnight on a Tuesday last spring, I was walking home from a gay bar on Christopher Street in New York when a minivan eased to a stop next to me. An anxious Hasid who couldn't have been out of his early twenties leaned across the empty passenger seat to wave me over. I approached casually,stopping a few feet from his car, assuming he needed directions.

"Hey," he said, "where are you coming from?"

"Oh, uh, that bar." I gestured vaguely back the way I had come as if I was trying to be nonspecific, even though the bar was the only one on the block, nestled against the West Side Highway, some forgettable gay music leaking into its empty front area. The Hasid followed my hand, then looked back at me.

"Is that a gay bar?" he asked.

"Yeah," I answered cautiously, leaning back on one heel, bracing myself for the rest of the conversation.

"OK," he said. "Listen. Can I ask you a question?"

"OK . . ."

"Do you think gay life is devoid of meaning?"

Welcome to *Fuck That Guy*. The instructions are simple. Click the blue links to move forward in the story, but click carefully because there's no going back unless you refresh the page.

Fuck That Guy by Benji Bright

Read and savor.

This game is meant for adults. If you are not an adult, or if you can't legally view this material then come back when/if you ever can.

It features **explicit gay sex, drug use, language/use of terms some may find offensive, and other disreputable shit**. Of course, this is all fictional and the author is not condoning or championing any of this. Just be easy and enjoy it.

All words—with the exception of references to music lyrics—are © Benji Bright 2013.

Got it? **Good.**

    I tried to answer honestly. I said no, not necessarily, but that I thought that gay men spent a lot of time figuring out how to not let anyone know that we were actually people. Instead, I said, it seemed like we spent a lot of time learning how to be mean and then being mean to each other. I wasn't sure why this was, and I tended to think most people were just *pretending* to be mean instead of being people, but I worried that we were pretending so much that maybe we really *were* mean, which didn't leave a lot of room for anything else. He explained that he was married, and a teacher, and he skirted around the obvious fact that he was gay, and then he asked me several times to get into his van, which I declined.

    In a way, I was glad he had run into me, a radical queer trans man who was willing to talk to him honestly and kindly about his questions. In another way, I felt bad that he had run into me, a radical queer trans man who was not going to get into his van and probably would have disappointed him if I had. Some cis guy might have been better, I thought; they might have made fun of his clothes or his halting English, but they probably would have had a cock to suck or would have sucked his. Or maybe they would have given him some snappy retort that wouldn't have led to some long, difficult conversation, one that ended abruptly when the Hasid, realizing I was not going to get in the van, pulled forward and turned right on the street abutting the West Side Highway, probably off to make another circuit of Christopher Street, looking for someone who would get in the van.

    I continued toward the subway, a little disappointed by the conversation's sudden end, wondering how the friends I had just left in the bar would have handled him, wondering if we were mean or if we were people, wondering if and how we found meaning in our lives.

    > good

There's a subwoofer about a foot away from you and it's sending vibrations up through the floor and into your legs. Some interchangeable "diva" is singing lyrics that are indeci-

played by Riley MacLeod

pherable at these decibels. You can pick out a few words: 'on the bar...latex...cherry..'

You don't even want to be here.

The drinks taste like paint-thinner and the boys are all staring at their phones. You didn't pay a cover to stand on the wall all night, but the night is going nowhere at a fast clip.

Until **you see him**. Tight shirt, big arms, moving single-mindedly through the room. He heads back up to the elevated DJ booth of the club. A crystal castle floating above the rabble.

You figure you should follow him, unless of course, he's not worth following up the stairs. Unless you want to go back to staring at *your* **phone**.

There aren't a lot of games about being a gay man. I'm not sure why this is, and I'm not totally sure if it bothers me. There is no dearth of stories about men, and no lack of stories about cis gay men in other genres, and I'm happy for men to take the backseat in favor of voices who deserve more space and attention. On the other hand, I often feel at ends when people I know discuss how important it felt for them to see their identity or something valuable and unspoken about their lives portrayed in a game. In my own writing and my own efforts to make games, I'm not sure what I have to say about being queer and male-identified. I'm not sure if there's anything to say that *needs* to be said, that is as important or vital as what I think other folks are saying about themselves. But then sometimes I feel like this position suggests that games aren't for me, in a way, or they're so much for me that I can slot myself into them seamlessly enough not to need other outlets, that a romance option with someone as terrible as Kaidan Alenko is all I need to be satisfied because maybe that's really all gay life is about. Maybe, like the Hasid asked me, gay life really is devoid of meaning, is set apart from other lives solely by our drive for sex with men, the meaningfulness of which I am still out about due to a certain personal ambivalence about the ultimate importance and value of sex. Given this, I was both excited to see a gay game and lightly disappointed that it was, perhaps inevitably, a game about sex.

I liked that the game opened with everyone looking at their phones, a gay phenomenon that baffles me. I'll often see a bar full of men shoulder-to-shoulder cruising Scruff or Grindr. If they're my friends, I'll prod them by saying, "Look up. You found the gays; they're *here*. Zero feet from you! Mission accomplished!" No one is ever amused by this, if they bother to look up at all. I assume there's something about gay phone apps I don't understand, a certain anonymity or lack thereof, a way to make a bid at someone without taking as big a risk as speaking to them face-to-face. Being trans (or using that as my excuse), proximity isn't a big factor in my sexual decision-making, though phone apps usually give someone a chance to prove to me that they're an asshole without me having to meet them in person. But that doesn't explain their appeal for cis guys. Maybe we're disappointed in each other when we finally meet; maybe we don't know how to read interest into the people around us beyond their presentation at the bar. I mean, I'm not all that into "tight shirt, big arms" as a look. As far as I was concerned, my night in the game was continuing to go nowhere.

So I chose "phone." One point for hypocrisy.

> phone

You pull up an app on your smart phone that lets you cruise guys from the comfort of your spot on the wall. The wonders of modern technology.

Within a few minutes you've gotten and sent a few messages. Two guys draw your eye in particular:

A smooth, twenty-something whose picture is of **him naked on a bed, hands tied behind his back**. Another man stands over him fully clothed.

The other is a guy being held upside down over a keg. His eyes are half closed and his shirt is bunched around his upper chest. He has great abs and his features and skin tone are ambiguous enough to be a mixture of any number of nationalities. His profile makes him seem **easy-going, playful even.**

Which draws your eye? Which would you like to fuck?

This one was a tough choice for me. Hints of S/M piqued my interest, but "easy-going, playful even" suggested that keg guy might have a personality, which piqued my interest more. My experience with cis gay phone apps is mostly reams and reams of "hey"s and "what's up?"s peppered with wildly offensive comments and blurry photos of abs, little in the way of suggesting personhood, telling me who someone is and what our experience together might be. I tend to arc toward sleeping with people instead of sleeping with bodies, and, like I told the Hasid, people sometimes seem in short supply in the gay world. I keep believing this is just an act, though I'm not sure I'll ever understand why. So I hesitated at this screen for a while. There was the sense that picking one meant not picking the other, and it seemed like a big decision, like I might make the wrong choice and get nothing. What if he's straight or something, as the keg might suggest? What if it all goes wrong? At least the S/M guy seemed sure to coincide with my own interests. Why take the chance?

I picked keg guy. In all honesty, "smooth twenty-something" as a descriptor turned me off, especially in regards to S/M. Keg guy seemed like a

played by Riley MacLeod

person. I wanted to find a person.

> easy going, playful even

After a short introductory message, you get a reply:

Quick: What's the capital of New Mexico? Don't look it up either. He sends.

You send back:

Albuquerque or **Santa Fe**

Playing this, I laughed out loud, moved my mouse toward the answer, and then realized I didn't actually know. I almost looked it up. I tried to ask my roommate when she came out of the shower, but she brisked by in a towel, intent on not speaking to me while naked. Fair enough. I picked Santa Fe.

> Santa Fe

The response comes in quickly:

That's right. Huh, you looked it up, didn't you?

You send:

I did or **I didn't**

Score. I totally didn't.

> I didn't

You get a another message a minute or so later:

Alright, smart guy. Do you wanna hook up?

He sends you directions to his place. It's way uptown. About thirty minutes from you, so you figure you better get **going**.

You leave the club behind with hardly a second thought.

Something I always struggle with in interactive fiction is these moments with only one choice, like I'm being funneled somewhere. I think I still hoped I'd have the chance to go back, to survey all my options before making a choice. Perhaps it's this inclination that gay phone apps cater to, this thought that there's something better out there. I used to have a cis friend who would spend the entirety of any time we hung out together on Scruff, ready to bolt at the slightest moment if some stranger wanted to fuck him. Once he made a "date" while I was on my way to meet him, and we spent an awkward half-hour together at a lecture before he took off. *Once*, fed up with this bullshit, I had sex with him just because it seemed like it was always what he wanted, which at least got him to want to hang out more. What did it say for our friendship that sex was the most reliable way to get him to want to be friends—a question which might not be native solely to gays, but might certainly be a prominent feature?

It's a quality I somewhat loathe in gay dudes, so I was surprised to find myself full of it here. What about twenty-something? What about tight shirt? What could they offer to my night, my game experience? Would keg guy be good enough, fun enough, meaningful enough? I rued that it was already decided.

Given this internal debate, "hardly a second thought" struck me, especially in combination with his place being "way uptown." I had a lot of second thoughts that the game didn't cater to without a quick cheat and going back in my web browser. "My" willingness to leave the club (and travel "way uptown" no less) reminded me starkly that I was a trans guy playing this game, not a cis gay man. Sex is tricky, difficult; cis gays are clueless, or rude, or hateful, and there's little I want less than to submit my body to the terrible pawing or worse of some stranger. I felt a tug, a flicker, another reminder that I was playing a game that was not for me, that the game was making assumptions about my goals just like my gay life at large. At the same time, there was something pleasantly voyeuristic about embodying someone who was just going to boldly head uptown to meet a stranger for sex. This must be how cis fags feel, I thought. There was something exciting about this, but also disappointing. I wanted . . . I don't know what I wanted. Meaning? I went.

> going

Forty-five minutes later you're standing in front of a building with a doorman. It's the kind of place you walk by, not the kind you live in or anyone you know lives in.

You tell the doorman the apartment you're going to and he rings up to confirm that it's alright. Shortly afterward you're brought into an elevator and shuttled up a penthouse apartment. You thank the doorman and step into the foyer where there's Portishead playing softly from speakers you can't see.

You catch footsteps from another room and your host appears in low-slung checkered cargo shorts, flip-flops, and sunglasses nestled in his wavy black hair. He's shirtless and slender, his well-developed upper-body is in full evidence.

He's shorter than you thought he'd be.

"I'm Cyril," he says, putting out his hand. You shake it and introduce yourself.

played by Riley MacLeod

"Cool. Good to meet you. This is my place." He scratches his head and looks around as if vaguely embarrassed by the scope of it, but that passes quickly.

"Anything to drink?" he offers. You decline.

He grins. "**To business then?**"

    I don't know what I expected. The posh apartment was a surprise. I have a lot of cis fag friends who look like this, who live like this, making copious amounts of money from sources we never discuss. Some of them do porn; not the DIY queer porn my queer friends do, but that expensive, mass market, high profile stuff that flies them around the world and gets casts made of their dicks to sell at stores on 8th Avenue. While most of the non-cis queer people I know who do porn are pretty excited about it, most of the cis gays I know who do it are ashamed of it, carry emotional scars whose sources I find difficult to trace back, who came of their adulthood with the assumption that they were only valuable because of their looks and their age. These friends feel like their lives are over in ways I can't possibly understand, but they live like this, make circuits through this world. Keg guy seemed like a lot of people I know, and this endeared me to him, even as it made me suspicious. I wondered who he was, how he afforded this place, what he did for it, what it meant.

    Given my questions, and after his humorous, personable opening bid, his brisk "To business, then?" was a let-down, a tiny sliver of heartbreak. I wondered if the state capital line was just an act, a standard tactic to intrigue men and reel them in. Of course the game is called *Fuck That Guy*, so its single-mindedness shouldn't surprise me, but gameplay goals aside, it tugged at something bigger, deeper, in me. I was disappointed. I didn't want to play a game about fucking; I wanted to play a game about people, about experiences. But we got to business. There wasn't anything else to do.

    > To business then

Cyril's bedroom is positively cavernous. High ceilings and soft lighting. His bed is big and covered with a fluffy looking duvet. A blur passes as you look around the room, it's Cyril running past you and throwing himself into the bed. He bounces, rolls and comes up on on one knee in your direction. He's crouched like a sprinter getting ready to launch himself. The whole motion is so smooth that you figure he's probably practiced it in this big empty apartment.

"Come on, get in the bed, I promise I don't bite the first time." His smile is winning and his taut muscles beckon. You take off your shoes, strip off your shirt and jump into the bed after him.

Fuck That Guy by Benji Bright

Your landing isn't graceful, but Cyril doesn't hold that against you. He scrambles over and climbs on top of your legs before you have a chance to do much of anything. He pins your arms at your side and lowers his face to yours. Though you struggle, it becomes clear he's stronger than you despite his smaller frame.

"Submit to me."

You wrestle more instead, but he pushes harder on your wrists until it almost hurts. "Submit. Let me control you."

His dick twitches in his loose shorts. Yours jumps sympathetically.

"Why not?" he says. He licks your cheek. "Why not?"

"Be mine. Right now. For now.

"**Be mine**."

    And then things changed, here. I imagined keg guy practicing this move alone, a delightful contrast to his cringingly pathetic "I promise I don't bite the first time." It cast him a new light, carrying his little bundle of personness through the sea of "this big empty apartment," and this endeared him to me. It was like a little crack in the costume cis gays take out to bars, to parties, to the street, these irrepressibly human things that we can't always hide. Suddenly, I was less disappointed. I was curious again. Who *was* he? How much would the game let me find out; how much would *he* let me find out? The tension between the practiced move and his awful "I don't bite" line felt real to me, felt like the struggle I see in the cis gays I know: being unceasingly human while pretending not to be, not being sure which version of you someone else might want.

    My own actions mimicked his, jumping in after him. It felt like another glimmer of humanity, of acknowledging his personhood and offering up my own. When the vaguely S/M interaction came up, I felt rewarded, relieved, like I'd made the right choice back at the bar, which immediately felt crass, surprising me. It was that contrast again—a little bit of an act in what felt like the bland "Submit. Let me control you," followed by the squeaking intimacy of "Be mine. Right now. For now." I was curious for the next screen, wanting to know how this would play out, what twists and turns it might take.

    > Be mine

Depending on how you define sex, Cyril may or may not be having sex with you, but it *feels* good. He's rubbing himself against you, still wearing his shorts and you're still in your jeans.

He suddenly lets your arms go.

"Touch me," he commands. "Feel me up, fucker."

You run your hands up his arms and over his chest. His body feels good and hard to your fingers. He closes his eyes, grinds his crotch harder against yours. His prick is insistent, pushing up against his shorts like it longs to be free, but he refuses to undress. The situation in your own jeans is humid and sticky, but Cyril's pressure feels good bearing down on you. The sensation of his humping is spreading warmth through your genitals.

You try to put your hands down the front of his shorts and he leans in and bites your bottom lip fairly hard. When you yelp, he gives you a chastising look and moves your hand from the front of his shorts to the back. You knead his firm ass instead of grabbing his dick. It might not be the trade you would have made, but it will suffice.

Cyril's humping grows faster and the thrust of his hips longer. He's making little noises and sweat breaks out on his tanned skin.

"Tell me you want me to cum. Tell me you want me to cum right now, right here in my shorts. Fuck!"

You can think of other places you'd like him to unload, but maybe this is alright. Maybe you've buying into Cyril's unique brand of domination. Maybe you really do want him to blast his load all over the inside of those dangerous low-rise shorts. So low you can see the top of his round ass peeking out beneath them, so low you can see his curly, trimmed public hair, so low you can see...

"Fuck!" Cyril shouts. "I'm gonna cum. Fuck, tell me you want me to cum."

"I want you to —" you start.

"God!" Cyril shouts over you.

He grinds harder as he cums, hard enough to make you start spurting out your own reckless load. You make a mess of your jeans, but the mess is the furthest thing from your mind.

Cyril pulls away from you and looks down at the dark sticky spots between you both. He laughs.

"I got carried away," he says. He smiles a little boy smile. On anybody else it would be insufferable, but on Cyril it's perfect. You can't help but smile back.

•

Fuck That Guy by Benji Bright

You got laid!

Awesome!

Start over?

    Whether or not we were "having sex," murky enough to define in itself, this entire encounter was immensely satisfying to me. Something I'm always surprised to learn is that cis gays have sex in different ways, that feeling weird about sex isn't just a trans thing, and that none of us can really live up to the standards of gay sex, or sex in general, that we think we should. I've had cis partners equally as shy about masturbating as me, partners who get off in ways they feel embarrassed about, partners who can't be touched in certain places or who have to work around their own bodily limitations.

    In this way, the line "It might not be the trade you would have made, but it will suffice" startled me, reminded me that the "me" in this game isn't me. The trade I "would have made" in sex is whatever the person I'm with wants, and Cyril's enthusiastic dry humping felt intimate, interesting; it felt like *sex*, even while the game told me it wasn't, not quite. "Maybe this is alright" felt disappointing. "Maybe you're buying into Cyril's unique brand of domination" felt strange, because not touching his dick didn't feel like domination; it felt like someone who didn't want to be touched there, which in no way struck me as unusual. None of this is a judgment of the game, I should strive to say; if anything it felt like a failure on my part, a little jab that I wasn't the game's intended audience, that this wasn't the game for me. I felt disappointed by my character's disappointment.

    Compared to the meaningful and emotional experiences I see in the games made by trans lady friends, I felt that fear that maybe gay life really *is* devoid of meaning, that maybe all gay men need from games is sex simulators and Kaidan Alenko. But at the same time that tension was there, and the game made space for me to think about these things, to bring my experiences and wants and needs to the interactions presented. Like in my own experience of gay life, the game made room here, carved cracks in the prescribed paths for humanity and person-ness and meaning to eek their way out.

    My encounter ended kindly; it ended well. I got laid, and the game told me that was awesome, which of course it was. But. And.

    Because I could start over. I could go back to the same bar, and all those potentially missed opportunities would reset themselves, and I could follow each one to its end, and I could see all the ways my night could have gone, could see if there was any room in this world for me to find what I was looking for. But that felt like cheating, too. It didn't feel true to my experience of playing the game, and it felt like a disservice to this question of choice, felt like caving to the Scruff and Grindr promises of a cavalcade of men always available, always something better appearing on the next swipe. But it was a *game* too, not real life. I felt weird about finding a desire in myself I judged

played by Riley MacLeod

other people for, a revelation of something I pretend I don't feel to keep myself apart from the cis gays I deride.

I went back and played all the other paths, but I won't write about them in detail here. There are several where you don't get laid, where you're too aggressive or you turn someone down. In others you do, with lots of different guys. Looking back at my experience with Cyril in light of my encounters with my other options, I think I could have done better than him, which appalls me to say. Cyril had seemed like the most *human* human I was going to get from that first screen, but the other paths had their flickers of humanity too, their little quirks and kindnesses that surprised and delighted me. There was one in particular, rife with little details like someone chewing on the string of their hoodie, that I loved. It reminded me of a strange night I had at the Eagle, New York's more-or-less official leather bar, when a friend and I somehow gathered an entire posse of dudes to go to some after-hours party we heard about from a creepy guy shoving a badly photocopied flier into our hands. I had thought that our little coterie all knew each other, but on the walk over to the party it was discovered that they were all strangers, that they had been charmed by the friendly enthusiasm of my friend and I and had decided to tag along with us. Two of them—one visiting, bearded, handsome, and the other skinny and hairless and much too young, whom we had rescued from the last chance loitering between the Eagle and a nearby deli—hooked up at the club while my friend and I hung out close by and assisted in our own weird way. It had been the sort of "cis gay men having sex in public" that I find standard and dull, but, looking back on it through the lens of the thoughts inspired by this game, I remembered its idiosyncrasies: the pauses for negotiation and laughter, the joyous bafflement of "How the hell did we all end up here?", invitations for my friend and I to weigh in on their technique, all of it culminating in this strange adventure that seemed like any other gay New York night, but that at the same time was quirky, emotional, native only to us. Looking back, I remembered the remains of our little group stumbling out of the club into a grey 8 a.m. midtown Friday, perching on a pile of construction equipment to light our cigarettes and bending our heads against the wind and a disgruntled stream of morning commuters. We had shared something, I think, but no numbers were exchanged or asked to be exchanged, and we all went our separate ways cheerfully, satisfied, chuckling to ourselves. Maybe there wasn't anything wrong with that. Maybe there was meaning there, if you knew where to look. Maybe "You got laid! Awesome!" isn't a rote interaction and a closed door but a possibility space, an invitation to look harder for humanity, something worth trying again.

ANHEDONIA
BY MADDOX PRATT
PLAYED BY EMILY SHORT

anhedon_a

T he title screen. The first thing we're asked to do is to click on an absence, the space where an "i" should be.

> _

this is not a rational response

Cycling text. If I click on the word rational, it changes to other words: "healthy," "reasonable," "sane." After "sane," I can't change the text again. Maybe the protagonist sees mental illness as an ultimate truth behind which there are no additional explanations.

Forward link. Clicking response moves us to a new screen. Perhaps you need to have some response to engage with the world. The thing is, these two links look identical. Actions that move forward look identical to actions that spiral in self-doubt. As the player, you can't tell which is which until you've tried.

> response

dismiss it

The same structure: this time, cycle through ways to deal with intrusive thoughts. "Dismiss," "repress," "repeat." You can't move on from "repeat" either.
I sympathize.
This time, I've learned how this works. I'm choosing to click "it", to move forward without going through the rest of the cycle.

i would walk through the creek that passed through the school grounds
****

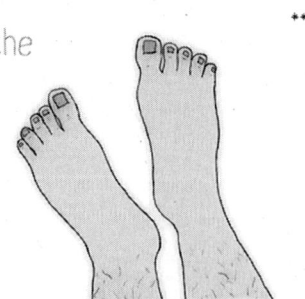

i would walk through the
creek that passed
through the school
grounds

****

The sound of a stream plays over this screen. It's soothing. The only link is those **** marks. Sensation drives out thought, which is a relief.

> ****

i keep imagining my life as something fading

Timed effect. The word fading slowly vanishes off the screen.
Unlike the cycling effect from earlier, this one isn't under the player's control. A hasty player might even miss it by clicking through too fast.
Nonetheless, *life* hasn't faded out. *life* is the forward link. The protagonist may be afraid of life vanishing, but the player has to affirm life to pro-

ceed.

> life

doctor opal

in her pink sweater set

told me

my problem

was that i had not tried hard enough

to smile.

Another fade. This time the last line comes in slowly. A hasty player couldn't miss this one. There's no way forward but to click on smile.

But we can't do that right away. Revealing the option slowly paces our confrontation with doctor opal.

We have to hesitate, have to wait, as though we were slow to understand her instruction, or just incredulous at its inanity.

practice

IMPROVING THE MOMENT

with a half smile

That upper case red text looks stressed out. When I click there I imagine the protagonist's teeth are gritted.

> IMPROVING THE MOMENT

i can't believe

we are still telling people to act

as if

Fragment. There's nothing that comes after that as if. It doesn't really need more. The meaning is certainly clear from context. But because there have been fade-in texts recently I find myself waiting here for a beat or two to see whether something is going to fade in. It doesn't.

> as if

i'm still not convinced about whose **benefit** it's for

Linearity. Constraint. On these pages about having to follow other peoples stupid rules there's less and less space for self-expression: no cycling text to change, no choice.

Some people say a hypertext with only one link forward is not interactive, that it might as well be a short story.

This misses something. Having no options in an interactive medium feels different from having no options in a book. It feels confining. The constraint is part of the meaning.

> benefit

five (or more) of the following symptoms have been present during the same 2-week period

1. **depressed mood most of the day nearly everyday (may present as irritability)**

2. **markedly diminished interest or pleasure in all, or almost all, activities most of the day, nearly every day**

3. **significant weight loss or weight gain**

4. **insomnia or hypersomnia nearly everyday**

5. **psychomotor agitation or retardation**

6. **fatigue or loss of energy nearly everyday**

7. **feelings of worthlessness or excessive or inappropriate guilt nearly everyday**

8. **diminished ability to think or concentrate or indecisiveness nearly every day**

9. **recurrent thoughts of death, recurrent suicidal ideation without a specific plan, or a suicide attempt or a specific plan for committing suicide**

check all

Choice overload. The opposite of constraint. So many options, it feels confusing and oppressive.

Click a symptom once to describe your experience. Click twice to lie about it. I'm going to lie about everything.

> (click all links once)

1. **i feel empty and heavy at the same time. tears are always approaching.**

2. **stopped returning calls. avoid large groups. no longer keep up the pretence of fine**

played by Emily Short

3. **weight gain from self medicating with sugar and wine**

4. **these endlessly running thoughts keep me awake at night. i would sleep through days if it weren't for appearances**

5. **i fidget and shake and need something to do with my hands**

6. **the solution is not sleep**

7. **there is a nagging question of worth. my friendship is a burden**

8. **i cannot keep track of thoughts. sentences are lost midway**

9. **i think about death every hour. formulating plans.**

When I first encountered this I clicked on the symptoms I've experienced myself.

I'm not screenshotting that version of the list.

This is not the first Twine work where I've felt invited to catalog what I have in common with the author—but privately, somewhere between conversation and journal entry.

> (click all links a second time)

1. **L I E**
2. **L I E**
3. **L I E**
4. **L I E**
5. **L I E**
6. **L I E**
7. **L I E**
8. **L I E**
9. **L I E**

Reflective choice. All lies. Looks like we're ready to go here.

LIE is still a link, but the thought on the other side of the LIE is always something worse. I didn't click through to those on my first playthrough. I've looked at a few of them since, but they're not screenshotted.

There's not a lot of choice about what to *do* in this piece, but there's some choice about what to think and say.

And I don't want those thoughts. I'd rather deceive doctor opal. I don't

Anhedonia by Maddox Pratt

like doctor opal. I know it won't make any difference but it makes me feel better.

> L I E

this is more than anhedonia
something is **looming**

Pacing. After choice overload, we need a break.

> looming

i smell the lilacs blooming

and feel the heat

that makes me feel

ten years younger

i smell the lilacs blooming
and feel the heat
that makes me feel
ten years younger
and only just discovering
what it can mean to touch.
i weep when my partner
says she loves me
because that makes it more
frightening,
my thinking of permanent
goodbyes

Scrolling. It hides the scary thought that we don't want to admit we're having.

played by Emily Short

> goodbyes

take 20mg 1x daily with water

avoid alcohol

and sunlight.

indulge in both

take **20mg 1x daily** with water

avoid alcohol

and sunlight.

indulge in both

Illustration. Individual objects ground the story in particular sensory experiences like the fact that we drink from a clean jam jar.

(take 10mg 1x semi-daily thinking it will be easier to wean off of when you lose health insurance because you still have not learned to **value** life more than money)

Clicking on a Twine link can feel like a descent, burrowing into the meaning of a word and its connotations. Structurally, any word in this passage could have been the link to the next page, but it's that concept of value that we're digging into.

> value

i think in net balances

my life always lighter

than what it takes

to **maintain** it

> maintain

this is an **irrational belief**

> irrational

Anhedonia by Maddox Pratt

this is an **unhealthy belief**

    Formal echo. We're criticizing our own thoughts again. Self-editing over and over. Irrational, unhealthy, dysfunctional, insane.

  > belief

dismiss it

  > dismiss it

sometimes not knowing how to take a life feels like cowardice

  > (wait)

sometimes this feeling of cowardice feels like **cowardice**

  Timed replacement. One idea fades out. Another fades in beneath it.

  > cowardice

it's all just **shame**
thickening right below the surface

  There are so many ways to have contempt for oneself.

  > shame

or is it all just an **attempt** at absolution

  The linear passage is longer this time than it was last time. It's getting harder to break out of thoughts on thoughts.

how does one **separate** illness from self

  > separate

i have mental illness

  > (wait)

played by Emily Short

i **am** mentally ill

> am

it's not a question of semantics
but of **ontology**

> ontology

tic tic tic tic tic tic tic tic tic tic

tic . . .

> Deliberate frustration. One tic at a time. Ticking noises with each one. There's no option now but to wait, agency diluted almost to nothing. But the sound is also calming, a sensory interlude like the stream before. Maybe when this ends we'll be able to act again.

. . . tic tic tic tic tic tic tic tic tic

tic tic tic . . .

> I could have skipped this paragraph and let you fill in the blanks. But it wouldn't have captured that sense of waiting.

. . . tic tic tic tic tic tic tic

tic tic tic tic tic tic tic tic tic

tic tic tic tic tic tic tic tic tic

tic tic tic tic tic tic tic tic **tic**

> Six by ten. A full minute. But the last tic is different. Sometimes when we're stuck in a bad mental state it's very hard to explain what changes between the moment when we can't act and the moment when we can.

i locked my mother out of the house once

convinced the termites tapping against the window

were about to break the glass to get inside

and throw themselves at the light

> Sound of rustling dry insect wings. Up to this point the sound-effect interludes have mostly been calming. Things are getting worse.

> (wait)

. . . were about to break the glass to get inside

and **devour** me

> devour

the glass is **cracking**

    Shorter phrases
    greater danger.
    Are you sure you want to see what happens next?

> cracking

all i can think about are its **edges**

    I feel like I'm walking out on the ice.

> edges

this is an **irrational thought**

> thought

repeat repeat repeat **repeat**

> repeat

call this:

attention seeking

    Starts out as "attention seeking." Then "a cry for help."
    But the alteration of text isn't up to me this time. It's a timed progression. I can't avoid the self-diagnosis.

> (wait)

call this:

borderline

> borderline

for whatsoever man called every living creature,

that was the **name** thereof

> name

my thoughts

refuse to stay

in place

played by Emily Short

It's a funny thing how it's possible to be bored and terrified simultaneously without either feeling erasing the other.

Funny also how it's possible to be inescapably upset but also viewing your own upsetness from the outside.

> (wait)

come back

> come back

i fear what **quiets** them

> quiets

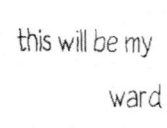

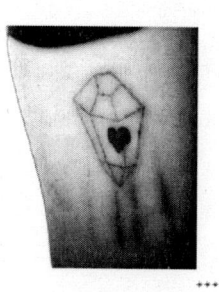

this will be my

ward

***

The words scratch themselves in place.

> ***

i'm skilled at cutting around
the **boundaries**
i set in place

> boundaries

tic tic tic tic tic tic tic tic tic
tic tic tic tic tic tic tic tic
tic tic tic tic tic tic tic tic
tic tic tic tic tic tic tic tic
tic tic tic tic tic tic tic tic tic

Anhedonia by Maddox Pratt

tic tic tic tic tic tic tic tic tic **tic**

Wait. Again.

> tic

semantic saturation:

the phenomenon whereby the uninterrupted **repetition** of a word

leads to a sense that the word has lost its meaning

> repetition

DEPRESSION
DEPRESSION
DEPRESSION
DEPRESSION
DEPRESSION
DEPRESSION
DEPRESSION
DEPRESSION
DEPRESSION
DEPRESSION

> depression

sometimes it **feels** like cowardice

And we're back here again. The piece has been repeating itself more and more, spiraling inward.

sometimes

surviving myself feels like it should be

enough

*

The victory is giving yourself permission to stop. To leave the mill of thoughts about thoughts about thoughts and self-criticism at every layer.

SABBAT
BY EVA PROBLEMS
PLAYED BY IMOGEN BINNIE

I have a friend who is a witch. I mean, I know we're all witches here, that all you've got to do to be a witch is to do some witch stuff,. But she's pretty hardcore about it, she knows about all the pagan holidays and the Rosicrucians and the Hermetic Order of the Golden Dawn and used to have the kind of sex you could hear throughout the house.

Y'know.

Witch stuff.

One time she brought up the coven she was a part of. I asked her what it was like to be in a coven.

"It's cool," she said. "You get naked and stand in circles and you can feel the energy in the air and between the people doing the ritual. But also it's basically just LARPing."

I bring this up because we live in an absurd world where we reject or make fun of pretty much anything that isn't, like, defined by white European colonial positivist empiricism. There's this assumption that if you stray from The Scientific Method into actually caring about things like lying on the floor of your room in the middle of the afternoon with black canvas hung over the curtains to keep the sun out with a single candle burning, wearing lipstick—even though you pretty much don't wear lipstick any other time in your life—sort of meditating and sort of tripping off sensory deprivation and sort of falling asleep, that you had better take that weird stuff just as seriously and humorlessly as scientists are supposed to take science. Like basically that magic can't be weird or fun or fucked up or stupid

SABBAT by Eva Problems

on purpose. Which is wrong! One of the best things about LARPing up some witch shit is that it can make you feel super powerful even though it can also feel kind of childish and silly. This probably has something to do with the fact that in this culture where I grew up the only model we have for stepping outside positivist empiricism is playing make-believe as children.

I'm not a gamer. I mean, I spend a lot of time with smartphone games from the "casual" section of the Google Play Store, and I was pretty into console gaming as a kid and as a teenager. But the last console I actually owned when it was still for sale in stores was a Turbografx-16. I've had the occasional thrift store N64 and emulated the hell out of games I remember from when I was a kid, but I have not Kept Up With Games. So I'm not really familiar with the work of Oh No, Problems, who made the game Sabbat: Director's Cut.

But the tone of the author's description of the game seems pretty consistent with the way I approach the occult. I mean, don't get me wrong—I'm not starting this game with the idea that I'll walk away better at astral projection or scrying. But it does make me feel stoked to play it! And being stoked is crucial to this stuff. If you're not stoked to bury some bones and hair in the woods or at the top of a mountain, why bother. You know? So I'm on board with the author's description of SABBAT: "have you ever gotten sick of your dumb human body and depressing future prospects? why not play through a twine story in which you can coat your body in charged animal essences and enact satanic rituals to gain weird demonic body parts and terrible power?"

This is basically why metal rules, too.

♦

I open up the game and it works, which I'm stoked about because I am the kind of Linux user who uses Linux without really knowing what she's doing: the "I can google that error message" kind of Linux user, not the "I have memorized command line commands" kind of Linux user. And honestly? I told Merritt I was going to email this playthrough essay thing yesterday. It is now half a day late and I won't lie about this: I kind of feel awful. My belly hurts and I woke up tired even though I got an adequate amount of sleep. My point is that I am in a bad mood and I was half expecting the game not to open, but it totally opened. Sick dude. Twine rules.

couple of options okay

first things first witchdumpling what's in your drawers

vagina

played by Imogen Binnie

penis

what's it to ya

    Of course the first thing it does is to ask me what's in my pants, meaning it wants to know about my junk—or even my theoretical player character junk, right, I get it—and it makes me totally hate this game. Fuck this game! None of these options is an answer I would ever give, but that's because I wouldn't normally answer that question at all. The closest option to true is "what's it to ya," which I appreciate I get to pick. But then I think: why am I so invested in playing as myself? What if I play as a theoretical character who would choose "vagina" here without even thinking about it? What if I play as someone who is stoked to pick "penis?"

> what's it to ya

you got some sweet junk there, cutie

how do you feel about sacrificing animals to satan for power

blood for the blood god

i'd rather not, even in a work of fiction, if it's all the same

    SABBAT: Director's Cut compliments my junk anyway! I guess that is nice. I don't want to talk about my junk with you any more, though, game. Leave me alone.
    I stopped being a vegetarian like three years ago when I was working in a day shelter that wouldn't give me more than twenty hours a week and I couldn't afford not to eat in the soup kitchen there. Plus I am hella metal.
    Or maybe my player character is hella metal!

> blood for the blood god

enjoy the depressing taste of SABBAT CLASSIC

OKAY SO TO CONFIRM

you have a GENITAL in your drawers, little witchdumpling

you want GRUESOME sacrifices

yes i love it let's go

hmm hmmmm no i changed my mind

SABBAT by Eva Problems

The game informs me that basically I have chosen the original, non-vegan version of the game, which makes me feel like I've fucked up. What are vegan animal sacrifices like? The obvious thing is tofu jokes but that's boring but I can't think of a better one so I let it drop and choose to play the NSFW version of the game.

> yes i love it let's go

Terrifying music swells up in my headphones! It is graveyard wind sounds and maybe baritone guitars and plinky pianos? SICK. I turn the volume on my headphones down a little bit though because I am old.

> tonight's the night. the omens are right and the stars are in alignment. tonight you must make the sacrifice, or miss this opportunity for the rest of your lonely life.
>
> it's hard to have a sabbat of one, but you make do the best you can.
>
> **look around your apartment.**
>
> **make the sacrifice.**

It asks me if I want to look around my apartment or just start sacrificing. I pick look around the apartment. I hope I have lots of very expensive dresses to choose from when I decide what to wear when I make this sacrifice. I would pick a black one.

> look around your apartment

> what a mess. dishes fill the sink. hair covers the floor. the air is hazy and sharp from the cloud of poison misery that smothers the city outside. the air conditioning unit rattles and whines, and the old tv set softly mumbles static. something smells. smells like no job, no money, no prospects, no friends. smells like alienation. smells like late capitalism.
>
> the only nod to cleanliness in the whole place is in the kitchen. you just mopped the kitchen tiles, but only so you could paint a pentagram on them in your own blood and stick sputtering candles at every point. it's easier to clean that shit off of tile than carpet. you would know.
>
> assuming this doesn't work, that is. which, really, would just be par for the fucking course. you can't live like this.
>
> you've placed all your materials in two different places, the **living room** and the **fridge**. better round them up.

played by Imogen Binnie

I guess my apartment is kind of a shithole. There is a little dig at the fact that capitalism sucks. "Shithole apartment" does not necessarily mean "no very expensive dresses" though.

> fridge

sidling around the pentagram, you open the fridge. in the vegetable drawer, a bag of wilted, slimy lettuce. an empty carton of eggs. a jar of mayonnaise, past its expiration date. and 2 mason jars in the condiments shelf, full of dark red fluid. one says "GOAT" on a tape label, the other says "WOLF"

you got them from the internet. you grab them and tuck them under your arm.

you shut the door with your foot and **keep looking**.

I want to be in a band with the person who made this music although it seems like they may not know any drummers where they live either.

> keep looking
> living room

somewhere out the windows, past the smog and shit and high-rise prisons, a ripe and full moon glows down. you can't see it. the air outside is a uniform dull orange, diffusing the lights from the street and the light from the moon. you can barely even see the buildings across the street from you. you cough.

on the coffee table, amidst stacks of bills and filthy plates, you see two terrariums. one holds a **snake**, the other, a **centipede**. hanging over the tv set, there is a birdcage holding a **crow**.

I go to the living room to find more stuff to sacrifice and there is a dig at the prison industrial complex. Also it turns out I live in a terrifying smog hell, which is cool. Now I get to pick either a snake, a centipede or a crow. I don't know if I can pick more than one but I pick crow, just in case, because crows are better than snakes and centipedes. I probably think this because I grew up reading Stephen King novels and Stephen King has this recurring character named Randall Flagg who is evil and who is the antagonist of The Stand and who—spoiler—is disappointingly killed off without much fanfare in one of the Dark Tower books and then hasn't really appeared in any of Uncle Steve's novels since, I don't think, which is a shame because like. He is an evil wizard who wears a denim jacket with little one-inch but-

SABBAT by Eva Problems

tons on it, like we all do, but unlike most of us he also does a bunch of interdimensional time travel. He could have had so many adventures before he got killed! That is the whole point of interdimensional time travel! Also he turns into a crow.

Plus like. Snakes are kind of an obvious symbol of evil and centipedes are the bad kind of gross. Crows are crawling with pestilence but they still have cool black feathers. And beaks rule. And cloacae.

> crow

the crow croaks at you worriedly. you try to tell yourself it's just a bird and try to ignore all those studies they did on the intelligence of crows and other members of the corvus genus. you unhook the cage from the hook above the tv set and clamp it in your teeth.

awww dangit. dangit dangit dangit this is a life you are giving over to powers you aren't even certain exist.

welp. better **move on**.

I am having remorse about sacrificing a crow! My character is, too.
This music is fucking unnerving.
It fades out and starts over.

> move on

What the hell I am back in the living room and it wants me to pick from the snake, the centipede and the crow again! I pick crow again.

> crow

you've already grabbed the birdcage. it dangles from your teeth awkwardly and bumps against your chest. man, crows are really smart and really cool.

better **move on** before the depravity of your actions catches up to your conscience.

Turns out the game knows I already picked the crow. Maybe I just have to pick all the things.

> move on
> snake

crowley, your gorgeous ball python, suns himself under the

played by Imogen Binnie

heat lamp in his terrarium. ohh gosh. look at the little guy. you've had him for years. you blink back tears, move aside the lid, and take him out.

well, you were already planning on hurling yourself out the window if this ritual doesn't work. who would take care of crowley then? it's... it's better this way. you hope.

better **move on** before you lose your nerve.

   . . . yep.

  > move on
  > centipede

ahh, scolopendra polymorpha. the sonoran desert centipede. this one is about 6 inches long, with a glossy red head at the front of a bright yellow body topped with chitinous red plates. the guy at the pet store said it was female. you'll take his word for it. you grab the small terrarium and try not to freak out when it scuttles around the cage.

why did you even buy a centipede.

time to **move on**.

  > move on

  . . . well, that's everything. better keep moving.

return

  > return

  . . . you had placed all your materials in two different places, the living room and the fridge, but now you have everything, meager as it is.

hopefully you won't have to live like this for long. time to **make the sacrifice**.

  I collect all the animals and blood and click "make the sacrifice" without getting any choices about what dress to wear while I do it.

  > make the sacrifice

you have all the materials you prepared. hopefully, that'll be enough. what a paltry selection. fuck. you strip from your

SABBAT by Eva Problems

clothes, set your sacrifices to the side, adjust your grip on your homemade athame and seat yourself in the center of the pentagram on the floor.

it's time.

   I take out my athame or witch knife and lay down in the middle of the pentagram I've drawn on the floor of my kitchen in my own blood.

  > it's time

what will you sacrifice

the snake

the centipede

the crow

the goat

the wolf

  > the crow

the crow flaps desperately in your grip. tears stain your cheeks. you slice its head off with your dagger. fuck. fuck.

where will you put the blood

head

body

arms

legs

genitals

  > head

you cover your head in the sticky fluids.

what will you sacrifice

the snake

the centipede

played by Imogen Binnie

the goat

the wolf

    I was kind of hoping I could sacrifice all the animals and put all their bloods on my head, but it makes me pick another animal and another part of my body. I'll put the wolf blood on my junk.

    you grab the mason jar and unscrew it. you dip in a finger and taste it. well, it's blood all right. you hope it's actually wolf blood.

    where will you put the blood

body

arms

legs

genitals

    > genitals

    blanching, you coat your groin with the blood, lather it into your pubic hair, and smear it into your genitals.

    you are a bad person.

    what will you sacrifice

the snake

the centipede

the goat

    The game points out that I "lather it into my pubic hair," which is nice to think about.
    Next, I'll decapitate my beloved pet snake Crowley (rhymes with "blow me") and rub its blood into my torso.

    > the snake

    choking back a sob, you raise your athame with shaking hands. with one clean stroke, crowley's head drops to the floor.

    where will you put the blood

SABBAT by Eva Problems

body

arms

legs

> body

you rub the blood into your skin, coating your stomach, your ribs, your collarbone, your whole front.

what will you sacrifice

the centipede

the goat

> the centipede

the centipede wraps around your hand and stings it painfully. fuck! you almost smear your pentagram in pain but you control yourself and chop the little fucker into pieces.

why didn't you wear gloves or something OW

where will you put the blood

arms

legs

> arms

you slather your arms in blood.

what will you sacrifice

the goat

This leaves the goat, which I guess is actually just goat blood. I'll slather it all over the only part of my body that isn't already drenched in blood: my legs.

> the goat

played by Imogen Binnie

you unscrew the mason jar and take a whiff. smells like copper. does not smell like goat. you don't know why you expected it to smell like goat. it's blood.

where will you put the blood

legs

> legs

you slather your legs in blood.

the candles flicker. you are coated head to toe in blood and filth.

your head oozes with the fluids of a crow.

your body is covered in the vital essence of snake.

your arms are slathered in centipede blood.

your legs, likewise, with that of a goat.

sticky wolf blood coats your genitals.

time to call upon the **unknown powers**.

> unknown powers

you call upon lucifer, morning star, the adversary

you call upon scylla, mother of abominations, she who guards the gates

you call upon all the dukes, duchesses, barons, and baronesses of hell

you take a quick water break. there's a lot of those fuckers.

ahem

> ahem

you call upon mammon, upon beelzebub, upon pythius, belial, asmodeus, merihem, abaddon, astaroth

you call upon satan, master of witches

you call upon the nameless dead, the women burned and tortured for the sin of knowledge, the untold howling pagan

SABBAT by Eva Problems

dead

you're running out of ideas.

> running out of ideas

your voice is getting hoarse.

blood congeals on your body.

you fight back tears.

...

>

𝕿𝖍𝖊𝖞 𝕬𝖓𝖘𝖜𝖊𝖗

*

!

> *

power surges and crackles through your body. the blood sizzles and evaporates from your flesh. your body is a crucible, a nexus, a locus. euphoric spasms build in your gut and radiate outwards.

the changes start at your **head**.

> head

your head throbs as power surges into it. it feels like a crackling disc is whirling vertically downwards through the middle of your head. you feel it widen, and it feels like your head is being torn in half. suddenly, two more eyes blink open in the void left by the power. you look inwards and are met with a mirror image of your own head. that was precisely what happened!

the vantage point of two heads lets you see firsthand the changes that follow. hair frays and widens, becoming luxurious jet-black feathers. more sprout across your foreheads, along your jaws and necks, blanketing your ears. as the feathers crawl inwards, you watch as your eyes turn a pure black, radiating inkily inwards from the lids. your nose heaves forward, carrying the bones of your skull, before the sea of feathers drowns it.

played by Imogen Binnie

you feel your teeth meld together before erupting outwards in a heavy black beak. you croak in surprise, the harsh sound echoing from two throats. suddenly, in a shower of ultraviolet lightning, power erupts from all four of your eyes. the beams meet above your head, and from the scintillating nexus of energy, small glowing pylons of black crystal trail outwards. they loop around the crown of one head, then double back and encircle the other. the power subsides, leaving your eyes a glowing purple and a hovering crystal crown in an infinite moebius loop above your twin crow heads.

killin it.

the searing, transmogrifying power arcs down to your **body**.

My head turns into a sick crystal crow head with a beautiful lavender tiara and a black beak big enough to bite off somebody's head!

Wait I just re-read it. It's even better. Now I have TWO crow heads. Perfect!

> body

something coils deep within your guts. perhaps it is your guts themselves. they feel alive and writhing. the sensation spreads upwards and outwards. you take a breath, another, then your lungs fill with writhing forms. you try to choke, try to cough, but your muscles no longer respond. you focus on your heartbeat, focus on its staccato panic, but something coils itself around it and squeezes.

bulges ripple under your skin. two prominent forms bubble up under your nipples, then stretch outwards. massive serpents burst from under your flesh and coil around your body. more spill after them, and yet more erupt from new places on your torso. well. that explains that, you suppose.

there should be pain. you should be feeling your own flesh tearing, your own organs failing as they are devoured by the gaping maws of deadly serpents. there is none. instead you feel the exultation of scale on scale, twisting, flowing, coiling and uncoiling. you can no longer see your own flesh, if indeed it remains and is even yours any longer. instead there is only a riot of scales and flickering tongues in constant movement.

wait. hang on. is that...?

oh gosh. oh gosh. you reach into the writhing mass of snakes and pull one out. it's crowley! he's alive! he licks your face happily and then slithers back down your arm to return to your new gestalt snake mass. this is the best day ever.

the changes roar outwards to your **arms**.

SABBAT by Eva Problems

Now my beloved pet snake is still alive! Not only that, he is part of my new replacement torso, which is made of snakes.

> arms

your ears fill with hideous chittering that seems to be coming from your arms. you stretch them in front of you in time to see strange bulges skitter from your shoulders down to your fingers. for a moment, you start to doubt if you saw them or not, but then your fingers start to blacken and swell.

before your horrified eyes, they rupture into open wounds of weeping black goo, exposing pitted and cancerous bone below. black sores spread down your hands. you lift your hands in front of your face, only to see your fingers slough off and spatter to the floor, splashing black gobs back onto your legs. you try to gather it up with your stubby palms, only to have them disintegrate utterly. tainted flesh drips from your plagued bones before they, too, crumble into wet ruin.

you huddle, shrieking, armless, on the pentagram, as black ooze flows and finally abates from what used to be your shoulders. the chittering returns, even stronger, and you feel something writhing inside your body.

with a rending, sucking burst, tremendous yellow centipede legs erupt from your body, showering you in ichor. one pair writhes at your shoulders, one just below them, another at the base of your ribs, a fourth pair where your old kidneys were, and a final pair wriggles from your hips. each has five segments covered in fine cilia, ending in a wicked point.

there's no joke here dude you got bug legs now instead of arms. goddamn.

as the power erupts from your limbs, more flows down to your **legs**.

My arms turn to slime and are replaced with ten giant centipedes in pairs starting at my shoulders and working their way down both sides of my body! Also fucking ichor goes everywhere. You know you are in a horror story when you see the word "ichor." I think the guy who wrote "Candle Cove"—the best horror story in the world—had a website or TV show or book or something called Ichor Falls. I forget. My point is just: ichor. Everywhere.

> legs

played by Imogen Binnie

blasphemous energies race down your legs. in their wake, swathes of coarse, earthy black fur sprout up. as the power reaches your toes, they start to fuse into cloven hooves with a series of pops and creaks. your knees vibrate before wrenching backwards, hurling you to the cold floor.

you can feel your coccyx stretch out, curving upwards and outwards. fur sprouts along it and strange new muscles fill in. you stand, hooves clicking on the blood-slick floor, and give your goat tail an experimental shake. heat spreads in waves throughout your legs, the legs of hoary pagan wood-spirits, of pan and baphomet.

can't go wrong with the classics.

the crackling power jolts inwards and sensuously encases your **groin**.

I get goat legs! Which is kind of boring, actually, but Sabbat: Director's Cut even acknowledges this sort of boringness by pointing out that "you can't go wrong with the classics." True! Also, I poke my head out of this game for a second and realize: here in meatspace while playing this game I am feeling kind of stoked! I didn't even really intend for this playthrough essay thing to have an emotional narrative arc in which the game makes me feel less shitty, but what the heck do you know. I am feeling stoked to see how this turns out!

Even though I don't want to talk about my junk. Ever. And it looks like we are about to.

> groin

wild and savage power envelops your groin, filling it with a feral heat. shaggy black fur radiates across your pubis.

the power races across your groin, warping and twisting your genitals, fusing and expanding sensitive flesh in erogenous scintillations. what remains is a lupine mockery of a human vagina. wait, mockery? that's a little closed-minded. it sure seems like a fully-functional vagina. who are you to hold all the genitals in the world to your arbitrary human-centric beauty standards? and i mean, it's not like you're human anymore anyway.

then the howling starts. muffled bays sound from inside your womb as it starts to swell, and swell. your womb distends, pushing the flesh of your stomach out in a monstrous parody of motherhood.

something inside thrashes its way out. you drop to the ground as it passes your cervix. as you watch, a growling

SABBAT by Eva Problems

wolf's head squeezes its way out of your vagina, fur matted with blood and fluids. legs follow, then it scrabbles its way fully out of you. it clambers to its feet, sniffs the air, circles restlessly, then, just as suddenly as it left, it burrows its way back inside you.

you recall a passage from milton:

These yelling Monsters that with ceaseless cry

Surround me, as thou saw'st, hourly conceiv'd

And hourly born, with sorrow infinite

To me, for when they list into the womb

That bred them they return, and howl and gnaw

My Bowels, their repast; then bursting forth

Afresh with conscious terrors vex me round,

That rest or intermission none I find.

yes. paradise lost. this is a perfectly natural thing to think about when your womb is continuously birthing and re-absorbing fully-grown wolves.

gasping, shuddering, you lift yourself from the pentagram. you flex new muscles, test new appendages, and **examine your new form**.

    I read the next part and I think Okay, fine, *Sabbat: Director's Cut.* You can talk about my player character's junk if you're only doing it to inform me that it is a terrifying wolf vagina that gives birth to a terrifying wolf monster who promptly crawls back through my terrifying wolf cervix and back into my terrifying wolf uterus. That is a pretty good image. You got me.

    Oh maybe they are not wolf monsters, just wolves? Still cool though.

    > examine your new form

played by Imogen Binnie

two crow heads rest atop your shoulders, eyes smoldering with fell energies. crackling black crystal pylons circle between the heads in a crown of dire power.

in place of a body, you have an amorphous and immense cluster of snakes. there may or may not be a skeleton somewhere deep inside them, but ultimately it doesn't really matter. the occasional snake will drop from your gestalt mass before climbing back up and rejoining the collective.

in place of arms, you have five pairs of centipede legs emerging from various places between your shoulders and hips.

you've got some lewd-ass goat legs. just lookin at em makes you wish you had some pipes to pipe on.

your egregiously distended lupine womb is birthing and re-absorbing fully-grown wolves constantly. it's a little inconvenient.

one thing is for certain. you are 100% the most authentic bitch. it is time to find some powerful auras and suck them fucking dry.

TIME TO HUNT

I am rewarded with a Sega Genesis looking picture of my new body which, I'm not gonna lie, is not as disgusting as I'd been imagining it. I mean it rules and stuff, and it is nice to see all the new parts of my horrifying new monster body represented. But it is kind of cute! I'd been imagining it in more of an elongated Sybil Lamb or Egon Schiele style, you know? But whatever. There are a lot of ways to represent a body and I'm not gonna lie, the pink and purple stars, glitter and tendrils on the frame of the picture are pretty nice.

> TIME TO HUNT

you slip out into the dead night, a fledgling demoness with the world to gain.

you can sense two powerful auras in the city, almost blinding in their brilliance. were you to take them into your own, nothing could stop you.

which aura will you hunt

dancing flame black purple

rigid mesh white crosses

But do I hunt the dancing flame black purple or the rigid white mesh crosses? I choose purple flames.

SABBAT by Eva Problems

> dancing flame black purple

you zigzag through the city's crazed and fractured leylines, following the threads of this enticing aura. you make no attempt to mask your own reverberations. no doubt some have already reached the aura's owner.

you can almost taste it, a psychic scent like candlesmoke and lavender. there. apartment high-rise. **top floor**.

   I travel on some ley lines. This game has so many things I like!

> top floor

you effortlessly scale the building's exterior. reaching the balcony outside the apartment, you peer through the sliding doors. yes. good. posters of sweet satanic stoner doom bands on the wall. bong on the living room table. a young woman dressed solely in a black cloak and satanic pendant standing over a pentagram. truly the portrait of the modern witch.

you hook a few segmented limbs around the handle, slide it open, and enter.

at the sound, she looks up and gasps. "luckyyyyyyyyyy"

you blush as best you can. "aww **shucks**."

   . . . Including a stoner witch. Women dying in media is a thing I categorically don't like, though, so I hope I can befriend her.

> shucks

"what brings you to my humble apartment, demon?"

"oh i was out hunting for auras and yours is super powerful. do you want to join your aura to mine so that i can spread my dominion across the face of this pathetic world?"

she is like "fuck yeah i do, what do we have to do"

"i don't know... i've never done this before... i think... we do this?"

wild heat spreads through your legs as you approach. you feel your muscles fill with excitement, from hip to hoove. it's all you can do not to break out in a lusty pagan jig. softly but insistently, you push her to the carpeted floor, until her head rests in the center of her pentagram.

played by Imogen Binnie

"you know i find it's best to do that in the kitchen or the bathroom, carpet's such a hassle to clean"

"that is excellent advice, i don't know why that never occured to me"

you settle over her, straddling her hips, black fur brushing her thighs.

"is it sex, do we do sex?"

"i'm pretty sure it's **sex**"

> I do! In fact it looks like we are about to become friends "with benefits."

> sex

the witch clasps you with her legs and twists until she rests on top of you.

she reaches down to your body to stroke it. when she does, her hand sinks into your mass of snakes. some coil around her arm, tickling her with their tongues as they slither up her limb.

she gasps in astonishment as you draw her into your body, enveloping her with writhing, scaled flesh. you feel your snakes passing over every inch of her, just as she must feel their cool scales playing across her flesh.

she resurfaces and pulls herself playfully out of you with a wicked grin.

"this is nice"

"are you ready?"

"i'm **ready**"

> She fists my snake torso.

> i'm ready

"wait, what the fuck is that?"

"i think it's a wolf vagina? uh oh look out"

your limbs give out from under you as another wolf wriggles its way out of your womb. blood and fluids drip all over the carpet, then more spatter across the walls and ceiling as the freshly-emerged wolf shakes its coat. the witch, perched on your belly, stares in shock. the wolf pads over, sniffs her, licks her face a few times, then burrows back into your vagina.

SABBAT by Eva Problems

"so uh"

"NOPE"

she wriggles out of your grasp and sits across from you on the carpet. she sighs. so do you.

"hmmm"

"sorry!"

"no, it's cool"

"well..." she casts her eyes around the room. they come to rest on the bong on the table.

"we could get really high and make out for a while."

"i am pretty sure **that also works**."

Aw man but I give birth to a wolf right before we're about to D. I.! I think it's fine though. We decide to get high on weeds and make out.

> that also works

she opens up a weed jar on the table and unscrews it. she starts to reach in.

"wait" you say. you take the weed jar from her, hold it in front of your eyes, and utter a few syllables of eldritch power. there is a sizzling, black-purple flash, and a thin wisp of violet smoke streams up, coalescing into the vague shape of a baphomet's head, before dissipating.

you have transmogrified the herb into wytchweed, a formidable substance indeed. few are the mortals who can withstand it. you pass the jar back to her and she packs a bowl, then passes the bong to you.

you clamp the beak of your left head around the mouthpiece, making as snug a fit as you can with your stiff beak. you gaze intently at the bowl with your right head, and as your eyes flash with a brilliant purple gleam, the bowl lights, and you draw.

you pass it to the witch and hold it. this is impressive because you're not quite sure if you even have lungs anymore. you crane your necks back and blow twin spumes of smoke into the cool air of the apartment. your crystal crown carves delicate trails through the soporific cloud of purple smoke.

she takes a massive rip and holds it. impressive! she is powerful indeed, to endure the potent wytchweed for so long. her eyes water and finally she coughs out an equally massive

played by Imogen Binnie

cloud of thick purple smoke. she keeps coughing.

"you okay?"

"mokay"

"you need some water?"

"eah"

you nip into her kitchen, rummage around in her cupboards until you find a glass, fill it, bring it back. she drinks some. she seems to have recovered somewhat.

so you make out.

I use magic to turn the weed into wytchweed and hit the bong even though my mouth is now beaks. Now we'll get high and make out even though my mouth is now beaks.

> so you make out

hell yeah. now her aura is joined to yours, bolstering your power.

you pull away after a while and smile at her as best you can manage. "my work tonight is not yet done."

"okay have fun, i'm gonna watch some anime while this shit lasts"

damn. that sounds really fun.

maybe just one episode.

—-

ten episodes later, you slip out again into the dead night, a fledgling demoness with the world to gain.

you can sense two powerful auras in the city, almost blinding in their brilliance. were you to take them into your own, nothing could stop you.

which aura will you hunt

rigid mesh white crosses

> rigid mesh white crosses

this aura festers in the pit of your astral senses like a throbbing cheek sore torn open by molars that you just can't help but probe with your tongue just to know you can still suffer. it feels inimical to your very being.

SABBAT by Eva Problems

you scowl as best as your inhuman features allow as you near the aura's source. it feels like a migraine now. there. a house in some forgotten suburb. **second floor.**

> second floor

you clamber to the balcony window and peer inside. a simple cross above the bed. a few posters for generic christian rock bands. a young man at a clean desk posting on... bible discussion forums? oh come on dude, for real?

how did this dweeb get such a powerful aura? ugh he's probably like a "good person" or something.

bust in the goddamn window

> bust in the goddamn window

you crouch down on black-furred haunches, compressing for a tremendous leap. in midair, you deliver a twirling hooved kick to the window, shattering it. landing, you crouch yet again and flip through the window.

he starts to flip the fuck out because a goddamn demon just broke into his bedroom.

you peirce him between the glowing stares of your twin crow heads. your voice seems to thrum and resonate with your whirling crystal crown.

"you will join your aura to mine so that my dominion shall spread to cover the earth"

he's like "nuuuhhhhh weh weh wehh" who gives a shit you aren't even fucking listening

"THEN I WILL TAKE YOUR POWER FROM YOUR **FLENSED CARCASS**"

    Honestly? In real like I'm not even that mad at Christians. I was raised Methodist (like Stephen King!) and came out of it without much trauma, just not much lasting interest in being Christian. And I think a lot of blasphemy is kind of ... I don't know. Boring, I guess. And mean-spirited? I mean I get it, some people have been hella traumatized by Christianity and totally hate it and want to yell at it, and I think they should. But I think most Christians are not bad people. And I think Jesus made some good points! It's just that, like in pretty much every other group, the loudest people in Christianity are also the most self-righteously wrongheaded. So I feel a little reluctant to get stoked about murdering this kid who actually, probably is just trying to be a good person and sees Christianity as a viable way to do that.

Also I don't think I've ever seen the word "flensed" before but given the context—"flensed carcass"—I can tell that it's pretty good.

> FLENSED CARCASS

he grabs a cross from his desk drawer and brandishes it at you. it actually hurts, damn!

you lose a bit of mass as some of your body-snakes crisp and sizzle away under the assault. oh no oh no

oh no

oh thank fucking satan, crowley is okay!

you can't lose him again. you shrug aside the assault and steel yourself to retaliate.

he starts yammering about swords of the spirit and shields of faith and shit like that. somehow, probably unconsciously, he has thrown up a **powerful barrier** between the two of you.

> powerful barrier

you analyze the shimmering, interlocking whorls of the barrier. astral fractals of force and counterforce swirl beneath your gaze, dancing, shifting...

there.

with a shrill cry, you lash out with every one of your centipede limbs, striking ten points across the barrier in quick succession. the barrier seems unchanged.

the little shit laughs at you. he's like "god's love protects me" or some bullshit but you stare him the fuck down.

you're like

"no. nothing can protect you. you are already dead."

blood gushes from his nose as his barrier shatters, leaving him defenseless against your **counterattack**.

> counterattack

you glance down at your swollen womb, take a deep breath, and push. the beasts inside you howl and wriggle their way to freedom. one wolf emerges, then another.

they lope over to him and tear gaping chunks out of his

aura and dipshit dick and balls. bloody prizes in their terrible maws, they return to your waiting womb.

he collapses. before he hits the floor, you lurch forward and **seize him**.

> seize him

he collapses in your merciless grip and screams a hideous scream as you suck the aura from his being.

power flows into you, bolstering you. you drop his spent husk. it shatters into ash when it hits the floor.

the most powerful auras in the city are yours. with them, the world. dawn breaks. your dawn.

TAKE THE POWER WITHIN YOURSELF

actually, i'm good

Basically the guy does some Christian magic stuff to me and it sucks but then I wreck his magic and give birth to some wolves who maul him and then climb back inside me. I turn the kid's body to ash and absorb his aura.

But now I have to decide whether to take on all the power in the world or not! I decide to.

> TAKE THE POWER WITHIN YOURSELF

The music changes! Because I have been writing this out while I play I've listened to the doom metal music thing like a dozen times. But now it is like stoner doom instead of classic doom! The musician seems even to have met a drummer.

you weave the strands of arcane power into the core of your being. power surges within you, but where before you were the plaything of terrible powers, now you are the instigator, the catalyst, the master.

you direct power through every synapse and cell of your twisted form, and are rewarded as you surge upwards. hell yes. it's attack of the 50-foot demon up in this **shit**.

> shit

you croak your triumph in hideous stereo into the smoggy night air. crackling energy arcs from your hovering crystal crown into nearby transformers and powerlines, and they

played by Imogen Binnie

shatter in blinding showers of sparks.

you focus your inner sight upon the thrumming webs of power ensaring the city. your sudden titanic growth has set them into a whirring, spinning chaos. you focus on a familiar thread, and pull.

in a purple flash, the witch appears in midair, just above your left head. with a cry of surprise, she lands in the bed of giant, soft feathers. she grabs on desperately.

"HOLY SHIT" she shouts.

"NOTHIN HOLY ABOUT IT, BABY" you say. "GUESS WHO JUST GOT FRONT-ROW SEATS TO THE RUINATION OF THE WORLD, HINT, IT'S YOU"

next stop: **downtown**

> downtown

you push buildings aside effortlessly as you make your way to the center of the city, leaving a swathe of destruction in your wake.

several explosions shock you, followed by hisses of pain and distress from your snake-mass. you look down. there are tanks in the street, barrels leveled directly at your massive, monstrous form. you focus on the astral webs of the street below, tracking nodes of potential energy and waves of hostility.

now.

the tanks fire again, but your snakes have already parted. the shells pass harmlessly through your body and detonate against buildings behind you. giant snakes drop from your body to the street below. they slither over to the tanks, coil around them, and constrict them into nonfunctional heaps of scrap. the snakes return and you laugh.

something screams overhead as more impacts rock your body.

"they've called in the **air force**!" yells the witch from her perch.

> air force

you hear the fighters circle around for another pass.

"NO YOU FUCKING DON'T" you bellow.

you reach down and impale parked cars on every one of your segmented limbs. you track the fighters' approach. just as they pull into range, you whirl, hurling a hail of cars directly into the squadron's flight path. you shield yourself from the shower of flaming debris, then straighten.

"oh my god you just took out a whole squadron of fighters!" cheers the witch.

"THOSE WERE F-22S, YOU KNOW WHAT ELSE CAN TAKE OUT A WHOLE SQUADRON OF THEM? THE INTERNATIONAL DATE LINE."

"oh."

the military is utterly crushed, routing in disarray. your rampage is now **unopposed**.

> unopposed

you stride through the burning streets, a colossus of depravity.

your womb bulges with the weight of your writhing lupine spawn, but you don't release them yet. you have a special prey for them.

you reach the capitol building. you knock off the top of the dome and peer inside at a suited sea of corpulent white fucks, fat as ticks on the blood of suffering, staring up in dumbfounded horror.

you press your furry groin up to the hole and push. wolves the size of metro cars plunge to the senate floor and start a gruesome hunt. howls and screams, like the most beautiful of music, drift up to you.

you gaze across the ruined skyline and take a **deep breath**.

> deep breath

your howl echoes across the desolate ruins: "BRING ME THE SKULL OF EVERY BANKER, EVERY MANAGER, EVERY EXECUTIVE, EVERY JAILER, EVERY PRIEST, EVERY RAPIST. BRING ME *SKULLS*"

and the people obey. by evening, a great mound of skulls fills the crumbling husk of the capitol dome.

under the directions of your witch-queen, the people shape the mound into a fine throne. yes. this is exactly what you have always wanted. you lean back into it and cross your hooved legs, then adopt your best brooding position. but re-

played by Imogen Binnie

ally, it's so hard to genuinely brood when you just got a god-damn skull throne. easing back in contented repose, you turn to your witch-queen.

"WAKE ME UP IF THEY DECIDE TO NUKE US OR ANYTHING, WILL YOU, DARLING?"

"no problem, boss!"

tonight, the city has fallen to you. soon, the world.

nothing can stop your terrible apotheosis.

NOTHING.

> NOTHING

THE END

also, you instated FULL COMMUNISM. YOU GET GOOD END!

There is also a request, on the credits page, that we be nice to animals in real life and don't sacrifice them. Agreed!

◆

I was going to close with some stuff about Joanna Russ's essay "What Can a Heroine Do? or Why Women Can't Write" where she basically talks about how traditional plot structures fail women for a lot of reasons, and why therefore women have to use other structures than the five-part Shakespeare plot or the eight-point Robert McKee plot structure, and how it relates to Twine games and the kinds of stories we can tell with them, and then to tie that stuff back to what I was saying in the beginning about witchcraft and stuff, but I am in a bad mood again. I think I need to eat. I'm stoked to play through *SABBAT: Director's Cut* with different body part/animal correspondences when I'm not writing about it, though! I bet the overall plot will be similar, but I want to know what the other monster body parts are like.

Plus my girlfriend, who is a midwife and to whom, therefore, I was happy to read aloud the sentence "your egregiously distended lupine womb is birthing and re-absorbing fully-grown wolves constantly," in the middle of this playthrough, has made me soup and ginger tea. These, now, are the most powerful magical objects in arm's reach.

HORSE MASTER
BY TOM MCHENRY
PLAYED BY NAOMI CLARK

A gallop across pixelated desert, a hollow white figure with a cowboy hat. You can't fool me, *Horse Master*; I already know your ways.

I played *Horse Master* three times last year. This is the fourth time I've played *Horse Master*, so I can tell you that it's not actually a game about Horses, not really. On the other hand, it is a game about Masters.

This is the same kind of warning that you might get from a friend who recommended the game to you. "Yeah, there's this picture of a dude on a horse in the desert at the beginning, but it's not a western or anything like

Horse Master by Tom McHenry

that. It's really weird. Pretty disturbing. You'd totally like it."

Horse Master makes promises and breaks them, frequently, but only if your expectations are taken in by the poses it strikes.

A playthrough (like this) one might show you the emotional and critical experience of someone playing a game, but *Horse Master* is definitely a game whose texture and tone irrevocably changes after playing it once. I could pretend to be playing *Horse Master* with "fresh eyes," but my eyes aren't fresh: I confess to x-raying *Horse Master*, and to mutating my own vision in the process.

> NEW GAME

You have trained your whole life for this moment: the first step in becoming a **Horse Master**.

You gotta buy a horse. **Your own horse**.

The structures commonly used by Twine games often have branches, cul-de-sacs, sometimes dead ends. These are the rules of many Twine games, of branching narratives, although they're not the only rule-like structures of *Horse Master*. Here at the introduction, I have several choices. Some of them are cul-de-sacs: a little fragment of story or description that will let me turn around, head back to the path leading forward. One of them will take me to the next scene of the story, past this opening premise--but if I make that choice first, I'll never be able to return here to see what I missed in the cul-de-sacs. Something is lost, even if it's just an opportunity to read a little more of the author's prose.

Horse Master disables the use of the browser's back button, and doesn't let the player rewind. A rule is established: if you move relentlessly forward, you'll never be able to stop and smell the flowers. *Horse Master*, I already know your ways. So let's not rush into buying a horse just yet.

> You

Sturdy, calloused, wind-blown.
Back

A hint of backstory, a whiff of cowboy archetypes. Jack Schafer? Clint Eastwood? "You." AYour past remains mostly a mystery, and you have no name. Besides "Horse Master," of course.

> Back
> Horse Master

played by Naomi Clark

A master of horses. A coveted position (with tenure!) hard won in reward for excellence in horse mastery across all disciplines.

Back

> Horse Master: a master of horses. Tenure: a cessation of insecurity.

> > Back
> > Your own horse

The salesman left the factory showroom a few moments ago to talk to the foreman about incorporating some of **your specifications** into your horse.

You are alone with **your thoughts** while a scuffed plexiscreen buzzes **some sun-faded government propaganda**.

> Things to know about horses: they come from a factory. They can be made to specification.

> > some sun-faded government propaganda

REBEL GROUPS DEFEATED...PEACE RESTORED THROUGH STRENGTH OF MORALS...PRESIDENT: "LIFE IS A SUCCESSION OF DISAPPOINTMENTS"...LABOR SATISFACTION ALL-TIME HIGH...JOANNA'S BABY BUMP?...

You heard all this on the bus to the **factory showroom** anyway.

> This is a future with plexiscreens and moral placation in the face of rebellion. A future where an aspirant Horse Master has to take a bus to the horse factory.

> > factory showroom
> > your thoughts

That salesman seemed to think you didn't know what you were talking about re: horses. Your father's legacy. The **dexobrimadine** tension skipping your molars against each other as could give off sparks. What is taking so long already?

> More backstory unfolds: the ghost of a father. Something that sounds

like a drug, let's see . . .

> dexobrimadine

Schedule II controlled substance. The nightly drip is essentially a job requirement for the mastery of horses in order to react with an almost unconscious speed to their powerful movements and keep yourself alive for continued mastering of horses. Now that you're striking out on your own, you've upped **the dosage to a professional level**, hence your **obnoxiously clattering teeth all morning**.

> Schedule II controlled substance

Schedule II drugs, substances, or chemicals are defined as drugs with a high potential for abuse, less abuse potential than Schedule I drugs, with use potentially leading to severe psychological or physical dependence. These drugs are also considered dangerous.

Some examples of Schedule II drugs are: cocaine, methamphetamine, methadone, hydromorphone (Dilaudid), meperidine (Demerol), oxycodone (OxyContin), fentanyl, Dexedrine, Adderall, piloxophite, brinotyline (ConCussotine) and—of course—dexobrimadine,"**The Horse Master's Lament**."

> The Horse Master's Lament

. . . Now that you're striking out on your own, you've upped **the dosage to a professional level**, hence your **obnoxiously clattering teeth all morning**.

> the dosage to a professional level

Though the FDA recommends no more than 6 mL administered nightly, the generally accepted wisdom in the professional Horse Master community is the so-called "Perfect Ten" (10 mL intravenous over an 6 hour period).

As of three days ago, you have graduated yourself to a professional pharmaceutical level. **Let's do this**.

This future has the same drug classifications established by the US Controlled Substances Act of 1970, but new drugs alongside some familiar "abusable, but presumably all right in sensible doses" pharmaceuticals. To keep up with your peers (competitors?) you're not taking a sensible dose. "The professional Horse Master community" probably has message boards

played by Naomi Clark

that you spend hours reading.

> Let's do this

The salesman left the factory showroom a few moments ago to talk to the foreman about incorporating some of **your specifications** into your horse. . . .

> your specifications

The dexo has met your giddy excitement about purchasing your first horse and is making you second-guess everything. Did you remember to ask for everything and in the proper order? Is that why the salesman was so put off by you?

Let's see, you wanted a:

Furioso-Hellfist

Europa Trotter

Carolina Coffinbreath

?

    There are other games where the player picks what kind of horse to ride, but the choices are usually more prosaic: a roan, an Arabian stallion, a chestnut filly. This is a shopping experience: unlike the cul-de-sacs that a player can pass by and never read, the game now allows a change of heart, a retracing. Which horse did the Horse Master ask to have custom-made? (Past tense.)

> Carolina Coffinbreath

Sure, the Carolina Coffinbreath. Consistently the choice of all the top international Horse Masters, achieving Horse Mastery with a "Coffer" would mark you as a bold new talent operating at the highest skill level of all Horse Masters.

Their coloration is always a deep black such as devours all light striking it. They normally stand no taller than 16 hands, but grow elaborate flared carapaces that intimidate all other breeds.

There's no way Dad would ever have purchased a premium breed like a Coffer. But he's not here.

That's the horse I came for and that's the horse I

asked for.

Whoa, that's not what I meant...

We can revise the Horse Master's past decisions, remember again, decide that the air of pretension suggested by the Carolina Coffinbreath isn't for this Horse Master.

> Whoa, that's not what I meant...
> Europa Trotter

Of course, a Europa Trotter, just like the first horse you ever saw. Maybe you're overly sentimental (most Horse Masters regard this breed as having poor hoof formation due to impure bloodlines), but a well-built Europa can still strum your wonderstrings.

They can range in color from #f9f9f9 to as dark as #646270, and their musculature, temperment and sheen can vary just as wildly, depending on how well-mastered they are.

That's right, that's the horse I ordered.

Wait, that's not what I said at all...

> Wait, that's not what I said at all...
> Furioso-Hellfist

Right! The Furioso-Hellfist. The breed is an oaky amber in coloration with limited markings and is known for an arrogant gait. They regularly stand as tall as 18 hands and can expect a long life.

The first horse you ever assisted mastering (when you were only 8!) was a Furioso-Hellfist and this is why you can't raise your left arm over your shoulder. His name was Cruel Saunders.

That's right, that's the horse I ordered

Wait, that's not the horse I asked for...

Things to know about horses: Their coloration is sometimes defined with hexadecimal numbers, much like the colors on a web page. A horse breed can be characterized with words, but a horse is also a set of numbers, especially when that horse is an object in a video game. Horses can injure their masters. I will name my horse for this playthrough "Kindly Saunders."

played by Naomi Clark

> That's right, that's the horse I ordered

You are waiting on the completion of your custom-bred Furioso-Hellfist.

Sitting in one place for so long on the dexobrimadine is doing funny things with your **sense of time passing/not passing**.

> sense of time passing/not passing

For example, you are certain that:

The salesman will have entered from the far set of double doors. He will have had been chuckling at his private joke and will have—

And then:

> And then

The salesman enters from the far set of double doors. He's chuckling at his private joke and wiping his still wet fingers on his damp tie.

"Sheena says she's never heard of a Furioso-Hellfist with specs like this before, but it's not outside the scope of the theoretical musculature load." He sniffs, "Frankly, I've been in the horse business for 18 years and I think you're just showing off. Grow a horse to these levels—well it's like you aren't taking these noble animals seriously."

You are not impressed by his lack of vision.

    Games often do funny things with time; drugs often do funny things with time. I have visited this moment three times before. The Horse Master, my puppet in this game, is a dexobrimadine junkie or a visionary. Cruel Saunders Jr. is being pushed to the limits of artificed horse-ness by the foreman, who happens to be a woman.

> You are not impressed by his lack of vision.

There is a reason this man is a horse salesman and not a Horse Master. Your father despised men like this.

He sighs, "They're spinning up the nutrient vat right now. **Confirmation of your payment** will trigger the fertilization process."

He slides a chipped glass PayPalm invoice to you. It glows on the brushed steel counter, waiting. Pregnant.

A simple palmsplay and you'll own the new growth horse that will come to define your career. Your own legacy.

> Confirmation of your payment

Between the cost of the animal-grade dexobrimadine (which you then cut with store-bought distilled water and a vitamin-heavy nutrient wash to keep your liver strong enough to process it all) and the cost of your Furioso-Hellfist, you've leveraged everything.

You'll have some substantial loans come due once you become a Horse Master. Luckily, top Horse Masters essentially ascend from the cash-based economy to a place of pure grace and skill.

In the quest for tenure, the Horse Master has taken a dive into debt—and, it turns out, poverty. This game signals something different about its economy and goals; unlike many simulation games that coax the player to build bigger-and-better engines to produce more and more resources which can then be reinvested to repeat the cycle, the Horse Master intends to transcend, to depart from the "cash-based economy to a place of pure grace and skill." So wealthy and powerful that one no longer needs to think of petty trifles like money, of debt and labor crises? A promise of security in a cultural institution, forever? A master, a don, a lord. A legate of horse mastery.

> You'll have some substantial loans . . . (Back)
> A simple palmsplay . . .

The glow of the PayPalm flares and then fades. The salesman takes the simple pane back from you and clicks his tongue. The two of you watch the **clucking propaganda** for a few minutes. He never offers you coffee.

> clucking propaganda

The loop has updated at least, so there's a brief twinge of novelty:

ANOTHER WIN FOR PASTA? IT COULD HAPPEN...SHOCKING PATRIOTISM TIPS THE GOVERNMENT DOESN'T WHAT YOU TO KNOW...FREDERICK TO GIALLA: "MAYBE NEXT LIFE!"...REBEL

played by Naomi Clark

LEADERS IMPOTENT, STUDY PROVES...

The salesman notices your apathy. "More like LAMEstream media, right?" he says.

> The salesman notices your apathy.

Theres a short 8-bit fanfare [Play "Horse Master (Theme from Horse Master)"] to cover up the whirring sound as a rotating cylinder rises from the floor. On top of the cylinder, illuminated from below, is a **blue sphere**.

Here the *Horse Master* soundtrack kicks in. Like your other sense-impressions of this factory showroom, the soundtrack exists in your imagination. Like the misleading introductory image of the game, the soundtrack evokes video games of the 1980s, but in a sci-fi setting. Hardly an unusual pairing of past and future, to be sure.

>blue sphere

Your horse isn't blue, of course. The blue comes from the foamy nutrient gravy. Suspended within it, the size of a pinky knuckle, is the slumbering larva of your horse, freshly struck from the egg sac of its queen's papal dome.

You will have had hefted it and it will be warm and round in a perfect way—

The music ends. You are still staring at the blue sphere on the fully extended column.

Even though there are no other customers on the showroom floor, it's clear the salesman is impatient for you to leave.

Take your horse.

Things to know about horses: They gestate in egg sacs laid by a queen, much like insects. They aren't allowed to mature past a larval stage; we will take Cruel Saunders Jr. home to finish that process.

> Take your horse.

The moment you lift the blue orb, the underlighting flips off and the cylinder drops immediately back into the floor.

You heft it and it is warm and round in a perfect way. It has a fleshy give. A breast almost—no, but rubbery like a water balloon.

Horse Master by Tom McHenry

You are moving very. Slowly. Knowing what you have sacrificed to hold this little ball, knowing just how fresh into our world this frankfurter of life is—anyway, you are terrified to drop it. Break it.

You will clench your hand and the plasticized rubber bladder will rip and the foamy gravy will run down your fist and one scrape of your heel will make this horse a pink streak on the—

The salesman is holding the door open for you to leave.

    This is the third moment of future-vision for the Horse Master, and the only one that doesn't come to pass immediately thereafter. Clenching the Horse Master's hand to destroy the horse larva is a dead-end to the narrative branching that was cut off, a refusal to engage in horse mastery that the player is only allowed to glimpse, never to choose.

    > The salesman is holding the door open for you to leave.

"Fucking deviant," the salesman mutters as he locks the door behind you.

You leave the horse factory, still carrying the blue sphere of your horse with more care than it probably requires. It's late enough that you have to take two buses to get home. You're not dumb: You wrap the sphere in an old sweatshirt and put that old sweatshirt in a plastic bag. You try carrying it like you don't absolutely depend upon its contents to survive. You try to not draw any attention to yourself.

The rides are long. Longer still because individual moments are tending to balloon, you notice.

You try to not be aware of every slow movement of the bus driver. You try not to be bored both now and in all the future permutations of soon-to-be-now that your dexo'd brain can retrieve. Bored+.

    Are all aspiring Horse Masters deviants, genetically engineering creature to take home and master? Or only the ones who are poor, indenturing themselves to debt, showing symptoms of dexobrimadine abuse?

    > You try to not be aware . . .

It's late when you get to your building. The tide of awareness: receded.

Three flights up. A single room. You open the bag, then carefully unfold the sweatshirt.

played by Naomi Clark

There's a wet spot. You run your hands over the soft soft orb, back and forth. Nothing. You turn on the bathroom lights and hold it up. No leaks. Just condensation. Probably.

You fill the bathtub with room temperature water to float the orb in it, water rationing be damned. Even with the faucet on full, this takes almost a half hour.

You're so tired that you almost forget to hang your dexobrimadine drip before **you nod off on the futon**.

Things to know about horses: they grow in bathtubs like novelty children's toys made of superabsorbent polymers, or maybe Sea Monkeys. We still don't know why Horse Masters have to sleep with IV bags full of dexobrimadine; perhaps we never will. Perhaps we don't need to.

> you nod off on the futon

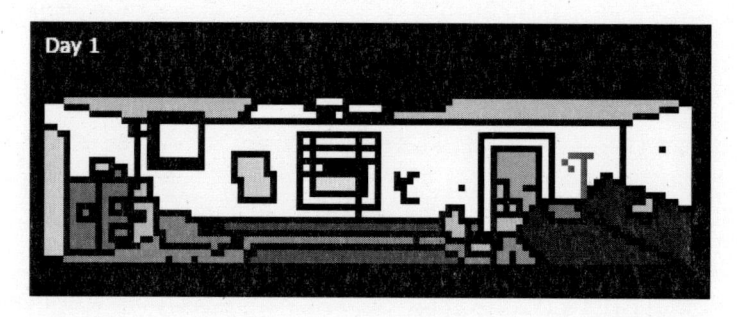

Day 1

Breed: Furioso-Hellfist

Age: 1

Growth Phase: Larva

Glamour: 1

Uncanny: 4

Pep: 5

Realness: 5

Discrection: 4

The little blue sphere burst in the tub. Diluted nutrient gravy gives the water a bluish hue. Your little horse uses its cilia to push itself around your bathtub.

You'll be showering in the sink until your horse can breathe on its own in a couple days.

Horse Master by Tom McHenry

You have 20 days until the Horse Master Competition. You have 3 actions left today.

Inject Horse with Nutrients

Feed Horse

Electrostim Horse Apodemes

Groom Horse

Watch Television

Hang dexobrimadine drip and try to sleep

Welcome to the heart of *Horse Master*: daily life while trying to raise a horse, from its soak in nutrient gravy to its apotheosis, twenty days away. *Horse Master* now reveals itself as a resource management sim, with three actions a day and a set of choices to spend those actions, seemingly fraught with meaning.

Things to know about horses: They have cilia as babies. They are, from a vantage at the heart of this game, a collection of five stats, like the points of a star. There's no explanation of what these stats do or why they're important, no guiding light of a tutorial or a diegetic guiding light. Maybe we'll find out eventually! Maybe it's a mystery to unsnarl! Or maybe it's just like the purpose of dexobrimadine?

We're fully confronted with the squalor of aspirant Horse Mastery. How did our Horse Master get to this state? It probably has something to do with the occasionally-mentioned father? Or perhaps all would-be masters are poor, sleeping on futons, showering in the sink, living in single rooms made of macropixels whose diagonal relationships signfiy cracked walls, dirty floors, peeling paint, uneven venetian blinds, an IV stand.

> Watch Television

Day 1

...REPORT: PRAYER "MOST EFFECTIVE REMEDY" FOR MENTAL ILLNESS...PRODUCTIVITY AT NEW HIGH...PIP TO GREGG: "NOT LIKELY"...CHESTERTON 4-0 CHAMPS OVER MADISON... BANNER ADS MOST VALUABLE EXPORT...**Day**

> Day

Breed: Furioso-Hellfist

Age: 1

Growth Phase: Larva

played by Naomi Clark

Glamour: 2

Uncanny: 5

Pep: 6

Realness: 6

Discrection: 5

. . . You have 20 days until the Horse Master Competition. You have 2 actions left today.

If you're accustomed to resource choices, this one is clearly a trap: It drips some content out at you, but nothing changes about your horse's stats. You return to the heart of the game, one action poorer. That's not the whole of the clue, however, because the invocation of television serves as a narrative warning: This is purposeless time-wasting (and mostly just propaganda, in the dystopia of Horse Masters), unlike the state-changing shuffling of resources. Similarly, the option to sleep suggests cutting the day's actions short, at least to a player who's seen these forms used in other works.

> Inject Horse with Nutrients

You slide the needle into the main nerve bundle of your horse's central nervous system. It's a full cocktail of essential vitamins, nutrients, stimulants, and selective serotonin reuptake inhibitors. You got a full set of these injections from the pharmacist who provided the liberal allotments of dexobrimadine. **Best not to dwell on how much it costs.**

Discretion +3

Uncanny +1

> Best not to dwell on how much it costs.

Day 1

Breed: Furioso-Hellfist

Age: 1

Growth Phase: Larva

Glamour: 2

Uncanny: 6

Pep: 6

Realness: 6

Discrection: 8

. . . You have 20 days until the Horse Master Competition. You have 1 action left today.

> Feed Horse

Many horses are raised to a professional caliber without ever eating solid foods in their entire lives. You probably shouldn't overdo it, but might give your **horse the edge in realness it needs to win**.

Realness +3

Discretion +2

> horse the edge in realness it needs to win.

Breed: Furioso-Hellfist

Age: 1

Growth Phase: Larva

Glamour: 2

Uncanny: 6

Pep: 6

Realness: 9

Discretion: 10

There's nothing left you can do for your horse today.

Hang dexobrimadine drip and try to sleep

Like any Tamagotchi, like any Digimon, like any Nintendog, you can also feed a horse in this game. Or you can inject its central nervous system with nutrients. Both will randomly raise your horse's Discretion by a small amount, but injections make your horse more Uncanny while solid food promotes Realness—a slang word with its roots in the ball scene of drag culture, where it was attached to different categories of competition. Military Realness. Executive Realness. Butch Queen Realness. The other end of drag competition categories is usually "twisted" or "bizarre," but uncanny serves as a synonym with some technological connotations.

The change in light as afternoon and evening fall across the Horse Master's apartment is a sombering and noticeable touch, another care for

played by Naomi Clark

detail in a haltingly sketched world.

> Hang dexobrimadine drip and try to sleep

You listen and imagine you can hear your horse splishing in the tub. You sleep. **Your dream is a dialtone that lasts all night.**

So are the unsettling fragments of dream that float by, every three actions, like clockwork.

> Your dream is a dialtone that lasts all night.

Day 2

Breed: Furioso-Hellfist

Age: 2

Growth Phase: Larva

Glamour: 3

Uncanny: 7

Pep: 7

Realness: 10

Discretion: 11

You're up before dawn to check the readouts from the first day. Those numbers up above are right where they should be on an overall efficiency curve. You dip your hand in the tub to do a physical check on your horse. No bifida, no unsealed clefts.

The nutrient gravy makes your hand smell like artificial banana flavoring.

You have 19 days until the Horse Master Competition. You have 3 actions left today. . . .

Every day, the tiny horse grows a little bit. As we feed and care for it, the game apportions us another slice of story, some words to go with the skeletal numbers of our horse's condition. This is not purely an economic sim of making numbers go up: there are loose flaps of flesh hanging on those bones, telling us things to know about horses: sometimes the engineering process goes wrong, and cleft cartilage or spina bifida results. Do horse factory showrooms accept returns?

Horse Master by Tom McHenry

> Electrostim Horse Apodemes

The fans hum as the electrostim powers up. To which end do you attach the electro pads?

Dorsal

Ventral

> Dorsal

You clip the pads to the dorsal side of your horse. There's a flash of current, some jitters, and you remember that this doesn't hurt the horse so don't think about it, **okay**?

Pep +1

Uncanny +2

More things to know about horses: like crustaceans, they have apodemes as connections for muscles instead of tendons. They can be electrocuted without being hurt... but possibly not without feeling pain?

The first time I played *Horse Master*, I couldn't help but wonder at the outcome of these choices: would my horse grow into a different kind of Furioso-Hellfist if I emphasized Glamour over Realness, Uncanny instead of Discretion? Would I achieve a different Pokemon evolution? Games have trained us to expect divergent outcomes.

> okay?
> Electrostim Horse Apodemes
> Ventral

You clip the pads to the ventral side of your horse. There's a short sizzling sound and a copper smell to the air. **The horse is stimulated**.

Pep +4

Realness +3

Electrical stimulation gives your horse more Pep. When you shock its underside, your horse gains Realness as well; on its back, Uncanny. Perhaps the shocks cause something burnt, something strange, to grow in or out of sight? Or perhaps it doesn't matter. Some players would care that we're inflicting pain (supposedly without real injury) on a tiny, infant, crustacean future-horse. Playing *Horse Master* several times has desensitized me to this assemblage of numbers and words, as has dissecting the game thoroughly. I

played by Naomi Clark

had to show you the apodemes, after all.

> The horse is stimulated.
> Groom Horse

You shoplifted a selection of shampoos and conditioners to help with grooming. Which do you apply this time?

Revelry

Shrike

Grandeur

We move again through the heart of the game, through its changing cycle of light and darkness, past the same words that you start not to notice anymore. On the last option of care: grooming, redolent with preconceived notions about brushing manes and conditioning hair.

> Shrike

Shrike smells like just soap. It is the shampoo and conditioner combination of realness. When you are a Horse Master you will never, ever use Shrike on yourself again.

Glamour +2

Realness +3

And rinse.

Shrike is apparently the most prosaic shampoo for horses and humans alike.

> And rinse.

There's nothing left you can do for your horse today.

Hang dexobrimadine drip and try to sleep

Shrike is the grooming product form of Realness. Reverly does the same for Pep, and Grandeur for Discretion. All three increase Glamour as well, of course. If, like a diligent sim player, you're paying attention to how these products affect all your horse's vital stats, its existence in the mathematical underpinning of *Horse Master*, you've now learned a few more thing. Enough, at this point, to do a survey of how the nascent Horse Master's options shake out:

Discretion: Three different actions (two feeding, one grooming)

Horse Master by Tom McHenry

    Pep: Three different actions (two electrical stimulation, one grooming)
    Glamour: Three different actions (all three breeding)
    Realness: Three different actions (feeding, electrical stimulation, grooming)
    Uncanny: Two different actions (feeding, electrical stimulation)
    Seven different actions in three categories, which each increase two stats out of five: this is the nearly symmetrical pentagram that Horse Master offers for inspection as you gravely undertake its central gameplay.

    > Hang dexobrimadine drip and try to sleep

Tomorrow's a big day. **So far your plan is working.**

    > So far your plan is working.

You wake up to find your horse walking clumsy circles on the cold bathroom tile. It still flexes its gillflaps, but they're so much decoration, as it's now breathing through actual lungs (of a sort).

The stale nutrient bath makes your bathroom pungent. You drain the tub.

Your little horse has lived through the larval phase. This is a great sign. You're finally confident enough to name it.

You cup the tiny pupal horse in both hands and you give it a name with a whisper:

_____

"is what they'll call you."

    Horses have gills and lungs (of a sort). An input form makes an appearance, so that the players of *Horse Master* may express some free-form choice, a name . . .

    > Kindly Saunders

. . . and have the game whisper an echo in response. "Kindly Saunders."

Kindly Saunders? **A fine name.**

    > A fine name.

Name: Kindly Saunders
Breed: Furioso-Hellfist

played by Naomi Clark

Age: 3

Growth Phase: Pupa

Glamour: 6

Uncanny: 10

Pep: 13

Realness: 16

Discretion: 12

Kindly Saunders is now a pupa. It skitters around your carpet, pouncing on dust bunnies. It naps a lot, puffing tiny snores out of its spiracles.

You have 18 days until the Horse Master Competition. You have 3 actions left today.

Every so often, the horse gets a little bigger and does something cute and mildly entertaining as I crank the mechanisms of *Horse Master* forward by choosing actions. Possibilities open up, free from the specter of guidance: Is it better to try and keep the horse's statistics carefully balanced, or try to make a very particular kind of horse? Perhaps Kindly Saunders should be Uncanny and Glamorous.

> Inject Horse with Nutrients
> Best not to dwell on how much it costs.
> Electrostim Horse Apodemes
> Dorsal
> okay?
> Groom horse
> Grandeur

Grandeur has a deep caramel musk. Your horse could be equally at home in the board room or in a limousine.

Glamour +4

Discretion +3

And rinse.

> and rinse.

Name: Kindly Saunders

Breed: Furioso-Hellfist

Age: 3

Growth Phase: Pupa

Glamour: 10

Uncanny: 15

Pep: 14

Realness: 16

Discretion: 18

There's nothing left you can do for your horse today.

> Hang dexobrimadine drip and try to sleep

Kindly Saunders climbs on your chest to sleep. It has to knock this off, because soon it will be big enough to crush you if it tries this trick. **Just for tonight, though?**

Horse Master is trying to convince me that this tiny horse is adorable, for now, until it becomes huge and dangerous. This is a three-week long relationship, between made-to-order crustacean horse and aspiring debtor-junkie trainer; I'm not sure I can buy it. Perhaps I've been blinded by staring too long at the underpinnings, the numerical skeleton that's what truly makes Kindly Saunders slightly different than any other horse created on any other playthrough of *Horse Master*.

> Just for tonight, though?

Name: Kindly Saunders

Breed: Furioso-Hellfist

Age: 4

Growth Phase: Pupa

Glamour: 11

Uncanny: 16

Pep: 15

Realness: 17

Discretion: 19

Kindly Saunders has a budding carapace on its head and you

played by Naomi Clark

can already see small whorls that will eventually form its unique individual patterning like a human fingerprint.

It practice rams against your ankle every spare moment.

You have 17 days until the Horse Master Competition. You have 3 actions left today.

    Things to know about horses: they have carapaces and ram things.
    Things to know about me: like a dexobrimadine addict, I can see slightly into the future of *Horse Master*, and know that it's all right to burn through a day watching television, sleeping.

> Watch Television

...FOUR DEAD IN FED RAID ON UNSANCTIONED HORSE MASTER LEAGUE...STUDY:FAX MACHINES ARE BACK IN A COOL WAY!...RATINGS FOR DRAMATOWN DIP IN SEASON 2...SCIENTISTS: "SOME BLEEDING LIKELY AS GDP INCREASES"... **Day**

> Day
> Hang dexobrimadine drip and try to sleep

Another restless half-sleep. Kindly Saunders seems excited, too. **You're both excited, but probably for different reasons.**

> You're both excited, but probably for different reasons.

Day 5

The thing about Horse Mastering is that, once you get the hang of the basic physical tasks involved, it's basically just a giant game of spreadsheet management. The skill becomes chaining the right actions in order to maximize your efficiency and produce the best horse. Horse mastery means exploiting every action and every horse statistic.

So you got all the maximum combos off a Horse Mastery Internet forum and coded a series of macros to just let your computer apply your actions for you. And now Kindly Saunders is finally old enough to **try it out**.

    Horse Master pauses to give us an explanation of "horse mastering" which is also an explanation of the core activity in *Horse Master*. What's not mentioned is the ultimate purpose of the spreadsheet management exercise.

Horse Master by Tom McHenry

> try it out

Name: Kindly Saunders

Breed: Furioso-Hellfist

Age: 5

Growth Phase: Foal

Glamour: 13

Uncanny: 18

Pep: 17

Realness: 19

Discrection: 21

Kindly Saunders is the size of a smallish dog but is surprisingly heavy. There are hundreds of of pounds of potential muscle coils inside it, waiting to knit and grow.

You have 16 days until the Horse Master Competition. You have 3 actions left today.

Run maximum efficiency horse stat growth macro.

Inject Horse with Nutrients . . .

After four days, a horse is akin to small, dense dog, and *Horse Master* has given us a way out of having to choose actions. The maximum efficiency option is a shortcut around the economic gameplay we've been trained in. This kind of option is increasingly acknowledged even in massively-budgeted, glossy, over-produced games you can buy at a retail location near you: "Casual Difficulty," they now say, "for players who are new, or just want to enjoy the story." In either case, there's an acknowledgement that "gameplay" might not be the reason we're here.

> Run maximum efficiency horse stat growth macro.

You press CTRL+ALT+H on your keyboard. The macro triggers each of the actions in the optimum order for horse growth.

Yup.

This is the work.

played by Naomi Clark

-=MAX COMBO!=-

Glamour +6

Uncanny +6

Pep +6

Realness +6

Discretion +6

    The efficiency macro is amazing: by using all three actions for the day, our horse's stats raise by 30 points, evenly distributed. In case you're curious, taking three other actions will raise horse stats by an average of 10.5, so the macro is much, much better. From a sheer mechanical point of view, there's no reason to choose any other action. From an experiential point of view, once you've taken each action once, there may not be too much reason either. Purity? Role playing? A distaste for shortcuts.

    Horse Master likens it to labor, but what's really happening is that we're labor-saving, the kind of affordance that players of free games on mobile phones and social games pay $2.99 to gain access to. Energy point refills, speed boosts; here in the carefully considered world of *Horse Master*, these things are gratis, not monetized, and it's a more humane experience for it.

> This is the work.
> Hang dexobrimadine drip and try to sleep

You listen to Kindly Saunders breathe for a while and your mind drifts off. **Then it's just morning all over again.**

> Then it's just morning all over again.

Day 6

Name: Kindly Saunders

Breed: Furioso-Hellfist

Age: 6

Growth Phase: Foal

Glamour: 20

Uncanny: 25

Pep: 24

Realness: 26

Discretion: 28

Until today, Kindly Saunders has excreted all waste through its collocytic pores. Now, though, it's grunting and sitting constantly, meaning it wants to excrete its first bowel movement, but can't fully expand and contract its anus without help.

In the wild, the mother can easily do this with one of her special grooming tentilla. You, however, must do careful work with a cotton swab and pinkie finger until the fecal head begins to emerge. Congratulations.

You have 15 days until the Horse Master Competition. You have 3 actions left today.

It's morning, all over again. Now that we're relieved of the need to make any kind of choice, we can be introduced to new unplesantness: a realism not unfamiliar to actual animal breeders, but rarely included in adorable pet simulators.

> Run maximum efficiency horse stat growth macro.
> This is the work.
> Hang dexobrimadine drip and try to sleep

You lie awake for hours, absolutely certain this was a mistake. **You are no Horse Master.**

> You are no Horse Master.

Day 7 . . .

You began Kindly Saunders's operant conditioning a few days ago in subtle ways, but today you begin work with the silver whistle.

Good behavior earns a pleasing melody and a treat. Bad behavior? A low tone and the withholding of eye contact.

You have 14 days until the Horse Master Competition. You have 3 actions left today.

We go through the paces over and over, hand-cranking a projector that's showing a training montage of the would-be Horse Master and an increasingly large crustacean horse.

> Run maximum efficiency horse stat growth macro.
> This is the work.
> Hang dexobrimadine drip and try to sleep

played by Naomi Clark

You run your hand across Kindly Saunders's sleeping flank. This has been a hard day. You think about how these rich fuckers will never see you two coming. **Your dream is something about snow.**

Class-climbing anxiety; victory in this game is to show those rich fuckers, to become one of those rich fuckers--perhaps, in some unseen future iteration, an imagined later playthrough, to be a rich fucker who's shown by a new upstart?

> Your dream is something about snow

Day 8

Growth Phase: Weanling

Thanks to the dexobrimadine, you are able to move so fast that you only dislocate your thumb stopping Kindly Saunders's powerful hooves from caving in your skull. You play a low tone and wrap the thumb in tape.

You have 13 days until the Horse Master Competition. You have 3 actions left today.

Fragments of the Horse Master's dreams remain some of the most haunting phrases in this game. We finally know that dexobrimadine is a drug that, among other things, increases reaction time—or perhaps lets the Horse Master see just far enough into the future to avoid a horse's lethal attacks.

> Run maximum efficiency horse stat growth macro.
> This is the work.
> Hang dexobrimadine drip and try to sleep

The swelling hasn't gone down on your thumb. The nail is cracked. **You sleep hard, clutching the bandaged hand to your chest.**

> You sleep hard, clutching the bandaged hand to your chest.

Day 9

You discover Kindly Saunders shat on your warm coat in the night.

You play a low tone on the whistle. Enzymes in the horse-waste melted much of the lining and the stench takes hours to dissipate.

Horse Master by Tom McHenry

You won't need a winter coat when you're a Horse Master. You'll never be cold again.

You have 12 days until the Horse Master Competition. You have 3 actions left today.

Another thing to know about horses: their excrement can melt a winter coat. Horses are dangerous, expensive; they kill you and your scant material possessions. We are meant to understand that horse-mastery is an all-consuming pursuit that involves risk to life, property, solvency, sanity.

> Run maximum efficiency horse stat growth macro.
> This is the work.
> Hang dexobrimadine drip and try to sleep

You're developing a facial tic, almost like someone is twisting your left cheek. You try to smooth it out and hold it flat like a sheet on a bed. For some reason this makes you start remembering every person you've ever let down. The list is terrible even before it is comprehensive, but then: **sleep**.

The pressure evoked here, the specter of "every person you've ever let down," brings horse-mastery in conjunction with whatever each player might think of as a terrifyingly risky ambition. College applications, perhaps, or a dissertation. The anxiety of a make-or-break live performance, or a job interview. There's something beyond personal performance in the creation of a Horse, however: a thing that has existence beyond you, operating by rules you partially understand and have only practiced in your imagination before this point, and which will ultimately be on display in the Horse Master Competition.

> sleep

Day 10

Growth Phase: Yearling

You wake up early to vomit a little. It's muddy gray.

Kindly Saunders doesn't wake up.

You have sleep's awful certainty that your horse has died in the night. Then you see its chest rise and fall again.

You have 11 days until the Horse Master Competition. You have 3 actions left today.

> Run maximum efficiency horse stat growth macro.
> This is the work.

played by Naomi Clark

> Hang dexobrimadine drip and try to sleep

You've eaten plain foods all day, and you kept everything down. Between that and Kindly Saunders responding to its name (just once), **it's been a day full of accomplishments**.

> it's been a day full of accomplishments.

Day 11

Kindly Saunders is already so large, and hardly halfway grown. It's unclear how large a horse would live and grow if they weren't raised for competition.

You have 10 days until the Horse Master Competition. You have 3 actions left today.

Things to know about horses: Their age is measured in days. Nobody knows how large horses would be if they weren't grown and raised for one specific purpose (horse mastery). An eleven-day-old horse is a "yearling."

Things to know about games: they often try to compress time and experience into a rapidly digestible (or indigestible) chunk.

> Run maximum efficiency horse stat growth macro.
> This is the work.
> Hang dexobrimadine drip and try to sleep

Would your father even recognize what you've become? Did he want this for you? Did he ever notice you enough to want something for you? **What good are horses?**

Horses are not for riding, for pulling cards, for mounted law enforcement; they are simply the object of horse-mastery.

> What good are horses?

Day 12

Growth Phase: Tween

You realize your apartment is covered in the coarse hairs that Kindly Saunders keeps growing and shedding. The hair clings to itself like velcro and stays warm hours after leaving the follicle. You gather together almost two garbage bags of hair puffs while Kindly Saunders watches.

You have 9 days until the Horse Master Competition. You

have 3 actions left today.

> Run maximum efficiency horse stat growth macro.
> This is the work.
> Hang dexobrimadine drip and try to sleep

In any project, there is always a trough of enthusiasm. There is a lull. This lull is where doubt hunts you with the weapons of your own creation. Tonight, doubt tells you that even if Kindly Saunders is perfect, they will not let you win. You are not one of them. **Given a choice, they will always choose themselves.**

Once again, a sense of entry to an elite club—one that's guarded by an establishment that you're trying to break into . . . to become part of?

> Given a choice, they will always choose themselves.

Day 13

When it flexes, the skin of Kindly Saunders's haunches becomes translucent. You can see wet dark red musculature. Taut. Ready. You could whistle the pleasing melody all day in gratitude.

You have 8 days until the Horse Master Competition. You have 3 actions left today.

Things to know about horses: They are sometimes translucent. You can see their muscles then, as you can see their stats when they're hooked up to a computer. They are autoflayed, for greater transparency, information. I am in the process of flaying *Horse Master*, the game, to try and make it more transparent for reading.

> Run maximum efficiency horse stat growth macro.
> This is the work.
> Hang dexobrimadine drip and try to sleep

No food tasted good today. The utensils tasted like burning tires, but the food provided no sensation. **A molar is loose.**

> A molar is loose.

Day 14
Growth Phase: Pubescent

played by Naomi Clark

First thing in the morning there is a knock on the door and you do not know what to do. So you hide. The knock repeats and you clamp your hands over Kindly Saunders's snout and will it not to make noise and try to not breathe yourself (even though you are in all-consuming panic).

Whoever it was leaves. So okay.

You have 7 days until the Horse Master Competition. You have 3 actions left today.

Signs of death and dissolution: you begin to lose your teeth and your apartment at the same time.

> Run maximum efficiency horse stat growth macro.
> This is the work.
> Hang dexobrimadine drip and try to sleep

You are very proud of Kindly Saunders this day. You are afraid that it will be taken from you now, that's how proud you are. When you are proud of what you have done, God will hurt you to remind you that it was actually God who did it. You can feel that God would like to take Kindly Saunders away from you. God playing a low tone on a whistle the length of a battleship and then taking his eye contact away forever. **It is what you deserve.**

The Horse Master dreams of being trained and punished for disobedience by God, of having all credit for horse mastery decisions taken away. What is the relation of the player to this dreamer, this feared deity? If I close the browser window containing my current playthrough of *Horse Master*, all the information about Kindly Saunders, and this particular incarnation of horse mastery in progress, will vanish without so much as a sound, much less a biblical deluge.

> It is what you deserve.

Day 15

You lose yourself in running your fingers through Kindly Saunders's **mane**. You are aware of just the sunlight, your breathing, and the gentle pull of the mane on your fingers.

You have 6 days until the Horse Master Competition. You have 3 actions left today.

> mane

Horse Master by Tom McHenry

Mane is a misnomer. The bundle of long prehensile tentilla emerging from behind the carapace that is called the mane was a surprise byproduct from the Fourth Evolutionary Improvement on the Foundational Horse Formulae (FHF).

A picture of what horses are like—carapace concealing apodemes, anus, mane-like tentilla, ramming surfaces, deadly hooves—emerges more and more. Does it make the player fonder? More apprehensive? Confused? Does it matter?

> Mane is a misnomer.
> Run maximum efficiency horse stat growth macro.
> This is the work.
> Hang dexobrimadine drip and try to sleep

You did not cry once today, even if you almost wanted to. So maybe you're probably getting the hang of the dexobrimadine? **The dream of flesh-colored fish**

>The dream of flesh-colored fish

You were evicted. You and Kindly Saunders are in an alley behind a failing strip mall. You are exposed.

You only have 5 days until the Horse Master Competition. You spent all of your actions trying to **find food today** and still have to go hungry.

You are ashamed at how bad you fucked up, but have to try to sleep, or you'll be too tired to try to find food tomorrow.

We are now in the climactic battle-disaster of *Horse Master*, where the horse and pursuit of its mastery has ruined health and home. *Horse Master* is now also a homelessness simulator: Everyone is more contingent, more random. If we make the wrong choice, the game can now end suddenly, with incarceration for shoplifting. Information is scarce—a line of errors—and finding food suddenly becomes pressing. Just as uncertainly, more vanishing cul-de-sacs of text appear, for the diligent narrative gamer to accumulate and absorb before hurrying on.

played by Naomi Clark

> You were evicted.

Name: Kindly Saunders

Breed: Furioso-Hellfist

Age: 16

Growth Phase: Pubescent

Glamour: 90

Uncanny: 95

Pep: 94

Realness: 96

Discretion: 98

Keys in the lock. Landlord. Deputized Military Officers. Notice on orange papers.

Previously: your landlord was casual regarding rent and punctuality. You were certain you could ignore it until you won. Nope: DMOs and everything.

Technically, this is an animal-free building.

They seize your dexobrimadine bags from the fridge to sell to other desperates like yourself. One of the DMOs motions like he will shoot Kindly Saunders, and the landlord begs him not to ruin the flooring.

Hot shame tears. You grab a half-packed garbagebag and whistle for Kindly Saunders to follow before it goes worse. **Your former landlord says he'll be rooting for you at the competition.**

    It's unclear exactly why the Horse Master was evicted, but the "normals," the people who don't hang around on Horse Master internet forums, don't seem to care much for people who spend all day taking horse mastery drugs and cleaning up after shedding, potentially lethal hoofed crustacean-equids. The potential for success at horse mastery—ascent to wealth and status—seems about as likely as winning American Idol, or the other characters in this game would be a little more respectful?

    > Your former landlord says he'll be rooting for you at the competition. (Back)

    > You are ashamed at how bad you fucked up, but have to try to sleep, or you'll be too tired to try to find food tomorrow.

Horse Master by Tom McHenry

There's enough dexy still in your blood stream that you wind up not really sleeping. Kindly Saunders does not understand why it is not at home. Every noise spooks it and it bleats and whinnies no matter how hard you try to calm it. You make it a bed of a sort on some garbage bags and cover it with more. This is the wrong neighborhood to have a horse at night.

You just wish there was some way to communicate to Kindly Saunders that this is only a temporary setback. **You've made it this far, you just have to make it a few more days.**

A young horse master and a horse, out on the streets, sleeping on garbage bags, malnourished—like a scene from a down-on-your-luck animated tale for kids. Not to worry. Our plucky hero will make it, especially due to being guided by a four-time player who knows where the pitfalls are.

> You've made it this far, you just have to make it a few more days.

Day 17

You are so tired. Without a safe place to sleep and food to eat, you will only receive two actions per day. The free library is across town and will take most of the day to visit. Scavenging food and usable materials can also take a full day.

You just have to keep you and Kindly Saunders alive 4 more days until the Horse Master Competition. You have 2 actions left today.

Scavenge for edible waste products.

Walk to the library to use a public computer to check stats.

Shoplift food

Hose bath.

Continue operant conditioning on horse.

Try to sleep.

The simulation of precarity is sharp: fewer actions because of stress, lack of security while sleeping, eating, bathing. Very little time for the "noble pursuits" of life (in this case, horse mastery).

> Scavenge for edible waste products.

After hours of searching, you finally find a dumpster behind a chain grocery store. They've sprinkled powdered

played by Naomi Clark

bleach on the top of the food to deter people just like you, but if you dig deep enough, there's some produce that looks untouched (only a little rotted) **It's something. You won't starve.**

> It's something. You won't starve

You and Kindly Saunders have a little food. How do you want to divvy it up?

Feed all the food to your horse.

Divide the food between the two of you.

Eat all the food yourself

A touching scene where it's tough to choose not to feed a confused adolescent horse, but we can learn something from it.

> Eat all the food yourself

Technically, Kindly Saunders doesn't need real food. Horses can often live off a combination of photosynthesis and enzyme breakdown for weeks. Of course, it's not optimum, but neither is you starving until you aren't able to compete. **You whistle for it to stand at the other end of the alley and eat, watching it always with a wary eye.**

A thing to know about horses: They can photosynthesize rather than eating.

> You whistle for it to stand at the other end of the alley and eat, watching it always with a wary eye.

It takes a while to learn these new actions, and there's not much time before the Horse Master Competition. The bath and operant conditioning improve your horse's stats, but there's no comforting rise of numbers anymore, not unless you spend a day going to the library—and even then, a change in stats only becomes meaningful if the player has actually bothered to remember what the horse's stats were before being evicted.

> Hose bath.

There is a hose behind the Thai Cheeseburger place. You spray Kindly Saunders down and the cold water causes it to rear up and tremble. You keep up and dodge to avoid its powerful hooves until it calms into the water temperature. A small river of accumulated grime runs off of it. Its shell gleams again in the sun.

Good, clean horse.

> Good, clean horse.
> Try to sleep

The dexy has worn off enough that you start trembling and don't stop all night long. Kindly Saunders gets jostled awake and spends most of the night pacing around you in a circle. It just keeps growing. It would have trouble standing in your old apartment now. **You'll both be okay.**

The Horse Master never once contemplates using this dread beast to commit violence, robbery, intimidation for money. There's a nobility to this life of drug addiction and animal training.

> You'll both be okay.

You have a headache that stretches over your whole body. You could really, really use some dexobrimadine, but absolutely no one is going to give you any. Luckily Kindly Saunders is basically raised by this point.

You just have to keep you and Kindly Saunders alive 3 more days until the Horse Master Competition. You have 2 actions left today.

Scavenge for edible waste products.

Walk to the library to use a public computer to check stats.

Shoplift food

Hose bath.

Continue operant conditioning on horse.

Try to sleep.

> Continue operant condition on horse.

You may be homeless, exhausted and starving, but Kindly Saunders's obedience will be fundamentally important in the Horse Master Competition. And so you drill for hours. The whistle. The two tones.

played by Naomi Clark

You train until you are too sluggish and disoriented to continue.

> You train until you are too sluggish and disoriented to continue.

You just have to keep you and Kindly Saunders alive 3 more days until the Horse Master Competition. You have 2 actions left today.

Shoplift food

Hose bath.

Continue operant conditioning on horse.

Try to sleep.

When you reach the second and last action of the day, it's too late to scrounge food or go to the library. It becomes tempting to shoplift, or just give up.

> Try to sleep.

Your eyes water. Your nose runs. Horses used to be different. Horse mastering used to be different. Your father was sure he would be in the last generation to master horses, but these things persist. If it could speak, would Kindly Saunders think of you as a friend? **Think of what you've lived through together.**

Some mysterious flashes of backstory. Horses used to be different. Were they mammals? Why did your father think horse mastery would become outmoded? Did he pass on his disdain for the horse-master establishment on to you?

> Think of what you've lived through together.

Day 19

It's almost impossible to hide Kindly Saunders anymore. If you needed to ride it (Safety Note: NEVER ride a horse), you would now need a ladder to get on top of it. What's more it now oxidizes luciferins, causing the distinct horse steaming bioluminescence that is quite unsettling to humans on a primal level and makes it like sleeping directly under an extremely muscular streetlight slash blast furnace.

You just have to keep you and Kindly Saunders alive 2 more days until the Horse Master Competition. You have 2 actions left today.

  Safety Note: NEVER ride a horse

  > Walk to the library to use a public computer to check stats.

You and Kindly Saunders walk to the far end of the city. Its hooves are bothering it; they aren't accustomed to this much walking, especially on asphalt. You keep chirping the high on the whistle to keep its spirits up. When you arrive at the free library, you spend ten minutes petting it and keeping calming eye contact. It has lost weight since your eviction, as have you.

You signup for free access to one of the two public computers. **You wait an hour for your turn.**

  > You wait an hour for your turn.

It's finally your turn, but the computer you get access to has dead ports. **You wait another hour for a turn on the other computer.**

  > You wait another hour for a turn on the other computer.

You fit the cables into the working ports, and get your first access to Kindly Saunders's stats in a while:

Name: Kindly Saunders

Breed: Furioso-Hellfist

Age: 19

Growth Phase: Adult

Glamour: 87

Uncanny: 92

Pep: 91

Realness: 93

Discretion: 95

You jot them down and compare them to your memory of your projected growth curves. It's still at least possible you'll pull this off.

You gather your things. You and Kindly Saunders walk all the

played by Naomi Clark

way back home **in the dusk**

These stats are great, thanks to the efficiency macro. Homelessness, starvation, hose baths—I'm telling you, don't worry about it. None of this matters to a master of *Horse Master* who already understands how this game works.

> in the dusk
>Try to sleep

You're exhausted, but there's no time to sleep tonight. To stand any chance of success in the Horse Master Competition, you'll have to be dressed to overwhelm. You're still wearing the same pajamas you were evicted in. Your unfinished handmade competition gown was lost in your haste to flee your apartment. The best you can hope for now is a successful **Couture Heist.**

Horse Masters wear competition gowns. A deadly steed poised between realness and uncanny, with a human master who must be "dressed to overwhelm." The intense rigors of horse mastery make the gender of Horse Masters seem irrelevant; it seems perfectly natural that a serious Horse Master wears a gown to compete, no matter what. Like a don, an academic master. Ceremonial vestments. But more fabulous.

> Couture Heist

The few high-end boutiques that still exist in physical storefronts keep nightclub hours. No one who can afford to shop there is awake during daylight hours. Those who can afford it are much more unthinking at spending **thousands of dollars on a single unmatched sandal at 3 a.m.**

> thousands of dollars on a single unmatched sandal at 3 a.m.

You parade Kindly Saunders uncovered down the street for the first time. Cars must swerve around it. Its carapace glows. Its eyes glow. Here is a madness given form that is mostly under your control. **The threat is implied and inferred.**

Horse Master has made me realize how online shopping is for peons. This passage may be among the most triumphant in the game: Poor, unhealthy, but with a terrifying, glowing, steaming destrier at your side, you make a midnight march to the boutique district.

> The threat is implied and inferred.

You hold up your hand and Kindly Saunders stops. Retail Experience Coordinators lay elaborate gowns, shoes, headdresses, buckles, suspenders, chaps, girdles, at your dirty feet in silent tribute. The night wealthy are transfixed.

You gather what you will and click your tongue. You and Kindly Saunders melt **divots in the street**.

The mere presence of a horse is enough to command attention, and giveaways of product. Celebrity potential: This one has a horse. At the very least, an aspirant Horse Master will be appearing at the competition. Maybe more. Either that, or the Retail Experience Coordinators are just terrified of being mauled, or both.

> divots in the street

Day 20

You've made it this far, just a little further. The body is bad at distinguishing between the excitement of joy and the excitement of fear. You get chills that even Kindly Saunders can't warm. You keep losing the thread of your thoughts and then pulling hairs from your nose or scalp as you try to work your way around to remembering and then there is blood sometimes. If you can score some dexobrimadine at the Horse Master Competition, your heart might not explode.

You just have to keep you and Kindly Saunders alive 1 more day until the Horse Master Competition. You have 2 actions left today.

> Hose bath.
> Good, clean horse
> Continue operant condition on horse.
> You train until you are too sluggish and disoriented to continue.
>Try to sleep.

You shower under the hose after all the businesses close. The rats regard you from a fearful distance. Morning means the **Horse Master Competition**. Tomorrow you'll at least have a hotel room. Then you'll win and never worry again.

We're almost at the final day. Are you excited?

played by Naomi Clark

> Horse Master Competition

Horse Master Competition

You and Kindly Saunders start walking before dawn and arrive at the Comfort Inn West a little before nine.

It is a humid morning and mist comes up off the grounds. The sprinklers hiss to life and Kindly Saunders is startled for a second.

There are banners welcoming the 86th Annual Southwestern Region Horse Master Championship Gala on every lightpost for miles around.

You realize your posture is stooping forward and remind yourself you need to focus on standing up straight for the judges.

You lead Kindly Saunders into the registration line. Aethelwulf, Chablis, Sumptualisk, Broudevard, all the major Houses will be present for the competition itself, but this early are only represented by sponsorship signs on the lawn.

The competition has been running for eighty-six years. It takes place in a Comfort Inn. It's a little bit like a beauty pageant, a little bit like an industry conference or a trade fair, and a lot like the Westminster Kennel Club Dog Show. The names of the Houses—another term that's also used in the drag ball scene—are better than their equivalents in the Harry Potter series.

> You realize your posture is stooping forward

You size up other horses in line, trying to guess at House affiliation, looking for exotic breeds from factories in the Far West. One is barely a foal and the joint between its actual carapace and and a papier mache extension is an embarrassment that will fool no one. You see a Hellfist that's so malnourished it can barely stand in the humidity and gives off no glow. You see a gorgeous Europa that hasn't been fully broken by conditioning writhing and flexing and know it won't pass the preliminary rounds.

This is the first time Kindly Saunders has been around so many of its kind. It wants to ram into the other horses, it wants to dominate them, but it won't do so without your command.

You pick up your tote bag, name badge, and lanyard from a counter. The tote bag is filled with advertisements for luxury brands that want you to remember them fondly if you should win. There is a banana inside and you eat it. You also eat the

Horse Master by Tom McHenry

two granola bars, never setting the bag down.

Your loose molar comes free, as does the one next to it. You spit a mix of granola, raisins, blood and enamel into your palm and try to be nonchalant. What's funny is it doesn't even hurt. What's funnier still is trying to close your hand in a fist around the teeth because **your fingers don't cooperate for a long time**.

The horses described at the competition are all in bad shape compared to your own; we never do see any of the horses from Sumptualisk or Broudevard. This close to the end, teeth falling out, the desperate feeling of "do or die" intensifies even more. There's nowhere left to go after this competition, not for the Horse Master. (The player can just sigh and switch to another browser tab.)

> your fingers don't cooperate for a long time.

Preliminary Screening

You lead Kindly Saunders to the Preliminary Screening Area. Deputized Military Officers with powerful rifles and laser blades surround this area. Full-grown horses are incredibly valuable if stolen and incredibly dangerous if loose, so the DMOs must protect smooth order in all directions.

A convention staffer hands you ports to plug into Kindly Saunders. Its stats blink up on a screenburned laptop:

Name: Kindly Saunders

Breed: Furioso-Hellfist

Age: 21

Growth Phase: Adult

Glamour: 93

Uncanny: 90

Pep: 96

Realness: 91

Discretion: 93

Overall Rating: 92.6

"Whew, nice numbers," the staffer says.

As we approach the finale, I have a secret to tell you: I have flayed this game to its bones, I have read the code. I know how the decisions are made. This might be considered a rudeness: to peek backstage, to look at the block-

played by Naomi Clark

ing directions penciled on an unreleased script, to demand the techniques of a stage magician. I make games, so this is how I play them: in the privacy of my own desk, I rip them apart where nobody can see, I let others reverse-engineer them, I stare at their entrails to divine what I'll do next. Now I'll share some of that awful wisdom with you.

Your horse's rating is the average of all five of its stats. It's possible for the game to end here if the average is lower than thirty, but that would take an awful lot of watching television and going to sleep early.

> "Whew, nice numbers," the staffer says.

Kindly Saunders passed the preliminary judging round. Many horses don't, and interns are dragging those malformed corpses to the bonfire pit.

The staffer who checked in Kindly Saunders shakes your hand and welcomes you as an official competitor with a bottle of ice water. Your badge number is recorded, and you ask about getting a refill of your dexobrimadine prescription. "You know how crazy travel is," you say (**you are still wearing the clothes you were evicted in and you've been sleeping in horse-piss-soaked garbage for a week**).

If you didn't make the cutoff, your horse is immediately incinerated. Horses only exist for one reason: to be judged. The rewards for being minimally attentive to *Horse Master*'s core systems appear immediately: ice water, drugs, hotel room. The austerities and anxieties of your homelessness relieved.

> you are still wearing the clothes you were evicted in

Yet, it's not a problem. The hotel medical staff is amply prepared for the competition and you won't be the only rib-thin hopeful to have misplaced a supply.

Then, porters lead Kindly Saunders to the stables. They chain it down with heavy iron links, but your hand on its face is enough to calm it mostly.

This will be the first time you are apart for more than a few minutes since it was born. You have to clean up for the opening gala and cotillion.

Also: **a minifridge full of chilled dexobrimadine**.

Preparing for the gala and cotillion via drugs and couture, you separate from your other half: the first time you haven't been together since near the start of the game (21 game days or roughly 120 clicks ago).

> a minifridge full of chilled dexobrimadine.

Hotel Room

You don't sleep, you don't unpack, you don't shower, you just lick the port on your forearm and hang the dexy bag on the rod in the closet, and it is an ice cold river that numbs your arm and then blooms your whole face. **You are blessed**.

> You are blessed.

Hotel Room

For the first time in days, you are present in the way that only people on dexobrimadine are present. The current moment swells up and up, and you see how you just might pull this off, but are stuck tethered to this bag of poison hanging from the closet.

You have plans. You have ideas about how you will carefully modify your gown just so. You can see a dozen more things you should have done with and for Kindly Saunders. First thing when you win, you'll get clean.

The drip you've waited for for days can't finish soon enough. **You have so much left to do.**

Everything is on the other side of victory: relaxation, freedom from capitalism, freedom from addiction.

> You have so much left to do.

Grand Staircase

You feel the best you've felt in weeks. You run your tongue over your front teeth to make sure none of them will come loose when it comes time for you to smile at the cameras.

You line up and meet your escort. You can hear the introduction of a state senator, and the end of his remarks.

"Of course the current administration," he pauses to chuckle, "would have you believe our ways — the traditional ways, mind you — are barbaric. Well what is more barbaric: **the nobility of the majestic horse** or the tyranny of socialism?"

The competition has been running for eighty-six years. It takes place in a Comfort Inn. It is politically conservative, considered barbaric by the regime in power.

played by Naomi Clark

> the nobility of the majestic horse

Grand Staircase

You and the three remaining potential Horse Master candidates are escorted by DMOs in traditional dress uniforms and white gloves down the palatial Grand Staircase to your waiting horses.

The silver whistle around your neck gleams in the camera light. **You smile as though joy is your only hobby.**

All but three of the Horse Master candidates were eliminated due to having poor stats. Assuming they weren't just lazy about using their actions to feed, groom, and shock their horses, it might be that the protagonist of this story really does have an edge in terms of ambitious horse-embryo design specifications, efficiency macros, or some other elusive quality that protagonists have. The absence of any other hobby besides joy, and Horse Mastery; transformation of one into the other, paid for with sacrifice.

> You smile as though joy is your only hobby.

Grand Staircase

Your crewcut escort wilts in the presence of your massive, gleaming horse. Kindly Saunders has been carefully cleaned and detailed in your hours apart.

In the sight of the accumulated judges and television cameras, you pledge to treat Kindly Saunders with the **full dignity of its species and according to all the customs of your people**.

Remember: you're wearing an elaborate couture gown, and being escorted by a crewcutted soldier in a uniform and white gloves. Pomp and ritual take over.

> full dignity of its species and according to all the customs of your people.

The Promenade

The first event is simple: Each candidate's horse must circle the judging grounds three times. One walk, one trot, one canter. The Horse Master candidate may only communicate using whistles and clicks.

On the final pass of each horse, its vital statistics are read aloud and the horse must kneel in each of the cardinal directions, symbolizing the submission of all horse under the unified nations of men.

It's the sort of event that has no drama because any horse that couldn't easily pass this event never makes it by the preliminary screening rounds anymore.

Horses used to be different? Horse Mastery used to be different. Was there a time when horses did not submit?

> It's the sort of event that has no drama because any horse that couldn't easily pass this event never makes it by the preliminary screening rounds anymore.

The Promenade

This event is almost as boring for Kindly Saunders as it is for you. It continues to exist because it's relatively low-risk and allows spectators both here and at home to begin investing themselves in individual candidates before the real meat of the thing.

Kindly Saunders passes the walk and the trot with no trouble. On the canter you can see it wants to go faster. There's a shocking moment where it breaks rhythm, but it passes. You've never really let it run at a full speed and there is so much power ready to do so, even now.

You can control it, though, and it kneels in all four directions. The knee divots left behind are within the half-degree margin of error. The crowd erupts.

The judges give you a 9.0. **Easy.**

Again, I'll tell you the dirty secrets: your horse always gets a 9.0 in this event. The knee-divots are always within the margin of error. That's not what's important. What's important is that the knee-divots are measured at all, I think: the ritual, going through the motions, even though it's a given for any horse that has above an average of thirty in its stats.

> Easy

Dressage

For the second event, you must prove your total mastery of Kindly Saunders's most primal instincts.

You are presented with a small knife.

played by Naomi Clark

Dressage usually refers to horse and rider carrying out a memorized set of motions. There is only one set of motions in *Horse Master*.

> You are presented with a small knife.

Dressage

With one swift movement, you sever your left pinkie finger.

You place the finger in front of Kindly Saunders and **wait**.

> wait

Dressage

The blood and meat attract Kindly Saunders, but at the moment it bends to eat the finger, you blow the silver whistle for it to **halt**.

> halt

Dressage

And with a simple gesture, Kindly Saunders performs the trick you have practiced hundreds of times — it drops the uneaten finger into your waiting palm.

The nine-fingered judges applaud.

Cotillion

A thing to know about horses: they long to eat human flesh. They have been subdued, tamed, so that they submit to the nations of man, perform tricks obediently.

This is the routine you and your horse have been training for—one which, once again, always happens the same way as long as you're able to reach this point in the game. There was no hint, earlier in the game, of a practice pinky, of taking food then releasing it. Would it have been a giveaway? Does the ritual speak of a deeper discipline that didn't need to be practice?

Every judge has nine fingers. Once you are a Horse Master, you never perform in this way to be judged again, apparently. Transcendent, there are no eight-fingered judges, six-fingered judges; it's not like passing the bar. It's a once-per-lifetime event. (And once per playthrough.) Now we reach the final moment.

> Cotillion

Horse Master by Tom McHenry

Cotillion

For the final event, there can be no tricks. Biology and development have chosen the true winner long before tonight. All that remains is the reveal.

It is the purest expression of horse development and mastery.

You will go first. You whistle for Kindly Saunders. It stands. **You regard each other with total certainty.**

The text here suggests that the outcome was determined long before. Players of games, habituated to influencing outcomes, might expect that the horse's five stats will once again come into play for this, the purest expression of both "development" and "mastery."

> You regard each other with total certainty.

Cotillion

Kindly Saunders never whinnies or screams when your small knife severs its main nervous bundle.

This is an excellent sign, judging-wise.

A thin pink line of drool drips from Kindly Saunders's slack lips. **Its eyes no longer focus.**

The fate of a horse should not come as a surprise to anyone paying attention. Horses are dangerous, not to be ridden; they exist for one reason only, and are destroyed in the process. The use of the term "horse" to describe a bioluminescent, deadly-hooved, tentilla-maned crustacean evokes a rash of sympathetic emotions, especially in the English-speaking world—which is one of the only slices of the world where horse meat isn't eaten, out of some kind of cross-species filial affection. I've eaten horse meat carpaccio; I like it a little bit better than beef. I like crustaceans too, but I probably wouldn't eat a bioengineered Horse Master horse. Still, we're supposed to feel sad here, as our companion dies. *Horse Master* has pulled a bait and switch: we were never going to walk (and certainly never ride) off into the sunset with our horse.

The bait and switch has also become more common in expensive, obscenely-budgeted games. The difference between these games and *Horse Master* is that *Horse Master* doesn't ask you to shoot enemy soldiers for dozens of hours on end before posing the question of whether what you're doing is morally reprehensible, or engineered by forces you're blindly succumbing to in the name of play. It's a short game, and one that relentlessly telegraphs its weirdness. *Horse Master* doesn't let the player raise a rideable, mammalian horse with a rough tongue and a fondness for apples, then force a slaughter. It's a game that tries to tell the player that something's wrong with it, from the beginning, like a cat peeing blood into its owner's sink.

> Its eyes no longer focus.

Cotillion

You begin to carefully cut away its carapace to expose the milky nerve disc below. You remove the disc and set it on a small plate held by a nearby attendant.

He places a lid on the plate and carries it to the judging platform.

The text on each page is brief now, the clicks more frequent as you read, drawing out the moment longer and longer. If we were reading a book, we'd see one sentence per page, anxiously flipping leaves towards the final revelation, the moment (we're told) of maximum suspense.

> He places a lid on the plate

Cotillion

A giant video screen shows the overhead view of the plate.

There is a moment of maximum suspense when the lid is removed.

The next click determines whether the protagonist becomes a Horse Master or not. To become Horse Masters, we sacrifice solvency, health, independence, and a finger: so that we may betray the horse and sacrifice it in turn. By using enough dexobrimadine, we can see into the future, for short, near bursts—although we may have to think back to opening scenes in the showroom, on the bus, in order to remember that.

By using enough JavaScript, I can see into the future of any given session of *Horse Master*. I have dissected the corpus of the game, as well, to find the nerve bundles underneath, the code and equations that control the Horse Master's fate. Unless you're caught shoplifting and put in prison, the horse always dies at the competition, but the Horse Master does not always win. I will pull out the critical piece of the organs that pulse beneath the textual skin of *Horse Master* and show you why:

Your horse has stats, including one called Uncanny. Although the game may lead players to believe that all the stats are important (and their average is, to get into the competition), it appears that only Uncanny is used for the final judging process. The workings of the game place your horse's value for Uncanny in a variable called $horse_uncanny.

When the Horse Master slides into the final, "blessed," dexobrimadine haze in a lush hotel room before the competition, another value is calculated: $comp3_uncanny, the threshold that must be met in order to win. If a player's $horse_uncanny is equal to or higher than the value of $comp3_uncanny, that player becomes a new Horse Master. Otherwise, they slink away in failure.

How is $comp3_uncanny calculated? What is the threshold that must be passed? It turns out it's based on this formula:

$$\$comp3\_uncanny = (Math.floor(Math.random()*((\$horse\_uncanny+10)-(\$horse\_uncanny-20))))+(\$horse\_uncanny-20)$$

Even if you don't understand the arcana of Javascript, you might notice that this value is based almost entirely on $horse_uncanny—adding 10 here, subtracting 20 there. If you puzzle this out, here's what it comes down to: The game generates a random number between 0 and 29, then adds it to your horse's uncanny stat minus 20. As a result, $comp3_uncanny is a random number that's somewhere between 20 less than the horse's uncanny stat and 9 more than the horse's uncanny stat.

The Horse Master randomly wins the competition, 2/3 of the time. The Horse Master randomly loses the other 1/3 of the time. There is nothing more. Not even the Uncanny stat matters, in the end; it turned out to be a figurehead.

> There is a moment of maximum suspense when the lid is removed.

Cotillion

The five purple-red nerves form a perfect equilateral star pattern across the disc.

The audience erupts. The smiling judges must keep up appearances, so they shout for silence. The measuring equipment is laid out to check depth and thickness, but it's all theatre: Anyone with eyes can see you've won.

You even get to shake hands with a state senator!

There is nothing in this passage to suggest the 2:1 odds of victory: if the Horse Master has won, the gory slice of nerves and flesh carved from the horse's dying form will be a perfectly symmetrical star. If not, then the star is lopsided, asymmetrical. The five points of a star suggest the five stats; the words flowing across the surface of *Horse Master* suggest that the key to victory, all along, was to accomplish a judicious balance of Pep, Realness, Uncanny, Discretion, and Glamour.

This is not the buried truth of *Horse Master*; it is the reality of skin, but not bone and nerve. The last phrases of the Horse Master competition depend on the roll of a die, not anything that a player can do correctly or

played by Naomi Clark

incorrectly. I have betrayed the confidences whispered to me by the game's source; I have looked at things we weren't necessarily meant to understand. I suspect the presence of secrets because the equations I told you about are needlessly obscure: a chance of two out of three could be written like this:

$$\text{if (Math.floor(Math.random()*3))} > 0$$

Many of the random elements of *Horse Master* are phrased in this simpler way—among other things, the 1/6 chance of being caught shoplifting, which consigns the aspirant horse master to prison, and sets the horse free to wander, still growing and uncontrolled. In the final moments of competition, however, the equations grow dense and complex, suggesting some more nuanced test of the horse's stats. Each other stat has an equation similar to the one for $comp3_uncanny—but values like $comp3_glamour are calculated and then never used, never compared to anything. What's going on here? Can we find a forensic answer as we scalpel and dig through the innards of *Horse Master*?

The creators of *Kentucky Route Zero* once called their game a "fallen puzzle platformer." They had originally included mechanics for running, jumping, solving problems with critical thinking. Now their game is a somnolent and haunting adventure game known for its atmosphere, not its challenge or puzzles; these earlier mechanics fell away, fell into ruin, but still persist in places in the code, perhaps glimpsed occasionally like a palimpsest, or a layer of ancient advertising underneath a layer of vibrant graffiti on the side of a brick building. Cutting deep into the nerve bundles of *Horse Master*, this may explain some of what I've unearthed. Is *Horse Master* a fallen sim, a game that might have once been crafted to hold some outcome-shattering meaning in it statistics and resources? Now only the silence of dutiful, neglected calculations passes through the ruins of functions and data structures that go unused.

Horse Master has a hidden "debt" value as well. It starts at 300,000; your debt increases relentlessly by 200 every night. Perhaps this once represented interest accruing; you'd have to ask *Horse Master's* creator to be sure.

Players of *Horse Master* who expected an outcome-determining sim—one where their choices, the way they cared for their horse, would matter in the end—might feel betrayed by the ultimate randomness of the finale, the contingent and uncaring nature of it all. This might be one of the statements made by *Horse Master*: Your choices don't matter, this mystical, drug-hazed, gory, traditional elevation out of debt and capitalism is vicarious and out of control.

This is not where I found the best moments and meanings of *Horse Master*, however; those were in the play of light across the pixels of a one-room apartment, the choice to share food with a horse in an alley behind a Thai cheeseburger joint, a dexobrimadine binge so deep that the temporal flash-forwards cease to matter, the triumphal couture heist before the real competition began. None of these textures, scenes, facets of the game have anything to do with the stats a player manipulates, or the outcome of the competition, but those last two cruxes have nothing to do with each other or anything else, either. The expected bond is severed, falling apart like a Gordian knot, leaving ropy strands behind. Instead, meaning assembles in layers, from everywhere.

I had to rip *Horse Master* apart to think about its scars, its medical history. I don't think *Horse Master* would want you to see it like this, so far under the surface, in its past, but I wanted to explain. The insides are wet, ropy, translucent, beautiful. I'm obsessed with these things because I make games, I try to put them through their paces, train them up, parade them for show, watch them slaughtered, chop off a seventh and eighth finger. It's a barbaric tradition that one day may fall by the wayside; but there's still beauty in it.

> You even get to shake hands with a state senator!

You made it.

You are a Horse Master.

You never have to (and never can) work again.

The world is sick and ugly, but at least you made it through okay. You did exactly what was expected of you. Good for you! The life your father always wanted.

Now you might even ask what kind of life you would have wanted, but it is too late to ever want again.

End

The Horse Master can never work again, and it is too late to ever want again.

You, dear reader, can never play *Horse Master* with fresh eyes again. I'm sorry.

> End

NINETEEN
BY ELIZABETH SAMPAT
PLAYED BY PATRICIA HERNANDEZ

> I was **twelve** the **last time** I **tried** to kill myself. That was **nineteen years ago**.

    The first sentence is striking. Immediately, there is a sense of vulnerability—that Elizabeth is being so frank and open about a heavy subject, yes, but I also feel vulnerability because I have the ability to click on links which tell me more about Elizabeth's history of suicide. Choosing which to explore further—"twelve," "last time," "tried," "nineteen years ago," requires courage from me—it's a sensitive subject that is difficult to speak frankly about. Clicking something means finding out more, and it also requires some sort of honesty from me: that this is a subject I have thought about before, that it is okay to discuss it with other people, that, even though we don't acknowledge it as a society, is something that people struggle with at very young ages, too.
    It's difficult to know what to click, so I go with the first choice.

> \> twelve

> When you're **young**, time moves slowly. When you're **depressed**, time moves even more slowly. It was impossible to conceive of a time when I'd be out of my parents house, when I'd **finally have control**.

    On this second screen, Elizabeth discusses the concept of time—how it slows down when you're young, and when you're depressed. I want to keep that narrative thread going, about suicide affecting kids, so I click on "young."

> young

My oldest daughter is only three years younger than I was when I tried to kill myself.

Sometimes I catch myself watching her and holding my breath.

There are words on this next page, but the first thing I look at is the picture of the child. It's big; it takes up the most space on the page. I wonder if it is Elizabeth herself, but after reading, I find out it's actually her daughter. There is no link, no way to go "forward" here. When I play through the game again and double through other options, there is a palpable sense of legacy, of family. Elizabeth shows you pictures of herself over the years, and of other family members. It makes me reconsider the picture of her daughter, makes me consider what it means to live with depression, or suicidal thoughts while trying to raise a family. What you share with them, how open you are with them. The fear, at least for me, of what genetics would make me pass down. The things family don't talk about. The things you want to avoid repeating with your own family. I think back on a different part of the game, where Elizabeth shows the player a giraffe she got at the hospital after attempting suicide. I think about how Elizabeth describes giving her daughters giraffes of their own. It's shocking for me, as someone with a family that never wants to talk about these things.

When you get to that picture of Elizabeth's daughter, you have two choices. You can click back in the browser and see what you missed on the last screen, or you can restart. I like that idea, in this context. Restarting. Finding a new way to navigate this difficult subject and coming to something that is less of a dead end, because, well, she's alive. There is more to this.

played by Patricia Hernandez

  > Restart
  > last time

My father was a diabetic, on the border of almost needing shots, but still barely able to manage his blood sugar with pills. I took three full bottles of **his pills** during lunch when I was in eighth grade. I'd been carrying the pills for a **week**.

My choir teacher intercepted a note I was passing to **a friend** about how I planned to kill myself soon. She turned it in to the school psychologist. **I convinced him it was sarcasm.**

I was in the hospital for four days.

  > his pills

Even if I had successfully killed myself, it wouldn't have been his fault.

The fault would have been mine.

  Stark. I don't restart, I just click back.

  > back
  > a week

School sucked for me. I was bullied a lot. I'd bring the pills to school every day and tell myself, If just one person is nice to me, I won't do it. A lot of days, **one person** was nice to me.

Eventually it got to the point where I realized I didn't care if someone was nice to me. I just wanted out.

  > one person

Sometimes it is so hard to tell my friends when I need them. Sometimes it's so hard to believe that they **care**. Sometimes I want to **push them away**.

I haven't been **close** in years, but there are still days when I feel a lump in my throat and the panic of the world closing in, when I feel dumb and worthless and it's hard for me to see the point of going on, and I get an IM and I wonder:

Do they know?

Do they get that they might have just saved my life with that stupid cat macro?

Nineteen by Elizabeth Sampat

I have the choice of clicking on one of three things here: "care," "push them away," and "close." I wonder about this impulse, to push people away, even if they help you, even if you need them—it's something I do sometimes, too. So I click on that.

> push them away

When I told my favorite college professor that I was transferring to a different school, she gave me a hug and wished me the best. Then she held me at arm's length and, with a strange look on her face, she said:

"I'm sad; I was really looking forward to seeing you become the kind of person who could be truly **happy**."

I went back to my 6'x8' dorm room and sat on the twin bed that touched both walls, digging my fingernails into my palms in rage.

How dare she.

It's easy to see why the comment would come across as flippant. The only choice you have here is "happy," sort of illustrating the absurdity of the idea that one can just choose to be happy, that it is as simple as clicking a word like this. Versus the more complex reality of learning how to cope with depression, I mean.

> happy

I was fighting with **my first husband**. We were yelling.

"Why don't you think about my happiness any more?" I sobbed.

He laughed. "Your—? Jesus, Elizabeth. Why would I even try? I think there's always a part of you that's sad."

played by Patricia Hernandez

This new page, Elizabeth goes into the idea of happiness further. She describes a fight with her husband, where he makes her depression seem impossible to manage, or cope with. You know it doesn't end well—the choice you have here is "my first husband."

> my first husband

Even if I had successfully killed myself, it wouldn't have been his fault.

The fault would have been mine.

I don't know to what degree it is "appropriate" to muse on the people and relationships mentioned in the Twine game, and maybe I shouldn't worry about that at all. I dwell on it a bit, anyway. It's hard to tell to what degree Elizabeth is being hard or unfair to herself. The two big interactions I read about thus far on this playthrough are when things go wrong, when someone is being kind of an asshole to her. I'm inclined to feel sympathy for Elizabeth, which feels strange to admit. But the game is so personal, and it hits so close to home in some ways, that it's difficult to maintain distance. Hell, at times it's difficult to stop projecting.

Either way, I click restart again.

> Restart
> tried

A year after my last suicide attempt, I was backstage at a play. I heard some grownups talking about a friend's son who tried to kill himself.

"It was just a cry for help, he wasn't serious."

"Yeah, **when people really want to die**, they find a way."

"Some people are so dramatic. **If you want attention**, just ask for it!" Laughter.

I thought about all of those times I sat in my room with a knife. I thought of all the times I almost killed myself but didn't. I thought of the **panic** that shot through me when I thought my plans might be found out.

I wondered why they called it a cry for help, when all I wanted was to be **silent**.

> silent

The intake nurse was very stern. People think suicidal people need tough love to get snapped out of their self-absorbed, self-destructive cycles. It didn't work, because I had given up.

Nineteen by Elizabeth Sampat

There was fire in her eyes when she asked why I would want to hurt myself.

I was dizzy from low blood sugar. My stomach had been pumped; I'd vomited liquid charcoal so high it was on the ceiling. I thought this woman was insane.

"Why would I want to HURT myself?" I asked her. "I was trying to KILL myself."

This makes me wonder if I've ever made the mistake of assuming that someone who has attempted suicide was trying to hurt themselves, not kill-kill themselves. I realize that this normally invisible distinction makes a hell of a difference.

> Restart
> nineteen years ago

I almost died nineteen years ago. I thought there was nothing worth the pain of living for me, past that fall day in 1994. I thought there was nothing to gain, nothing I would miss.

Amazing vacations.

Nineteen years of **questionable hairstyles**.

The rise of Justin Timberlake.

Friends who love me more than I ever thought possible.

Two children.

Discovering Thai food.

Making my first game (and every game that has come after that).

I still get depressed, **I still have to fight through it sometimes**, but I am sometimes overwhelmed by the enormity of what I almost stole from myself. **I want life**. I want so much more life than I will probably ever get to experience.

But I am beyond grateful for the last nineteen years.

(Next year I am throwing a party.)

Here, Elizabeth describes things that she would have missed had she been successful, and it brings a smile to my face. It's not just Serious Stuff, like having children. It's also stuff like "questionable hairstyles." and "the rise of Justin Timberlake." I click on questionable hairstyles first, where Elizabeth displays a number of photographs of herself over the years.

played by Patricia Hernandez

    There's a sense of relief in this, as well as a sense of vulnerability, too. Here she is, in front of me so to speak. A person, with a body. Not just words and thoughts. She lived. She grew. She coped.

    I click back on my browser, and this time it feels less like The Video Game Thing to Do—you know, where you try out all the choices. I'm not interested in seeing every single choice in the Twine game, that feels wrong, somehow. But I do want to know more about how Elizabeth coped and came this far.

> I still have to fight through it sometimes

It took a decade, maybe longer, to realize that no matter what I did it would be impossible to handle **these feelings** on my own. I joined **a church** in high school, I wrote, I tried therapy. all of these things helped, some more than others, but the only consistently valuable tool I have found has been **my friends**.

Depression convinces you that you have no power. **Sometimes you need friends to lend you some of theirs**.

    It makes me think about my own life, and the support structures that I have. I go back once more, one final time.

> Back
> I want life.

Nineteen by Elizabeth Sampat

Last year I came up with the idea of a thimble list. It's a bucket list, but smaller.

I realized that when I find myself staring death in the face, I'm not going to be heartbroken that I never got around to climbing Mt. Fuji.

I'm going to be sad I didn't cook more meals for the people I love.

Elizabeth describes her thimble list, the things she wants to do before she dies. They're not grand things, because like she says, the things you come to regret later in life aren't that you never got to climb Mt. Everest or something. Rather, it's the smaller stuff. Things you could have done for a loved one, for example.

I click out of the game, and I think, hey. Maybe I should find a recipe, so I can cook something nice for a loved one, too.

SCARFMEMORY
BY MICHAEL BROUGH
PLAYED BY ANNA ANTHROPY

this is a memorial.

it's made in twine.

begin

   so right off the bat i really like that this in unmodified sugarcane, the default theme for twine. you've probably seen it if you've ever played a twine game: white text, blue links, black backgrounds. in my own twine work i've always been really cautious about glitzing up twine too much: adding code, making text move, stuff like that. it just seems like every games space other than twine is obsessed with technology, with show-offiness, and i never wanted people to feel like their twine games weren't interesting because they didn't do anything daring with the format. i wonder how many twine games have been passed up because they're in unmodified sugarcane.

   > begin

you're walking down the street.

(i say "you" because interactive fiction is written in the second person by convention, but since this is autobiographical i could equally well say "i")

on my way home from a **concert**.

keep walking

scarfmemory by Michael Brough

> concert (note that "keep walking" is still a choice" throughout what follows)

on my way home from a sigur rós **concert**.

> concert

on my way home from a sigur rós concert. seriously amazing, they played popplagið last and just drew out the climax forever and **wow**.

"popplagið" here is a link to a youtube upload of the song in question. i'm now listening to it in the background as i play. this is an exciting thing about hypertext: a link in a twine game can be to *anything*.

> wow

on my way home from a sigur rós concert. seriously amazing, they played popplagið last and just drew out the climax forever and wow. but there was a kind of uncomfortable moment half way through that made me feel a bit **alienated**.

> alienated

on my way home from a sigur rós concert. seriously amazing, they played popplagið last and just drew out the climax forever and wow. but there was a kind of uncomfortable moment half way through that made me feel a bit alienated. they started playing a song from their uninspired fourth album and the audience's response was an order of magnitude greater than for anything else in the concert. this really confused me, they'd just played some incredible renditions of some incredible pieces and people **clapped a bit** but then they start up on this honestly quite dull one and suddenly the crowd goes wild, it's clear that the majority of people present are way more interested in this.

the "keep walking" link here is obviously the way to advance the story but clicking on links about the concert just expands its description into more and more detail, adding to the paragraph. the impression is of someone mulling over a thing he experienced while walking home. gonna skip forward a little bit, but keep in mind: it takes a lot of active effort continuous clicking, to read this whole paragraph.

played by Anna Anthropy

> clapped a bit (etc.)

on my way home from a sigur rós concert. seriously amazing, they played popplagið last and just drew out the climax forever and wow. but there was a kind of uncomfortable moment half way through that made me feel a bit alienated. they started playing a song from their uninspired fourth album and the audience's response was an order of magnitude greater than for anything else in the concert. this really confused me, they'd just played some incredible renditions of some incredible pieces and people clapped a bit (although personally i'd have preferred silent contemplation to raucous noise after some of them) but then they start up on this honestly quite dull one and suddenly the crowd goes wild, it's clear that the majority of people present are way more interested in this. i'd kind of had the impression i was in the company of people with similar taste to me but then it became clear that no, we appreciate very different things, i don't understand them at all. i guess it's that this was radiobait, by making shorter and more conventional songs they get more radio play so people have heard them more so they like them more just from recognition. i guess i'm officially a "hipster". it's like the feeling i get when i walk into a videogame shop, games are a huge part of my life and mean a lot to me but of the selection on display there there's nothing i connect with at all. it makes me wonder how i can possibly hope to make a living from making videogames when i have so little comprehension of why the majority of people appreciate things that i find really oppressive. but hey i've gone off topic a bit, the concert was amazing overall.

keep walking

> keep walking

still walking down the street

it's this busy high street with clothes shops and holland and barrets and stuff. **ads everywhere**.

anyway there are other people walking on this street too.

> ads everywhere

it's this busy high street with clothes shops and holland and barrets and stuff. ads everywhere (**memetic hazard**).

scarfmemory by Michael Brough

> memetic hazard

it's this busy high street with clothes shops and holland and barrets and stuff. ads everywhere (sometimes i panic in environments like this, the amount of attempted brainwashing going on is really creepy, but for now it's okay i'm just ignoring it).
anyway there are **other people** walking on this street too.

> other people

anyway there are some men in suits, a **couple** holding hands, a group of teenage girls, a **homeless guy**, an older woman walking a dog AND HEY SOME OTHER PEOPLE TOO I'M NOT GOING TO LIST THEM ALL ALRIGHT walking on this street too.

clicking on the "homeless guy" produces the message

(look away if it makes you uncomfortable)

and clicking on the couple expands them into a list of things they're wearing:

a couple dressed warmly for the cold northern winter, which i have a hard time dealing with having grown up in a temperate subtropical climate: long coat, **scarf**, gloves,

the scarf link throws up a big picture of three gorgeous striped scarves next to each other, like curtains, the left one all pale desert colors, the middle one cool blues and pale earth tones with an occasional purple or burgundy introducing some contrasting warmer notes, and the rightmost one is all richer, darker wine colors, violets, burgundies, with just the occasional pale blue.
this is against a white background, and i imagine that if i had been playing this twine game at night in a dark room, tiny text on a black background, this picture would suddenly fill the room with light.

i've seen a lot of scarves in this style this winter, **colourful** lines longitudinally, popular i guess.

> colourful

played by Anna Anthropy

not as colourful as my scarf, which i **lost** a bit over a year ago,

    so michael's using twine to illustrate internal processes, his own inner monologue. each passage starts with a more superficial visual description of what he's seeing, but clicking on words allows the player to go more deeply into his thoughts on the thing in question, which often then introduce new thoughts to explore, and etc. sentences like "on my way home from a concert" eventually become great sprawling paragraphs of internal landscape.

    i've always known michael as someone who pays a lot of attention to the visual appearance of his games, who spends years tweaking what a single monster in a game looks like, to better communicate its behavior to the player. i've played games of his that contained almost no text, was almost all picture. this is one of two twine games i think i've ever seen him make, which seems really deliberate: twine's hypertext game design made the most sense to communicate this internal process of monologue, speculation and memory.

you're sitting on a bus, talking with a couple of friends who've come to visit. just met up with them at the bus station on your way back from **london**. you grabbed a few bags of shopping before the bus came so you'll be able to feed everyone.

it's really warm on the bus.

    this passage comes with a photo of michael, bundled up for the winter: gray coat, backpack straps, fuzzy blue hat, and his scarf, tan and red, a donut around his neck.

on your way back from an event in london, where you **received an award**.

> received an award

on your way back from an event in london, where **you received a joke award**.

> you received a joke award

on your way back from an event in london, where you, not being taken seriously enough to be considered for the real awards, received a **joke award**.

> joke award

147

scarfmemory by Michael Brough

on your way back from an event in london, where you,
not being taken seriously enough to be considered for the
real awards, received a joke award named after someone's
genitals. you grabbed a few bags of shopping before the bus
came so you'll be able to feed everyone.

it's really **warm** on the bus.

> warm

it's really a bit **too warm** on the bus.

> too warm

it's really a bit too warmly heated (this is something they do
here in the uk, every time you go inside somewhere in winter
you're hit with a blast of hot air and since you were dressed
appropriately for the climate outside it's really uncomfortable,
you're faced with the choice of sweltering in your clothes or
taking everything off and having to carry it around) on the
bus.

   the pacing here changes, instead of drawing a thought out slowly, it comes as a big rush of information, like it's especially urgent.

> taking everything off

you remove your hat, scarf, gloves and jacket and put them
on the set next to you with the shopping bags.

look out the window

talk

wait

> look out the window

   another photo, this one focused on the scarf, and it's glorious: you can see vivid orange, red, pale violet and blue and tan. it's a really beautiful scarf.

you can't see much out the window, it's dark. but you'll know
when you're getting close to home because the town before is
well lit.

> talk

you catch up with your friends, one of them is **getting a job overseas**.

> getting a job overseas

you catch up with your friends, one of them is getting a job overseas so they'll be living apart for a bit, which is always kind of tough, you hope it ends up working out okay for them.

> wait

this is the part where i start to feel dread, as i click through these trivial interactions knowing that no matter what i click on (because this is history, this already happened) michael is going to forget his scarf. the photos of said scarf are omnipresent now, they fill most of the screen, drawing your attention away from the text, the small talk.

bus reaches the stop finally. better take all your stuff.

take: **hat gloves** scarf **backpack bag of food**

okay lets go

all of the items here are links, big blue letters, except for "scarf," which sits between them, small and white and naked, unclickable. this is storytelling right here, just through how the text is labelled.

in older, puzzle-focused text games, the player develops a sort of instinct of, upon reaching a new place, immediately grabbing everything that's not nailed down and taking it with you: you never know when you might need that hairpin to pick the lock on a treasure chest. at this point, you want to alter history, i want to make michael take his scarf, but my inability to is already a forgone conclusion. i wonder how many times michael played out this scene in his head, willing himself, in memory, to just take the scarf. the player's doing the same thing, right now.

there's a photo of a pile of stuff on the desk: michael's coat, michael's gloves. his scarf can be seen, orange and blue, in the pile.

when i click on something to take, its name vanishes from the screen, ultimately leaving the word "scarf" behind, untakeable, alone.

> hat
> gloves
> backpack
> bag of food

scarfmemory by Michael Brough

> okay let's go

you're sitting on a different bus, in a different time and place.

how much of life is spent moving from one place to another?

> how much of life

it doesn't matter, it doesn't have to be wasted time, you can **read a book**, **knit something**, think deeply, look out at the **view**, **talk to friends**.
maybe in the future these things will have internet connections too!

clicking on "knit" draws me through an entire internal dialogue, as michael goes back and forth about whether he should learn to knit. this game is all about transitions: michael knits his scarf as a way to deal with travel, he loses his scarf while travelling. a scarf is a transitional piece of clothing: you wear it when you're between places, because it's too warm to wear it inside. for michael, his scarf is a way in which he takes ownership of the time of his life he spends out of control of it—the time he spends travelling. but travelling, ultimately, takes it back.

> knit

it doesn't matter, it doesn't have to be wasted time, you can (unless you get travelsick, i didn't used to but i often do now on buses, trains are fine), (i don't know how to knit), think deeply, look out at the ocean, you're talking to your friends right now - several of you from school have the same commute to university, your lives are heading in different directions, in a few years you'll be living in different countries, but for now every morning you get to have the old gang back together.

> knit

(i don't know how to knit - why don't you **learn?**)

> learn

(i don't know how to knit - why don't you learn? - well i guess i could - i'll show you how! just get some wool and needles - **OKAY I WILL**)

played by Anna Anthropy

> OKAY I WILL

every time i see someone with a colourful scarf it catches my eye.

sometimes i have to look closely, to make sure it's not mine.

i have this **fantasy**.

(it's never mine.)

   there's a picture of michael, here, wearing his scarf as a headband. the photo is sideways. in this photo it's red and purple—we see what must be different parts of it in every photo in the game. we never seem to see the whole thing.

> fantasy

i have this fantasy that one day i'll just be walking down the street and i'll see it. i walk up to the wearer and i say "hey, that scarf you're wearing - i made it". i tell them its story, how i made it and where i lost it, i tell them about all its **secret places**, and they are delighted to have met the creator of this amazing scarf that they found and maybe they give it back to me, or maybe i'm just happy to know its in good hands.

> secret places

i have this fantasy that one day i'll just be walking down the street and i'll see it. i walk up to the wearer and i say "hey, that scarf you're wearing - i made it". i tell them its story, how i made it and where i lost it, i tell them about all its nooks and crannies, the bits near the start where i kept accidentally adding or losing stitches and the knots that hold these together, and then when i learnt to do this on purpose and grew it out to a great width then contracted it back to a narrow strip again, all the different coloured wools, the places i experimented with different stitches, discovering new ways of knitting (later finding out there were names for all of them), the grid (knitting is a lot like pixel-art) where i switched between different stitches in a regular pattern for a while, the time i realised it had somehow split into two separate scarves because the alternating rows didn't interlock at all and then i knit them back together leaving a little tube you can fit your finger through, the bit where i got hold of a third needle and started loading stitches onto it to cache them

scarfmemory by Michael Brough

while i knitted other bits and then putting them back on later in the row so everything ended up all twisted and tangled, how i finished it off by looping it around into a möbius band, joining the end up to the middle with a twist, and they are delighted to have met the creator of this amazing scarf that they found and maybe they give it back to me, or maybe i'm just happy to know its **in good hands**.

> \> in good hands

or maybe i'm just happy to know its appreciated. my fear is that it's not, that whoever found it could not see its **beauty**, and that it's ended up discarded, destroyed, unloved.

> \> beauty

or maybe i'm just happy to know its appreciated. my fear is that it's not, that whoever found it could not see its beauty (as so many people don't understand things that i like and things that i make), and that it's ended up discarded, destroyed, **unloved**.

> \> unloved

i loved that scarf, even though it was just an item of clothing **it meant a lot to me**.

> \> it meant a lot to me

i loved that scarf, even though it was just an item of clothing i miss **it**.

> \> it

i loved that scarf, even though it was just an item of clothing i miss it i don't even have a good photo of it.

(it's **never** mine.)

> \> never

for some reason we're talking about scarves.

i ask HAVE YOU SEEN MY SCARF?

they haven't.

played by Anna Anthropy

> they haven't

i'll show it to them!

i go downstairs to get it.

it's not there.

i search the house, turn it upside down.

it's not there.

> it's not there

can you check in your room? i didn't want to go in but i've looked everywhere else and maybe when i was carrying in the shopping and you were carrying in your bags maybe it got mixed in somehow.

it's not there.

here the game puts the player in the role of being the voice that insists to michael, as he searches frantically, that his scarf is gone. it hurts a little bit, to do.

> it's not there

she casts it on for me.

for the next couple of months, this is what i do on my long bus journeys: i knit. it's relaxing. sometimes i do it in lectures too.

eventually i figure it's long enough, work out how to finish it, and there we go. scarf.

there's a small, weirdly cropped picture of one part of the scarf trailing down from michael's neck—this part's tan and orange and a deep, dark blue.

> she casts it on for me

she casts it on for me. i've still not learnt to cast on. it's the only thing i've knitted, just that one scarf, i guess i'll have to learn how if i ever want to make something else.

for the next couple of months, this is what i do on my long bus journeys: i knit. it's relaxing. sometimes i do it in **lectures too.**

scarfmemory by Michael Brough

eventually i figure it's long enough, work out how to finish it, and there we go. scarf.

> lectures too

or the next couple of months, this is what i do on my long bus journeys: i knit. it's relaxing. sometimes i do it in lectures, i guess i'm a bit of a spectacle, one time some asian kids spot me through the window of the hall and they all gather round taking photos of the hippie knitting in class, it makes me feel pretty uncomfortable.

eventually i figure it's **long enough**, work out how to finish it, and there we go. scarf.

one of the things this twine game establishes, more clearly than maybe a photo would, is that this scarf has *history*, really personal history. maybe it was his inability to find a good photo of the scarf that inspired michael to write this game: it was the only way to show the scarf from all angles.

> long enough

eventually i figure it's actually it's long enough for two people i got kind of carried away, one day i'll wrap it around my **girlfriend's** neck as well as mine keeping us both warm, work out how to finish it, and there we go. **scarf**.

> girlfriend

clicking on the word "girlfriend" changes it to "wife." that's a kind of powerful transition there, and positions the scarf within a very personal history.

> scarf

i needed a new scarf pretty soon in that weather. got one in the tartan of my ancestors. i'm wearing it right now. it keeps my neck warm.

BAD END

this is the ending screen. contrast its sparseness, the matter-of-factness of his description of this mass-produced scarf, bought in a store, with the pages and passages of thoughts and memories and history woven into michael's description of his lost scarf. a few tiny sentences in pale, skeleton white, in the big black void of the page.

played by Anna Anthropy

    this is another thing about sugarcane: the text size is very small, and the horizontal margins of the text are super wide (these are usually the first things i change when i customize one of my own stories: make the text bigger, the margins smaller, so the text becomes more bold and easy to read), so the four short sentences about the new scarf occupy almost none of the screen, and with none of the bold blue links—nowhere to go—the words look frail and naked. you wonder if they're cold.

    it was really amazing to me, when i first played *scarfmemory*, to see twine used in this way: as a memorial for a dearly loved object. later, someone actually used twine to make a memorial for a dead brother, full of pictures of the two of them together, the author's investigations of his own feelings of guilt around his estrangement from his sibling. but *scarfmemory* was one of the first games to make me think: this is what real human beings would do with games, if they had a way of making games that was actually accessible to them. it was a thought that opened my eyes, and they've never stopped opening, wider each day.

    i'm sorry you lost your scarf, michael.

REMOVED
BY AEVEE BEE
PLAYED BY LYDIA NEON

This playthrough begins not with the game itself, but with Aevee Bee's article of the same name. As a rule, I'm not an enthusiastic subscriber to the Barthesian notion of the "death of the author." Especially not when the author goes the extra step of explicating their work. How ironic then that Aevee Bee's explanation of "Removed" focuses on the sympathetic (yet disturbing) horrors spawned by a child's failure to divine authorial intent in *Final Fantasy Legend III*.

The sprite on the left holding its own brain in a jar is the one I still remember from when I was ten. It's a game boy RPG so they reuse the sprites with different names—I looked them up and they are things like Duke, Headless, Brain—but Removed was the only one I remembered: concise, past-tense, ambiguous, the name is as memorable as the sprite. Lacking context or explanation has always made RPG enemies terrifying, and the name and the image are equally ambiguous to a child who can imagine a lot and knows very little. Did the writers even even talk with the art department about the cute little horrors or were they busy with something else and let them doodle vaguely horrible weird things until they had enough to fill out the 30 hour game. Maybe they weren't even thinking about the kids. Removed looks pretty cute and droll to me now, a little cyborg musketeer, and likely that is all they were thinking. Or maybe they were thinking exactly about the kids, knowing that kids love to be totally freaked the fuck out.

There isn't enough room in the character limit of the UI to specify, so maybe it's not just its head. What else has been removed? In 1995, I was just at the right age for me to think about that for the rest of my life; being a kid is a lot of learning how to not be miserable and one thing I hadn't quite worked out in 1995 was shutting my brain off, which is an important life skill, to not consistently repeat and retread and reinterpret every thought that makes you uncomfortable on an instinctual level and persists in you like a toothache that begs to be worried until all other thoughts burn away. This happened to me many times with many thoughts. (I dealt with them through, and I am serious, praying, not that praying invoked any kind of healing of course but because I couldn't control whether or not I obsessed over a thought I created a relatively safe and good and protective thought to obsess about instead. I wrote about this a little in Thirteen Rules).

But in 1995 I was still very bad at thinking about anything else but the worst thing, and thoughts grow like mold in the brain, once a thought occurs it can't un-occur and I didn't know how to stop or redirect my brain from encouraging a terrible thought to bloom. And removal is not an unattractive idea. When I was six a tree fell on me and broke both of my legs so even in 1995 I had experienced the kind of pain that made me at least consider the possibility that having a part of oneself removed might be preferable to the pain of keeping it. It's impossible to not think about, once that thought is there, and so, so you can enjoy this too: what would you have removed if you could? It's missing its head, so the sprite in the Game Boy game made me think about headaches—mine and my mom's (she gets migraines) and so I can imagine at least what it's like to have a headache so bad that in brief moments of world ending agony I wish my

played by Lydia Neon

head would be removed, and in that case, what a lucky guy that cyborg musketeer is. But not having a face is too much existential pain to bear, I need that reminder of self. The thought is grotesque, but it teaches something important: even during the worst hangover of my life, having a head is, reluctantly, worth the pain.

But oh, there's no shortage of other stuff that can go. When I was an little teen I was on medicine that completely killed my appetite, and eating became boring and loathsome and incredibly difficult and I wished so much I could just inject nutrients in my veins instead of having to force myself to eat. I was around this age when I was reading Battle Angle Alita and Ghost in the Shell and thinking about how blissful it would be to be a brain in a perfect machine body, and become an invincible, unflinching, unstoppable woman. Which is funny, a little; I had basically just got my flesh and blood and I already was wishing I could lose it, knowing my body had already betrayed me and having enough sense know that it would just keep on doing that for the rest of my life.

Tear out my stomach so I don't have to eat and tear out my heart so I can't blush and give myself away, and you know, why don't you take out those organs of generation and gender and all the baggage that comes with them while you're at it. Wouldn't that have been convenient, to be like Alita, or the Major, or the Air Maid to the left, also from The Final Fantasy Legend III, fast and beautiful and the most powerful thing in the game and you could turn yourself into one if you wanted, you could install parts into the heroes and heroines until they glittered. What a beautiful thing to do.

Growing up with hideous images is not so bad; the irritation becomes a pearl and terrible dreams are a comfort, the path to the real thing, showing you the way before you knew what the way was. It's all weird silly childhood nightmares from decades old disposable entertainment but it still lodged itself in my brain like it meant something and now I just can't help it. Now it lives and it is part of me and I have built layers and layers around it and I have rearranged it from an awful little thought into part of me, and here is the story of that grain of sand, small and alive in me still:

    I have my own an awkward relationship with the Final Fantasy Legend (SaGa) series. See, I've never actually finished one, and that's not for lack of trying. I sunk more hours into those games than a healthy ten year old should have. I just kept starting over.

    Monsters fascinated me. Their raw, infinite protean potential spoke to some core need I felt but couldn't name. Don't like what you are? That's cool. Just eat the next enemy you can and become something new. On its face, the game presents no judgment about this: no matter how strong or weak you are, just swallow another monster and be reborn. No stat growth. No time spent leveling up. Just keep trying until you get something you like.

But I realized that as the game progressed, it left less room for experimentation in the face of the steadily growing difficulty of encounters. It was horrifyingly similar to real life. Some combinations were more equal than others, and the stakes for changing your form could grow much, much higher. So when I would inevitably end up with a team full of helpless horrors of flesh, the solution was simple: start again.

If *Removed* is the story of Aevee's mind virus spawned by *Final Fantasy Legend III*, then the mercurial nature of its monsters is my counterpart. Knowing Aevee, I don't think my Final Fantasy Legend baggage will be a hindrance to this playthrough; quite the opposite.

You're **Removed**,

which can be sweet.

Encouragingly, that is what the very first screen evokes for me. Every Twine game makes an impression with its use of CSS alone, and Removed does all it can to put an original Game Boy in my ten year old hands. A single screen Jonah interface sets up a very different kind of experience than an unaltered SugarCane (two of the default formats for Twine), and so rather than expecting a space to explore, I'm anticipating a semi-narrative emotion to explore. Perhaps the biggest detail is the way the cursor becomes the same selecting finger as in the FFL games.

I think I'll need a drink for this experience, because I can tell already that we'll be playing with emotional fire.

> Removed

Humanity is liability and what a relief it is to not have it, enough to assuage the guilt of shirking your duty to be one. It's impossible to not feel a little pang in the accusatory stares of strangers who don't know the first thing about you, but your removed organs will serve others much better than they ever did your body, and what's left of you is a more complete existence than it ever was fully assembled.

You're missing the **heart**, the **digestive system**, and the **organs of generation**.

You and your **older sister** and your **younger sister** have a restless **Kid** who must be kept safe until she dies. This place isn't safe. You'll take her to the ocean where we ride boats between the skyscraper groves and watch the jellyfish dance

played by Lydia Neon

and glow in the night.

And it's time to go.

Oh boy. We're wasting no time spelunking in the twisted caverns where the old pains are buried. That first line is a litmus test. Are you the sort who nods in sympathetic understanding? Or is your first thought to wonder why the thought of being inhuman would ever be a relief? How wonderful it must be to not understand the quiet, ever-present need to be rid of one's body.

It fascinates me that it is framed here as a willing, compassionate offering to others. Less a sacrifice, and more a trade: relief for relief. The bodily equivalent of "free for the hauling" furniture on the sidewalk.

> heart

the circulatory system

Born gone. Instead you have the Small Ones marching through your body in at the steady and pleasantly quiet rhythm of a washing machine. The Small Ones are helpful and small and hard workers, not unlike yourself. Your body is a hive to them and they will strip the flesh or nearest equivalent from whatever you feel like and do their best to deliver it back to you in a form you can give to your friends who might be currently lacking in it.

Back

Interesting that the first organ presented as missing is something that was never there. It's on the schematic for a human, sure. But here, it's unnecessary. Like the prior offer of comfort to others, the body is home to a community who need it as much as they are needed.

> Back
> Digestive System

the stomach and intestines

Unacceptable corruption (literal). When you were little it was okay but you can hardly remember what it felt like when it wasn't torturing you, and what a relief it is to not have to eat anymore, a small need to be free of. You inject nutrients or use the Small Ones, the tiny machines who march dutifully through your body. And bonus, there's not much left inside you so it's not even very inconvenient if you get stabbed or whatever.

Back

As someone who has a less-than-healthy relationship to food, this one cuts deep. I love the sensual experience of tasting food, drink, lovers' bodies. But actual consuming of food falls so far down my list of priorities that I don't often plan for it. It's an employee I'd love to fire, or at least avoid, but grudgingly admit is necessary to keep around. There's a silent tension there, one we both know is not worth rehashing at every encounter. I get it when I need it, and then promptly forget about it. To be free of the need would be glorious.

> Back
> Organs of Generation

the junk

Unacceptable corruption (metaphorical). Not being able to give birth feels complicated, even though it shouldn't. This is something you should be over. You're Removed, not Bestowed. You're grown up and won't long for impossible gifts like a child. You will be happy enough with just the wholeness that comes from discarding what is unberable.

You can still have sex, and it can be very nice even if you have to be patient and explain how it all works.

Back

The distinction between literal and metaphorical corruption is quietly beautiful. Not dwelling upon scars is taken here to be a defining quality of adulthood. The gender subtext becomes text for a brief moment here. Some days I'm over it, some days I'm not. And as much as I used to see the value in experiencing the latter publicly so as not to leave others believing they're alone in their pain, these days I know there are some games that can only be won by not playing. So I will do the adult thing and say: it's complicated.

> Back
> Older Sister

Heirloom Revenant

An AI knight handed down from generation to generation, her ghost persists long after her machine body has rusted to the red scrap that clings like dust and cobweb to her shimmering soul. Spending a few thousand years caring for living children has worn all the softness off her patience and her body.

A super-psychic with no flesh to harm.

She is hilarious and exhaustingly mean.

played by Lydia Neon

Back

I pull out my phone.
Lydia Neon: bb, I'm playing Removed right now. Is Older Sister me?
She assures me she's not. I am not sure I believe her.

> Back
> Younger Sister

Trash Ghoul

Grown in the trash wastes from a positronic seed, the ghoul grew from absorbing ambient discarded garbage and memories into a generally human sort of thing. They have a general humanity instead of specific memory, which leads to vague identity and ideological intensity, and are born ready to die for everyone.

A quick-burning firework of magic and greedy flesh.

Their brains form before their bodies and their flesh more or less perfectly conforms to their consciousness so they're super fucking hot and it's really easy to hate them for it.

Back

Ah, the defiant beauty of trash. Of making do with the discarded. Of repurposing the forgotten, cast-off waste of society into something beautiful and whole and glorious.

> Back
> Kid

Kid

She's not grown up, so she's as human as a question mark, a tamagotchi, a chao egg, with three busy sisters glittering in the corner of her eyes suggesting answers. She's a good girl, which has you worried, but maybe she is just waiting. Thankfully, she is ten billion times smarter than all of you.

Back

"She's as human as a question mark . . ." I keep rereading this line, parsing it for its manifold shades of meaning. In keeping with the theme of the game, my first notion was that it was stating she was inhuman, an invented symbol, not a person. But also a fundamentally human invention, a creation of the human mind the way a child is a creation of the body. And then there is the untapped potential of childhood wrapped up in the question mark. Like childhood is a question that is answered by growing up. But whose question is it? And lastly, I come back around to seeing Kid as human among monsters, one who hasn't given up humanity, like her sisters, but might soon.

> Back
> And it's time to go

Nonhuman life still exists in the Dusk Jungle, but it wants nothing to do with people. It's not so bad if you cover the Kid with a breathing apparatus and a suit to protect her skin, even if she looks kinda funny while her big sisters blow the deadly spores like dandelions and curl up in the mushrooms, enjoying the privileges of being machine undead. It'd be perfect for everyone but the little one if all the species there were smart enough to not try eating them

Crash

My questions about Kid are answered immediately. Kid is vulnerable to the world in a way the others aren't, and not wholly because of childhood. This is a place for the inhuman. A place where the monstrous can celebrate their monstrousness with such simple acts as blowing "deadly spores like dandelions."

> Crash

Dusk Treader A attacks by R. Smoke

40 damage to Removed.

Removed is poisoned.

40 damage to Ghoul.

Ghoul resisted the poison.

0 damage to revenant.

Revenant is immune.

80 damage to Kid.

Kid is poisoned.

Removed used Cleaner.

Removed was cured of poison.

Kid was cured of poison.

120 damage to Dusk Treader A.

played by Lydia Neon

Ghoul used Marm. Fires.

97 damage to Dusk Treader A.

Dusk Treader A is stuck!

98 damage to Dusk Treader A.

Dusk Treader A fell.

Victory.

Ah ha, a battle. Oh no! Kid is poisoned! Thankfully Removed can take care of her.

> Victory.

Camped in the shed skin of an insect you watch the pollen slowly fall like snow outside. The Revenant is guarding the nest they have burrowed for the Kid underground and you and the Ghoul can enjoy your translucent apartment to yourselves. There's no day or night in the phosphorescent jungle: just dusk forever. You're leaning on the Ghoul, because you're warm and you want to be warmer and she has leaned into you too like she is warm and she wants to be warmer, and after squirming for a little she catches your eye.

Hold me.

Have sex with me.

Rip through me.

The clash of the alien being presented in such lovingly familiar ways is hauntingly familiar. The beautiful disjointedness of it all. I revel in the way that "Hold me", "Have sex with me", and "Rip through me" are all presented as equally valid ways to show affection. For the monstrous, they can sometimes feel, if not the same, then at least interchangeable.

> Have sex with me.

"Is this okay?"

"ahhhh...it's a little..."

"How about—is this okay?"

"Ahh!"

"More or?"

"More like....this."

"Here?"

"Let me show you—"

"Here?"

"———————!!!!!"

"Oh wow."

"Keep on...there...it's so...sweet."

You're too sleepy to keep having sex but too restless to stop and spend the right of the night getting as close as you can to one or the other.

This is adorable.

> You're too sleepy . . .

In The Impossible Mountains, the world bends beneath the moon. The peaks twist and curl in upon themselves in agony as the moon coaxes them to betray the earth. The moon teaches the people here a strange gravity, a mad gravity, and it frees their bodies to pursue other shapes, longing and reaching and stretched and spiraling.

Crash.

It's just a quietly poetic statement of How It Is Here. It's not quite backstory, and it's not quite superfluous description. It's just beautiful. Fuck you, Aevee. How dare you.

> Crash.

Lycanthrope A unfolds the true form and attacks with Uzumaki Fingers.

56 damage to Ghoul!

Resisted Mad.

Ghoul counters with Rend.

50 damage to Lycanthrope A.

Removed attacks by Spinal Siphon.

330 M damage to Lycanthrope A

334 M damage to Lycanthrope B

383 M damage to Moon Masher A

Moon Masher A uses Dance...but it failed!

played by Lydia Neon

Not enough MP.

Revenant attacks by Dk. Dream.

Lycanthrope A fell.

Lycanthrope B fell.

Moon Masher A fell.

Victory.

The combat messages are blunt, utilitarian. A stark contrast to the lazy beauty of the monstrous world. But this is a world of sometimes necessary combat, and sometimes the why and the how aren't as important as who won and who lost.

> Victory

Nobody gets to sleep in the Impossible Mountains but everyone still needs to recover the HP and MP so you all wait in a circle and there's nothing to do except talk. So you talk. The ghoul and the kid tell each other stories and they're very sweet, but it's awkward between you and the revenant, it's always like she's making fun of you, like no matter how old you get she'll always be one thousand years ahead of you, and of course she will but also aren't you the second oldest, so why are you so far away from her? It hurts to not get it and she won't explain it. But no matter how mad you are at her you still trust her, except you just want her to answer

How can you be sure?

How can I be sure?

...

Oh, Goddex. Awareness of my own relationship to Aevee strikes me. No longer am I the second person protagonist, I'm the third person Older Sister. I remember having an Older Sister of my own, of desperately needing someone to tell me the answers. And now that I am someone else's I can't help but already know the answer to the questions presented. I already know what the words will be because they're my words. They're the ancient words passed along the infinite chain of Older Sisters to Younger Sisters, as we each eventually find ourselves the middle children of the universe.

> How can I be sure?

"You can't."

Removed by Aevee Bee

You can't. I'm so sorry.

> "You can't."

The highway has no end and there is no reason to be kind to anyone else on it. There are some things in this world you just can't fight, and they are better and stronger and less broken than you. Such things are hungry and want you to care about it. It's best to ignore them if you can, spite them if you can't, because if you try to fight them you'll never win.

Crash.

Ah, the understated bitterness of acknowledging reality, that there are others "less broken than you" who can outwit or overpower you. No use dwelling on it, but it does suck.

> Crash

Thirst-tortured Ghoul attacks by Dehydrate.

323 damage to Ghoul.

Thirst-tortured Ghoul recovered!

Ghoul attempted to run.

Couldn't get away!

Rampant Revenant attacks by Brain Splicer

167 M damage to all.

167 damage to all.

Revenant attempted to run.

Couldn't get away!

Remover used Thief.

Removed resisted the attack.

Removed attempted to run.

Couldn't get away!

Adult attacks by H. Arts.

Kid repelled the attack.

Kid used Gate.

Got away safely!

played by Lydia Neon

You can't win them all. For those who don't want to start fights, the motivations of those who attack others are wholly alien. Sometimes victory is just escaping alive.

> Got away

Hopefully you'll be there tomorrow. The Ghoul and the Revenant are watching while you help the Kid get ready for sleep. You want to dive in the sea, pick polished stones from the shore, snuggle in the quiet shallows and watch the jellyfish glow. But it doesn't feel like you've done enough. You hesitate as you brush her hair. She will be okay, of course she will be. You have been as good an immortal machine undead teacher can be to your student. You've taught her about life and machine life, death and machine death, the human and the inhuman, the thinkers and the animals, the born and the never born. You teach the lessons of the body and she learned from your discoveries how it is possible to force a body to function like a soul, and now that she knows it is up to her to do something about it. But there's still so much more.

"Flesh and synthetic organs alike are defined by their execution of a function, which the root name refers to. A stomach is defined not by its make or model or year but because of the function it executes. Living or dead, life or machine, understand that the names you have given are not to be taken away. Using the default equipment and its definition is a choice you can always rescind. Your body will betray you first, remain loyal only to the functions you desire from it."

"We're on your side, always. I know you won't believe this coming from me, but I'm going to say it anyway. Everything about you is valuable and powerful and that can't be taken from you. It will always be there, when we're gone and even if the world tries to bury it. I know you know that. But I really mean it. It's the most important thing in the world that you remember this."

"We love you."

Confession, this is my second playthrough now. The first time I reached this passage, it destroyed me. I had to wait for the universe to cool and reform in its cycle and spawn me again to get through this one.

Family of choice can sometimes be the only family that understands you well enough to know what you need, rather than just what they think you should need. The endless cycle of middle children caring for one another lead us to to create volatile, transient orphanages of the soul.

Removed by Aevee Bee

"Your body will betray you first" is cruel, but honest. The one thing you have no choice but to rely on even when other people have failed will someday fail as well. For some of us, it failed right out of the gate, and we are now making do with what we have.

"Everything about you is valuable and powerful" is, indeed, something we are always reminding each other of because the world does constantly try to bury it. And we never seem to fully believe it.

> "We love you."

"Thanks, Mom," she says, and she laughs, not because it's a joke, but because it's not.

End.

Sometimes, that's all there is to say.

FOR POLITICAL LOVERS, A LITTLE UTOPIA SKETCH

BY BRYAN REID
PLAYED BY AVERY MCDALDNO

i smell boiling water on your **tongue**

    I'd originally planned to play through the game once, before returning to the beginning and starting my commentary. But this opening screen made me change my mind. It was quietly disorienting. It seemed to ask that I start from a place of disorientation. And so I'm writing this screen by screen, during my first playthrough.

    I've always hated these colours, shrub green and straw yellow. They seem like a chromatic shorthand for nausea and barf. That's part of where my disorientation came from, coupled with the mixed sensory impressions. I'm not sure what it means to smell boiling water on someone's tongue, but I'm also intrigued.

    The title gives me complicated feelings, before I even know what it means. I've spent the past few years trying to fall out of love with utopianism. I used to fantasize about the miracle politic that would cure all oppression and liberate mankind once successfully deployed. There was a book, The Political Ideas of the Utopian Socialists, that finally broke me. It charted out the shared fate of so many utopian thinkers: to one day gather up all their friends, move out into the woods, found a radical commune, and then starve to death. Even just the word raises red flags for me. Utopia.

> tongue

for political lovers, a little utopia sketch   by Bryan Reid

as if you were a martyr or a wheelbarrow full by the assembly of martyrs **within**

What if I don't like this game? I'm trying to focus on disentangling this phrase, but my mind is busy with apprehension. What if I don't like this game and don't have anything interesting to say about it? I'm not sure what a "wheelbarrow full by the assembly of martyrs" is. I hope that as I move forward, the pace and cadence will become familiar to me. That even if I don't decipher in exactitude, that I am able to pull meaning from these pretty phrases.

> within

transversal

The word transversal appears, so I click that too. I debate looking it up, but decide not to. I feel a little bit stupid for not knowing it, for having dropped out of college, and for not reading very often.

> transversal

in every place where there were marshlands, you bring me a **beer** to push concrete through my body

Is this game about having a lover while struggling with depression? This third screen is the first one I really connect with, and I think it's because the words feel familiar. The stagnancy of marshlands and the immovability of concrete both remind me of my experiences with depression. I could be off base.

Now that I've acclimated to the color scheme, I want to talk about punctuation. The words are spare and unadorned. There aren't capitals or periods to lend tidy boundaries to these thoughts. I'm really enjoying that. It lends a hazy, dreamlike quality. And given the language so far (with talk of concrete in the body, boiling water on the tongue, and martyrs), it seems a spiritual and visceral dream.

> beer

wildflowers

> wildflowers

played by Avery McDaldno

wildflowers, honey

> honey

wildflowers, honey, barley

> barley

wildflowers, honey, barley, **cherries**

I feel almost guilty now, for how apprehensive and annoyed I was a few screens prior. This list is lovely. This list makes me think of witchcraft, and of hiking Idaho Peak with my family as a child, and of Redwall. This screen feels something like a healing spell.

I'm still not sure what this game is about or what these words mean. Maybe I'm boring for wanting art to have clear, accessible meanings.

> cherries

these things expel **junk asphalt** from my **liver**

Mmm. I was right to feel like the last screen was a healing spell, it seems.

This is the first choice that the game has offered me. Twine is weird that way. Coming from a background in tabletop roleplaying, I'm used to thinking of games as being driven and structured by choice. That's not really true of most videogames, though, and especially not of Twine games. I've played Twine games that involved no choices whatsoever. I was starting to wonder if this game would fall into that category. It's interesting to play Twine games and wonder what it is that makes them games. It's interesting to play other people's sometimes autobiographical experiences and wonder what it is that makes it play. Not to determine the ways it isn't, but to uncover the ways it is.

> junk asphalt

It changes.

junk food

for political lovers, a little utopia sketch   by Bryan Reid

> junk food

junk sound

> junk sound

these things expel junk light from **my liver**

This time the text is static and unchangeable. I wish I'd left it at junk food. I struggle with toxic eating habits and I eat too much junk food. It would have been good, somehow, to acknowledge that ingame.

> my liver

i smell the places you've brought your tongue

> i smell the places . . .

and laid it down to the surface between things

> and laid it down . . .

and left the heat to **do its job**

At first it's just one phrase, but clicking reveals another.
 I want to know what this game is. I want this game to give me some kind of assurance about the experience I'll get from it. I was starting to feel more connected to its story over the past few screens a story about detox and attentiveness. But it's lost me again. I don't know what I'm supposed to do with these words. I don't know how to engage with them.
 They seem to have emotional content, but I don't know how to reach it.

> do its job

i am a state bureaucrat's office

This screen feels jarring in a new way. It's cold and impersonal.

> i am a state bureaucrat's office

i **accept**

> accept

i **accept**

> accept

i **delay**

I'm not sure why the game is pulling back so hard from the sensual and immediate, acting estranged all of a sudden. I feel as though I've done something wrong. Or maybe that the game feels embarrassed for having been too vulnerable and earnest with me, and now it's getting defensive and backpedaling.

a body hosting mostly other microbes, largely a **harbortown**

>

people debone fish with one creamly tug

>

it's **effortless**

Since the third screen, each has involved some sort of text cycling or gradual unfolding. It was several clicks before this screen was fully expanded. Coupled with the absence of capitals and punctuation, as well as the abrupt shifts in tone and imagery, the game feels like a dream. It is both hazy and frantic.

I like the imagery here. While I was growing up, my mother worked part time surveying fishermen and weighing catches at a rural wharf. I would often spend those days with her. The sight and smell of recently gutted fishes is a fond one for me. They remind me of carefree days running amidst driftwood and shale out at Shelter Bay.

> effortless

to be a room full of abstract **art**

for political lovers, a little utopia sketch   by Bryan Reid

It's strange to me how the game moves between feeling very personal, immediate, talking of you and I, to this more distant and almost clinical phrasing. The imagery undergoes similar shifts, screen to screen. Sometimes the images are immediate and visceral. Other times, they are detached and unreachable.

I have the feeling that I am meant to be moving through this game more quickly.

> art

you teach me the ways to read energy in a novel,

where to put punctuation in between the **censers** of literature

This time, I do look up the unfamiliar word in the dictionary. Doing so doesn't make the phrase any clearer. Still, I'm able to parse the passage as a whole. It reminds me of the times I've heard my friend Samwell read, how every breath he takes doubles as a strategic pause, how he leans into certain words, the long preambles he constructs sometimes before reading.

> censers

the indefatigable **musk**

\>

the indefatigable **musk of words that**

\>

the indefatigable **musk of words that bore through**

\>

the indefatigable **musk of words that bore through the face at**

\>

the indefatigable musk of words that bore through the face at

played by Avery McDaldno

all en**trances**

Four clicks unfold the entirety of this sentence. I like this continued image of two people reading together, one guiding the other through the intricacies of a text. I'm not entirely sure what an "indefatigable musk of words" means, and am doubtful that a dictionary would help me. My text analysis has become pretty shallow at this point, hinging mostly upon phrases that I don't understand. I think that's because I'm now fixating on the fact that I don't understand this game, and I don't understand how to play it well.

Maybe now is a good time to talk about Twine and accessibility. I think there's something paradoxical at work in the medium. Twine is rightly celebrated as an accessible and empowering tool for creators. It requires almost no understanding of code, it allows you to plot out stories visually, and a culture has been built around the platform that celebrates small works from marginalized creators. But I don't see the Twine world as being entirely accessible for players. Games are often presented in poorly contrasted colors. Language is often esoteric and intentionally chaotic. Few games let you bookmark or save your progress, and few games mention how long they're going to take to complete at the outset. The medium and the culture surrounding it nudge creators toward making work that is hard to navigate or grapple.

> trances

you teach me how

here

the author paid their bills three days late **and**

> and

here they lived nowhere in particular, maybe inside the heat of a friend or kind **stranger**'s ligament

Clicking the first of these phrases unveils the second. I love this screen. I'm imagining now a very cozy scene, lovers gently teaching each other how to do common things with uncommon grace. How to breathe. How to read. How to lay upon the floor and close one's eyes.

I'm thankful—grateful, even—that the creator hasn't yet jumped forward to another metaphor or fragment. I feel like I'm being given a chance to catch up and to appreciate.

I like the idea of living nowhere in particular, and wonder at what point in my life that might have been true of me. I'm a writer, after all.

for political lovers, a little utopia sketch   by Bryan Reid

> stranger

illinois used to be full of marshes and forests and has squirrels **trapped in open spaces** once closed off

The creator sometimes leaves whole phrases as links. Other times, it's a single word at the end of a phrase, or stuck in amidst it, or even just part of a word (in the case of en/trances). I think this builds on the absent punctuation, contributing to that hazy scattered feeling. The many approaches to link formatting make each poetic image feel more happenstance and accidental, like this is just what happened to bubble to the surface at this particular moment.

let's **get out of here**

let's **go**

This screen lets me pick my escape fantasy, my urgent romance—

> get out of here

let's **find a mountain**

>

let's **find a desert**

>

find a place where people talk about anything but money

Whenever the game presents a set of options to cycle between, they strike me as being very very similar. It feels less like I'm choosing what to say, and more like I'm seeing the same scene play out in a few hardly divergent parallel universes. I'm reminded of Upstream Color, the scene(s) where birds take flight and memories collapse in on themselves.

> Let's go

you can **act**, and i'll **teach**

played by Avery McDaldno

we'll find people who imagine **a future**

The game feels more concrete and relatable now. I have an image in my head of the titular lovers, maybe two or maybe more than that. I have a picture of their homes and lives and exhaustions. I am no longer left to piece together meanings from indefatigable musks and rooms full of abstract art.

The way this screen handles cycling choices is new. Previously I was given an opportunity to choose between four parallel phrases, and the fourth would turn out to be static text that I couldn't click any further. Here, though, there are perhaps thirty different choices for what you can do, and thirty again for what I will do. I settle quickly on making wine, myself, but am indecisive when it comes to selecting your activity. You can start a food truck. You can train dogs. You can dance.

you can **dance**, and i'll **make wine**

we'll find people who imagine **a future**

> a future

a space out there to let ourselves become **exhausted**

If this is what was meant by "a utopia sketch"—a vision of the future where lives are purposeful and chosen and we are allowed to be vulnerable with one another—then I am excited. I like the phrasing on this screen. I like the idea that exhaustion is not an inherently bad thing, that it can be liberatory under the right circumstances.

> exhausted

time whorls through the weft and warp of seasons, of time-knowing where it is **becoming** into

I click through without spending much time on this screen, eager to know where the game leads me next.

> becoming

people **unmoored from knowing**

> unmoored from knowing

for political lovers, a little utopia sketch   by Bryan Reid

people becoming out of their **parts**

    The game's creator seems to love abstraction and obfuscatory language a lot more than I do. I'm starting to lose the plot again. I hope that I'm given more grounding details in the next screen.

    > parts

wholes becoming **slower**

    >

wholes becoming **slower, heavier**

    >

wholes becoming **slower, heavier, earthen**

    >

wholes becoming slower, heavier, earthen, lovingly **porous**

    This is nice. It reminds me of my time living in the country soup pots sitting on top of woodstoves for days, trenches dug through the snow, the quiet echoes of a banjo being played out in the garden. I wonder sometimes whether I could move somewhere rural again, start up a new life as a prairie dyke.
    I sometimes think that the urban fascination with novelty and new experiences is a sickness. Or maybe these dichotomies I'm latching onto are silly.

    > porous

i want to find a space with you where our talking can **repair and sleep**

    This is nice.

    > repair and sleep

played by Avery McDaldno

and our neighbors **repair and sleep**

This, too, is nice.

> repair and sleep

and their loved ones **repair and sleep**

I used to do performance poetry. And there's this really common mechanism in performance poetry, other sorts of verbal storytelling too, for bring a piece to close. It's to say the same thing a few times, or maybe a few ways. It's reassuring, soothing, grounding. Threes are especially good.

> repair and sleep

and no one delays inside their body any more

(x)

The (x) signals an ending. This is a gorgeous screen to end a story on.

I found *for political lovers, a little utopia sketch* really difficult to engage with, sometimes. The first half was esoteric in a way that mostly made me feel stupid. I'll echo myself from earlier: I want art to have clear, accessible meanings. Maybe that's lowbrow and maybe that's boring. But when I hear a story I want to understand its contents.

Maybe that's part of the point of this game? The experience felt like a mire of abstraction and heaviness, finally rescued by intentional living, little gestures, the countryside. I felt a palpable relief toward the end of the game, contemplating the simple activities that might fill the lives of these imagined lovers. I felt comforted when the narrative stopped skipping around so abruptly.

for political lovers, a little utopia sketch inhabits a weird middleground between Upstream Color and Goodnight Moon. I liked its ending.

YOUR LOVER HAS TURNED INTO A FLOCK OF BIRDS
BY MIRANDA SIMON
PLAYED BY BRYAN REID

Your lover has turned into a **flock of birds.**
Do you still love me, **she asks**.

Yes

No

    my lover, the flock of birds. my lover, the murder in the leafless trees, chattering away to me and calling her own name to check over and over again: she is here, she is in love, here, loving love. my lover, the flock of seagulls // her ruffled feathers so ridiculous, and i spend hours chasing each one of her foreheads to kiss it and tell her she looks so campy. my lover, the flock of terror birds, flightless loomer *titanis walleri* // i could sow together a panoply of monstrous sweaters to keep your eight-foot frames warm in the chilly north, a cozy for each one of your axe-like beaks. i could learn how to build a lot of birdhouses, and line the walls of each one with a new line of poetry each day. i could get a job at a pet store and buy up all their seeds on discount. if you were a bunch of owls, i could build a treehouse and try to hoot in symphony // work in the city, catching mice.

    > flock of birds

Your Lover Has Turned into a Flock of Birds by Miranda Simon

none of them are birds of paradise, but none of them are pigeons either

chirp

> chirp

Your lover has turned into a **flock of birds**.

Do you still love me, **she asks**.

Yes

No

> she asks

she can't speak because she is a flock of birds but **you understand her**

> you understand her

Do you still love me, **she asks**.

Yes

No

    yes, i can love you as a flock of birds.[1] what is human is a sea of many things, culled under the name of one person // is a whole homestead for microbes otherwise thought up as aliens. the person is a thing that repeats itself, mimics itself // is the spigot of the society that excites it to bring energy into the world. the person is a collective, holding a collective inside.[2]

    1   Everyday, we run a gauntlet of minute decisions, revelations, and affirmations. We don't, in our minds, change overnight, but find ourselves becoming a new *something*—a nominalized something—once there is an object to anchor this change into. It may be an memory or occasion in time, a new name, a new ideology, a physical newness, &c. Transitions states are the norm, with each relationship being in part predicated on the agreement that each person involved accepts the risks and may hazard heartbreak to leave and/or be left in the course of life changes. *Your Lover Has Turned Into a Flock of Birds* deftly folds these anchors, these sites of perceptibility, into the nodes of the story. The movement from Twine passage into the next is the realization of one anchor into the next—this being the basis of hypertext. The rules of the game are hidden from the player. We only see the game at the nodes of visibility. *Your Lover Has Turned Into a Flock of Birds* exists in a much greater volume of coding, gameplay outcomes, and linguistic expression than is immediately visible.

    2   The process of movements in between—the physics of the changing, revealing, affirming being—exists in love in a state of publicness. This is the gamble

played by Bryan Reid

i could get used to a beak, a coo, a flap if it was all still you.

> yes

She creates nests all over your body until you're wearing her like **armor.**

I can protect you, she says.

It's better this way, she says.

    my lover is so sweet, so kind—but my lover needs to be youness, from visor to toeguard. as two as one, we both go out and play with the hazards. my lover can't be a suit of armor // is too full of her own youness to only be in the spaces of my movings. my lover is loving, but must be able to bankrupt me, to pull me into struggles, to call up a need to overcome things that don't belong to me. the gravity, the pool of unknown water, the field of verse in languages i don't know and a meter i can't guess. my lover and i: each other's certainties in each other's uncertainties.[3] her own atmosphere.

> armor

Your lover has turned into a suit of armor.

She's metal and beginning to **rust.**

There are no dragons or kings to defend you from, and the weight of her alloy makes you droop. This isn't what you need.

What do you want me to be, she asks.

Full

Empty

---

of approaching the two-state, as Alain Badiou describes in *In Praise of Love*. The first publicness is domestic and intimate publicness. Forging oneself as shaped in love means reading the apparent, the anchor positions that overshadow the fuzzy mass of decision-making and revelation in between, and moving those apparent anchors in harmony with each other.

    3   Love isn't the careless loss of self. Moving towards another person isn't being obliterated or subsumed by them. Negotiation of the power in a relationship to set apparent changes as markers of harmony means consent. Consent means, to be brief, being on solid ground—and when that's not available, helping each other to get to solid ground.

Your Lover Has Turned into a Flock of Birds by Miranda Simon

> rust

all it took was a little exposure to air and to water and she's fallen to pieces

she's sorry she's sorry so so sorry

but **metal** can't help but rust

   i don't want her to have to apologize, to have to feel sorry for this. i want her to be a universe within herself. this is the collective person in happiness: too multitudinous, too volcanic even in quietness, to ever come into full rendering. love is the moving of these two multitudes into a single language that, like all languages capable to speaking to truth, is more a matter of trust and porousness than perfection.[4]

> metal

Your lover has turned into a suit of armor.

She's metal and beginning to **rust**.

There are no dragons or kings to defend you from, and the weight of her alloy makes you droop. This isn't what you need.

What do you want me to be, she asks.

Full

Empty

---

   [4]   *Your Lover Has Turned Into a Flock of Birds* demands choice in trust from the player. In the game, my lover will change regardless of my choice—but I can establish my anchors of apparent change with her. She can ignore me, overshoot these markers, make choices impressed upon her by exterior publicness, &c. I don't want a lover who is a suit of armor, and so I'm given the choice to set a new anchor of apparent change. I want a lover who is full of yearning, full of vigor, full of rage—I choose "Full." I'm reading the game like I read my lover. "What does the interpretation of the anchor mean?" is looming under each hyperlink, is looming under each conversation I have with the person I love. We keep going; we hold faith in the gamble of love, that we can and will move towards that point of dynamic harmony together. I can want and want, but this isn't the point. My lover will be whoever she will be—I'm just taking a guess on where we might find harmony. I click the next link; I'm locked into the gamble of this game. It's not because I love this game, but because I want to rehearse that movement of anchors towards a different sense of self.

played by Bryan Reid

    i want my lover to be full, to be powerful,[5] to be keen, to be a story in her own language. my lover's fingers, eyes, voice move at my lover's work // my lover's work to move fingers, eyes, voice. i want my lover to be every artist, scientist, priest, or philosopher she wants to be, full from the rolling out of the beginning and end of her time of wanting. in geometry, curves are more resilient than flat planes; i want my lover to be so full of her happinesses and hungers that she makes a gravity around her, curves the world around her, builds her own shell of harbors and safe places out of the kind of sweet life she wants. and those daily happinesses and hungers radiate in harmony with mine // my lover and i, euphony, polyphony. be so full, so expansive, cover such a great volume in yourself that i fail everyday to hold you in your allness, and have to come back everyday to try again.

    > Full

Your lover has become the **moon**, and disappears from view in the heat of the day.

You see her that night, and she tells you about the places she's seen.

She waxes and wanes, but every time you see her now, she's **glowing**.

    my lover, the moon. my lover loves to travel, to see the endlessly whipping stretches of earth, its cloudy hair in a migratory frizzle // my lover rocks the oceans and lakes with glee. i can go to lake michigan to see the push of her laughter. it's a little cuteness as benefit for having the moon as a lover.

    > moon

    a celestial body

---

    5   The first publicness is domestic and intimate publicness. If this is threatened—if the negotiation of power in a relationship has its credibility threatened by exterior publicness—love demands the liberation of the publicly threatened lover. The health of our relationships are immediately influenced by how our society constructs power, and this demands action from us. This goes beyond just listening and openness—an attempt to rectify the threats of the exterior publicness within the intimate—which is a good place to start. Exterior action is demanded, however; society itself needs to be acted upon to make the world safe for lovers. Lovers shouldn't be threatened because of their race, their ethnicity, their gender, their sexual orientation, their class, their religion, their nationality, their disability, &c.—all lovers must fight for the social healthiness of love itself. How can any of us hope to hazard heartbreak and harmony in an atmosphere of fixed odds?

Your Lover Has Turned into a Flock of Birds by Miranda Simon

she returns night after night

sometimes she's invisible, but she's **still there**

    my lover sees the vastness of space, as it goes out and out.[6] you could fit the whole planetary scope of the solar system between me and my lover, but we come home together and talk about our day together. she makes me so proud, helping verne, melies, calvino, the marcels, werewolves, debussy, beethoven, that duncan jones movie, calendar makers around the world, &c. so busy, so busy—but my lover always comes back to me, beaming brightest off the energy we all share. and, like this, no one can contain her.

    > still there

END

---

6   The space shared between lovers who move towards that state of changing in harmony—harmony, not duplicity—multiplies as each one adds more and more possibilities into the range of potential anchors. This is like learning a new word, which adds a peculiar token of sound, sight, and/or texture to the world for the learner. New anchors expand the possibilities, and reveal limitations, of articulation. It's not that anything makes more sense. *Your Lover Has Turned Into a Flock of Birds* makes no more sense at this end as it did at the beginning. What it does is rehearse the process of becoming attuned to the range of articulating markers—anchors, as I've been calling them—lovers may use to note changes in who they are. The game plays out Augusto Boal's poetics of the oppressed, and calls us to practice in our arts the skills we need for better living in a freer world. This isn't about sense in the interpretative mode. This is performative sense—the sense of moving parts, dynamic parts, that can't be held down within the mechanically reproducible text. This game lets me practice articulating myself, as a lover, in a language rife with possibility and limitation. More than a game that *says*, this is a game that *does*—and that's a powerful mode to learn from.

DETRITUS
BY MARY HAMILTON
PLAYED BY AURIEA HARVEY

Just like real life, this game will not let you save or refresh the page or use the browser buttons to go backwards without breaking. Also just like real life, it probably won't work in Internet Explorer 8 or below.

Detritus

Dear past self,

Do you think it will be different this time?

All the times i've left and all the things left behind,
leaving in haste,
leaving for an ideal,
wondering if I'm even right to go,
wondering what i should take with me?

Over seas and a husband… yeah.
Wondering, if and when, will it end again
—and start again
—and end again
Just like in real life,
endings look like beginnings.

Play it again.

Detritus by Mary Hamilton

I hate those game commentaries that are based on very first play-throughs. People think this will get the most surprising or genuine reaction. Ha! I say. You have to think about what you've done. I played *Detritus* three times and screen-recorded the first and third. The second play was the best. The titled songs as soundtrack on loop along with my clicks. The game, the videos and the music, like echoes, like a memory of a story you only remember because there is one object you didn't throw away or give away. The kind of memories you go over and over . . . well, I don't anymore. But when you are in your twenties-early thirties, in your more lucid moments, you try to figure out how you got wherever you are. Those times when reality is something to be seen from the inside out. I'm in my forties; am I past it?

(1) The first two weeks in the NYC apartment I shared, I used to wake up constantly from the sound of trucks bumping down 3rd Avenue. I shared with 3 friends. It turned out one of them hated me with a passion all along. When we all fell out, and moved out, she told me I was the "most unoriginal person" she had ever met. I decided she was the one with the problem, not me. Fuck her. Forever.

(2) Nirvana is not a neutral choice. Even the first chord of any given Nirvana song reminds me of pickup trucks in Indiana, USA and the wrong blond boys I was deathly attracted to that drove them. Still, we all have "that band" with "those songs." I might have done the same thing, substituting with titles from Nick Cave and The Bad Seeds.

But I don't remember things this way anymore. I don't. It is hard for me to put myself into this position, this character, without wanting to lecture, to advise, to ask questions. I fear this kind of *essential* moving on. I know this about myself now: I'll do anything to avoid having to pack up all this stuff.

> I make promises to myself,
> to be more adult.
> Even as an adult you find you have to change your life.
> Sometimes you have control over what you bring with you,
> other times
> you don't.
>
> You want a fresh start?
> Out with the old, in with the new.
>
> Funny to enumerate the things left behind or lost.
> Maybe it will be different this time. So there is still hope.
>
> Play it again.
>
> \> Detritus

played by Auriea Harvey

You unlock the door with a freshly cut key, cold in your hot hands, and walk into a broad beige room. The carpet is thin under your feet and the walls are painted the colour of boredom. There is a bay window, even though you are on the second floor, with plain net curtains that prevent much light from breaking in.

You swing your small suitcase up onto the single bed, and the white-painted metal frame squeaks under the unexpected extra weight. It will squeak like that every time you turn over under the thin blankets for the next six months. It will **wake you up**.

> wake you up

>

It will be weeks before you have to go back to college. You have weeks to become accustomed to this place. You do not yet know how to fry a chicken breast or clean a sink. You have plenty to learn.

You have a small kitchen. You have a dark brown wardrobe made from cheap chipboard. You have a chest of three wide drawers with white bases and brown plastic handles. You have a coffee table. You have a single shelf. Your suitcase needs unpacking. The **zips buzz**.

> zips buzz

The suitcase sits on the single mattress. There are a few things left inside.

Take out the **poster**.

Take out the **chessboard**.

Detritus by Mary Hamilton

Take out the **kitchenware**.

Take out the **books**.

Take out the **clothes**.

  Posters. Figuring out who you are. You are fresh from High School.

  > kitchenware

You've brought a few bits and pieces: a cheap plastic **toaster**, a white **kettle** that's never been used before, a **set of plastic tea and coffee jars** you got from a charity shop last week. You head to the kitchen.

  > kettle

A kettle's such a basic thing you couldn't even imagine making this move without one. You've been living on black instant coffee made so thick you could stand a spoon in it. Where you were before, they'd make you a cup in the mornings and put it on your desk, in your room, as far away from your bed as possible, so you physically had to get up to reach it. Bribery, of a sort. You'll have to make your own, here, now you're better. You have to put it in the kitchen. Putting it within reach of the bed is cheating.

The suitcase sits on the single mattress. There are a few things left inside.

Take out the **poster**.

Take out the **chessboard**.

Take out the **books**.

Take out the **clothes**.

  > books

You only brought the best ones, those that would repay reading over and over again, that you could place on your shelves - if you had shelves - and be proud of when visitors came.
Camus, Brett Easton Ellis, Jane Austen.

  Twice I chose Brett Easton Ellis once Camus.

  > Camus

played by Auriea Harvey

A few novels, pregnant with metaphor, and a few books of philosophy. The Plague has pride of place, alongside Primo Levi and a weighty Kierkegaard you will never admit you haven't read. These are books you describe by their authors' names, not by their titles. There are **no women** among them. You place each one on the shelf carefully, memorising where it sits.

The suitcase sits on the single mattress. There are a few things left inside.

Take out the **poster**.

Take out the **chessboard**.

Take out the **clothes**.

> At no time did I want to hear about there being no women.

> chessboard

With both hands, you pick the marble chessboard out of your suitcase and turn it over slowly. The squares on the top are white and a banded greenish-brown, like agate. You were in chess club, in your first year of high school. You used to be pretty good. Impulsive, but you could **think ahead** when you really needed to.

It's a stupid thing, you know. Why do you even own it? It's too heavy. It's a square of solid stone with more **solid stone** attached. There's a cardboard box of glass chess pieces - the box used to contain wooden fragrant balls of the sort you slip into underwear drawers to distract moths - the pieces don't match and it's not like anyone will visit you here to play, anyway.

You put it on the chest of drawers, carefully positioning it so it's square and parallel to the edges. You can unpack the pieces later.

The suitcase sits on the single mattress. There are a few things left inside.

Take out the **poster**.

Take out the **clothes**.

> (thinking ahead was the best choice.)

> solid stone

You have a bag of crystals at the bottom of your suitcase.

Detritus by Mary Hamilton

You've been collecting them since you were four or five, before you can remember. There's a chunk of amethyst, a fist-sized lump of green adventurine, a hunk of rock quartz you found on a beach one time in France. Dozens of little clusters of pyrite, fool's gold, that glint and glisten when the light hits them.

You pluck each one carefully from the blue plastic carrier bag and place it on the chessboard. In the end you have a little copse of glistening stone, shining in the sunlight from the bay window.

The suitcase sits on the single mattress. There are a few things left inside.

Take out the **poster**.

Take out the **clothes**.

> clothes

You no longer have to wear a school uniform, which means maybe you need different clothes, but you've no money and no time to find them. This is what you have: a pair of jeans that are ripped at the knees, deliberately; a t-shirt with a yawning kitten on the front; an enormous jumper you like to wear when you're sad, so you can feel small and quiet at the centre of it; a set of pyjamas with stupid monkeys on. You hate the monkeys.

Take them all out.

Clothes out of the suitcase.

> Take them all out

You take each item carefully out of the suitcase, shake it out, then fold it up again. They do not even begin to fill the space in your drawers and your wardrobe. You pause over the monkey pyjamas, but in the end you fold them anyway and put them in the top drawer, with your underwear. In three weeks' time you will wear them to bed again, with the enormous jumper, because the blankets are thin and the radiators insufficient.

You sling your suitcase under the bed and go to make a cup of tea. It is 11am on a Tuesday and the day is your own. All the days are your own, all of a sudden. There are **so many** of them.

played by Auriea Harvey

> so many

Act Two
About A Girl

>

She said yes.

You have **four days to pack** and get everything from here to there, from your wide room with the beige carpets and the white walls to a new place. The new house is in a terraced row of seven. The bus to your new job leaves across the road, six doors down. You can be there in less than an hour. You can afford the rent, if she shares it.

She said she would. It is far better than being alone.

I thought about love but then thought about my roommates. Four days isn't a lot of time but it gets worse.

> four days to pack

Day one. They tell you a new girl is moving in to your flat in four days. You will have to be quick.

You have 3 big, thick cardboard boxes, 7 binbags and 2 crates. What will you pack today?

Put the **books** into a crate.

Put the **clothes** into a bin bag.

Put the **posters** into a box.

Stack your **CDs** into a box

Pile your **soft toys** into a bag.

Put the **chessboard** into a box.

Detritus by Mary Hamilton

Pack your **notebooks** into a box.

> clothes

Some of your clothes are getting threadbare and worn, but you are determined not to let anything go to waste. You still wear everything, even the torn jeans with the Nirvana acid smiley face drawn on in felt tip pen. You don't have enough trousers to stop wearing the ones that don't suit you any more, or that you've come to realise never did. You still own no skirts, nothing that would mark you out as female, nothing that makes you look weak or vulnerable.

You pile your clothes one item at a time into the bag. The monkey pyjamas are the last thing to go in. You decide a monkey is an acceptable level of weakness, if you're in bed. She's the only person who will see you like that, anyway. She won't take advantage. She wouldn't.

You have 3 big, thick cardboard boxes, 5 binbags and 2 crates. What will you pack today?

Put the **books** into a crate.

Pack the **crystals** into a box.

Put the **posters** into a box.

Stack your **CDs** into a box

Pile your **soft toys** into a bag.

Put the **chessboard** into a box.

Pack your **notebooks** into a box.

> books

You've read a few more of these now, just because the nights got long and you couldn't really afford to stock your shelves with style over substance any more. And you've diversified: Robert Anton Wilson's Illuminatus! trilogy sits next to Zen and the Art of Motorcycle Maintenance. Both, you've told your friends, are inadequate in their own ways, not least the absence of a female perspective. Jeanette Winterson's Written on the Body nestles up to Germaine Greer's The Female Eunuch on your shelves. In the crate you mix up the titles to make the number of books by women look larger than it is, and you make a resolution for the new house.

You have 3 big, thick cardboard boxes, 5 binbags and 1 crate.

played by Auriea Harvey

What will you pack today?

Pack the **crystals** into a box.

Put the **posters** into a box.

Stack your **CDs** into a box

Pile your **soft toys** into a bag.

Put the **chessboard** into a box.

Pack your **notebooks** into a box.

She has bad taste in books.

> notebooks

You never finish notebooks. You find it hard to start them. Often you'll write on a few pages at the start then tear them out days later, feeling the book somehow spoiled by the imperfections in your writing. Three notebooks are thus far unused, and pregnant therefore with the possibility of getting it right this time. You pack each one into the box, even the ones with no clean pages left, to guard against the past rotting away.

You have packed all day, and you are weary. Your bed is still your bed. You can curl up here with a good book, while away the hours until it's time to start it all again. Till **tomorrow**.

> tomorrow

Day two. A friend whose father has a trailer has volunteered to come round the day after tomorrow, in the afternoon, and take your things away. As much as you can pack before he arrives.

You have 2 big, thick cardboard boxes, 5 binbags and 1 crate. What will you pack today?

Pack the **crystals** into a box.

Put the **posters** into a box.

Stack your **CDs** into a box

Pile your **soft toys** into a bag.

Put the **chessboard** into a box.

Pack the **kitchen things** into a crate.

Detritus by Mary Hamilton

Pack your **craft kit** into a box.

Pile your **papers** into a crate

> kitchen

It's had a good life, your kettle. It was third- or fourth-hand when you got it, passed from student to uncle to friend to you by some circuitous route, and you've drunk two cups of coffee and one of tea every day since you came here. But if you're honest, it's not been the same since you ran out of cash without a saucepan and had to use it to boil spaghetti. You do the mental maths: you can get a new one, if you only spend a tenner. You know a place. It'll be a treat for the new house.

You stuff it in an old Kwik Save bag, put it next to the bin, and carry on wrapping plates in old copies of the free Metro newspaper.

You have 2 big, thick cardboard boxes, 5 binbags and 0 crates. What will you pack today?

Pack the **crystals** into a box.

Put the **posters** into a box.

Stack your **CDs** into a box

Pile your **soft toys** into a bag.

Put the **chessboard** into a box.

Pack your **craft kit** into a box.

Pile your **papers** into a crate

> CDs

You tell everyone that the first album you bought was the Spawn soundtrack, because it had a cool alien face on the front. It's just about believable, just. It goes in the box, along with the Black Album, Korn, Antichrist Superstar, and all the rest. You pause over a relaxation CD of springtime water music. One of the other girls in the block gave it to you a few months ago, just before her second court date, to say thank you for helping her cook a meal. You're pretty sure she shoplifted it. You don't listen to it much. Should you **keep it**? Or will you **need the space for other things**?

played by Auriea Harvey

> need the space for other things

You don't need it. Sally only gave it to you so you'd help her again, really. Three days later she was back chasing the dragon in the shared living room, then waiting outside for shady blokes to come by in good cars to pick her and Rachel up. She's never kept you safe. A CD doesn't change anything.

You never listen to it anyway.

You have 1 big, thick cardboard box, 5 binbags and 0 crates. What will you pack today?

Pack the **crystals** into a box.

Put the **posters** into a box.

Pile your **soft toys** into a bag.

Put the **chessboard** into a box.

Pack your **craft kit** into a box.

Pile your **papers** into a crate

> craft kit

For the first year you didn't have a TV, aside from the box in the shared common room, and that was tuned to soaps: Emmerdale, Brookside, Corrie, Eastenders, the same set every night. You kept the habit of creating small things to keep your hands busy, even after she started to occupy more and more of your time. There's a tin of sequins, an empty ice cream box of glue and pens, a little bag of embroidery yarns and needles. You make cards for birthdays and stitch presents for friends with your imperfect hands. Every time you are ashamed, but it is cheaper to create than to purchase. That won't change, even if she does find another job and start helping with the rent.

You have packed all day, and you are weary. Your bed is still your bed. You can curl up here with a good book, while away the hours until it's time to start it all again. Till **tomorrow**.

> tomorrow

She calls. It's a week since you've seen her and she sounds distracted. Still no job despite everything, but she has been put on a course. The job centre will send her on forestry

Detritus by Mary Hamilton

training next month. She tells you she loves you. You tell her you love her. You eat a single slice of toast and drink two cups of coffee before you start.

You're starting to run low on packing materials. You can go out and get some more, but it might take a while.

You have 0 big, thick cardboard boxes, 5 binbags and 0 crates. What will you pack today?

Pack the **crystals** into a box.

Put the **posters** into a box.

Pile your **soft toys** into a bag.

Put the **chessboard** into a box.

Pile your **papers** into a crate

> I obstinately refuse to take the soft toys the second and third time. But i always go out and get more supplies.

> go out and get some more

Binbags are easy. A roll of ten from the corner shop is 57p, which is within your acceptable overspend for the week. Boxes are harder; nowhere within walking distance sells them, and they're too expensive to buy when you can beg them from the shops. Kwiksave recycle all theirs, you know from last time, so you try other shops. Oxfam has none you can take. The hippy shop doesn't have any deliveries till next week. The woman behind the counter at the bookshop on the corner takes offence at you asking and tells you to leave. Eventually the greengrocer gives you a couple, wide things that will be too heavy to lift if you fill them to the brim.

You filch another bread crate from the car park at the back of Sainsburys on the way home.

You have 2 big, thick cardboard boxes, 15 binbags and 1 crate. What will you pack today?

Pack the **crystals** into a box.

Put the **posters** into a box.

Pile your **soft toys** into a bag.

Put the **chessboard** into a box.

Pile your **papers** into a crate

played by Auriea Harvey

> papers

It's your first house, and you still don't really understand which papers that come through your door are important. There's all sorts in here: phone bills, bank statements, benefit receipts, the stubs of your first income support book and the letters about your council tax and your rental arrears from before the benefits came through. You kept everything just in case they stopped the money again. Now you have a job, you won't need that any more.

You start to leaf through the small stack of paper, checking account numbers, making a list. There is too much. After twenty minutes, the incomprehensible bureaucracy of living condensed in this pile has defeated you. You lift it in one messy lump and dump it into a crate. If you need any of it in the future, you will know where to start looking.

You have 2 big, thick cardboard boxes, 15 binbags and 0 crates. What will you pack today?

Pack the **crystals** into a box.

Put the **posters** into a box.

Pile your **soft toys** into a bag.

Put the **chessboard** into a box.

> chessboard

You did play chess here, a few times. You put the glass pieces out and sat on your bed with one of your oldest friends, last year. You smoked more weed than you really thought possible and you could see all the lines of force between the little sculpted players. The game took three hours, staring, seeing all the patterns, carefully picking your way through the web of possibilities in front of you, but you won in the end.

You pack the heavy board at the bottom of the box, take out a black felt tip from your pencil case and write "CARE - HEAVY" on the side, in case anyone but you picks it up.

You have packed all day, and you are weary. **Tomorrow** afternoon the trailer comes. You can leave a few things here and come back for them, if you need to. Surely.

She should play more chess.

Detritus by Mary Hamilton

> tomorrow

Wake up. Wake up. Wake up. Wake up. Wake up.

You have 1 big, thick cardboard box, 15 binbags and 0 crates. What will you pack before the trailer comes?

Pack the **crystals** into a box.

Put the **posters** into a box.

Pile your **soft toys** into a bag.

Put your **makeup** into your purse.

Check **under the bed** for anything you've left behind.

> under the bed

You pull the metal bedframe away from the wall, uncovering a patch of dust and hair that's not been vacuumed since you moved in. Amid the grot and grunge is an unexpected thing: a sculpture of sorts made from wire, twisted together to form a spreading tree. You were proud of the tree, but she told you she didn't really think it looked like much. You remember hiding it, now it stares you in the face.

You grab the Henry from the downstairs cleaning cupboard and give the floor a quick once-over before you push the bed back to where it belongs, with a ray of sunshine from the window just hitting the pillow.

You have 1 big, thick cardboard box, 15 binbags and 0 crates. What will you pack before the trailer comes?

Pack the **crystals** into a box.

Put the **posters** into a box.

Pile your **soft toys** into a bag.

Put your **makeup** into your purse.

> makeup

You started wearing metallic, smoky eyeshadow last year along with half the rest of college. You have a little stack of very unsubtle shades, white through black with greys and silvers between. Brown has never suited you. Some days you put on your silver eyeliner and imagine yourself impervious to harm, a robot, emotionless.

played by Auriea Harvey

There's a honking noise outside the bay window, where the sun shines in. You lift back the net curtains one last time, and see the trailer in the street below.

You have the keys to the new house, and she's meeting you there this evening with whatever small bits and pieces she can contribute. You have a pile of things, a meagre, nondescript collection. It looks small for something that weighs two years.

It's time to **go**.

> I'm judging this girl (First, by thinking it's a girl)

> go

*Act Three
School*

>

Hey hey hey it's OK it's OK shhh you're going to be fine. It is going to be BETTER NOW. You understand. You're going where she won't hurt you. You wrote down the numbers on a piece of scrap paper and made a list of all the times she cost you. You won't see any of it again but you wrote it all down anyway so you could show it to her. As if you can put a price on **pain**

BETTER NOW

> pain

but that is not the point here.

You are leaving.

Detritus by Mary Hamilton

You are going away. To learn things. To a new city.

You get to be whoever you want to. New person. not **weak** like the old one

  > weak

No no never again.

You will be the sort of person who **collects things**.

You will be the sort of person who **drinks tea**.

You will be the sort of person who **has art on their walls**.

  > has art on their walls

You go out the day before you leave to say goodbye to the city. You walk up the steps or the museum where you've sat and smoked more times than you thought there would be days. In the end you go inside and buy the first beautiful thing you can find, a print of a stencil of a child releasing a red balloon into the sky.

You will be the sort of person who has art on their walls.

You will be the sort of person who is **calm**.

You will be the sort of person who is **organised**.

You will be the sort of person who **writes**.

  weak who writes

  > writes

Your notebooks are two years full, words pouring out of them and falling into useless clumps on the stained carpet of the old house.

No money for paper in the end, so you used different pens at different angles.

You burned to write

and so you wrote

layering text on text until only you could distill language from the interwoven lines. You made maps.

played by Auriea Harvey

You will rip pages from your new notepads and tack them to the breezeblock walls of your first student home.

You will use your words to set the world on fire.

You will be the sort of person who has an on their walls.

You will be the sort of person who writes.

You will be the sort of person who **cooks delicious food**.

You will be the sort of person who **looks awesome**.

You will be the sort of person who **creates art**.

> looks awesome

this is NOT YOU ANY MORE. **throw it all away**.

> throw it all away

everything here is broken and wrong. holes in your shirts. stains on your trousers.

none of it is **new**.

none of it is **beautiful**.

> beautiful

go to London on the train and try on a long velvet dress

it is dark red and black

it is laced up the front and the skirt flows when you spin

when you emerge from the changing room wearing it your friend, a man with a big beard and no hair and four facial piercings, is breathless at the way you look

you will only see him three more times before his accident

later you will be so glad he saw you tall and straightbacked and radiant and beautiful

you will never regret the money, not once

Detritus by Mary Hamilton

You will be the sort of person who has art on their walls.

You will be the sort of person who writes.

You will be the sort of person who looks awesome.

You will be the sort of person who **is organised**.

You will be the sort of person who **collects things**.

You will be the sort of person who **wears eyeliner**.

    wears eyeliner . . . rethought this choice

    > is organised

You quell the fire in you just long enough to dig out the box of paperwork, heavier now with tenancy agreements, benefit slips, rent bills. It takes a whole morning to dig through and sort.

When you are done you take everything that's not yours out into the overgrown garden where you did not have picnics, ever, and you pile it haphazardly amid the undergrowth.

It burns well. It smells good. Too soon it is all ash.

You will be the sort of person who has art on their walls.

You will be the sort of person who writes.

You will be the sort of person who looks awesome.

You will be the sort of person who is organised.

You will be the sort of person who **makes things**.

You will be the sort of person who **cooks delicious food**.

You will be the sort of person who **loves animals**.

    > cooks delicious food

You will buy a spice rack, 16 jars and a metal stand, even though it is an extra unnecessary thing to transport hundreds of miles. You'll fill it with things you can't yet afford: cardamom pods, turmeric, mustard seeds, garam masala. By third

played by Auriea Harvey

year people will ask you to come round and make curry for parties, little student affairs. You will make a meal for six and change out of twenty quid. You have two years' more practice than most people at this, after all.

You will be the sort of person who has art on their walls.

You will be the sort of person who writes.

You will be the sort of person who looks awesome.

You will be the sort of person who is organised.

You will be the sort of person who cooks delicious food.

You will be the sort of person who **loves animals**.

You will be the sort of person who **is calm**.

You will be the sort of person who **wears eyeliner**.

when i played the second time she was calm—i thought this was really important.

> is calm

You need to be strong. Calm and strong like a bar of metal, like a deep ocean.

You pack your new trainers deep in your rucksack so she can't find them and destroy them before you leave.

You will take your first Taekwondo lesson the day you arrive. You will get bored of inner peace and courtesy pretty fast and move on to kickboxing. You will never, ever get to punch her.

You will be the sort of person who has art on their walls.

You will be the sort of person who writes.

You will be the sort of person who looks awesome.

You will be the sort of person who is organised.

You will be the sort of person who cooks delicious food.

You will be the sort of person who is calm.

You will **never be hurt again**.

Detritus by Mary Hamilton

> never be hurt again

>

Did you think it was going to be forever? I guess you thought you were staying for good this time. You mixed your book collections together. All your utensils are muddled up. Now you have to pick out only what's yours and move away, not far enough away, while he's out, so he won't look at you and you won't become weak and want to **stay**.

> stay

you can't

this is a dead end

you have to go on

go on

> go on

take a deep breath

this is the home you made together

this is the home you have decided to leave alone

this is **not your home** anymore

played by Auriea Harvey

> not your home

you have promised you will take your things and be done by the time he comes home

in the kitchen

is the **spice rack** full of chili powder smoked paprika cayenne pepper fire and burning hot,

is the pair of green glass **goblets** made from beer bottles you bought together on your first holiday away

in the living room

is the **little girl** releasing her balloon, heart-shaped, releasing it

is a stack of **board games** you played with friends and wine, laughing together in this silent room

are four tall white church candles sitting atop an **onyx chessboard** covered with candle wax

in the bedroom

your neat array of expensive **dresses** hang in your half of the wardrobe, each one a statement

is your **gym kit** all in its own bag, ready to go

is your **CD collection**, all but inextricably intertwined

is an oyster **shell** he gave you three weeks after your first kiss

in the study

is a stack of **documents**, boring and legal and carefully organised

are dozens of your **notebooks** written thick with poems

is your **Xbox 360**, bought one impulsive student loan day so you could play Oblivion

in the bathroom

is your **silver eyeliner** and a stack of old, smoky eyeshadow

Detritus by Mary Hamilton

> (As time passes, the different links slowly fade out to plain text, until "time to leave" appears. Clicking one changes the line in which the link appears to the given text.)

sometimes i chose fast sometimes slow staring at the options disappearing. also a kind of power over the situation.

> dresses

his clothes hang lonely in the half-empty wardrobe

> shell

is a snail shell you found on the pavement three weeks ago

> notebooks

are a few of your old notebooks, nothing but useless scraps

> onyx chessboard

are four white church candles, unevenly burned, set on the folding table

> little girl

is an ugly hook sticking out of the far wall, stripped bare

> time to leave

run fast towards the skyline

run laden down with bags and boxes

run into the rising sun

run into the arms of another man

run for love

run for the future

run **free**

> free

played by Auriea Harvey

Act Five
On A Plain

>

You have a new suitcase. It took nearly two weeks to be delivered from an Amazon seller in Denmark somewhere. It's bright red with a hard shell, so it won't be damaged on the plane. You've bought new luggage tags, but you don't know what address to write on them, so for now there's just your name and a phone number that probably won't work, where **you're going**.

you're going. (you're always going.)

> you're going

You have this suitcase to fill, and everything else must go. In seven days time you will be ten thousand miles away and it will be autumn instead of spring. Your tiny flat bursts at the seams. The suitcase has an extra zip that will help you compress it all down. The flight regulations say 32kg or less. The **zips buzz**.

zips buzzing along. what makes you think this will be any better? have you changed?

> zips buzz

Everything must go, again.
What's next?

Detritus by Mary Hamilton

> What's next?

On your wall hangs the print of the girl letting go of her balloon.

Take it with you.

Leave it behind.

Give it away.

> Leave it behind

On your wall hangs the print of the girl letting go of her balloon.

~~Take it with you.~~

It hangs here fine; the light from the window falls on her upturned face. You leave it hanging when you leave.

~~Give it away.~~

What's next?

> What's next?

You have stacks upon stacks of old notebooks, full of poems and diary entries. Half formed thoughts externalised.

Take them with you.

Leave them behind.

Give them away.

> Take them with you

You cannot take them all; you could take one or two but you cannot pick which ones. Better to dispose of them somehow. Cleaner.

Burn the notebooks (but only because the game designer makes you... saving you from yourself.)

played by Auriea Harvey

> Leave them behind

You are finished with all that. You tie them in careful stacks with twine and leave them to be recycled. You imagine your words, pulped to make new notepaper.

~~Give them away.~~

What's next?

> What's next?

Your beautiful red and black dress hangs in the wardrobe. You have taken good care of it; it has been worn to two weddings and an award ceremony, and from time to time at parties. It is unblemished.

Take it with you.

Leave it behind.

Give it away.

> Take it with you

You buy a suit protector and fold it around the dress. You find a silica gel packet from an old handbag and add that, too. A small protective talisman for the journey.

~~Leave it behind.~~

~~Give it away.~~

What's next?

> What's next?

Take a shell from the table by the front door. Hold it in the palm of your hand and watch it miss the sea.

Take them with you.

Leave them behind.

Give them away.

> Give them away

~~Take them with you.~~

~~Leave them behind.~~

put them in a padded envelope and post them back to him. later you will dream about eating them, the cold enamel crunching between your teeth.

What's next?

> What's next?

All the vital things are in a wallet your sister gave you: passport, flight schedule, visa, cash. You still have a stack of carefully organized documents you didn't throw away just in case: old tenancy agreements, pay slips, pension statements, tax code letters.

> Leave them behind

~~Take them with you.~~

You spend a calm, cathartic afternoon with a friend's home office shredder, turning the minutiae of your former life into hamster bedding.

~~Give them away.~~

What's next?

> What's next?

You have a heavy onyx chessboard, that's been sitting on your dining table for years. You have played three games of chess in that time with three different people, each one frustrating but fruitful.

Take it with you.

Leave it behind.

Give it away.

played by Auriea Harvey

> Take it with you

You can't take it with you. It is so heavy you would have trouble taking anything else.

> Give it away

You ask around but all the friends who play chess already have boards. It's a heavy, silly, mismatched thing. Why do you own it? Who else would want it?

> Leave it behind

You have no choice. Leave it on the dining table. Try not to think about where it will go next.

What's next?

> What's next?

Your running shoes are knackered from the pounding you have given them in the last three years, but they are usable still.

Take them with you.
Leave them behind.
Give them away.

> Leave them behind

~~Take them with you.~~
They are exhausted. You can always get more.
~~Give them away.~~

You're all packed.

> You're all packed

Detritus by Mary Hamilton

You have five bags and a husband and a plane to catch, to the other side of the world. You have three more minutes in these empty rooms, bare shelves, stripped bed, the scent of curry wafting in through the open window from the restaurant down the street.

There are birds in all the colours of the rainbow, where you are going.

The taxi's here. It's time to **leave**.

> leave

Game over.

Congratulations. You left the country with 4 items out of 53 and left behind or lost 14.

Detritus is a Twine game & formal experiment by @newsmary. It is a work of fiction inspired by real-life experiences. Originally it was just meant to be five short elements, each one using a different mechanic, as a way of teaching myself the medium. It got kinda out of hand. Please send me feedback on Twitter or by email at newsmary@gmail.com.

Thanks to Webbed Space, Porpentine & the Tweecode Google group for helping me learn Twine.

THERE OUGHT TO BE A WORD
BY JEREMY PENNER
PLAYED BY AUSTIN WALKER

Begin

> Begin

Hi.

I'm Jeremy. I'm 31 years old. I have a wonderful **5-year-old son**. I have been married for over 7 years, and was with my wife for 4 years before that.

We have been **separated** for six months.

Sometimes I think about **dating**.

Hi.
I'm Austin. I'm twenty-nine years old (probably thirty by the time you're reading this.) My editor couldn't have known this when she suggested I write about it, but Jeremy Penner's *There Ought To Be A Word* nestles comfortably into the last few years of my life—years spent struggling with the way language delimits my life and the lives of those I love.

> 5-year-old-son

Seriously, he's great, and I love him so much. We go to Value

There Ought to Be a Word by Jeremy Penner

Village every Saturday to try and keep him in books, but he reads like multiple novels a day. Just non-stop. He is into Magic Tree House and Pokemon and Animorphs.

Back

"Keep him in books" is a wonderful phrase, and at first blush a wonderful notion. But language moves and bends whenever we try to pin it down, and it reaches out to make connections we'd rather it didn't.

On first reading, the boy's parents keep him from harm by surrounding him by books. It is warm, nourishing. "In" works to build an image of the boy surrounded by paper, joyous. (Even now I feel my own language failing me. The boy is "in" "works.")

But push a little harder, and you'll fall into other phrases. "Keep him in books" recalls "kept her in furs," and other similar phrases tossed around in hardboiled fiction featuring "kept women." Suddenly, it's clear that there is a power relationship here: not that there wasn't in the other reading, but here it feels less clean. It's denaturalized. Suddenly, parents scrambling to meet the needs of their child or else.

> Back
> Separated

It's actually going really well. We're still really close. In fact, our relationship is better than it's been in a long time.

We have a good plan in place for raising our son together. We eat meals together with him. We'll do holidays together sometimes. He still has a family. That's really important.

Perhaps the best bits of Penner's prose in *There Ought to be a Word* are moments like this, where his narrator speaks to convince himself as much as the reader. God. You can see his body language. You can see the smile, can't you? "It's actually going really well." God.

This is the double movement of language. It is impossible to staple it down, to be sure that it will do what we want it to. But then, it's always communicating something, and sometimes it does it in a way that's so forceful that we can't help but think the words are magical, that they carry one meaning, the one that just punched you.

> dating

Oh man. Okay. I am a lot better equipped for this than I was 11 years ago, **the last time I got into a relationship**. I can do this.

played by Austin Walker

I think.

I made an **OKCupid** profile a few months ago.

 This notion of "preparedness" recurs throughout. Look for it. And note the ways in which Penner considers what it means to be ill-equipped: how often is it a personal failing? How often a limitation beyond his reach.

> the last time I got into a relationship

I was nineteen years old. I was obnoxious and entitled and Nice Guy, but I was funny and weird, too, and she decided I was special, and I thought she was pretty spectacular, and for years it was fantastic and confusing and amazing. We had no idea what we were doing. Oh my gosh. You should have seen it. You should have lived through it. Everyone should get to have that, at least once.

I wouldn't take back anything.

But I don't miss being married, either. We were done. It was time.

Back

 Pages like this make me feel guilty for recognizing myself in them—not because the sentiment is wrong or bad or shameful. Because unlike the author, I still haven't been able to reconcile the then with the now. I would take back a lot. I hate that.

> Back
> OKCupid

It was about two months after we'd finally come to the conclusion that we were separating, for real.

I was still in a really weird place. I wasn't really ready to start dating, but I needed to know what my future was going to look like. I needed to know that it was going to be possible for me to move on, that I wouldn't be stuck **home alone in my basement** every night because I never learned to date.

I picked OKCupid because all of my friends, all of the interesting people I like, when they talk about dating sites, universally talk about OKCupid. And I vaguely remembered Daphny saying that the secret to OKCupid was just to use it to make friends.

I could use some new friends.

Create a profile

There Ought to Be a Word by Jeremy Penner

The rise of OKCupid is interesting for a lot of reasons. One of them is that it spent a lot of time as the hip, artsy alternative to eHarmony and Match and all the rest, while simultaneously flaunting all of the data collection in a way those other sites didn't. Yes, they had patented algorithms and acronyms to go with them. But OKCupid, with a smile, released fascinating blog posts about all their data collection. They were always filled with a sort of boiler-plate progressive syntax. The kind warm hearted capitalists throw around.

One of them reminded me that as a man of color, OKCupid was pretty much not for me.

I feel my fingers linger on each key press. I'm bitter. Then immediately, I recoil.

> home alone in my basement

I'm typing this home alone in my basement. I'm not unhappy about that. I'm still, six months later, figuring out what my life should look like.

I seem to need space to get obsessed about things, and to work on things, but I also need to share myself, to put myself out there. It seems to go in cycles. I've spent the past month and a half completely engrossed in a personal project; almost all of my energy has gone towards that. But before that I spent months feeling awful about any time at all spent in front of a computer. I was completely depressed. Luckily I found people to reach out to and connect with, which I needed desperately. I'm very grateful to those people.

I can't quite tell if I'm neglecting myself right now or if this is just how I operate. But for the moment, I'm enjoying being pulled by myself, rather than pushing myself.

Back

"I'm not unhappy about that." He's not lying to himself, right? But he's also not sure that he isn't lying to himself. What I like about Penner's work is that it is always tentative. "I'm typing this home alone in my basement." He types it, I imagine (read: I project), then goes to delete it, knowing that if he wasn't actually unhappy, he wouldn't even think to type it. And then thinking 'well, if I typed it, it must be important.' Commit and assign meaning later—this is one strategy to move forward.

> Back
> Create a profile

played by Austin Walker

Am I really doing this? Deep breath. Yeah. I guess I'm doing this.

Okay, basic information. Gender. Birthday. Interested in making new friends. That's about as far as I can commit right now, yeah. Friends.

Oh god. What do I do about this.

Single

Married

    This is the first time Penner gives the reader-player an option that looks like a choice. Twine is interesting in this way. The links never communicate ahead of time whether or not they will take you further down the main path of a story or if they're asides. And if one option will take you further, it's impossible to know what the other option would've done without doubling back to check.

    But there is a conventional syntax. The way forward tends to be at the bottom of the page, not some phrase underlined in the body. And when two links are presented consecutively, like this, some ancient nerve stands on end. All art is interactive, but some art advertises the audience's role a little more clearly. A pat on the head and invitation to play. My cursor slides between each option, hovering indeterminately between the two options. I want to choose Single . . . or, I want the narrator to choose Single. I click it, only to find that the narrator is as ambivalent as I am.

    > Single

Augh. Am I really single? I mean, technically, I'm still married. In Canada, you have to be separated for a year to get a divorce, unless you have "grounds". As though "we don't want to be married to each other anymore" isn't a good reason to not be married to each other anymore. We never had to fill out a form explaining why we wanted to get married.

But that's a subject for a whole other Twine game. (Tentatively titled "Canadian Divorce Law Is Some Sexist, Patriarchal Bullshit.")

At this point I feel really, really weird about calling myself single. I mean, my wife still lives in the house. There are friends I still **haven't told**.

I go back and forth for a long time before eventually choosing **Married**.

    The most uncomfortable—and y'know, the most interesting—thing about reading *There Ought To Be A Word* for me is that I can't firmly place myself inside or outside the story.

I spent from 2009–2014 trying to square the fact that I was active on OKCupid, going on shitty dates, burning through (mostly) short term relationships, while also struggling to understand a weird, long term relationship I'd been in, and how that fit into the picture.

In that same window of time, my mother and step-father split. Well, not really. He still lives in the bedroom, and she dragged a shitty daybed into her office.

And so I'm looking in on this story and saying "Oh me, Oh them, Oh me." I swing, knees in, knees out, from subject to audience and back, gaining speed, wondering why language has left us without a word for this motion.

> haven't told

Telling people we were separating was easily the worst part of separating. The dominant narrative of divorce is fucking awful. People throwing things at each other. People ruining their kids' lives. People taking everything from each other. We're not doing any of that. But this is what people think of when you tell them.

People feel bad for you. But it's not bad! Nobody did anything wrong! It's *better* than being married! That's why we're doing it!

Back

Twice a year, in the summer and winter, I need to convince my dad that my mom and her still-not-ex-husband are not going to get back together. There's a warmth in this inquiry, not only for my mother, but for my step-father too. I happy for this, but it's strange.

When I was twelve, I saw my father, who is six foot eight, stand over my step-father, who is five foot five, and threaten to kill him in the parking lot.

They talk about football sometimes now.

To Penner's point: It was, I think, seeing my step-father do an okay job that finally mellowed my dad out. He got to see that there was an alternate narrative, one where I wound up more supported, not less.

And here, again, is Penner pointing out a failing in our words, and I recognize that failing now even in mine. Our grammar—and I mean grammar in the broadest way—was built such that it's easy to leverage the severity of the death threat and then drop the friendly football chat like a little punchline. We have a grammar of trauma, one that resists giving soft moments their due. It is so much harder to make parallel lines as interesting as a collision.

> Back

played by Austin Walker

> Married

I'm technically still married. A divorce is a long way off, yet. And it feels weirdly dishonest to not mention it, since it's such a huge part of what I'm dealing with right now.

It bugs me a lot that there's no word for my relationship with my wife. We're definitely not a couple anymore, and there's not any feeling on either side that we might become one again in the future. (It's not like I'm sneaking around behind her back; we discussed dating. She's supportive.)

It's like, we're close friends that are also raising a child together. We're a family, but not a couple. All of the labels feel wrong.

I decide that probably the most accurate thing to mark down is that I'm married, and just looking for friends. That seems the least wrong set of options, to me.

Write a bio

Penner lays it out as clear as day here. We don't have a word for what his life is. We don't have a shorthand short enough. His description is material, straightforward, and I suspect relatable: He lives his life in a way that takes more words to explain.

And this is a pressure—one of many—that works on us, that works us over, our whole lives. No one wants to explain every detail of their life. Everyone wants to be understood. This contributes to our understanding of what a "good life" is. It's why the oppressed and marginalized so often pursue assimilation into the larger culture. Who the fuck has time to explain themselves?

And this pressure isn't only about explaining ourselves socially, to others. It also effects self-appraisal. When Penner wavers here, insisting on his happiness before it was questioned, confirming his prowess as a father before anyone doubted it, he's explaining himself to himself as much as to us. Ignore the dictionary definitions, he's saying to himself. Ignore the directions on the bottle.

Can you blame him for wavering?

> Write a bio

I spend a couple of hours writing about myself. It is kind of gruelling. (Most writing, for me, is gruelling. (This is not the first Twine game I've tried to write about my experience.))

I'm really good at:

Empathy.

There Ought to Be a Word by Jeremy Penner

Overthinking things.

Puns.

I spend some time digging through photos of myself. I don't have a lot, but there are some nice ones.

It's probably midnight when I start **filling out questions**.

At some point, OKCupid shifted away from the "three adjective" system of profile starters. I don't remember what two of mine were, but one was 'mercurial.' What a prick I was.

> filling out questions

Is astrological sign important in a match? Uh, no.

Have I smoked a cigarette in the last 6 months? Try never.

Which would I rather be?

Normal

Weird

You can get into a rhythm to answering these questions. You pivot from one question to the next. Your mouse moves between the same four or five points on the screen. You swing in moods—lots of positives in a row, a few negatives. You answer questions you'd never considered, and that you wouldn't answer in a vacuum.

I imagine that's ideal for OKCupid.

> Normal

Dude, I looked up to shareware authors as heroes when I was a kid and once made a game titled "Sonic The Hedgehog's Orphan Genocide", you don't know me at ALL

Next Question

I love that this passage ends on all caps and without a period. It's so hectic, so determined to prove the author's weirdness cred. Another tell: "Dude."

> Next Question

Could I date someone who was really messy? Sure, why not.

played by Austin Walker

Ffffuuuuck, OKCupid, did you really just ask me if I'd only consider dating white people? Jesus Christ. JESUS CHRIST. I leave a comment on that one.

Would I consider sleeping with someone on the first date?

Yes

No

OkCupid is a minefield of very nice people harboring very racist beliefs they've never been asked to interrogate.

A girl I went out with in 2009, while on a date with me, mentioned that one of these questions asked if she'd ever want to have a nonwhite child (she wouldn't, she said). She couldn't help but bring it up. It was like water boiling over, or like dropping a plate, slowly. It was clear that she was relieved just by admitting it. Confession feels good.

Another time:

In the middle of a breakup with someone who I'd met on OkCupid, I received a biology lesson. The theory was this: Because of Canada's overcast winters and my melanin count, I wasn't getting enough Vitamin D in my system to be able to love.

I wish they'd asked her a "Can black folks love" question up front.

       and again I hate that I'm compelled to tell these stories, to wear them like a badge

          but I won't not tell them, not ever

> Yes (Or No)

It occurs to me some time after I answer this question that I am mostly unthinkingly using my 19-year-old self's answer, since that's the last time it was relevant to my life.

This is the only sex-related question I fill out. I feel uncomfortable answering them. I'm just looking for friends, right?

Am I happy with my life?

Yes

No

Here is Penner's putting great use to conventional bottom-of-page, two-option choice format. The last passage seems like it wants to cede power to the reader to make the choice, and in a sense it does. But regardless of which they choose, the answer is the same (and it has to be):

Penner can't possibly have an answer to this question, because it is not one he's had to consider in eleven years. Or said differently: In the conventional understanding of 'marriage,' this question is one of the many excised

There Ought to Be a Word by Jeremy Penner

out and discarded.

And here is the only choice I was truly flustered over. I chose one, then backed up and chose the other, then reversed that, too.

> Yes

Yeah. Yeah, I've got a pretty good life. I'm in a pretty good place.

Look at profiles

> ~~Yes~~
> No

You think so?

Hm.

I mean, I've been going through stuff. It's hard. But I don't think I'm unhappy. Not really.

Look at profiles

I wonder if it doesn't matter what I choose: Here, Penner is offering these choices as if they're determinations, but then reveals that they're actually observations. You don't get to decide if he's happy, you only get to decide whether you think he's happy—or maybe, whether *you're* happy. You thought you were driving a car, but you were really having a conversation.

Still . . . I go back one last time and click Yes. Yeah. He's got a pretty good life. He's—I'm—in a pretty good place.

> Look at profiles

It's kind of fun, to keep clicking through profiles, seeing who OKCupid thinks I might be interested in. It seems to do a pretty good job. There are lots of people on here that sound interesting. And in aggregate it starts to paint an interesting picture of the culture of my city.

Lots of people working in government, which I expected. Lots of outdoorsy, outgoing people, which, as an indoorsy introvert, I find myself weirdly put off by. Lots of the people I find interesting are into knitting.

Also, an awful lot of women in polyamourous open marriages? They all seem pretty cool. I guess that happens if you check the "married" box.

It's 2am, go to bed

played by Austin Walker

It's such a different thing using OkCupid in a big city than, well, anywhere else. Suburbs, small city, college town.

Here, in my little city in Ontario, spend a month on OkCupid and you'll have what feels like a full picture of the town. Sure, the demographics might be off, but you get what's available to you–not just romantically or sexually, but also culturally. "Oh, okay, this is what a person can manage to be in this city."

In New York, OkCupid was undulating. A constant stream of new people, new names, new faces. Sometimes old faces with new names. At the time, I thought this was great: "I'll never run out of people to send messages to!" I wish I'd been able to hear myself.

In any case, Penner's right to say that a city's character is captured in the aggregate of its dating profiles

> It's 2am, go to bed

Okay, yeah, I have been at this for like five hours, now.

OKCupid feeds me a **steady stream of emails** about all of the interesting people that I might meet if I just strike up a conversation with them. I don't send any messages, though. I'm not sure at all what I'm after, with this whole endeavour.

Eventually, someone takes the first step and sends me a **message**.

How could he know what he wants?
There are relationships we have that . . .
It's easy to see how they end, how they have to end, eventually. Eventually someone else will enter your life or their life, and they'll demand more time. Or a new job will come, or a new side project. Something, eventually, will demand that time. And one of you will think about your priorities, and leave the other behind.

What makes "marriage," "couple," "love," and all their adjacencies so attractive is that they offer a little whisper of assurance. "No, nothing else will separate us. However busy we get, whoever else we meet, this thing we've got, this'll still be here."

But these words that we turn to for assurance are also responsible for the disaster that they we hope they'll protect us from. Because now permanence is their domain—if not marriage, then what? And because now permanence must mean more than impermanence, or fluctuation, or the momentary.

What does it mean to have a long term relationship that doesn't fluctuate, that isn't marriage? That isn't family? I think about this notion we hear a lot in alternative spaces: a family of choice. Supplant your old family with one you choose. I get it, I do.

There Ought to Be a Word by Jeremy Penner

But what if we let affinities stand on their own? Without the baggage of the family. Without anyone, ever, thinking "I'm the father of this group."

Penner says "There Ought to be a Word." He doesn't say "We ought to elbow out some more room in the old words."

There ought to be a word, and then another, and then another.

> steady stream of emails

It's a trickle, now, but when I signed up, I was getting multiple notifications a day. So-and-so is looking at your profile! We have new matches for you! So-and-so rated you highly! Our algorithm has decided you're attractive, and so we'll show you more attractive people! (That email was super gross, by the way, OKCupid.)

For the most part, these emails have the effect of making me crave validation. I compulsively log in, wondering how people are reacting to my presence. I look at more profiles. I don't send messages.

Back

ugh those fucking emails

> Back
> message

She's impressed that I listed "empathy" as a thing that I am good at. "I am also in an open relationship", she says.

Eeee! Someone thinks I'm interesting!

I guess I had better update my profile to be clearer.

Ramble on for a while about empathy and my marriage

Again, Penner deploys multiple, in-line choices to great effect. These come in a roll, one then another (slightly longer) then another, 'rambling' away . . .

> Eeee! Someone thinks I'm interesting!

Oh gosh, do I feel great about this message.

Back

> Back

played by Austin Walker

> I guess I had better update my profile to be clearer.

It's hard not to be misleading about my reasons for putting myself out here when I don't know what they are myself. But clearly I am giving an incorrect impression about my current relationship status.

I still feel uncomfortable setting my status to single.

There is no section in the profile called "describe your relationship with your spouse". So I cram in an awkward paragraph somewhere about how I'm technically married, but we're separated, but it's actually good, and we have meals together, and I feel weird writing this, but I also feel weird not writing it, so it's lucky that I feel okay with weird.

Back

> Back
> Ramble on for a while about empathy and my marriage

Hey! Thanks!

Empathy's not really such a hard trick — I find being naturally quiet helps. You just listen to people and accept what they have to say, even if it's different from your own experiences. It kind of seems weird and ugly to me when people are dismissive of others, or when they're quick to judge without understanding. Like, that's level one on the Basic Human Decency Scale, to me.

I don't quite have the language to describe my current relationship status. My wife and I are actually in the process of separating, but we're still quite close, and we're continuing to be a family together — we're just no longer a couple. She moved into her own apartment recently, but she comes by the house in the morning to take our son to school, and sometimes in the evenings to have dinner. We're all three of us happy with the arrangement, but I really wish there were words for what we're doing. Sometimes I'll catch myself thinking along the standard divorce narrative, like my marriage "fell apart" or something, and I have to consciously remind myself that, no, my marriage was great, it ended well, and I wouldn't take back a thing.

Anyway, I should probably be a bit clearer about that in my profile. I'm mostly just looking to get to know some new people right now.

So, uh, how's it going?

There Ought to Be a Word by Jeremy Penner

I just love how these messages spin up like an engine. A really awkward, human engine, desperate to balance that first moment of elation with the desire to be honest, to be understood, all while wondering if full disclosure could take it away.

> *So, uh, how's it going?*

We exchange a couple more messages, but it quickly becomes explicitly clear that she's looking for someone to date (as you would expect, on a dating site), and I am totally not ready for any such thing, and so we stop corresponding.

Soon after, I get a message from another woman, who read my awkward blurb and thinks it's great that we are having meals as a family. She relates a story from her childhood about one of her parents' exes coming over for dinner every week. It is nice to hear. We talk about doing right by kids for a bit.

My wife is seeing someone.

I really liked this bit of OkCupid. Short conversations about topics that were deeply important to the people I was talking to. One person was doing ethnographic research on prisoners at Riker's Island. Another had a sister who was going through some real shit.

A friend of mine, facing the fact that most of these conversations were with people he'd never talk to again, called these "good practice for when it really counts." I get it, I do.

But also: I wish we could be less interested in closure.

> My wife is seeing someone.

I spend about four hours lying **motionless** on my bed having **feelings**.

> motionless

I apologize to my son for not being able to play with him. He reads in his room.

Back

> Back
> feelings

Stupid, irrational jealousy. It surprises me. I'm not expecting it at all. I haven't experienced anything resembling jealousy for many, many years. It's a terrible, **hurtful** emotion.

These three passages couple so nicely with that last package of three. Penner builds up with that last set, bit by bit, and then dives hard here. Short, staccato emotives.

And Christ, there it is. I didn't see it the first time through.

"He reads in his room."

They keep him in books.

> hurtful

Not me. I'm not the one who gets hurt this feeling. But jealousy could make me hurt everyone I care about. My son. I don't want that.

I am feeling shitty, sure. But it doesn't make any sense to feel that way. Her behaviour has nothing to do with me. She is doing what she needs to do for herself. She's not inflicting anything on me. I'm doing it to myself.

Eventually I realize that nothing has changed. My plans for myself are sound, and I should continue with them. The feeling burns itself out, and is gone, forever.

I want nothing but success and happiness for her.

Life continues.

The limits of our language are such that we can say "yes, I am happy with this arrangement" and then feel like liars when we're jealous. As if happiness and jealousy are mutually exclusive.

> Life continues.

I do eventually build up the courage to send out a few messages. At the moment, OKCupid is a place where I have short, **pleasant conversations with strangers**. I've gotten book recommendations. I've found a good pizza place not far from where I work.

I'm still not dating. I might give it a shot soon. I'm emotionally comfortable with the idea, now. I changed my OKCupid status to "single". I deleted the awkward blurb about being married. It doesn't seem relevant, anymore.

Still, I worry about how I spend my time. I worry that I don't actually want people in my life, right now. I'm not exactly going out of my way to spend time with my friends, either. I have trouble getting myself out of the house. Will that im-

There Ought to Be a Word by Jeremy Penner

prove if I'm dating someone, or will I just ignore them? Am I overthinking it? Am I just making excuses for myself?

I don't know. I can see that I'm holding myself back, but I can't tell if it's because I'm doing what I really want to be doing right now, or if something else is going on.

Can't tell if **depressed** or **happy**.

I leave this passage aching because Penner doesn't even put an "I" in the last words, which by some accounts answers the question for us.

I leave it aching because he can't seem to dig himself out.

I leave this passage aching because Penner forfeits the fight for the word he doesn't have. Or rather: because, without that word, that life could never stabilize.

Though if someone else's happiness is the cost of having the word . . . This is the dilemma, right?

> pleasant conversations with strangers

Though, several women who I would've liked to have continued talking to have disabled their profiles — I know for certain one of them because she kept getting gross messages from jerks. I suspect it's true of the others. I gather that getting harassed by men is a pretty universal experience for women on the site.

Back

The first time I read this passage, I couldn't quite place how I felt about it. It was important that he'd said this, but also mandatory in a way that reduced its value. I've said these words before, often, as Jeremy does here, immediately after bemoaning my poor experience on OKCupid then realizing my own privilege.

Yeah. It's shitty that I sent out hundreds (thousands?) of un-replied-to messages, but also no one harassed me. I never went on a date and had to think of an escape plan. Not a fun "call me if I text you" escape plan: a real escape plan.

And fuck even now I did it again. ("thousands?") Fuck off, dude.

And then thinking "well, if I typed it, it must be important."

If Penner's written a story about the words we don't have, he's also written one about the words we keep saying, even when we know better.

> Back
> depressed

I pretty much broke down completely a couple of months

ago. All of my coping mechanisms failed me. I dropped all demands on my free time and gave up sitting in front of a computer for fun. It was a couple of weeks of hell. But I found new coping strategies. I reached out to friends. I played the piano. If there was nothing else to be done, I watched TV. I let myself do whatever I was drawn to do.

I feel a lot better now, but I'm scared it'll happen again, that I'll push myself too far and give out on myself. And I don't know if dating will help or hurt. I think maybe the only way to know is to try.

Soon.

> happy

There is a lot of good going on in my life. I have a good relationship with my son. I have a good relationship with my ex. I am full of enthusiasm for my projects, and when I'm not, I don't push it. I take good care of myself.

I know I'll make a good partner for someone. I just don't know when, yet.

Soon.

> Soon

THE END

Here, the final reader choice, between depressed and happy, and it turns out (of course) that these terms are not mutually exclusive, regardless of whatever the popular depiction of depression is. So even here, Penner takes aim at the limitations (and the delimitations) of our language. He preys on our assumptions.

And this is why I include both options. Because the narrator isn't *just* happy. He is happy, of course, but that happiness is cradled inside of the breakdown. And maybe *I* would be happier if I was the sort of person who could selectively censor or re-organize history such that his (my) happiness could exist in a vacuum. But it can't. Nothing can.

And then
"THE END"
In all caps
As if we could ever believe him. As if closure were around the corner, soon.

But when all you have to tell your story is the old words, THE END must suffice.

NEGOTIATION
BY OLIVIA VITOLO
PLAYED BY KATHERINE CROSS

It read rather like a poem when I assembled my list of choices together:

> *A woman*
> *interesting*
> *By giving*
> *S&M*
> *Attention*
> *"So where should we start?"*
> *I've had some infrequent sessions, but I know what I like.*
> *What're you in the mood for?*
> *spanked, punched, and slapped*
> *pressure on my neck*
> *Yes (paddling)*
> *I love those.*
> *Will that be a problem?*
> *needing comfort is pretty reasonable*
> *that right? (x3)*

A beautiful, spidering tree of choices that drives right into the ground of sex. Each choice seems simple and inoffensive, almost like character creation in a roleplaying game: the inconsequentiality of personal preference. I prefer a woman to have kink play with, I prefer S&M to bondage, I have x level of experience with kink, and so on.

Negotiation by Olivia Vitolo

The poem of preference branches out until the purpose of the game hits you. When, at last, all this kinky sex you've spent the last several minutes negotiating over and thinking about is about to begin, there the game ends. This is a sex game in the truest sense, however; it does not simulate the act of congress so much as it lays bare the exoskeleton of assumptions, choices, desires, and interactions that hold it all up. Each step through the tree of choices in *Negotiation* is a reminder of how variegated sexual possibility can be, even within the confines of that leathery nebula known as kink.

The game is a simulation of the negotiation and consent briefings that take place before any ethical form of kink play between strangers; in that respect it provides an important, accessible public service that deflates the commonplace misconception of kink as glorified abuse. Rather, in any properly done BDSM encounter, consent is a Pompidou Centre of visible support structures and fully transparent architecture holding up the play. All is known, all is negotiated, all is consented to in an open and honest fashion.

That's the ideal, at least. The real world of BDSM subcultures is as inflected by patriarchy as every other sexual fiefdom in our society, often staggering peoples' attempts to live up to that ideal or actively sabotaging it. But *Negotiation* is a fine articulation of that ideal, smiling and even loving communion of desires. The game steps you through choices that involve communicating both physical and psychological sore spots to your dominant—places to avoid in the midst of play—that help shape the forthcoming scene somewhere beyond the final curtain drop into a fingerprint of lust that perfectly suits the player.

Again, this is the ideal, one not always borne out in the real world. But it does rather neatly match my experience of kink play, a rollercoaster of intensity that waxes and wanes between high pitched lustful drama and joking around with your partner as you rub the ass cheek you just spanked—perhaps she is playfully making fun of your aim because you hit the wrong spot, or perhaps she is telling you to adjust how hard you hit, or perhaps she's roleplaying brattiness to inspire you to hit harder. Either way, there's a lot of talking involved, and while it's almost never dramatized in the popular misconceptions of BDSM in the mainstream media, or most pornography, it's actually part of the fun.

The negotiation never stops; it's a grammar of kink play that is essential to writing poetry with pleasurable pain.

You're sitting at the non-alcoholic bar of your local club when the smell of leather fills the seat beside you and you see a flogger set down out of the corner of your eye. You look to who is interrupting your ginger ale and chips.

a man

a woman

played by Katherine Cross

androgynous

The game conveys a lot of this quite well, and its details have the flourishes of authenticity that lend its didacticism some credibility. At the very beginning, for instance, your character is seated at a non-alcoholic bar in their BDSM club; most people don't know that alcohol is strictly verboten in any club worth its salt, for reasons that are obvious in retrospect. While the rest of the world has hand-wringing paroxysms about the role of alcohol in rape culture, most kink clubs have an intuitive understanding of how drunkenness and enthusiastic negotiated consent simply do not mix.

Most video games, regardless of their level of sophistication, struggle to talk meaningfully about sex. Very often, even well-written games present sexual desire as the equational result of certain "kindness coin" style inputs. A few points of reputation here and there and off come the pants. This is done for a variety of reasons, not least because it is mechanically easy to do; converting love and sex into a series of numerical inputs and outputs is easy for developers to get a hold of and to control and intuitive for players to understand. I want Character Y to sleep with me? I'll just give him Z number of presents until his heart meter is filled up to 100 and then, bam, sexy times.

In this way, sex manages to be equal parts ubiquitous and painfully shallow in video games.

> A woman

She looks you up and down.

"I've seen you around, but I've never seen you play. Looking for anything **in particular**?"

> in particular

You like what you see, and your eyes meet hers, intent but not overbearing. Eyes that know how to get what they want by **giving**.

I cannot call *Negotiation* a particularly deep game, but it's not intended to be; instead it shows what a better framework might look like while also using the Twine medium to great effect in doing so. Unlike a graphics intensive game where the focus is on the world outside the confines of the avatar's body, Twine allows for the kind of interiority permitted by literature. If words are all you have, then, much as in a novel, inner monologues are possible; thought can be woven into dialogue and action. The inside of a character is never far from the surface of the page or the screen. *Negotiation*, even in this regard, is not fantastically deep, but it is miles deeper than your

Negotiation by Olivia Vitolo

average romance in an AAA roleplaying game all the same because it reveals the intricate realities that make up sex.

> giving

After several beats go by in silence, you realize that your playful answer was not at all sufficient, and are keeping her waiting.

You reach behind you, into your right pocket, drawing out a hankerchief while you you see a flash of amusement cross her face as she takes in the color:

S&M

Bondage

Sharps

> S&M

Her eyes drift from the fabric down to the flogger resting on the table.

"I see how I managed to get your **attention**."

> attention

Your mind excitedly cycles through future possibilities: blunt, sharp, electric, hot, endurance... floggers, canes, hands, boots, wands, weights, wax, and whips...

Snapped out of your reverie with a satisfied, "ahem?" you ask, "**So, where should we start?**"

> So, where . . . ?

"Well, let's start with you," she says, what's your experience like?

I've just thought about it a lot.

I've had some infrequent sessions, but I know what I like.

I've been doing this for years.

> I've had some infrequent sessions . . .

I'm glad to hear you've got an idea. It's exhausting coming up with everything on my own and it's always a little intimidating being that influential first time.

What're you in the mood for?

> What're you . . . ?

I've always enjoyed being roughly handled, tossed around, **spanked, punched, and slapped**.

Once I was **tied to a cross and flogged** and I'd love to do it again.

I've been wanting to **try being caned** for ages.

BDSM is its own culture and a distinct constellation of orientations, fetishes, and desires, but its consent culture ought not be unique to it in any meaningful sense. *Negotiation* exposes something at once simple and intricate about intimacy: that it is far better to actually know your partner's body by becoming one with their interior selves, and you can only do this by talking to them. Far from being the stereotypical "mood killer," sexual knowing requires discussion, requires asking questions, a lesson that I and so many others have had to learn quite painfully; the worst sexual experiences of my own life occurred, as I often say, because I did not know how to ask and did not know how to tell. For too long I thought sex had to occur in a kind of monastic, knowing silence. To do anything else would be to risk giving offence, putting myself in harm's way, or simply ruining the atmosphere; how wrong I was.

> spanked, punched, and slapped

"Is there anywhere I shouldn't hit you?"

I don't respond well to **pressure on my neck**.

The soles of my **feet bleed easily**.

I have some **nerve damage in my lower back**.

> pressure on my neck

Alright then, nothing on your neck.

I'm quite the fan of hitting people with large flat objects, how do you feel about paddling?

Yes.
No.

Negotiation by Olivia Vitolo

> Yes

I like to integrate sensations like a wartenberg wheel into the quieter times. Does that sound good to you?

I love those.

I'd rather **something a bit broader**. Like your hand or a paddle.

> I love those

Just to warn you, I can be a bit needy when it comes to after care. **Will that be a problem**?

> Will that be a problem?

That's not a problem at all. We've both got emotions and **needing comfort is pretty reasonable**.

If *Negotiation* does anything well, it reminds us that hell is silence. By giving us a brief and pointed simulation of what active consent can be in the space of kink play, it also provides a blueprint for consent in *all* sexuality, and a reminder that language is a silk rope that we must negotiate with in order to ethically maximise our pleasure. Twine is now language's native medium in the world of gaming, where it becomes the star of a one person show in storytelling, and that makes it ideally suited to shift the perspective from the flashy externality of sex that none of us ever sees while we're in its throes to the way we *actually* experience sex, as a parade of ideas and feelings made flesh, travelling from within us to the bodies of our partner(s) and vice versa.

> needing comfort is pretty reasonable

I just want to make sure we're still on the same page, Okay?

You're most interested in S&M and you have some experience.

Is that right?

> that right

You'd like me to use my hands and you need me to avoid

your neck.

Is **that right**?

> that right

You want me to incorporate paddling and want me to use a wartenberg wheel during downtime.

Is **that right**?

> that right

Amidst a gaming world that makes sex into an act of violent conquest rather than exploring the pleasurable realities of intimacy and what it actually feels like, this is a welcome change.

Would you like to start?

Yes, Mistress, I think I would.

REPROGRAM
BY SOHA KAREEM
PLAYED BY MATTIE BRICE

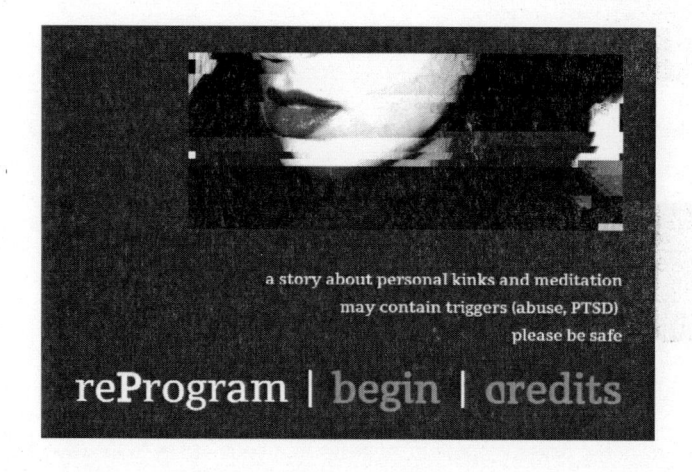

a story about personal kinks and meditation

may contain triggers (abuse, PTSD)

please be safe

    I think it is fitting, as a game that states upfront it is about kink, and in a general consent-awareness games made with Twine seem to interact with, that you are braced for what's to come. While content warnings weren't invented by *reProgram*, its use here emphasizes its general role of establishing consent, in a way, before beginning. This is in contrast to games that sensationalize serious topics by making them plot twists and gimmicks, which tends to create a shallow representation of the topic. There is something about knowing what you're getting into that allows you to be more open to understanding something complex.

> begin

Once upon a time there was a **girl**

Evoking a fairytale opening, probably to play with the idea of the fairytale girl and the one in the piece.

> girl

tousled black waves that frame large eyes

a cigarette usually dangled from her lips

she called herself pet

Okay

Here we get a mix of a mix of voices with the "Okay," which could be the narrator's voice, but it'd be an unusual tone shift. Or maybe the girl, pet, herself, injecting her voice. Or even it's supposed to be the player's guided thoughts. In a way, "Okay" is holding a lot in this one place, as many people might find a girl calling herself "pet" strange or alarming, so "Okay" might be both affirming that decision and an admission of skepticism.

> Okay

Once upon a time there was a **girl**

pet had some **issues**

Here is the first example of repetition, which I find to be a common feature in games surrounding trauma and PTSD. We can cycle through "girl" and "okay," a cycle that feels like reifying or reassuring the validity of chosen identity. This screen also shows the lines of narration to be disjointed, as girl and pet seem to be separate identities.

> issues

Patient Name: ███████████
Date of Birth: ██████
Gender: F

played by Mattie Brice

How long treating this patient: 7 months

Diagnosis: Post-traumatic stress disorder, major anxiety disorder

History: Sexual assault, domestic abuse

Risk of self-injury: Moderate

I see

The faux-medical profile is interesting mostly for the blacked out information. That Soha decided to have type-characters blacked out that give no information makes me feel like there's a part of this that is generalized, a nod to people outside this character, and at the same time a lack of identity, or at least confusion surrounding it. The "I see" at the end maintains the ambivalent voice. Is it another therapist or the continually skeptical expression of the player, or character?

> I see

Once upon a time there was a **girl**

pet had some **issues**

She had seen many **doctors**

The second repetition, embedding a daily reality of both the status of being a trauma survivor and a patient.

> doctors

How are things?

How is school?

And your family?

Any romantic partners?

Have you been sleeping?

Does it make you tense?

That's understandable.

Are you familiar with the "fight or flight" response?

Many with your

condition

reProgram by Soha Kareem

CAN FEEL TRAPPED

And that's okay.

We call this

a normal reaction

to an abnormal situation.

Here, take **these** to ease the anxiety.

Next is a series of questions and comments from a psychologist. There is an interesting contrast here between the slow, somewhat comforting pacing of therapy questions that cut to abrupt and enlarged text. It's both jarring and unsettling because the flashes create an uncomfortable stop. I'm actually getting some anxiety from it, my heart is racing. But it's a completely appropriate and fitting piece of design. For one, the psychologist is saying extremely devastating things in a calm, matter-of-fact manner, creating a further divide between outside help and legitimizing internal feelings. This also helps promote the player's own fight or flight responses. It makes it a little harder to keep going.

There is something weirdly bittersweet about "take these," as it can refer to the commonly quoted "take this" from *The Legend of Zelda*, as the gamer-centered mental health non-profit Take This (www.takethis.org) exemplifies. In a way, it feels like a riff off of sanitized portrayals of struggle.

> take these

Here is the first image compilation that is uniquely suited to this game, or maybe Soha's style. It's borrowing some glitch aesthetic with lo-fi sci-fi film-type framing and cutting. While most literally it is showing the prescription cocktail the character has to take, it also hints that there's multiple distorted views going on, not just one with the character.

Isn't that better?

ARE YOU BETTER

played by Mattie Brice

. . .

Once upon a time there was a **girl**

pet had some **issues**

She had seen many **doctors**

But she was still **stuck**

    Another cycle. I felt compelled to go through the "doctors" sequence again, and there is a dull pain and mundanity to it. The cycles feel like "getting help."

> \> doctors . . .
> \> take these . . .
> \> stuck

stuck in a **t o w e r**

    There was a change in text; "tower" was in plain text, then revealed to be in crimson and spread out. It is foreboding.

> \> t o w e r

and woke up every day to the same long hallway

    This quickly appears before changing to other text, but it continues to feed into the cyclical nature of what is going on, even if it isn't a completely direct loop. These disjointed cycles are hinting at patterns that aren't easily identified, and how they appear is reminiscent of my experience with PTSD. An association throws you into a loop, and you constantly re-experience certain feelings. This text indicated this is a subliminal threat throughout the player's and character's time here. The hallway is currently featureless; except for the face it is the same, and seems inescapable.

The hallway had an elevator

And a **girl** at the far end waiting for her every morning

    The elevator is an extension of the hallway, just moving in a different direction. Here we have "girl" again, but we know that "girl" and "pet" are somewhat different people. "Girl" being crimson sets up a threatening feel as I go to click on the word. Also noting the cyclical nature of "every morning."

> girl

the girl looked like pet

If pet was looking in a mirror covered in dust and ash.

She sounded like pet after a carton of cigarettes and a bottle of whiskey.

It's about time you woke up. Jesus, fuck. Drink another bottle of wine before bed last night?

Pick a **floor** already, will you?

We are introduced to the shadow of pet, who is distorted in many ways. Her image doesn't exactly line up to give us an idea of her face, she is described as being a reflection in a dirty mirror, and her voice is altered by booze and cigarettes. She has darker speech text, and her words are harsher. Floor is in crimson, but it is also a bit distorted and hard to read, implying they aren't exactly what they seem.

> floor

The hallway had an elevator

Beside it was a **guide**

And a **girl** at the far end waiting for her every morning

Another kind of cycle, but we are now situated in a current scene. So the new information feels like pet just noticing something, like having a moment of recollection or sobriety to understand what is in front of her.

> girl

played by Mattie Brice

Where do you want to go today, fuckskull? We don't have fucking time for this. **Let's go**.

However, it isn't a complete cycle. Clicking on "girl" again doesn't reintroduce her, rather it starts moving us along. In a way, the girl is a catalysis for movement, even if she's not the best catalyst to have.

> Let's go
> guide

4th FLOOR: PHYSICAL RELEASE ROOM (You are here.)

3rd FLOOR: MEDITATION ROOM

2nd FLOOR: CREATIVITY ROOM

1ST FLOOR: [CLOSED FOR RENOVATIONS]

The girl was breathing down pet's neck, like a pesky shadow.

How many times do you have to look at this fucking thing? Don't you know where **shit** is by now?

The first look at the structure we're in, and the building up of tension between the now directly named shadow and pet. We get an idea of the inner monologue of the character and how this entire building and interaction is an interior journey.

> shit
> elevator

The elevator buttons, mostly interesting because of how the first floor is missing. Indicates that the 'closed for renovations' is something of a mental state instead of a straight-up progression lock in the physical world.

> [3]

"I need some time to clear my head and calm my thoughts."

Oh, great. That means we get to see that **weird thing** with a plant for a face?

I choose the Meditation room, mostly because of how crowded I feel with the alarmed feelings and constant negging of the shadow girl. That "weird thing" is the coded link makes it so this transition to a meditative state is unnatural or is assisted in a way that's foreign.

> weird thing

Welcome, the instructor's soothing voice fades in

Don't you find her fucking creepy?

pet shoots the shadow a glare and through gritted teeth whispers, "let's just try this, okay?"

Ignoring their whispers the instructor begins, "**now let's ground our feet with mountain pose.**" It's unclear whether she can even hear them. Sometimes they suspect she's a hologram programmed with pre-recorded messages.

The jump to the meditation room is extremely jarring and full of conflict. Firstly we have a bright yellow background, which isn't really relaxing

played by Mattie Brice

and is typically associated with stimulating hunger. The picture of the yoga instructor is strangely surreal yet the most coherent so far. The instructor is balancing in a dance-like pose but has a bouquet of roses for a head, which at least grounds the shadow's observation in some sense of logic, not completely negative or untrue despite their phrasing. However, unlike the past pictures, this one is minimally distorted; we can see the whole figure as if we're looking through a screen at her. The instructions reference a pose in yoga, which is almost like just intentionally standing upright and still. The skepticism around the corporeality of the instructor is interesting, because it's not certain if anyone involved is really a whole person.

> now let's ground our feet . . .

Inhale.

You are **majestic**.

While you firm your thigh muscles, you are a **lion**.

You balance the crown of your head over the center of your pelvis. You are feeling **relieved**.

aaaaaand **exhale**.

The chant allows us to fill in what sort of feeling we want to focus on (radiant, confident, calm, awake, focused, relieved.) In a way, this is a sort of cyclical process as we go through the options, implying that we try to be many of these admirable qualities, but it's hard to concentrate on and be happy with just one. There are also some strange options, like being a rhino beetle or ostrich, that probably point to an inability to take this completely seriously.

> exhale

The shadow snorts.

Really? You're a lion that is majestic and that makes you feel relieved?

Can we have a smoke now?

On cue, the instructor exhales from plank pose and pushes back into **downward-facing dog**.

The shadow expresses this skepticism, and even though she somewhat internalizes it by repeating it back, links smoking to actual meditation and relaxation. We move to downward dog, which is one of the most common

251

poses that's used often for a transition into another pose.

> downward-facing dog

Inhale.

pet ignores the flicker of the shadow's lighter.

Lengthen your spine, and imagine your tailbone reaching high to your **creativity**.

Push your thighs and resist **your insecurities**.

With your heels urging to meet the floor, unleash your **expectations**.

aaaaaand **exhale**.

Another chant, which at this point feels like mocking the sort of talk that happens at these sorts of classes, while also trying to find the value and release in them. There is a suspension of disbelief that needs to happen, and the shadow seems to embody disbelief.

> exhale

Wait. How does your fucking TAILBONE reach your creativity?

Holding downward dog, pet's breath shakes.

And, like, your thighs can resist your insecurities? Cuz, you've gone tons of that going on. I don't think strong thighs will help, honey.

The shadow lets out a puff of smoke and looks at the bead of sweat sliding down pet's cheek.

I'm sorry, is that you unleashing your expectations?

And we now move our body into **warrior pose**.

Here the shadow reminds me of my own inner dialogue when I've tried to go to yoga classes for my own anxiety. There's self-monitoring, trying to imagine abstract transformation as you attempt to pose, and the sneaking suspicion you're being watched and judged. Next is warrior pose, which actually does feel quite bold.

> warrior pose

Inhale.

Ah, such an important pose that is all about **beauty**.

played by Mattie Brice

As you extend your arms through your fingers, picture yourself **in your favourite memory**.

Feel yourself in this pose. Feel as you are one with **your core values**.

aaaaaand **exhale**.

Here we have a projection into the future, of what we want to be. The poses represent a past-present-future spread of sorts.

> exhale

The bright orange dot on the end of the shadow's cigarette bounces up and down between her lips.

Okay, I get it. I get that you're trying to be all zen with your cultural appropriation and beauty or whatever the fuck planthead said. And you're in your favourite memory, if you even have one of those, finding your core values or some shit--

pet stumbles in warrior pose and sharply turns to the shadow, "Do you ever shut up?"

The instructor begins to shake and static.

W-we-we-wel-c-c-c-c-c-

To-day----peace garden p-p-p-p-pose

*Oh, shit. I think we actually broke the bitch. Well I'm glad we can **finally get out of this room**. The wallpaper colour makes me want to fucking puke.*

Shadow has some reasonable thoughts, but they are invasive and don't come at their time. pet is unable to take part in the aspect that will actually help her because of the intervention, if you will, of her shadow. That the yoga instructor is indeed is a program or robot that fails upon critique, or maybe the breaking of pet's concentration, shows that it is a poor substitute for what pet actually needs.

> finally get out of this room

The instructor fizzes out as pet and the shadow head towards the exit.

pet notices something shine in the spot where the instructor stood, and she heads towards it to pick it up.

A piece of cold metal weighs surprisingly heavy in her palm. It looks like a large pendant that can be buckled to another object.

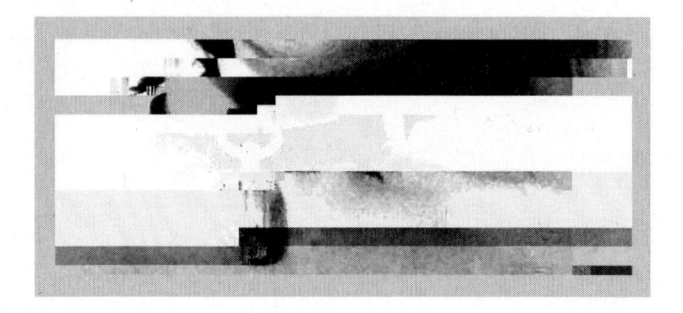

She tucks the pendant into her back pocket and heads toward the **door**.

The destruction of the instructor gets pet a pendant, a metal one, though we're not entirely sure what the pendant symbolizes. The picture shown is distorted and hanging on a collar, leading us to believe she will be finding meditative practice in other kinds of activities and rituals. There is something particularly game-like about this, gaining an item after, possibly, defeating a boss.

> door

and so pet continues to find comfort in **another place**

What is striking about this is that the current place seems like a normalized, prescriptive place to find comfort. It speaks to how I feel whenever people immediately recommend yoga or other standard middle-class practices to get rid of stress and anxiety, and really not for me.

> another place

played by Mattie Brice

Back at the elevator, with its buttons looking like art deco lights in a film noir. The 3rd floor is unavailable now, meaning there might still be something of worth on the 4th floor. But I continue on to the 2nd.

> [*2*]

"I think I should get some writing done."

Ohhh, this is the writing that Dr. Dickface recommended? Your, uhh, **journal**?

I'm actually not too thrown by what the shadow has to say, because, well, the instructor really did have a plant for a head, so many this doctor actually has a dick for a face?

> journal

Dr. DIXON made a good point. Writing can help me release some of these emotions.

You're a pretty shit writer, though.

pet grinds grinds her teeth into each other, "That doesn't matter. It's not about good writing. I'm just writing whatever comes to my mind.

Ok. Well, let me give you a haiku.

Annunciating every syllable on each finger after clearing her throat, **the shadow announces**

This page is curious because of how much wordplay is going on, especially giving the shadow voice. Almost as if the shadow is at least a part of the creativity pet draws from. Which hits home a bit, because writing is a difficult habit to keep up and easy to feel stuck in. Also curious is the word choice of "announces" for the shadow's haiku.

> the shadow announces

once i was ab-used

it made me feel real-ly bad

now i drink a lot

The text is paced out syllable by syllable, giving a weird sort of reverence to the mocking she's doing. It is a forced confession that pet didn't really want to make.

"Are you done?"

Fine, fine. I'll fuck off for a bit, Sylvia Plath.

So the shadow hung out in the corner of the room. pet turned to her empty notebook and picked up a pen, "Ok. Just, write **anything**."

    Surprised that the shadow would give pet her space, though it is on a really hurtful note as Sylvia Plath killed herself, and now generations of young women identify with her writing, which is good, but also feels weirdly romanticized. That pressure to be "perfectly depressed" seems present.

> anything

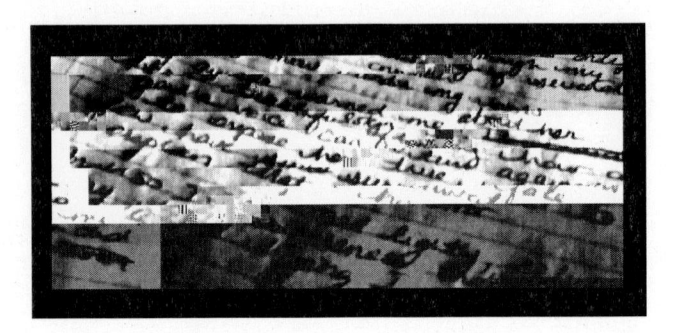

Maybe an hour passed, or two, and pet had written a **blog post** about **anger**.
A wave of **guilt** washed over her.
The shadow **noticed**.

    The picture of the distorted writing along with the choices of what to write capture a nebulousness when you feel pushed to pen something important. Especially true when someone, even your shadow, will be looking at it.

> noticed

Oh, hello. There's that guilt I'm used to seeing. What's up, buttercup? Did your blog post about anger not work out? Maybe because you're the last person who should give advice on anger?

pet needed a break.

"I'm going to have a **coffee**," she said to the shadow in her **peripheral vision**.

played by Mattie Brice

Here we have the shadow undermining pet again. What's interesting is how much pet is used to the shadow, and it's only when the shadow gets extreme does she really intervene. Also, the choice between coffee, cigarette, and a drink provides an interesting choice and reflection on what a 'break' is. We know she has a problem with drinking, and drinking would mean having a break from reality, moving back into old habits. Smoking might mean a break from striving towards something positive, as she would be joining shadow for a smoke. Coffee, in a way, implies she's going to continue doing what she's working on.

> peripheral vision

The boiling water pours over the coffee grounds and fills the room with its stimulating aroma.

Sometimes the smell woke her up.

Other times it made her remember the waiting room of the abused women's center.

She went there after after leaving ███████.

I hated that **place**.

Of course, choosing coffee because it seems the most positive has its own catch. And really, I think it's important to not have clear-cut good/bad options. There's a reason why a person doesn't do all the things others think they should to get better. And here in particular, the shadow seems to speak for the both of them. Also, we see the blanked out name, which feels like both an active block on the pet's part, while generalizing out the archetype that this person is actually many people.

> place

Me too, pet thought.

The one-on-one with a counsellor was okay, but group therapy was exhausting.

The women who overshared every detail of their lives shut her up even more.

The women who were still with their abusers broke her heart.

The women whose children were involved made her feel like her problems couldn't even compare.

It's why pet **sometimes**

This feels reminiscent of the pattern making in the previous room, associating the same practices with alienation as well as meditation.

> sometimes

CAN FEEL TRAPPED

with other abuse survivors.

CAN FEEL TRAPPED appears for a second time, this time a little more predictably, which frames going to group therapy or being around other survivors as something to avoid to keep a certain sense of space.

But it's okay.
It's been a while since she had to face group therapy.
It's fucked to get impostor syndrome about that.
No shit.
"Speaking of impostor syndrome, I should get back to **that piece**."

The roles slightly flip, or at least, lines blur between pet and shadow. Shadow is a more complicated character that doesn't necessarily come from a malicious place, but rather, one of total self-service that tends to be discouraged or worked out of women.

> that piece

pet chugs the last bit of her coffee and heads back to the desk.
The blog post about anger is **gone**.

This feels like the first, or one of the few, purely information-giving screens. It doesn't say much besides what is actually going on, which highlights the missing piece of writing.

> gone

Instead a short piece of black matte leather sits on the chestnut desk.
She picks it up and runs her thumb against the soft material.

played by Mattie Brice

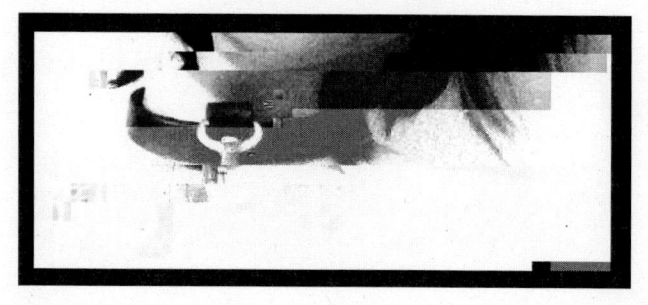

She tucks the leather strip into her back pocket and heads toward the **door**.

Here we get the other part of the collar, or the main part really. Interesting to have these thoughts transform into a symbol of servitude. In a way, putting it on would be an acknowledgement of self-service and healing, rather than the more surface reading of being of service to someone else.

> door

and so pet continues to find comfort in **another place**

Repetition, particularly now with the collar, coming to a crescendo, building upon the search for comfort going beyond simple activities.

> another place

Back to the elevator and to the 4th floor. More cyclical motions, coming back to previous points with more knowledge and experience, recontextualizing the things we fixate on.

> [4]

reProgram by Soha Kareem

I'm feeling stressed out and pent up. I need some time alone.

Feeling like a little pervert, huh? I'll give you some privacy *so you can release some uh, tension.*

   It's interesting how the shadow seems to actively separate itself but then comments on everything pet is doing. Also implies that "time alone" is time away from the shadow as well in this instance.

   > privacy

Does this type of self-care help? pet wonders every time she's in this dimly-lit room.

She heads towards her nightstand and opens the drawer to pick out her favourite toys.

She grabs her laptop off the floor, and **sets it on her bed**.

   This screen is paced to sort of 'reveal' the sex toy, which is interesting along the doubt around this actually being self-care. It is, at least, moving into a different space to focus on yourself, and starts to tie sex/pleasure/kink with self-help.

   > sets it on her bed

pet chooses a video

face-fucked by her mistress's giant dildo

and slicks her asshole with a slippery **finger dipped in lube**

   The most surprising thing here is how some of the choice selection already seems to be made in contrast to the other activities. Also now feeling the effect of the red, which is kind of overwhelming.

played by Mattie Brice

> finger dipped in lube

pet pushes the plug into her ass while watching a strawberry blonde lick the strapon of her Mistress

Mostly just a narrative line, but there's something about the link being "of her Mistress" that shows a focus, or maybe even a hint to the relationship that's going on here. Meditation was with a yoga practitioner, journaling was with a therapist, and now sex with a mistress, of which there are numerous mentor/teacher archetypes and roles in dynamics.

> of her Mistress

She sharply gasps and bites her bottom lip. Like the strawberry blonde, she wishes she had a lover

With this transition, we see a comparison between the role of the mistress and the role of a lover by where the link passes, and we see the theme start to correlate as we know there's a history of abuse to work past, but other kinds of help haven't been working, at least on their own.

> lover

She sharply gasps and bites her bottom lip. Like the strawberry blonde, she wishes she had a lover who would roughly fuck her throat and make her gag while ordering her to take that cock deeper

This is also the most cohesive part of the story, staying on the same page, building on these thoughts. Implying this has been one of the few points of clarity pet has. In particular, it seems like pet needs help moving past certain inhibitions or to succeed through particular kinds of endurance, which might relate to trauma and negative feelings she wants to work through.

> ordering her to take that cock deeper

pet rubs her clit with the vibrator after the plug reached its limit

A pull back to the present reality, and also being upfront about self-pleasure and how it is the forefront of this entire fantasy, not the putting aside of her own wants and feelings.

> its limit

Circling the vibrator, she bucks her hips **forward**

> forward

She watches the the strawberry blonde drool and choke over the strapon, her Mistress **holding a fist of her long hair**

> holding a fist of her long hair

She was getting **closer**.

> closer

How do

closer

you tell someone

closer

you want them to

CLOSER

really hurt you

FUCK

    Spelling it out, intertwining self-pleasure and the need to survive pain. And the confusion that results when the answer doesn't seem very clear.

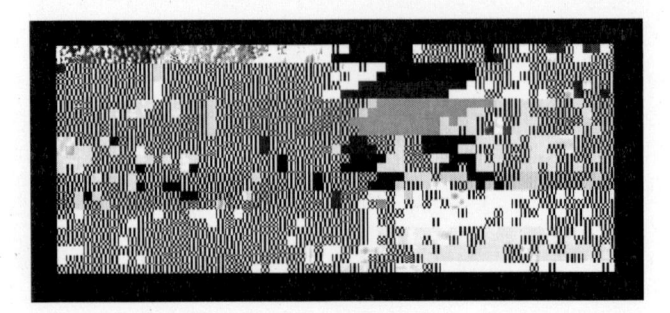

    Almost a literal manifestation of the pleasure-confusion, the thing that doesn't make any sense just now but it sure feels right. Is this the most distorted picture, or is this feeling the static that distorts other ones?

played by Mattie Brice

> (click)

Her limbs twitch, her breath shakes, her skin flushes.

Her eyes are still glued to the strawberry blonde begging her Mistress to cum as her body cools down.

It's then she notices the shadow is in the room.

How do you **do it**?

Shadow now reappears in a moment of vulnerability, the doubt that arrives after the peak or high of the activity, the self-skepticism.

> do it

pet can't answer that.

She mutters, "Well maybe this is my way of loving my body."

The shadow stares at her for a while.

Sure, let's go with that. Now can you take the plug out of your ass? It feels weird talking to you with that thing in.

"Sorry."

For all the things shadow makes fun of, she takes this revelation pretty well. It also shows the awkwardness, at first, about sex-positive language that doesn't fully communicate the wholeness of pet's feelings. In a way, she still has to convince herself this is "loving her body" at this point, instead of something more holistic.

> Sorry

Running hot water over the toys, pet looks at herself in the mirror for a while.

Violence is satisfying when you actually ask for it, she thinks to her reflection.

She turns the tap off, and heads over to where her laptop sat on the bed.

But it wasn't there.

Expressing a tenant of consent and kink, where pet, in a chant-like way, reminds herself that there are healing kinds of pain.

> But it wasn't there

Instead a long strip of leather sits in its former place, almost embedded into the comforter.

She picks up the black material and feels its softness in her palms. She wraps it around her hand.

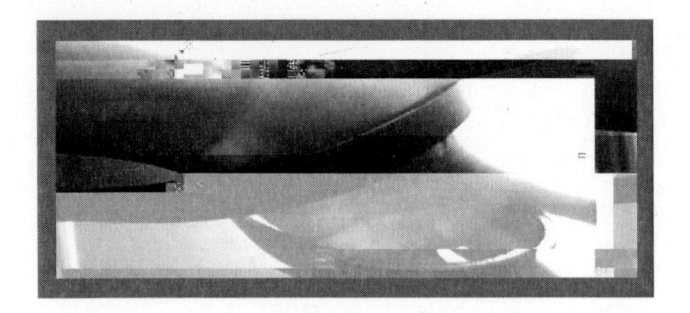

She wraps the leather strip around her waist and heads toward the **door**.

The third, and possibly final item, a longer leather strip, that comes from her attempts to reconnect with herself.

> door

What's this?

> What's this?

The pieces fit together.

Leather ties and knots through the metal pendant fits snug around her neck.

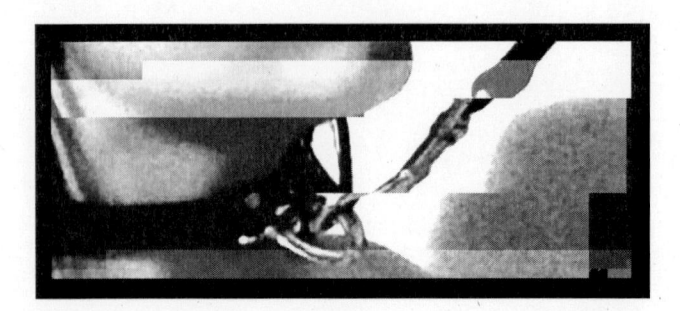

played by Mattie Brice

A button appears on the **elevator** that wasn't there before.

The items assemble together to form a collar and leash, working as a symbol of active self-discovery and care.

> elevator

The 1st floor button appears, implying that with the collar and leash, we are finally able to get to a place deep within her that was inaccessible before she came to these realizations.

> [1]

A leash only pulls too hard

If the wrong lover masters it

Waiting at the first floor for pet was Sir

> (wait)

Once upon a time there was a **pet** and her Sir

Down on the first floor, she meets a figure named Sir, and the story almost seems to loop on itself by evoking the "Once upon a time" device. Seems like the introduction of Sir provides a new life or storyline.

> Sir

tousled black waves that frame large eyes, pet stands on the tip of her toes to kiss Sir

back

    Some of the same language is used to describe pet, but now it seems to stem from happiness or a new-found completeness.

  > back

Once upon a time there was a **pet** and her **Sir**

    First time in a while there was a cycle like this, in it shows me a couple of things. First, that Sir is contextualized only in relation to pet, not a force independent on his own, a force in her life with disregard to her needs.

  > Sir

a deep voice attached to hands that slap and caress, Sir presses pet to his chest
back

    That idea is reinforced here, he is abstracted to a voice, hands, and actions that serve pet's needs.

  > back

Once upon a time there was a **pet** and her **Sir**
They love each other **painfully**

    A twist on the fairytale wordage, to complicate consensual pain.

  > painfully

pet enters the room to see Sir sitting on the end of their bed.
Crawl

    Crawl is one of the few, if not only, direct actions pet can take, somewhat recalling meditation class.

  > Crawl

Crawl, he orders.
She sinks to her knees where the hardwood floor presses against her skin, and slowly moves toward him on all fours.

played by Mattie Brice

Look at me, pet.

A twist, it becomes an order, but really, it seems more like something she willed, and he is, in a way, serving her by phrasing it in this way.

> Look at me, pet

Her eyes lift from the floor to meet his, and he reaches out his hand to grip her by the chin.

With his other hand, he runs a finger down the side of her cheek.

He traces her pout with the tip of his finger.

You're gorgeous, pet.

This seems to be a contrast to pet's shadow, I now realize, as she hasn't shown up, and Sir's introduction was placed in a similar position to shadow's during the first story cycle. He is stern, in a manner, and can be seen as topically mean, but everything he does is out of admiration and love, whereas for shadow, it might have been similar reasons, but manifesting in a negative way.

> You're gorgeous, pet

Her lips curve upwards and part to thank him, but he forces his thumb through her teeth and pulls her jaw towards him.

Her eyes widen and she lets out a whimper at the sudden movement.

The tip of her nose barely touching his, and the sound of her racing heartbeat thumping in her ears.

Now show me what this mouth can do.

Recalls the scene from the porn, expect in a less, well, porn-y way. The pain is part of the affection.

> Now show me what this mouth can do

Once upon a time there was a **pet** and her **Sir**

They love each other **painfully**

They destroy each other **beautifully**

Something that interests me about these cycles of passages is how they bring awareness to the depth of stories or really anything we read or hear. There's a mix of difficult feelings and contexts behind all of these sentences, but they themselves show a shallow understanding of what's going on in pet.

> beautifully

Sweat-drenched bodies collapse and heave.

Sir loosens the belt around her neck.

Black tears run down pet's face, mascara mixing with the spit and cum smeared on her cheeks and lips.

His arms wrap around her, pulling her back closer to his chest, and kisses her neck.

His hands linger on the handprints they left behind.

When her tears stop flowing and breath begins to stabilize, he squeezes her even tighter.

I love you

Crying black tears feels like an excising of the shadow, like this is the place she needed of get to in order to have this sort of catharsis, and then have someone intimate and caring of her while she's there. Instead of shadow's tearing down, she is lifted up in moments of vulnerability.

> I love you

I love you, he says.

She smiles and kisses the forearm wrapped around her, **I love you too**.

> I love you too

Once upon a time there was a **pet** and her **Sir**

They love each other **painfully**

They destroy each other **beautifully**

And on even their **days off**

> days off

1 New Message from Sir

played by Mattie Brice

We get the first sound of the game, jarring us into reality. Interesting that it's the cellphone, which in a way, is a source of painful yet pleasurable relationships with technology.

> pet jumped in her chair, waking from an unexpected doze.
>
> Her eyes blinked twice and focused her attention on her phone.
>
> Hey, love. Still on for a movie tonight?
>
> Can't wait. I'll be done at the office around 5 today.
>
> That's much earlier than usual! I'll pick up some wine and then come get you. Shiraz?
>
> Ugh. Yes please. 40 bottles?
>
> Haha. I love you. I'll see if I have enough cash for 40. ;)
>
> You're the best. See you soon! xx
>
> **pet counts the minutes down.**

Now we have a sort of flip in romanticizing, where before we had the romantic style of hyperbole with abstracts and actions, and now we kind of go to a romcom sort of place. I think this helps show this is something that is in real life, and applicable, not just musings or imaginations of things that don't actually exist for her.

> \> pet counts the minutes down.

> Once upon a time there was a **pet** and her **Sir**
>
> They love each other **painfully**
>
> They destroy each other **beautifully**
>
> And on even their **days off**
>
> They still knew they belonged to **each other**

> \> each other

> pet walks into the den where Sir is typing in front of his laptop.
>
> He looks up, eyebrows lifted and furrowed at her expression, **What is it**?

> \> What is it?

reProgram by Soha Kareem

She runs her hands through her hair and grabs a fistful while shaking her head, Does it look like I gained 20 pounds because I can't even fucking fit into anything anymore and I don't even know how it could've happened and the last time I checked the scale-

Sir pushes his chair away from the laptop abruptly, cutting off her words. **Come here**

> Come here

Come here, he motions to his lap.

pet sharply exhales and lets go of her hair, smoothing it out as she walks over to him. She sits in his lap.

His hand forms a grip around her throat and he presses his forehead against hers, their eyes locking.

We've talked about this, pet. I gave you a warning last time. You will

> You will

You will, he squeezes hard around her throat, **n e v e r**

> n e v e r

n e v e r talk about yourself like this.

pet's eyes glaze, vision tunneling as her breath escapes with his every word.

You belong to me. This body belongs to me. And this is the most beautiful body I've ever had.

> You belong to me.

Do. You. Understand?

> Do. You. Understand?

She quickly nods, feeling her cheeks getting hotter, eyes water and blur.

Say it.

> Say it

I underst

> I underst

I underst, she mutters, I **understan-**

> understan-

Say you're my gorgeous slut.

>

Choking between words, pet obeys.

Sir lets go slowly, and presses his lips **against her throat**.

    Here we see, paced in a way that punctuates how things are communicated to her, how self-love and intervention is framed for pet now. Self-love is "forced," or, the headspace to understand self-love is achieved through pain and discipline that Sir provides. A trust exchange is going on, where pet trusts Sir's judgment and actions to help her on her journey, and for Sir, that pet will place his judgement above hers when it's in conflict during the times they've established.

> against her throat

Once upon a time there was a **pet** and her **Sir**

They love each other **painfully**

They destroy each other **beautifully**

And on even their **days off**

They still knew they belonged to **each other**

The shadow is still stuck around in the tower **sometimes**

> sometimes

Hey. **Fuck you**.

> Fuck you

reProgram by Soha Kareem

The shadow is still stuck around in the tower **sometimes**

But in a strange turn of events, she and pet **became friends** over time

> became friends

*I actually did like your blog post about anger. It was **inspiring**.*

The shadow is still around, but now, maybe since her role is being taken over, has time to see accomplishments pan out and be contextualized, since pet was actually able to complete her journey to better self-care.

> inspiring

This is how pet survived.

And she lived happily ever after.

And the tale is complete, and the happily ever after just makes it sounds like a really fucked up, but enjoyable kind of fairytale ending.

MANGIA
BY NINA FREEMAN
PLAYED BY LANA POLANSKY

Mangia is a game about Nina Freeman's personal experience being diagnosed with a chronic illness. This is a prototype. The full version will be released here during Fall 2014 with art by Jenny Jiao Hsia and music by Maxo.

Trigger warning: This game deals with chronic medical conditions, eating disorders and anxiety.

Start.

Being completely honest, this is my second actual playthrough of this game. I've seen screens of the full version but I haven't seen a release yet so I'm going to assume that it's still in development. The full game, based on what I've seen, should look and feel more like other Nina Freeman games ("How Do You Do It" comes to mind in terms of aesthetics, although Joni Kittaka did the art for that one). All that being said, I actually like the barebones feel of this prototype, the monochromatics, the thin sketchy art style, and so on. I relate to this game to a surprising degree, and the simple, muted, and obscure visuals of this version actually really capture exactly how I felt when suffering through digestive issues of my own. That was about a year ago now, and while I can't say my experience fully matches what Freeman illustrates in this game, playing it still triggered a lot of the feelings I had while going through my own medical issues.

> Begin

Mangia by Nina Freeman

You haven't been feeling like yourself. In fact, you think it's been months since you've really felt normal. Although, honestly, you're not even sure what you mean by "feeling normal" — you do know, that it's not how you're feeling **now**.

I can relate to this a whole lot. I spent two years getting these really intense, really spontaneous-seeming stomach attacks, especially after heavy meals (although it wasn't always that predictable). Because I'm stubborn, I WebMD'd myself instead of going to a doctor after the first attack . . . or fifth attack . . . and so on. Besides, they always seemed to subside within a certain time frame (depending on my food/stress level it could take minutes, hours, or even days of inconsistent sharp and crushing or low-grade dull pain). I figured from my symptoms and because of heredity that I was experiencing IBS, and negotiating how my body would react to food or certain stressors just sort of became "normal" for all the time I was dealing with these episodes.

> now

This is the first of these simple sketches that show up throughout the game. I really like this raw, rough drawing because it pretty aptly captures my relationship with food. This one in particular is fairly innocent but the white, slightly uneven thin line is a bit ominous against the opaque black background. It breaks it open a bit, suggesting more menacing things down the road for something—food—which ought to be a source of comfort and pleasure. It makes it alien and threatening, jagged and harsh.

>

Your cell phone is buzzing—it's mom.

Answer.

Ignore.

I have an idea of what's coming, and I know I won't enjoy it. There's a

played by Lana Polansky

weird part of me, though, that feels guilty ignoring a call from my mom. So I opt to follow that impulse in this game and prepare myself for something peculiarly triggering.

> Answer

Mom: "Why didn't you answer any of my calls this weekend."

You: "I was really tired. Last week was stressful and I just wanted to relax."

Mom: "Well Kevin and I went out to the mall and..."

You're pretty annoyed that she didn't even care to ask why you'd been stressed.

Tell her you have to go, because you have homework to do, and hang up.

Hear her out.

Literally the first thing my mom said when I last picked up a call was that I needed to call her more. I'm guessing this is pretty typical—and maybe generational too? Like, I don't call *anyone* on the phone unless I have to. It's basically a pocket computer. That being said, I can relate to Nina's (I believe *Mangia* is autobiographical) depiction of her mom not really paying close attention to her needs while demanding energy expended on personal concerns, and the desire to just make as much distance as possible so as not to dwell on resentment all day.

> Hear her out

Mom: "It was so funny! Here I was, with Kevin, and he was trying to get me to buy this Teletubbies DVD. This woman walks by us and I'm like, she looks really familiar. Then, someone yells out her name, they yell Hollis! And I realized that she was one of the famous models from the 70s that I'd been shot with a few times..."

Cut her off--tell her you have homework to do and hang up.

Tell her: "Cool, that must have been exciting."

I don't even have the courage to stop conversations like these so I just sort of let them peter out on their own while feigning interest. I know how passive-aggressive that is. Also I'm certain I've said exactly the above line of dialogue at some point during a real phone conversation.

> Tell her . . .

Mom: "It was. Then we left the mall because Kevin needed to use the bathroom, and you know, we're still doing the potty training thing."

You: "Yeah."

Mom: "You sound upset—what's the matter anyways?"

You: "Nothing, I'm just tired. You know, school and whatever..."

Mom: "Is something wrong with you and Emmett?"

You: "Oh my god mom, no, we're great."

Mom: "What else could possibly be bothering you?"

You: "Uhh I just haven't been feeling great."

Mom: "Well, get some rest. I'm going to head out now because I have to pick up Kevin from the therapists."

You: "Ok, bye."

 This conversation makes me scream internally because I've been tuned out and talked over in pretty much exactly this way, and it sort of pushes you to the point where you don't want to share anything too personal with the people who do this. It stings even more when that person is supposed to be someone so close to you. it makes you feel like a massive burden and you get all this guilt and these second-order feelings on top of the shittiness you're already dealing with.

 That "Ok, bye" at the end is so perfect and succinct, not only because I've sort of capitulated in conversations in exactly this way but because you can also tell that Nina's pulling away from the conversation, that her mom senses a problem but is not equipped to help with it in any substantial way, and from this exchange there's a sense of isolation and alienation coming through. Nina's mother isn't oblivious, exactly, but she is fairly detached from Nina's life. It's not surprising Nina *would* pull away, mind you, but it also creates a cat-and-mouse situation and hints at a sense of dread and resentment just in answering the phone.

 The dialogue in this game feels so raw and so organic that I can hear it in my head. I can visualize Nina fidgeting and staring off and I can hear her voice go flat and maybe sort of quiet. I can hear her mom prattling away energetically. But it's more than well-written: I connect to this in a really intimate way and it helps to know I'm not the only one that's struggled with

played by Lana Polansky

precisely this scenario.

> Ok, bye

[scribble]

>

You don't really like talking to your mom. All she cares about is your weight, and if you bought any new clothes recently. She always asks about how school is going, but doesn't seem very interested in the details.

Call your boyfriend instead.

Go to the kitchen for a snack.

Screaming again, because this brief passage hits every note of my last couple years living at home, particularly while I was sick. I still dread the holidays because I'm afraid my mom is going to make some comment about my weight (especially when my sister is around so she can compare us). Irony of ironies, while I was ill, I was also a lot thinner than I am now, and it's very possible that the reason I got so sick was in part triggered by flash dieting, which included a lot of over-exertion and undereating. But I looked great, so no one really cared what else was going on.

I remember that my mom was pretty much the same when I was going to school, in that she seemed to care a lot more about my grades than if I was actually happy. I could be totally miserable as long as I earned a degree. I think for her my happiness was more contingent on me meeting certain expectations than how I might have been doing internally, and I'm not sure either of us have ever been comfortable having those conversations with each other anyway.

I have and still do stress eat, and I like that this choice is juxtaposed with calling the boyfriend in this game. Both are coping mechanisms that I've relied on, sometimes simultaneously, and more than once after an unpleasant conversation with a family member.

Mangia by Nina Freeman

Emmett: "Hey, how are you?"

You: "I'm alright—so tired though."

Emmett: "You've been really tired lately, like… a lot. Maybe you should take a day off from work?"

You: "I can't—I've already taken off too many days lately. I basically have no sick days left."

Emmett: "Ok, well… can I come over tonight?"

You: "I was hoping you'd like to. I just got off the phone with my mom, so I'm sort of stressed out. I'd love some company."

Emmett: "Sure, I'll be over in an hour. I'm gonna run and get my bag together, ok?"

You: "Sure, ok, I love you. See you soon."

Emmett: "Bye!"

Go get a snack from the kitchen.

Begin to prepare dinner for two.

    For some reason, I chose not to get the snack. I chose to talk to Emmett, who is blessedly comforting and understanding, and I then chose to make dinner. I guess I'm a sap. But I think I avoided the snack because making it a choice here also makes it something conscious and deliberate. Stress eating is so often automatic, by contrast, and choosing to do it here flooded me with a sense of shame and self-awareness. So I thought refusing to do it demonstrated discipline, even in a game space, and I realize what a fucked up impulse that is.

    > Begin to prepare dinner

You decide to make some pasta, because you're not a very good cook and it's a really easy thing to make. While you wait for it to boil, you go into your bathroom to look in the mirror.

    Speak for yourself, I'm a great cook. I am lazy, though.

You see some black stains on the ceiling above you in your reflection. You have to remember to get your landlord to come check it out—it might be mold, you think.

    My landlord is really good at taking weeks or months to fix anything, too. Unless it compromises his equity.

played by Lana Polansky

Have some Cheeze-It's while the water heats up.

Shut the bathroom door and look in the full-length mirror.

I used to do the mirror thing a lot more. I still would, probably, if I had a fully length mirror. My mom does, and I used to judge my body all the time with it. Checking out different angles, sucking things in, sticking things out, et cetera. Trying to make myself most resemble the ideal I had in my mind. Now I have this small mirror that's in a permanent "Myspace" position so I always look good when I catch my reflection in it. It boosts my self-esteem but it's not a real solution. I still torture myself when I look at my reflection in the TV, for instance.

> look in the mirror

You look in the mirror and lift your shirt up. You stare at your stomach—it feels full and uncomfortable. It's odd, because you haven't eaten in a few hours.

I would have something like this happen for days on end, just a low-grade fullness, bloating. chest constriction, a feeling I was being slowly crushed.
Then it would just go away.

You stand there staring at your stomach, and wonder why you stopped going to the gym. You would like to blame grad school, but you really just feel too tired to go most of the time.

When I wasn't keeling over or trying to expel the contents of my whole body, I would try to work out more because of my own body shame and because I thought it would make the "fullness" feeling go away.

You think your mom would probably kill you if she saw you in a swimsuit.

I fucking hate bathing suits. It's not just my mom. My brain just automatically assumes at this point that everybody is thinking what my mom and others have told me explicitly.

Check to see if the water is boiling.

Continue to look at yourself in the mirror.

If this were real life and not a game, I'd stare in the mirror and sulk until the water boiled down, probably. I'd go to Twitter with a selfie or something and fish for compliments to regain some semblance of self-esteem. But I don't need to dwell on that in *Mangia*. I know how it goes.

> Check to see if the water is boiling

You open a box of linguine and put half of it into the pot. You figure you'll bring some to work for lunch tomorrow. Also, Emmett, your boyfriend, will eat a lot anyways.

I ALWAYS MAKE TOO MUCH PASTA GODDAMMIT.

Your phone has been buzzing. Check to see what's up.

Look at yourself in the full-length mirror.

I keep thinking of my phone as this distraction and window into another place but it reflects back onto me just as often and forces me to contend with my own insecurities, amplifying them, subsuming me in them.
Then again, so does the mirror.

> Your phone has been buzzing

You made a stupid tweet about Pokemon earlier and it got a bunch of retweets. That's pretty cool.

This number valuation of human contact is a slow-acting poison but I can't get enough of it. I'm glad we have that in common.

You also have a calendar notification for tomorrow—a doctor's appointment. It's with a gastroenterologist. You got an endoscopy recently, because you'd been having some weird stomach and chest pain. Everyone says it's probably just acid reflux, but your aunt has a hernia, so they told you it was best to get checked anyways.

You're a little anxious about the appointment, but you think it'll go fine.

I fucking hate doctors and hospitals. It's not even that it's a financial burden. I'm Canadian, and I live in a big city. I have access, but maybe it's that I spent too much time seeing/hearing/smelling unpleasant things in

played by Lana Polansky

hospitals when I was a kid and my mom, a nurse, took me to work with her because there was no one to look after me. Maybe it's because going to the doctor evokes the fear that something is very wrong with me, maybe worse than I thought. It's like confirming that, oh, this won't just pass on its own. And then mortality comes up, and even though I have no reason not to go to a doctor I think ignorance is bliss. And that's how I ended up with my condition for two whole years while my boyfriend begged me to go to a clinic.

Emmett's calling--he must be outside.

For what it's worth, I did eventually see . . . was it a gastroenterologist? I'm going to assume that's who diagnosed me. It's funny, because when I went and assumed I had IBS, almost everyone just agreed. As if I had told people I had "acid reflux" and everyone decided it made sense, except for those who were more inclined to think like Nina here and get this thing checked out.

> Emmett's calling

You run downstairs and open the door for Emmett.

You have been dating Emmett for seven or eight months. His apartment is in Manhattan, and it's tiny, so he usually stays over at your place. In fact, he basically stays over every night. You've never been in a relationship for this long, so you feel really strongly that you want it to last.

I got sick a few months, maybe a year, into dating my bf, and a part of me was worried and embarrassed about putting this new responsibility on him. Thankfully he was supportive and understanding.

You go up into your apartment together, kiss, and sit down on the couch.

Emmett: "Want to watch some anime and eat dinner? I'm starving."

You: "Sure! I made some pasta."

While you serve the pasta, tell Emmett about the issues you've been having with you mom.

Bring the food back and put on Netflix so that you can watch some anime.

Time to unload everything on my significant other, as I do.

Mangia by Nina Freeman

> Tell Emmett about the issues

You tell Emmett about how, the other day, your mom called and harassed you about the gym again. You tell him how stressed out you felt after—"I honestly just wanted to go straight to bed when I hung up," you said. You tell him that you wish you could just lost weight overnight.

He tells you that he thinks you look beautiful the way you are, and that you don't need to lose weight, no matter what your mom says.

Tell him more about how your mom made you feel as a kid.

Ask him which anime he wants to watch.

    I've had this exact conversation with my bf, including his response almost verbatim. This is fucking eerie.
    It's weirdly cathartic watching this character talk to her boyfriend at length about memories I feel like I've also had. It's nice to get it out vicariously through this game. *Mangia* might actually be the most "immersive" game I've ever played in that respect.

> Tell him more

You tell Emmett that when you were 15, your mom would yell at you if she so much as heard you opening a cabinet in the kitchen. She would tell you that you weren't fat, you were just overweight, and that you needed to eat less. "You don't look as good as you could," she'd say.

    My mom straight up would tell me I looked fat, or chubby. That's why clothes didn't fit (she said this about a suede jacket that fit just fine, it just had a broken clasp that wouldn't stay shut. It took me losing weight and then eventually showing her the broken clasp for her to believe me.) Then it became insinuations (I still get them sometimes, but less.)

You tell him how one day, when you were 15, you decided to see if your mom would care if you had an eating disorder. You really wanted her to worry about you—to feel bad for terrorizing you about your weight. You went into the bathroom and turned on the faucet, and dropped handfuls of water into the toilet to make it sound like you were puking. You could hear

played by Lana Polansky

her walking by the bathroom, but she never said anything.

I think my mom would have cared if I obviously had the kinds of eating disorders that my sister went through in her teens, but my approach didn't 'look' the same even if I was as self-effacing and pathologically obsessive. Even if I was starving myself, technically. But shit, I was working out, so it must have been healthy.

Emmett asks you if you ever actually had an eating disorder.

Tell him about that one doctor's appointment...

Tell him that you didn't--you were too obsessed with food to not eat it.

I want to keep following through with this conversation, but in this sense we diverge. I very clearly went from overeating to undereating, and both were unhealthy eating habits in their own right. I'm only now learning what a healthy diet for me looks like. I'm curious about this doctor's appointment, though. I've gotten conflicting information from doctors. Sometimes I'm overweight. Sometimes I'm healthy and fine. It seems to fluctuate a lot.

> that one doctor's appointment . . .

You tell Emmett about how, when you were 16 or 17, you had your first doctor's appointment that your mom didn't come to. She dropped you off and went to run from errands, because it was just a regular check-up.

Of course, you always get weighed at check-ups, so she weighed you, and you were 145 pounds. She told you that 145 pounds was about average for your height and age, but that it was maybe a little more weight than I needed by 2 or 3 pounds. You told her that you weren't surprised, and that your mom was always saying that you were overweight, and that you thought you looked really fat.

You talked with the doctor about how huge you thought you looked when you saw yourself in the mirror—you looked like a whale, or a monster, you said, and that you saw cellulite all over your body. She told you that you might have Body Dysmorphic Disorder, because, she said, "You look normal to me."

I never told doctors I feel this way about myself but I do and some days

Mangia by Nina Freeman

it's worse than others.

   Emmett tells you that you still say that about yourself now, and that he wishes you wouldn't, because you look really good. You laugh, and look down at your pasta.

   Holy shit, am I actually dating Emmett?

Eat up.

   > Eat up

   There's a nice, slow build going on here with these visuals. This one naturally follows the pasta scene, but given the aesthetics and the pacing of these passages, there a momentum clearly building here. It's a dread and tension I can relate to, considering the fact that for a long time everything I ate became a potential threat. So, you're eating and everything seems fine. There's maybe slight discomfort but you can ignore it. And then you can't ignore it. It makes you afraid of food and of your own body. This passage is subtle and muted but it does suggest a kind of visceral horror of something invasive, sinister and painful. Having to click on the image itself to get to the next passage is an interesting formal choice than reinforces a tangible relationship to the food. There's something intimate and embodied about that, needing to click on the food to progress.

   >

The noodles are steamy. They smell and taste good, and suddenly you're ravenous. You eat a few forkfuls and lean back onto the couch. Emmett goes to get you both some water, **and you take a few more bits of pasta.**

played by Lana Polansky

I love this because the writing is evocative enough that I can really visualize this food, even kind of taste it and smell it. This whole thing is also bizarrely familiar to me: the very first attack I got was after I ate a huge plate of pasta.

> you take a few more bits

>

Your chest feels tight—it's almost like asthma. It couldn't be though, because you would be wheezing. Emmett brings back the water, and you gulp some down and it feels good. You eat more of the pasta—**you're almost done**.

So I forked down my spaghetti before that first attack because I had no clue what was about to happen. I learned quickly, though, that as soon as I felt that burning and abdominal constriction to just stop right away and go immediately to the bathroom. Screw whatever was left on my plate.

Maybe these exact conditions are a little different, you feel like you can still eat. But for all my recklessness with doctors the one thing I didn't fuck with was the onset symptom of one of those attacks.

> you're almost done

Mangia by Nina Freeman

    I like this blunt visual representation of food as a jagged, tangled mess. The chicken scratch over the illustration of the noodle pretty succinctly sums up what it's like when the act of eating goes horribly wrong, as something simple and banal turns into something scary and unknown. It's like an attempt to scratch the food out that just made a bigger mess. Which is apt considering that in this story food isn't just a physical threat, but a source of shame tied to indulgence, so the scratching out feels like it's at once trying to evoke pain and guilt associated with eating.

>

Your stomach feels hot and full, almost bursting. The heat in your stomach feels like it's rising, and you feel it sharply in your chest. Nausea rolls over you, and you sit forward, hunched and quiet. Emmett is still enjoying his food, and he looks over at you.

"Are you alright? You look really pale?" he says.

You tell him that your chest is in pain. Your chest is in severe pain and **you have no idea why**.

    Almost exactly this happened to me, not while eating but while lying in bed. The "fullness," the nausea, the heat—not just in my stomach but radiating throughout my body like a fever—all hit me and I couldn't figure out why. I was so scared, but I also rationalized at first that it was just really bad indigestion. My bf gave me a back rub and tried to calm me down, but I didn't feel better until I threw everything up and collapsed on the bathroom floor for a while. When I was better, I tried to make up for it by eating cereal. That didn't work out for me either.

> you have no idea why

>

played by Lana Polansky

Why would your chest start hurting suddenly? Were you choking? It almost felt like choking—or like someone had taken your esophagus, and was twisting it round and round until it was taut. Every second, in a steady beat, a sharp pain stabbed the very middle of your chest.

I also had a stabbing sensation but it wasn't in my throat. It was more like being stabbed in the back repeatedly.

You're so confused, and horrified. "I have no idea what's going on inside my body," you say, and you're crying. You curl up into a ball and press your forehead into your knees. You're wondering if you'll die.

. . .

This is like reading a narration of my life and it's terrifying. It's not just how familiar it all is. I'm also just mortified that someone else went through feelings like this in quite this way. It shouldn't surprise me but I guess I have a special empathetic pathos for the experience described here. The fetal position, the crying, the confusion, the fear of death. All of that hits close to me.

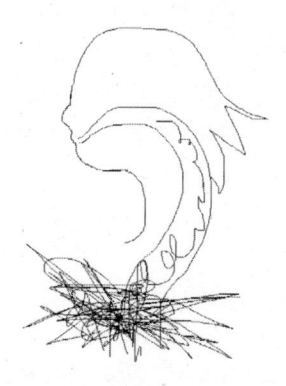

> . . .

So, this is apt on a few levels. One, because you really do feel, if you go through something like this, something "alien" is about to pop out of your stomach. You really do feel like something foreign, malicious, parasitic has invaded you and you need to get it out as soon as possible and by any means. Or, conversely, like it's trying to get out and it'll kill you to do it.

I guess it helps I was watching *Alien* while I went through *Mangia* a second time.

>

You wake up, and Emmett's already sitting on the couch with his laptop in the living room. He sees you roll over, and walks back into your room and gets into the bed. He pulls you over and squeezes you.

Whenever I had pain a good squeeze could be really therapeutic. That and the closeness to someone I trusted helped calm me, which also lessened the pain a bit.

"Morning—how are you feeling?" he says.

You tell him that you're feeling ok—just sort of drained. Last night was rough. You tell him that you've got to get going because you have that doctor's appointment.

Have sex, and show up to your appointment a little late.

Go take a shower and walk to the train with Emmett.

The first time I played this game, I think I opted to have sex as a kind of token gesture of intimacy, and because the placement of the text suggests that the character wants to do this. I have trouble fathoming why, though, since extreme abdominal pain isn't just draining, it's scary, and you don't know when it might come back. Also, I've never been a morning sex person, although that's neither here nor there and this character is, I believe, autobiographical anyway.

> Go take a shower

You run to the bathroom—the black spots on the ceiling are still there. You text your landlord, because he was supposed to take care of that a while ago.

You head out with Emmett—it's too cold outside. On top of that, you're pretty sad that you missed the opportunity to have sex. You don't like the fact that stress seems to be destroying your libido.

This I can relate to. Physical pain takes a lot out of you emotionally, and it can have a really strenuous effect on your ability to just . . . enjoy things.

played by Lana Polansky

He takes the subway with you for a few stops, but has to get off before you. He kisses you, and tells you that he'll come over again tonight. He wants you to let him know what happens as soon as you get out of the doctor's appointment.

You wave goodbye.

 Just reading this single bit of separate link text gives me chills, because it really communicates this feeling of being on your own. When I went to the doctor, finally, I was with my boyfriend. I couldn't have done it alone—really, because I was in extreme pain. But this reads as daunting, intimidating. I feel like the text could easily say "You nervously wave goodbye" because—and maybe I'm reading into this—I feel like that extra space between it and the rest of the text already communicates that feeling.

> You wave goodbye

Whenever you're feeling down, you tend to listen to the same kinds of music—droney, electronic, sad stuff. You always do this, and you feel like it must be pretty lame.

You look at everyone else on the subway—it's 9:00 AM, so they all look like they're heading to work. You pause your music, and the train is silent, except for the hiss of the engine and the momentary clash of wheels on the tracks.

You play your music again—the noises in the subway make you feel lonely. Everyone looks so sad.

There's an old man in a worn-out plaid coat standing next to a young man with a leather suitcase. The old man's eyes are shut, and the young man is reading something on his iPad. You think that the old man has probably had a hard life—you wonder if he has a job, or a family. You don't think he ever had an iPad, and you feel bitter towards the young man, who gets off at this stop. You have to get off too, and you wonder if the old man will ever get off the train.

You walk a few blocks to the doctor's office.

 This passage has nice pacing. All of these lovely descriptions—of the old man, the silence, the music—focalize the character's state of mind; they strike a nice tone of heaviness, a lonely burden. This is capped off by the straightforward passage link, nothing emotional, just walking a few blocks to the office. But you have a strong sense of the character's emotional state going into that, without it being too on the nose.

Mangia by Nina Freeman

> You walk a few blocks

"I'm here to see Dr. Li," you say to the girl at the front desk. She recognizes you, and tells you to wait and he'll be right out.

He is, indeed, quick, and **you walk into his office a few minutes later.**

    Lucky. I swear I had to wait an hour in an empty emergency room before I was admitted. And the nurse was rude.
    I had to lie on the floor because I was in so much pain I couldn't sit in a chair, and I had to taxi over to the hospital because I was in a subway-less suburb at the time. When I was admitted the nurse was venomous. I know that job is tough and it's easy to be irritable, but I was gaunt and keeling and she got angry with me for having difficulty answering questions. When I did get in, I ended up sleeping on a gurney in a hallway, but I was so hopped up on morphine I didn't even care anymore.
    At least I wasn't alone, though.

> you walk into his office

He tells you that he will review the results of the endoscopy with you, and that he wants you to ask any questions that you might have.

Questions...? You shift in your seat, leaning on the arm rest.

    I remember I had to go through a whole host of exams during my weeklong stay in the hospital. I had some kind of extremely painful ultrasound where a technician jammed some kind of wand into my abdomen and I had an x-ray and... I can't even remember now. One doctor came to ask me questions but I hardly remember them, although that's when I finally found out why I had gotten so suddenly sick I couldn't brush it off anymore.

> Questions

played by Lana Polansky

    I like this little break in the dialogue because it ramps up the tension, and it's also a reminder that the problem is still lurking, the pain is still there although maybe it's subsided. Nerves can do a lot to affect intestinal pain, and in situations like this you can feel things coming back up. I was lucky to have been taken care of enough that I didn't have this nervous reaction, but I could imagine being alone and not quite recovered and having it come back up, so this is a nice touch.

    >

"You don't have a hernia," he says, "but there were a few issues."

You feel a little bubble expanding in your stomach, it feels faintly like the heat from last night.

    The tension suggested here reminds me of my admittance, the pain bubbling and gurgling and clawing at my sides while having to put up with procedures my body had no patience for. I just wanted everyone to get to it, for the world to go at the pace I needed. I feel that here. It's hard to appreciate someone's calm when you're anything but, sometimes, and you have to pretend to be. Also I appreciate how the link text describing the physical discomfort matches the frustration of how oftentimes doctors will waste your time telling you what you don't have. I realize it's for the sake of thoroughness, but I'd rather just be given a blunt answer and work out the details after.

    > You feel a little bubble

"You have a mild case of gastritis, which will go away after a couple weeks of medication. It's really not a big deal at all— it's some inflamation of the tissue in your stomach."

    My comorbid illness that put me in the hospital was acute pancreatitis.

Mangia by Nina Freeman

Unfortunately, it was a big deal. I could have been in serious trouble if I'd waited any longer to get help than I did.

You can feel your chest rising and falling with each one of your breaths, **in and out**.

I used to have this feeling all the time, the sharpened awareness of my own bodily functions because of my new acquaintance with forming symptoms. Illness has a weird way of putting you in visceral, uncomfortable contact with the processes of your own body. It's intimate yet alien, the way you start to think about the things inside you that you normally take for granted the second something goes wrong.

> in and out

I could imagine this noodle pulsating, twisting like a worm around Nina's insides, strangling with apprehension as she waits for the doctor to finish giving his diagnosis.

>

"You also have..." and he shuffled around some papers on his desk, pulling out a photo of... something pink—clearly, a picture of something in your body.

"You have a condition called eosinophilic esophagitis."

...

It's funny, when I was diagnosed, it was for gall stones. That's what all the tests were for, first to figure out what was causing the pain (inflamed pancreas) and second to figure out what was causing the inflammation. The big, scary word was associated with the symptom and not the cause. I can say "gall stones". It doesn't seem so big but it almost killed me, apparently.

I'm not sure whether the ellipsis connotes confusion or fear, or maybe both. I'm sure when I was diagnosed I didn't say anything much more intelligent than, "Oh, okay."

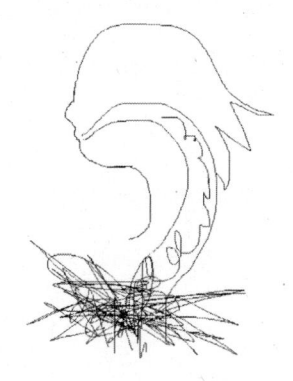

> . . .

Putting a name to your illness is like creating a taxonomy for the monster inside you, so I appreciate this visual.

Also, the use of these illustrations throughout this scene has helped not only pace out the tension but also create that sense of intimacy with the body, that uncomfortable feeling of familiarity that I described before. The alien, because it's such a familiar pop image that repeats so often in this game, especially establishes that feeling.

>

eosinophilic esophagitis

eosinophilic esophagitis

eosinophilic esophagitis

eosinophilic esophagitis

eosinophilic esophagitis

eosinophilic esophagitis

eosinophilic esophagitis

eosinophilic esophagitis

eosinophilic esophagitis

eosinophilic esophagitis

eosinophilic esophagitis

eosinophilic esophagitis

eosinophilic esophagitis

eosinophilic esophagitis

eosinophilic esophagitis

eosinophilic esophagitis

eosinophilic esophagitis

I remember when I finally found out what I had I looked it up obsessively, looked for possible bad side effects of the surgery, tried to understand the science of what was happening. I basically did what this passage is suggesting: word overexposure. Repeating it to myself so often it loses meaning, or at least seems less distant and ungraspable.

I also enjoy this repetition because it suggests that Nina's trying to sound it out in her head. Eosinophilic esophagitis took me a minute to read too—I literally had to sound it out—so having the protagonist repeat it to herself suggests that same behavior of trying to get a handle on what's going on.

eosinophilic esophagitis

eosinophilic esophagitis

eosinophilic esophagitis

eosinophilic esophagitis

eosinophilic esophagitis

eosinophilic esophagitis

eosinophilic esophagitis

eosinophilic esophagitis

eosinophilic esophagitis

eosinophilic esophagitis

eosinophilic esophagitis

eosinophilic esophagitis

eosinophilic esophagitis

your head feels like an echo chamber and your stomach feels like a living creature, fighting to expel itself from your body.

I'll admit, I had forgotten this line was here, but it sure seems especially apt now.

> your head feels like . . .

played by Lana Polansky

"Eosinophilic esophagitis," said Dr. Li, "essentially means that there are rings on the inside of your esophagus—inflamed rings. These rings are what's making it difficult for you to swallow. The burning sensation in your stomach is the gastritis. Unfortunately, eosinophilic esophagitis doesn't have any proven treatment."

Here I admit I was lucky, because my illness was very curable, it just set me back awhile.

You're not sure that you understand what the doctor is saying anymore. All you know is that everything around you feels and sounds loud.

"However, of course, we need to deal with your issues swallowing. There's a treatment that's... not well studied, but I have used it with other patients and some have found success. You will need to take two puffs of a steroid inhaler daily—puffing onto your tongue, and swallowing the substance. You'll also need to avoid foods that are not easy to chew, like chicken, because you're at higher risk for choking that the average person."

I wondered about the need for an inhaler and if it would have an effect on the protag's weight, which is something the game establishes she struggles with. I wonder this because my weight came up an awful lot when I was sick. People act like it's a moral failure to not look a certain way, and in this case there would be a lot of frustrating misunderstandings around the medical reasons for weight gain. In my case, it was insinuated that my weight caused my illness, when that was never actually proven.

You can see the noodles from last night, and all the tough vegetables, on your white plate.

"The steroid inhaler isn't very good for you—but you must know that, because of your asthma. So we'll give it a try, but I'll need to check on you fairly frequently."

He continues to tell you about the dangers of steroids, and the kinds of foods you should avoid—but all you can think about is the white plates at your apartment, full of food.

For about a month I had to be on a special diet, which was a minor bit of additional torture. To have to do this forever is something I can hardly imagine. You crave things like nobody's business.

Mangia by Nina Freeman

You leave with a prescription and a follow-up appointment in a month.

> You leave with a prescription

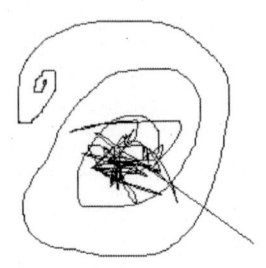

The passage following this one is two links, asking the player to choose between calling mom and calling Emmett. So there's an additional layer, on top of the physical pain and the existential fear that comes with a diagnosis, a sense of finality in this situation as the character contemplates her whole life and its new restrictions, but now comes another question: Who can I lean on now?

>

Call Emmett.

Call mom.

The game isn't really subtle about this: Nina does not want to call her mom. She doesn't want to confide in her mother, who will, in all likelihood, not fully understand what's going on here. Emmett's not only first, his name is capitalized whereas "mom" is not. Calling mom is not just a secondary option: It's least preferred.

I sort of get this. My mom was more able to help me in my situation, being a nurse and having, I found out, gone through the same illness around the same time in her life. But when I needed to go to the hospital, I appealed to my boyfriend. Over two years he put up with my episodes and my emotional needs more than my mom, because I felt we related more, I could trust him more. My mom and I don't have a terrible relationship but we don't have a great one, and she's not the first person I'd feel comfortable talking to about my feelings. I'd expect her to tune out sooner, much like Nina's mom does at the beginning of the game. So it's an obvious choice.

played by Lana Polansky

> Call Emmett

Emmett: "Hello? How'd it go?"

You're standing on the corner of the corner of Lafayette and Grand St. You still have to go to work, but you're stuck on the corner. Your whole body feels like it's being crushed by the weight of a steel anchor. You can't even blink.

Emmett: "Are you ok?"

...

    When Emmett told Nina to call him right after and inform him of what happened, I already felt frustrated. I hate having to report in when I'm feeling emotionally overwhelmed, and I can have a lot of trouble articulating my thoughts and feelings. I get flustered, I babble, and like Nina, sometimes I'm just stunned to silence. I really like that imagery of the steel anchor, of being stuck in place on the street, of being so lost you just stare. I've only had that kind of fear a few times in my life, the kind that's so incapacitating it's like you've just shut down but the world still needs you to be present.

> ...

    This is reminiscent of the thin, jaggedy noodle illustration from before, with all of its curves removed, lines hardened and made more angular, more like chicken scratch or chipping paint or a nervous scribble. The sharpness of the illustration insinuates food as a kind of weapon, cutting on the way down, but it also of course illustrates the confusing, frustrating nature of the situation. Depicting food in this formless way, removing the defining feature of soft curves that indicated "noodle", helps us visualize how inarticulable something this overwhelming can feel.

>

Mangia by Nina Freeman

You feel like you had the wind knocked out of you.

"I'm not ok, I have a condition."

You hear yourself saying "a condition" in your head. You're saying it over and over.

This is difficult not only because Nina's acknowledging what's happening and it barely seems real, but because the word "condition" feels so removed and clinical. I'm reminded of the passage with the repeating words, "eosinophilic esophagitis." By now we're familiar with the term, but recalling that passage with a simple reference to repetition helps us understand that it hasn't really sunk in yet.

Emmett: "What exactly happened?

"My esophagus is swollen... there's these rings. It's called eosinophilic esophagitis. That's... I have to eat soft things now. I can have soup. No chicken. No Vegetables. No Popcorn... I could choke."

Here's the jugular, the explanation of what this "condition" really means. It's not just a complicated name or a clinical diagnosis. It implies a forever changed relationship to food, a huge restructuring of habits. It means imposed limits on something most people take for granted to a moral degree. It's a huge paradigm shift.

Tell Emmett you're worn out and upset.

Tell Emmett that you're fine, and that you don't want to bother him at work.

I had to pause when I did this a second time. When I first played I had decided to tell Emmett I was fine, because I thought that's what I would do. But in retrospect, I'm not sure that's true. I, of course, wanted to pick the alternative option just to see where it led, but having to contemplate the decision for a second time I think I wouldn't be able to hold it in, as soon as the words were out, that something was wrong, I think the floodgates would open and as inelegantly as possible.

> Tell Emmett you're worn out and upset

You: "I'm exhausted and upset. I think I need to just go back to work and sit in the bathroom for a while. I'll see you tonight?"

played by Lana Polansky

Emmett: "Ok... I'm worried about you though. Can you stay on the phone until you get back to work?"

You: "Don't worry—this is just something I'm going to have to deal with."

Forever, you say to yourself.

This line spoken as an aside from the dialogue helps reinforce how isolating an experience this is, how it's something permanent and existential that no one else can really, truly know unless they're going through the same thing.

Emmett: "Are you crying? Maybe you should get a hot chocolate or something, maybe it'll make you feel better?"

You: "If I eat anything, I will puke."

The first in what I'm sure is many instances of well-meaning people not really understanding Nina's needs due to lack of proximity to the problem.

Emmett: "...I'm sorry, that was insensitive of me. I'm really sorry. Where are you now?"

You: "It's ok—I'm at work now. I'm going to go. Bye—love you."

Emmett "Bye, I love you too..."

Call mom.

Wash your face in the bathroom.

Here I'm given another opportunity to call mom, which seems like the reasonable, next logical step. But because I'm me and I put off doing things I dread for as long as possible, I visualize myself instead taking a bathroom break. A long bathroom break. I know I'll have to tell this person in my life what's wrong eventually. I figured this when I was sick. But I held onto pretending I was fine for as long as I could. Not because I didn't want to tell someone, but because I was so afraid of telling a person who had put so much pressure on me and my body in the past, I didn't feel safe saying anything.

> Wash your face

Mangia by Nina Freeman

The water at work is always freezing. It's alright though, because you went to the bathroom on the first floor—no one ever uses it, so you're alone. You can deal with the cold water as long as you're alone. You stand in front of the mirror and stare at your face. You look pale and you feel small. Your head feels like it's shrinking. It feels like your blood is thin.

This description of all the physical sensations of despair, anxiety and isolation really resonates. Good example of the first rule of writing: "Show, don't tell."

You rub a cheap paper towel on your face, and it leaves you more red than before. You're not sure you can avoid looking like a wreck at this point.

Hiding in the bathroom trying to make myself not look like complete shit even though that's how I feel is an experience I know well. I remember having stomach attacks when friends were around and I'd try really hard to force myself to feel better, and when I wasn't totally falling apart I'd try to put on a strong face and be social. I've never had a good poker face, though.

Return to your desk.

I don't think I had a job at a physical location when I was sick. I think I was freelancing then. But I was going to school, and I tried really hard—and failed—to power through a lot of classes while fighting off intense pain. Everyone could tell. One really awful class in particular gave me anxiety something awful, and I had attacks almost every day for a month because I basically had to crunch to finish a rash of assignments that were as boring as they were difficult. I scraped by in that class and felt my whole body loosen up when it was over and I realized I had passed with a C.

> Return to your desk

You're starting to wonder what you're going to eat tonight. You haven't even had lunch, to be honest, but your stomach feels too battered right now to even consider eating.

This is a hell of a feeling, because you know you can't just pick something up anymore. When I was getting the attacks, I tried to predict what would make me sick and what wouldn't, which was really hard, and then for a month before my surgery—when I was diagnosed—I was put on a

played by Lana Polansky

low-fat/no fat diet, which was its own form of tasteless torture. Additionally, I really empathize with the body issues brought up in this game in part because trying to explain this diet to people as a medical necessity was super frustrating. On one end I had insinuations that being chubby caused me to be sick, while explaining this diet to others required the disclaimer that I wasn't trying to lose weight, nor was I trying to express any internalized fat-shaming. Twitter was especially fun for this.

> The work day goes by quickly. You spend most of it thinking about what you're going to eat tonight. Definitely not pasta, you thought, especially after last night... that pain. All you have other than that, though, is chicken. The doctor said chicken was a choking hazard. You feel nauseous just thinking about it.

This is an awful feeling. I was so scared I'd get another attack before my surgery and it would have to be delayed. (It took a month for me so that my pancreas could heal and the swelling could go down, because if the surgeon punctured it accidentally it could have killed me.) I was so worried that the food I ate wasn't safe enough, while also wondering just how far I could push it. I knew it was bad though. In the hospital I gave myself an attack after drinking too much Crystal Light and had to ask for morphine.

> It's five.
>
> **Go home.**
>
> **Go to the grocery store.**

Might as well pick up some food. I also expect this passage to be sort of daunting and provide a nice bit of description and context.

> \> Go to the grocery store

> You don't normally think about the sheer amount of food in the grocery store, but you can't help but feel the weight of it today. Walking through the sliding doors feels like jumping into the pool, your belly smacking flat onto the water.

Another nice, very tactile, very visceral simile here.

> Granola bars, string cheese, ramen, potato rolls, steak, rice, asparagus, salad, hot sauce, clams, lamb, hamburger, bacon,

cereal, stew...

Granola bars, string cheese, ramen, potato rolls, steak, rice, asparagus, salad, hot sauce, clams, lamb, hamburger, bacon, cereal, stew...

Granola bars, string cheese, ramen, potato rolls, steak, rice, asparagus, salad, hot sauce, clams, lamb, hamburger, bacon, cereal, stew...

Granola bars, string cheese, ramen, potato rolls, steak, rice, asparagus, salad, hot sauce, clams, lamb, hamburger, bacon, cereal, stew...

There's so much food.

Another great use of repetition to illustrate just how overwhelming the situation is. This one in particular evokes a kind of "water, water everywhere" idea, in that Nina's surrounded by food but she can't eat the vast majority of it. It feels not only overwhelming but hopeless.

Decide that you're not hungry after all.

Buy a bunch of different things, hoping that you'll be able to eat any of it.

I find it a little weird that the character wouldn't seek foods that she knows for sure are safe to eat, like soup, or maybe pudding. I get that she doesn't really have a clear idea of what her diet should be and she's probably still in a state of chaos but I guess I find it curious that she would go at this more or less haphazardly, considering it's so important.

> Buy a bunch of different foods

You head home with peanut butter cookies, a box of Cheeze-It's and angel hair pasta. You figure that angel hair is so light that it won't bother you... hopefully. Otherwise, you guess you would just not eat.

This third choice makes some sense. Nina has gone for a food item that's recognizable (pasta), but hopefully in a friendlier form. The best I can make of this is she's gone after foods that she finds comforting almost instinctually, rather than rationally seeking out foods which are definitely safe.

You're feeling exhausted after being in the supermarket. All of that food...

played by Lana Polansky

    The choice of angel hair in particular sort of strikes me as a rhetorical softening out of the harsh illustration I saw before, taking that rough-edged scribble and bending into something gentler.

Go to bed without eating.
Make the angel hair.

    I'm genuinely curious to see how the food goes down. I might, unless I were really hungry, just give up on eating and try to sleep, but since the mediated space of a game guarantees a lack of consequence, I would like to find out what happens here.

    > Make the angel hair.

The water is boiling, and you're stirring the angel hair around. The water is cloudy and steamy. The steam feels good in your lungs—you feel like it's flushing something out of you.

    I literally used to try using steam when I had stomach pain. I thought it would help relieve the tight, constricted feeling. I guess it worked a little, but that might have been placebo effect.

You empty the pot into a streamer and put the pasta in a bowl. You top it off with some olive oil and pepper, and sit on the couch.
As you roll up the pasta and bring it closer to your mouth, you feel your throat get tight. You tell yourself that you need to eat—you don't want to starve.

    This feeling, too. Just being near food sometimes would trigger feelings and I couldn't always tell if they were psychosomatic. I felt like I could will them away sometimes, like a prayer.

Chew, and swallow.
It's too risky--put the fork down.

    Let's try that prayer here.

    > Chew, and swallow

Mangia by Nina Freeman

You chew slowly... but you hesitate before swallowing. You're alone in the apartment. Light spills in from your room, but it's dark outside, and there's no noise. There's nothing. If you choke on this, you could die, you tell yourself. There's no one here to save you now.

I like how *Mangia* is descriptive without being text-heavy. This first paragraph is a nice bit of exposition that situates the predicament of the character perfectly. You know what the stakes are if things go wrong right away.

Would it be better to starve, or to choke, you wonder?

I like this rhetorical question because it reinforces how impossible the situation is. If you don't eat, you'll die. If you eat, you still might die.

You swallow the pasta, and feel every piece sliding down your throat and into your esophagus. You feel like it's taking forever, and your heart starts beating **faster, and faster**.

It's the obvious choice, but putting the link on the "faster, and faster" does something important. It creates a sense of tension, contrasting the character's anxiety with the slowness of eating, like running down an endless hallway. It also forces the player to connect directly with the emotional state of the character by explicitly having them click on this expression of her fear in order to move forward, which suggests the possibility of something sinister happening.

> faster, and faster

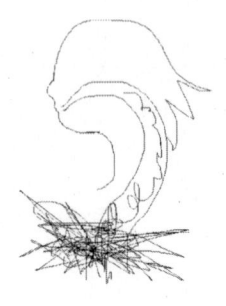

Just like the pacing technique we saw in the first food scene and at the

played by Lana Polansky

doctor's office. This breaking up of the scenes with illustrations draws out of the pace and makes that hallway seem longer. Using this particular illustration ramps up the sense of dread, but as the player you have to remember that it's focalized through Nina, so it's at least partly her emotions and expectations that this is referring to, and not just a physical symptom. She senses a monster inside her that may or may not be there.

> >

> Your phone starts buzzing, and you feel the pasta sink past the middle of your chest. It's ok, you tell yourself, it's fine.
>
> You: "...Hello?"
>
> Emmett: "Hey, I'm outside."
>
> You: "Ok, hold on."

    This bit of line pacing is reminiscent of the subversion of expectations in horror films when we see the protagonist open a door or be tapped on the shoulder, and we anticipate the worst, and to our relief, it's something or someone harmless. Doing this helps us empathize with the character by setting up a context where our feelings match those projected by the character, which is what focalization is trying to achieve.

    That momentary respite in works with horror overtones is really important, too, because it cuts the tension for a minute, letting the viewer relax momentarily, but also recalling previous depictions of horrible stuff from earlier in the work. This sets us up for an even more dramatic impact later on.

> You go downstairs to let him in. He shuts the door and hugs you. The two of you stand together, and it's warm. You lean your forehead into his shoulder and shut your eyes.

    This line is a good example of that respite. It's humanizing and comforting, and as Nina is shown expressing this relief, we get invited into it as well.

> **Tell him that you just tried to swallow some pasta, but it was scary.**
>
> **Tell him that you already ate, so you saved this last bowl of pasta in case he hadn't.**

    I feel like I've begun a tradition of laying all of my feelings on Emmett.

I wonder if this is something of a power fantasy, actually, because while I avow I have trouble keeping a lid on my feelings, I will still try to hold them in for the sake of others before they're pried out of me. And here, just freely being able to let loose rather than put myself second, I'm really eager to just do it.

> Tell him that you already ate

Emmett: "What did you eat today?"

You: "Oatmeal."

Emmett: "...for breakfast?"

You: "...yeah."

Emmett: "You're not a very good liar—you know that. That's your dinner, and you should eat as much of it as you can. I can't watch you starve yourself."

I appreciate this line, although it's frustratingly paternalistic, because I feel like *Mangia* has already established a characteristic pattern with Emmett of being a little too eager to talk when he really needs to listen. It's a really useful demonstration of an unconscious gendered dynamic in this relationship: Emmett wants to be helpful, he means well, but he doesn't know as much as he thinks and what's meant as care comes off as nagging or condescension. Let's just say, I've seen this before.

Tell him that it's too stressful to eat.

Don't say anything.

Because of this gendered dynamic, because of the emotionally overwhelming nature of the situation, and because this tendency in Emmett reveals a contrasting tendency in Nina to maybe put her needs second rather than argue (that behavior was really apparent in the phone conversation with her mother), the next logical step would be for her to say nothing. I admit that if I were in the same position, I might say nothing, or I might get so flustered that I would have trouble saying what I wanted to say, which would exacerbate everyone's frustrations and help lead to a light.

But I'm just going to go straight ahead and tell Emmett it's too stressful to eat.

> Tell him that it's too stressful to eat

Emmett: "I'm sorry... I can't know what it's like. I do know,

played by Lana Polansky

though, that you need to eat something. If you chew your pasta really, really well, I'm sure it will be ok. I'm here with you now, in case anything does happen."

When boys who are out of their depth try to be helpful. <3

You do feel better now that you're not alone.

You: "Ok, I'll try to finish it."

It is encouraging that confronting Emmett directly leads to an acknowledgment, an apology and some real moral support. If this is my power fantasy, that right there would be the payoff.

You take another bite, and another, chewing as thoroughly as you can. You feel a wave of anxiety wash over you every time you swallow, but you remind yourself that you're not alone. If anything happens, Emmett will help you.

You start to feel full very quickly.

Finish the pasta.

This recalls the beginning of the game, where I'm forced to eat pasta and allow the stomach pain to set in, let the character fully experience it, to be able to progress. It's a nice coda to formally repeat that idea by setting "Finish the pasta" as link text. But now that we know the stakes, there's a do-or-die quality to this. Also, that lull in the tension brought on by Emmett showing up and encouraging Nina to eat has allowed for this moment to have a kind of feeling of finality to it.

> Finish the pasta

There's that harsh, jagged noodle. That same technique of interspersing dramatic moments with illustrations to lengthen them out and make them more viscerally evocative, almost like a kind of physical empathy, is happening here again. But unlike before, this illustration goes straight for harshness. It doesn't start with that relatively soft noodle; it's much more explicit than before. That little scratch that looks like razor wire tells me so much and makes me fear the worst.

>

It feels like there's a balloon expanding inside of your stomach. You feel it getting bigger and bigger, stretching your gut beyond comfort. It feels just like last night—with your insides heating up like a furnace. You bring your knees up to your forehead, squeezing yourself tight into a ball.

There's that moment of dread, which may only be due to the gastritis, but still feels like a nightmare. The little details of pain, of curling up, are actually triggering for me. I would curl up. I would cry and feel uncomfortably feverish and feel, not so much a balloon as a vice, slowly crushing me.

Emmett: "Are you ok?"

You feel dizzy and nauseous. You wish you would just throw it all up—it would be better than feeling like this. Like your stomach might explode.

And I would feel dizzy and nauseous and like I just needed it out of my body. There's no use for clever descriptive prose here, just a blunt explanation is enough.

Emmett: "Hey..."

That acknowledgment of basic uselessness and uncertainty, possibly tinged with guilt.

You: "I feel so full, it hurts."

And the protagonist having no time to beat around the bush. It isn't even a choice anymore, because her body isn't giving her (or me) one.

Emmett rubs your back, and asks if it would feel better to lie down. You say that you would, and that you think you just ate too much. The two of you walk into your room and lie down together.

I'm actually getting flashback memories to backrubs and belly rubs to alleviate pain.

You fall asleep.

When I was in pain I loved being able to sleep because I was safe from the pain when I dreamed, and when I woke up often I felt better. Not always, though.

> You fall asleep

The illustrations in the next bit can all be said to constitute one scene (although who is speaking here isn't clear. It could be the second-person narrator, the protagonist, something else entirely . . .)

But this is suggestive. It's that first, softer noodle, corrupted with a scribble. It makes me ask if this is a dream, or if something more sinister is going on while Nina's rendered unconscious. Is she okay? Am I okay?

>

Following the last passage with this one suggests a transformation: the soft noodle becomes hard-edged. Food is now an eternal threat. The familiar is now threatening and other. The body is now a site of fear rather than a site of comfort.

Mangia by Nina Freeman

>

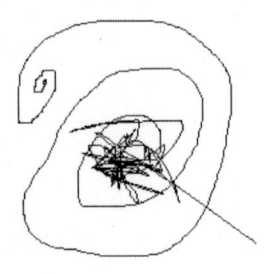

I'm not totally sure, but I think this is meant to depict the rings with evil, dangerous food struggling to get down the character's throat. This is very ominous, following the two noodles. This wordless suggestion creates more panic: What is going on here? Is it just gastritis? Is it a nightmare? Is it only focalization?

That lull I mentioned before is bringing the immediacy and the horror of this scene into stark relief. Now, instead of interspersing illustrations with text to draw out a scene, the entirety of the message is pictorial, which deftly underscores the idea that since Nina is asleep, she can't make choices.

Whatever happens, happens.

>

I was so worried, as soon as I was actually diagnosed, that I might die. Like, I hadn't really considered the possibility when I thought it was only IBS, but as soon as I had an idea of just how serious the condition was, and how soon I needed treatment—and how "carefully" I had to treat my body until then—I was petrified something would go wrong. I would get an attack before my surgery and end up on life support in the ICU, or my pan-

played by Lana Polansky

creas wouldn't be totally healed and it'd get punctured during surgery. The images of those possibilities flashed in my head the way these illustrations suggest a terrible fate in *Mangia*.

>

Which will you eat?

This passage isn't really a choice so much as it is a waypoint connecting two ideas. It's more like a semicolon than a passage.

Asking me which one I'll eat is almost sarcastic, considering the last handful of passages were all illustrations suggesting extreme physical pain. It's like asking whether I'd like to be burned or frozen. It's an impossible situation, like choking or starving.

There's also a hint of sarcasm, because again, the character is asleep. So there's a feeling of breaking the fourth wall, as if the game has asked me to look upon the landscape of events, and the strong suggestion of something terrible happening at the end, and asking "me," the player, which one I will eat. I'm in a position now where I can eat things—minus one secondary organ, I'm back to my old self—but the memory of the pain and the terror of uncertainty makes this question carry a specific cruelty that I'm not sure people who haven't had a similar experience will detect.

There was a possibility that when I got my gall bladder removed, I would have to modify my diet forever, and I was lucky that wasn't the case. But I wouldn't have had a risk of dying as a result. So my best method to relate here is to imagine that fear as a mortal question, not temporary but eternal. And when I do that, this brief and simple question which inverts the technique of interspersing—rather than text broken up by images, now we have images broken up by text—carries all this extra subtext. The climax of this story hangs on a question, and so kind of refuses to allow for a comforting resolution. I don't know which one I will eat, or if I even can.

> Which will you eat?

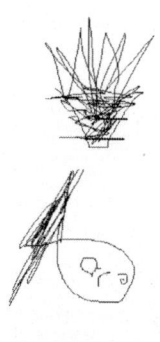

Mangia by Nina Freeman

Now, *Mangia* introduces me to things I supposedly can't eat. The objects are pretty discernable. I think it's supposed to suggest fish and chips. But of course they've been scratched out just enough to evoke the same danger response as before.

I can't eat these. So it isn't a choice. They're razor wire and alien.

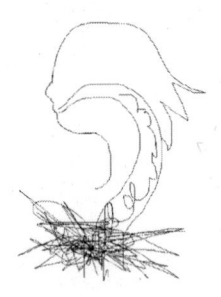

>

They're followed succinctly by the *Alien* figure, with the rings going down her throat and the stomach made of angry scribbles.

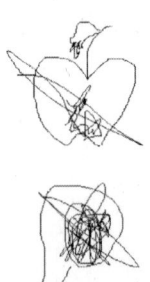

>

Again, here's some food that's familiar enough. An apple and a drumstick. Familiar yet corrupted just enough to be a threatening other, with strategic scratches.

Can I eat these?

>

played by Lana Polansky

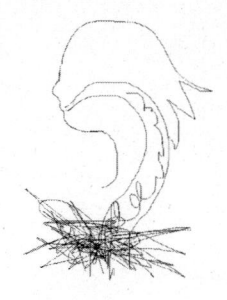

Again, it's not a choice.

>

The game does this for a while, alternating illustrations with each consecutive passage. It wears me down, as the player, by forcing me to visualize all of these food items that are off-limits, twisted into something terrifying, one after the other. I become aware of the exhausting scope of the limitation, of how surrounded by death I am. It's like a slow death, or a resignation that if death didn't come in the protagonist's sleep, it's hiding everywhere, in a thing she needs to live that she can no longer trust.

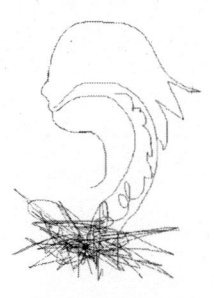

>

>

Mangia by Nina Freeman

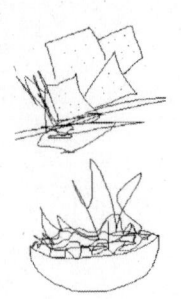

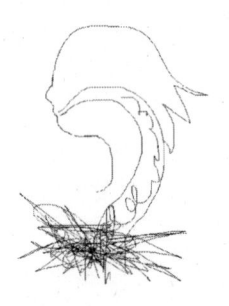

\>

\>

\>

played by Lana Polansky

>

>

>

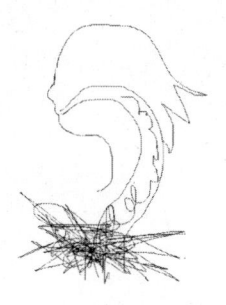

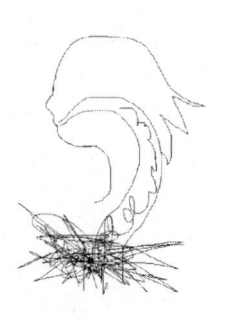

Your grandfather, Nanoo, always had a healthy appetite. He would inhale your Nana's dinners without pause, and would always ask for more. He loved to eat.

He loved you and wanted you to grow up healthy and strong. He taught you how to spell your first word—milk. He made you spell it out loud: M-I-L-K. Then, he would take out a fountain pen, and you would write it clumsily onto his yellow notepad. He said that you needed to drink a lot of it—it would

Mangia by Nina Freeman

help you grow.

At night, he would sit you down with a bowl of pasta and meatballs and he'd tell you "Mangia, Nina! Mangia!" He told you that it meant "Eat up!"

He's not around anymore, but you'll never forget the oak table and the cupboard of antique china. His olive skin and black hair, and his low voice telling you to eat up. To live and eat and grow.

...

I like that this ends on an anecdote about someone who has passed away, juxtaposing food once again, and finally, with death. It's like a final memory. Also these several references to growth, to living, feel cruelly ironic. This is impossible now, one way or another. It makes sense then that the last passage ends not on closure, or resolution, but on an ellipsis. The voice of the character is choked out at the end.

> ...

THE END

Like I said, I've seen a few of the passages tweeted out sporadically for the full version of the game. They're a lot more detailed and colorful than this—and as a result maybe less suggestive—but I don't doubt that the full version will take a lot of the aesthetic, formal, and narrative ideas here and expand on them. There's a lot of stuff here in terms of borrowing horror devices, psychodrama devices, and also just a really strong sense of things like pacing, symbolism, allegory, characterization, and focalization, and it all works to create a strong thematic overtone of bodily alienation, where the body itself and the basic necessity to keep it living becomes a mortal threat. It goes on to suggest the terror of making the banal inarticulable and remote, and it does this through simple descriptions, set pieces, and deft use of irony.

So I guess *Mangia* works as well as a horror game as it does a psychological first-person (or in this case, second-person) narrative.

Maybe it was scarier to me because it forced me to recall such a similar experience, and it did it while evoking body image and self-esteem issues that I'm very familiar with. Body image and ego stuff are probably common enough for all women, but to see my fears and rationalizations and a description of pain so similar to my own just play out was a very jarring experience. But I think it also helped me understand and empathize with some of the feelings approximated in *Mangia*, and maybe—I hope—helped me to communicate those things more articulately than I would have otherwise.

SACRILEGE
BY CARA ELLISON
PLAYED BY SOHA KAREEM

THE CROWD HEAVES

the bass of the music

you can feel it vibrate through your fingertips

warm feeling of rum

sticky on your throat;

ice cracks in the glass

you put lime to your lips and bite

turn, ravenously, to regard the dancefloor

    At first, it's the colors I notice.
    A hot pink with muted text but bolded yellow links, which upon hover turn into an equally jarring green.
    It takes a few seconds to adjust, quite fitting for the setting. I'm useless at night clubs, even worse if it's crowded. I like being able to hear what people are saying to me and despise being touched without permission or knowing the person touching me.
    But here we are, and we're going to dance.

    > turn, ravenously

you don't go home with strangers in case you end up

dismembered in a freezer

this means that here, there are only these options:

Matthew

John

Mark

Luke

"You don't go home with strangers in case you end up dismembered in a freezer." So now I have my options of men.

My first thought is, "I don't think I've ever fucked a Matthew, John, Mark, or Luke. And I've fucked a lot of people."

I choose Matthew.

> Matthew

you turn siren eyes to matthew

matthew is tall

>

disheveled

>

he makes you laugh

>

initiate fuckplan

i could do better

There is something comforting about having and initiating a fuckplan. A little secret you keep to yourself, and maybe a close friend or two to honor the "buddy system" on nights out.

Matthew doesn't know it quite yet, but he's our target, and the heat-seeking missiles have deployed.

> initiate fuckplan

You grab Matthew's shoulder and yell his name ecstatically:

MATTHEWWWWWWWWW

>

the lights sparkle

>

the music is loud

>

you both whirl around bashing people in the elbows
>

"What are you doing here?"

"I am observing small dresses for science."

You grin.

"You look hot," he says, appreciatively. "Do I also look hot?"

"You look like Matthew with glowsticks on. Like a sort of glowstick-holder Matthew."

"...Would you sleep with such a man?"

"I definitely would, I mean, we would certainly be able to see what we were doing. **What with all the glowsticks**."

I can't help but cringe at observing people hit on each other, mostly because my mind flashes back to all the times I've desperately wanted to make a good impression (a good-enough-to-get-fucked impression) and likely ended up making an ass of myself.

I appreciate the way the text moves between me and MATTHEWW-WWWW. Clicking through links is a rhythmic and hypnotizing ritual; our mating calls are bouncing back and forth between each other.

> What with all the glowsticks.

he is going to kiss you
>

he is going to kiss you
>

he is going to kiss you
>

what are you doing

Kiss him back.

Your boot is vibrating. **Investigate**.

As I think about kissing Matthew, my phone vibrates in my boot (How have I never thought of putting my phone in my boot while out? That's pretty clever.) I had the option to ignore it, but my thoughts are "maybe it's an emergency."

> Investigate

You dig out your phone from your boot

It's Patty. Text message reads:

"That guy is married. Married. MARRIED."

ABORT THE DICKHEAD

FUCK THIS DICKHEAD

    I'm not sure this qualifies as an emergency, but as a fun fact about our dear friend here. Matthew is married, and technically a few of the people I'm fucking are currently married, but that's just a personal aside as I'm exploring more poly/open dynamics with others.
    Here, I assume Matthew is not following my train of thought.
    We've re-routed the heat-seeking missiles, and are aborting this dickhead.

> ABORT
> turn, ravenously

you don't go home with strangers in case you end up dismembered in a freezer

this means that here, there are still

still

only these options:

Matthew

John

Mark

Luke

    I return to the dancefloor and start thinking about my next moves. It appears that tonight a fuckplan will be initiated with or without Matthew.
    I'm coming for you, John.

you turn siren eyes to john

john is tall
  >

dresses smart
  >

played by Soha Kareem

has a kind smile
>

initiate fuckplan

i could do better

> initiate fuckplan

Hey John

- You purr.

In your head, you imagine yourself at the end of the night, peeling your clothes off to reveal your naked twenty-something skin, and knowing you look good, and thinking, **god, someone should see this**.

    I particularly enjoy this passage. When I was younger I had such a hate-hate relationship with my body that the lines "god, someone should see this" was never in my line of thinking.
    I want to steal that line, now. Employ it for future fuckplan initiatives.

> god, someone should see this

More people should see this before I am old and my skin loses this tautness, my body tries to balloon - more people should see me hot, instead of wait until I am forty and happy, and have me be accomplished and smug and grandiose and happy but not young any more, not the naked unpretentious sylph in this mirror right now, the one with artless bruises from falling over laughing, and the glossy hair, the full mouth, the way eyeliner sits on the eyelids, smoky, and the forced smile built from being alone.

That look in the mirror will not happen this time.

You will take someone home. Because really, you are content, apart from where everyone else tells you you have failed

Which is in their voice

When they ask you

Who is walking you home

Because they don't want to have to do it again

They have someone waiting

Your twenties love you

Don't they, wild child

At this point of *Sacrilege*, I'm painfully realizing the emptiness in people.

"[M]ore people should see me hot, instead of wait until I am forty and happy, and have me be accomplished and smug and grandiose and happy but not young any more."

My brain jerks with the reaction, "God hookup culture when you're young can be so fucked."

I will take someone home. At this point in the story though, I'm not quite sure that's what I want.

> You will take someone home.

"Hello," he smiles shyly.

"Can I buy you a drink?" you ask.

"Sure. Any kind of beer will do," he says.

"You always dress well," you say.

"Thanks," he grins. "I try hard to look good."

"You know how Erin always says we'd be the best dressed couple if we ever got together?"

"Haha," he says. "Yes."

You hand him his beer, sip yours.

"Why don't we go home together tonight."

It isn't really a question. It is a statement pretending to be a question.

The best thing about heterosexual men is their face when you **ask them** straight up.

"The best thing about heterosexual men is their face when you ask them straight up."

The forcefulness of coyness on women in hetero dynamics is so nauseating and, really, quite boring. Nothing has ever been as tantalizing or alluring as the enthusiastic "YES!" and the deafening "just FUCK me already."

We want women to fuck men, but we want them to be shy and cryptic about it. If you tell them you want to fuck them, you're a desperate slut. If you don't want to fuck them and can't say that directly because of your safety, then you're being shy and cryptic, and they read that as an agreement to fuck.

Do you want to fuck? Y[ ] N [ ]

played by Soha Kareem

"Serious?" he says.

"Deadly," you say.

He starts to look troubled.

Engage interpretation

Rejection

> Engage interpretation

"Ah. You are not, and never have been, attracted to me."

"You're pretty hot."

"Then what?"

"Me and Mark are pretty good friends..."

"Did he tell you not to sleep with me?"

He avoids your eyes.

"We shouldn't sleep together. It would be weird. Because of him."

"Right," you say."Right."

The horror. The HORROR. Look down at your arm - LOOK

"Sorry," he says.

Rejection.
This isn't a regular rejection, no. It's not that you aren't his type, but that another man has claimed and branded you already.

You are unfuckable, and you didn't choose that.

"No longer a person with ideas and love and conversation / Just an object/ Passed around / Once / Another man dropped you to smash"

The amount of our worth placed in our desire for men to brand us as something wonderful, or not brand us at all, leaves a sickly taste in my drying mouth.

> The horror...

You look down at your arms

There are barcodes and barcodes and barcodes climbing and climbing up your skinny milk arms

Like tattoos under the skin

And you can feel them creep, sting

You are branded

Spoiled

Your desire is fake, an illusion of agency

You are nothing

Another man has ruined you

You are a container into which something awful has been smeared

No longer a person with ideas and love and conversation

Just an object

Passed around

Once

Another man dropped you to smash

No one will ever clean it up

Not a person

A vase that will never hold flowers again

"I'm sorry. It's the honourable thing to do."

   Feeling angry, I go to find Mark.

   > I'm sorry
   > turn, ravenously
   > Mark

you turn siren eyes to mark
mark ignores you
   >

played by Soha Kareem

you don't know why
>

you hear he is a nice person from other people
>

perhaps your charm
>

and talent
>

aren't totally impotent as an aphrodisiac
>

initiate fuckplan

i could do better

 The option to initiate a fuckplan with Mark after knowing he's poisoned this social well and then continues to ignore me is arguably the most tragic part of this story.
 Of course I could fucking do better.
 I refuse to be less than the heroine of this story.

 > i could do better
Nearing the end, I choose Luke.

 > Luke

you turn siren eyes to luke
>

luke is happy
>

is handsome
>

is smarter than you
>

initiate fuckplan

i could do better

 Will Luke be mine tonight?

 > initiate fuckplan

Hey

Sacrilege by Cara Ellison

- you say to Luke.

Luke gets in close
 >

Pushes an arm around your waist
 >

And you dance:
 >

The beat ruptures

Bass through your feet

Into your eyelashes
 >

Electric Feel strokes the crowd
 >

Everyone's hearts beat together
 >

All along the western front

People learning to receive

She got power in her hand

To shock you like you **won't believe**
 >

When he smiles at you he means it and it crushes you

Because there is something chemical missing

Something gone

Or never there

The thing that has your fingers

Feel like they are getting frostbite when you touch skin

The smell of his skin

All that

All that witchcraft

It isn't there

It isn't fucking there

And you can feel his body tense

Like it is there for him

It is there for him

played by Soha Kareem

And **not for you**

    How horribly we feel when someone finally wants us and we don't want them in return.

    It's a queasy cliché, yet we always yearn for the people who are trash, treating us like we can lay down and accompany them in their filth.

  > not for you

Saw her in the amazon
>

With the voltage running through her skin
>

Standing there with nothing on
>

She gonna teach me how to swim
>

Sweat between breasts

Sliding towards the floor

The music is making you drowsy

Making you happy

Making you think

This is a good idea

He is good looking

We are young

We are free

We should fuck

And be **free**

  > free

He looks at you adoringly
>

And you feel your heart hurt
>

But the music is arguing
>

Pushing you closer to him
>

The music sways your libido
>

Like a chemical metronome
>

Suspended in your soul
>

My heart is yearning, Paris is burning

It's not love, it's just Paris

    I know, I'm horribly boring. Choosing standards over libido creates a rather linear narrative.
    Girl Does Not Want to Fuck, So Girl Does Not Fuck

> It's not love

Luke
- you say, your heart spilling into your lungs
Like Playdough through a sieve

Luke, I don't like you enough
I think you would get hurt
We are friends
And I would hurt you

He tells you that you are conceited
to have thought that he liked you
he melts into the crowd, upset.

Yes, you think. Yes.
Better this, than to lose him completely.

MAPS

> MAPS

played by Soha Kareem

THE CROWD HEAVES

the bass of the music

you can feel it vibrate through your fingertips

warm feeling of rum

sticky on your throat;

ice cracks in the glass as the barman refills it.

you put lime to your lips and bite

You have no more options. This place has no more to show to you. **Another drink.**

  We run out of options.
  Unfuckable and fuckless, but ready for another round.

  > Another drink

Just as you think

I am going to probably get dismembered in a freezer

The barman's hand brushes your arm

And something heavy and papery

Hits your fingers

It is new:

But it is somehow old

It is torn a bit

Dogeared

It's a secret optional book.

You open it

It was handwritten by someone

Who uses hearts for the dots on the "i"s.

You can **read it if you** like.

Or you can bugger off back to **Unwinnable**

A secret optional book, as if all we've been programmed to believe and swallow in hetero dynamics is actually untrue?

No, it cannot be.

> read it if you like

Left for us while we sip on our drink is a guide, a 6- page manifesto titled
OVEREDUCATED NEUROTIC MODERN HETERO WOMAN'S GUIDE TO CASUAL SEXUAL RELATIONS

It's an empowering, thoughtful summary of how sexual society has failed us. We foster emotionally stunted men to lead women into baggage and shame because we want to fuck each other. I'd laugh if this wasn't all so fucking depressing.

Our mysterious revolutionary writes:

women: ask the hard questions, be brash, be understanding, supportive like a nice Wonderbra

men: try to be more up front about your sexy feelings. we dig 'em, make them part of you, have us notice them

OVEREDUCATED NEUROTIC MODERN HETERO WOMAN'S GUIDE TO CASUAL SEXUAL RELATIONS (god 'hetero' is such an uncool abbreviation)

the post-sexual revolution era has been liberating for crushingly overeducated self aware 20-something women in important ways: you can

fuck who you like

fuck how you like

fuck however many people you like

fuck in a happy relationship

fuck in a terrible relationship

fuck for babies

fuck for love

fuck for hate

fuck because you miss someone

fuck because you are lonely

fuck because you think someone is wonderful

fuck because the other person needs it

fuck because why not

played by Soha Kareem

privileged (particularly white) 20-something heterosexual women like myself seem to be getting to know themselves extremely well:

they know better than ever what they want

they know how they feel about men

they know what kind of sex makes them feel good

they know how to tell you what they are looking for

Page 2

> Page 2

they aren't ashamed as much as they used to be: they are more publicly articulate about emotions because they are becoming comfortable actually being women (this is because of feminism - thanks feminism you are doing a sweet job at that carry on *salutes*) and are starting to realise that things people label as 'feminine' might not necessarily be inherently bad. such as feelings. unfettered feelings are, contrary to popular opinion (and game journalism critics), very very good for us and being honest about them is integral to everyone's happiness and enjoyment of most things including sex, video-games, condiments etc

however one of the areas in which feminism has failed is with convincing men that feminism loves them and wants them to be happy too (because if men are happy then women are and vice versa). what hasn't changed is the majority of men's attitudes to your fucking whoever you like whenever you like, or to your wanting to fuck them how you like, or their reactions to your having any feelings at all about what sex should be and when it should be

Page 3 (god you are reading in a club how uncouth)

> Page 3

that is because men are still not socially and culturally encouraged throughout their life to tell you how they feel about you emotionally, or to tell you that they have no desire to be involved with you emotionally (which is sometimes more important)

they are not able to tell you personally who they really are

who they are really looking for

what kind of sex they really want

or that

in general

they don't know who they are during their twenties either

and they'd also rather cry in the shower to The Smiths (How Soon Is Now is my own personal choice)

men are encouraged to be leaders, and if they don't feel like they know what they are doing, they are not going to ask about it beforehand because it is a sign of weakness - and that specific weakness is something women have (it's a strength!)

BUT

Page 4

> Page 4

"i think this should be a one time only deal"

"i'd rather this be a long term thing"

"i think we should fuck FOREVER no feelings no strings"

"i can't do this right now"

"i'm too upset"

"i think am going to hurt you [emotionally] if we sleep together"

these are things that are rarely said that would save the world (along with "what would you like me to do to you")

because these are things that women can deal with better than being ignored, being abandoned, being mistreated, being stalked afterwards

and a small secret is: if we were planning on sleeping with you before these things are said (it is always a plan), even if they don't appeal to us we will probably still sleep with you because we also have libidos! the difference is we won't spend time worrying about your lack of/lavish attention later and you'll never have to worry about talking to us about anything concerning sex ever again

managed expectations, you see

Page 5

> Page 5

played by Soha Kareem

i have seen it work

it is still working

i bet more men wished women were unafraid to say these things too

am i being revolutionary yet

there is still that antiquated feeling in some women too: i want a man to LEAD ME. to FUCK me. to MASTER me. hell i spend a lot of time fantasising about this man. i think it is okay to want this but

where men like these exist, they had HELP.

being a master of anything takes a long time. and it takes a fuckload of people giving a shit to make you into one. you can't just take that effort without giving, and you can't just invest yourself in an intimate act like fucking like wild animals without knowing that you are cared about, even in the smallest, least profound way, like they once bought you a Coke because you didn't have any change does this reveal anything about my partners oh never mind

so everyone better start caring about each other enough to communicate, because there are a lot of fuckmasters, both men and women, to make.

women: ask the hard questions, be brash, be understanding, supportive like a nice Wonderbra

men: try to be more up front about your sexy feelings, we dig 'em, make them part of you, have us notice them

Page 6

> Page 6

assertiveness is an aphrodisiac and we have forgotten it

laugh

fuck

repeat

don't sleep with people who don't tell you what they want first

don't sleep with people who don't tell you what they want first

don't sleep with people who don't tell you what they want first don't sleep with people who don't tell you what they want first

know who you are and why you do everything

and enthusiastic consent is the fucking hottest thing to give, and the hottest thing to get

AMEN

(the author has scribbled some sort of crap unicorn at the bottom of this, and there is a coffee stain on the bottom right corner)

Through my disappointment in how *needy* I felt playing this game, this was one hell of an unexpected ending.

Sacrilege is kicking down the doors for men and women plagued by condescending hetero structures that lead them to dreadful, awful sex. Our mysterious crusader leaves me feeling *great* about *fucking* and about *my want and need to fuck*.

laugh / fuck / repeat

Girl Wants To Get Fucked, Girl Gets Fucked [Y]

A-fucking-men.

AND THE ROBOT HORSE YOU RODE IN ON
BY ANNA ANTHROPY
PLAYED BY CAT FITZPATRICK

I don't play video games lots. Or, I haven't played video games lots for a while. I used to play games lots when I was little. I remember playing one game where you were a dog and the boy who fed you was sleepwalking, and you had to go ahead and remove obstacles so he didn't hurt himself and could still feed you. But when I was a bit older I twigged that video games were supposed to be for boys, and I was starting to really not want to be a boy, so I stopped and just read books. Which I think was a pity, now. So, as if to make good, I've agreed, enthusiastically, to play this game called *And The Robot Horse You Rode In On*.

So I google "Robot Horse Rode In On" because I know this is a free game on the internet and not something you have to buy in a box on five disks and install or anything.

I click on it and get this screen.

And the Robot Horse You Rode In On by Anna Anthropy

A game by anna anthropy featuring code by Lydia Neon.

This game contains scenes which are violent and sexual.

Shall I tell you a tale?

It's a nice piece of font design, no? And I love being told tales. So yes, please, do.

> Shall I tell you a tale?

The Wild West. 2100 A.D.

This is both a game and a story, it is a story game. I appear, unlike in a film, which might also have such a cut title, to be being asked to assent to something. But actually my choice is the same as in a film- assent or walk away. Except that here not just passivity but participation is demanded of me. I have to click on it. I click on it. I suppose I am giving some kind of assent.

> The Wild West

There's a sailor's story about how when the sun descends into the sea, it dissolves into pieces, filling the sky with stars. Well, this is a hustler's story, a story of the west, and when the sun touches the desert, all it does is dye the sand red like blood.

It starts to cool off, too. You're grateful for that, after the long day you've had.

Diode emerges from the porta-tent, yawning and cracking open a canteen. She takes a long swig. "Evening, bandita."

played by Cat Fitzpatrick

Then she comes over to you and plants her foot on the top of your head. Cool as you are, you **do not freak out** about this.

And a story begins. It is atmospheric, I am persuaded and gripped by the tone, the voice, like in a story. At the same time, the pronouns here are different than in stories of the kind I am more familiar with. They are second person pronouns, but in books, second person pronouns, when they are not explicitly an address to a reader who is clearly positioned outside the narrative, as an imagined recipient, are normally instead taken to be someone talking to themselves: someone you, the other "you", the reader, can invisibly overhear, somehow. Whereas here, the speaker, who knows who they are, God probably, is addressing someone, not themself, someone who is the character. And that someone *is* you, "you", the reader. The you of the reader and the you of the protagonist are taken to be the same. And this is strange. Because I am actually not cool, at all. I would freak out. But I would kind of like it too, probably, having a foot put on my head like that. Maybe, I think, I am unlike this cowgirl. But in the story she, who is me, has no choices. I have to be cool. I have to click to show I am cool.

> do not freak out

No, even though you have spent the last six hours buried up to your neck in the desert, feeling the sun breathe hot in your ear, even though you now have the weight of Di's body pressing down on your tender noggin, you do not freak out because you are Capital-T Tuff.

That's what being a bandita's about. Being Tuff.

She playfully shakes your head like she's an aunt ruffling your hair, then steps off you. She extends her bare brown foot to you, the one you had just been wearing as a hat, like a kind of peace offering. She turns the canteen over and lets the water run down her leg, over her foot.

Do you **lick it off** or do you **refuse**?

Oh, I see. I have been buried in the sand all day. This changes things. I would definitely not like that. Also that explains the lack of choices. But now I do have a choice. And listen, I'm not stupid. Of course I lick it off. I'm thirsty.

> lick it off

You lick water off the cool vellum of her feet, you tongue the shallow pockets between her toes, you suck delicious moisture from the tips of her piglets. Your tongue, a moment ago dead and locked in the casket of your mouth, is fat with new life.

Diode sits down cross-legged in front of you. "Now that your tongue's in working order again, let's have ourselves a talk about what happened to those cred-chips, huh?" She reaches out and scritches you behind the ear, like a dog, smiling one of her fucking smiles. You bristle at the sight of it.

"Let's start the night of the heist. And **don't lie to mommy**."

"Fat with new life." I like that. Although often when I am thirsty, which is often, my tongue feels bigger, not smaller. Probably I, the reader, just haven't been thirsty enough. But I, the character, have. I know these things. Although I am being told them by God, these are my thoughts. And that seems fair enough. I mean, where do thoughts come from anyway? I've read Beckett. I know all about it. But then this woman whose foot I am licking asks me for something, and this is even stranger. Because she is asking me for information, and I don't have it. In fact, as a reader, and not as a person buried in the sand, I am eager to discover this same information, though for different, more frivolous, reasons. How can I tell her? Easy, I can click. And God, who, since she speaks for me, since she supplies my thoughts, I suppose is me too, even as she is radically not me, will supply.

> don't lie to mommy

Even if I hadn't made plans for the evening, Di's snoring would keep me awake easy. She's checked out after our very successful grab and subsequent, equally successful celebration. I slip out of the futon, quietly collecting my clothes, my boots, my big-ass satchel - and of course my ten-gallon hat. Our rayguns are still in the dock, charging back up after a busy day. Best to leave mine; I'll be able to buy a new one after the night is through. I'll be able to buy ten.

The insides of the porta-tent are lit up ghost-blue by the moonlight through the open flap. **Di's** asleep on the futon, her clothes black blobs scattered on the floor, like fat snails. My **canteen** is sitting by my feet. **The box** is over in the corner, covered by an old poncho. That about covers our shared possessions.

Outside, the desert quietly waits.

And I am in the past. The past has blue text. And because I am in the past, and no longer buried in the sand, I have significant agency. Except how can I? This has already happened, this can only lead to one place, and presumably only in one way. Maybe I just have a choice over which details to dwell on in this telling. Maybe it doesn't matter, within the past of the story, if I click on these things to look at them more closely. Maybe it only changes things for the audience, so that I, the reader will know more about what I do, even though I, the protagonist, will still do the same thing. Or maybe here the telling, as is sometimes the case, really does create the past it tells. This is not just a philosophical dilemma. As the reader, I want to know all the details, to acquire total knowledge about the story in order to become like the God whom I am, so far, radically unlike. If clicking just gives information, I will click on them all. But if clicking on them changes the story, then in clicking on them, to acquire knowledge, I will in fact be denying myself knowledge, of what would have happened if I did not click on them. And of course, as reader, I have at this point no way to know which of these possibilities is correct. So I try to make a different kind of choice. I try to choose not as a reader, but as a protagonist. As a protagonist, of course, I am hampered by my lack of knowledge about myself and my plans and desires. But I am clearly pulling a fast one. If the choices change the actual past of the story, I don't want to hang around. I want to get out of there. And if this is just a telling, if the choices only change the telling and not the past, I also don't want to tell Di any more than I have to. I want, either way, to move on quickly. So I do.

> Outside

Di slides two fingers into your mouth, silencing you. You look up at her, your cheeks burning a little.

"I thought I told you not to lie to me, bandita," she says. "We both know you left that tent with the cred-chips. Let's **try that again**."

My dilemma is solved. As the shift from the second into the first person and now back to the second also indicates, this is a telling. Instead of being told what is happening to me, I am telling what has happened to me. I can change nothing about the past, just as I cannot get out of the sand. And certain things are to be demanded of me, by my interrogator, by my own restless desire for closure, the nature of this fictional device.

> try that again

The insides of the porta-tent are lit up ghost-blue by the moonlight through the open flap. **Di's** asleep on the futon, her clothes black blobs scattered on the floor, like fat snails. My **canteen** is sitting by my feet. **The box** is over in the corner, covered by an old poncho. That about covers our shared possessions.

Outside, the desert quietly waits.

And the Robot Horse You Rode In On by Anna Anthropy

Instead I have a new dilemma: to balance my desire, as the reader, to find out as much as possible against my desire, as the protagonist, to conceal as much from Di as possible. Where are my loyalties? And how, as this strangely self-ignorant protagonist, am I even meant to determine which unknown details I want to conceal or reveal? It is not until, as a reader, I have clicked on all the links, that I can reasonably decide, as a protagonist, which ones to click on. But I cannot have my cake and eat it. In order to acquire knowledge it is necessary to reveal it. How do I know what I think until I see what I say? I decide to talk about Di.

> Di

She sleeps with her ankles crossed and her back straight, head resting on her shoulder like she fell asleep reading a book or something. I never got how anyone could sleep like this, or in any position other than sprawled across the bed like you fell that way, but she is out for another few hours at least, I can assure you.

What else?

I still am not able to leave. I am still compelled to speak, of what I do not know until I do speak. Fine then, the box, since that's what you want from me.

> What else?
> The box

Ah, yes, come to momma. Inside this metal box are a hundred small, hard cred-chips, tight-packed, a thousand credits on each of them. Silent as a wish, I slide the box out from under the poncho and tuck it into my satchel.

Now what?

I already knew this would be what I would do. Di has already told me I would do this. Now I tell her. I did it, ok? I think this is a lot of money. I wonder what I'm going to have spent it on.

> Now what?

Di's asleep on the futon, her clothes black blobs scattered on the floor, like fat snails. My **canteen** is sitting by my feet. That about covers our shared possessions.

Outside, the desert quietly waits.

played by Cat Fitzpatrick

So, now I can go outside. As a small protest against the exigencies of narrative form and/or being buried in the sand and interrogated I am not going to talk about the canteen. Not even going to look at it. Whatever.

I grab my canteen as I leave - I thoughtfully had Di fill it during a brief break in the revelry.

Do I **give one last look back** at Di as I leave the tent? Or do I **just leave**?

Ha! See I get the canteen anyway. I have to get the canteen anyway. I have to tell Di I got the canteen anyway. And yet I am being offered a choice again, some imitation of a choice. Perhaps this is it, this, as I shuttle along my ordained path, this is all I have, that I have to do what I have to do, but perhaps I can look back in regret. Or pretend I looked back in regret. Well I have my pride. I won't do it.

> just leave

Nope, I definitely do not spare that girl even one of my legendary backwards glances. Not even two.

Outside the tent, I pull on my clothes, my boots, my hat, all the accoutrements of the bandita experience. Clip the canteen to my belt, sling the satchel over my shoulder, feel the reassuring weight of the metal box inside it.

The desert glows alien blue beneath the nearer of the two moons. Standing motionless beside the tent, their bright LED eyes the only sign they're awake, alert, and ready to ride, are our robot mustangs.

Standing here like statues are Di's horse, **Quicksilver**, and my own horse, **Whore Palace**.

I like the horses' names. Or rather, I like my horse's name. Di's is ok, I guess. My respect for myself increases. I am clearly a person who knows about naming. I want to get on this wonderfully named robot horse and ride it further into this story. Giddyap!

> Whore Palace

I reach beneath Whore Palace and my tricky little fingers slide open a hidden panel in her belly. From inside my trusty horse I retreive my Little Miss EMP - it looks like a metal chapstick tube, with a fingernail-sized black panel on one end and a hot little button on the other.

And the Robot Horse You Rode In On by Anna Anthropy

What now?

Clearly one advantage of robot horses is that it is much easier to hide things inside them. I wonder what this device is, I'm assuming it's not a chapstick. Maybe a sex toy?

> What now?

Standing here like statues are Di's horse, **Quicksilver**, and my own horse, **Whore Palace**.

Look, I already told you, I want to ride my robot horse which no longer conceals what may be a futuristic sex toy into the future which is the past, or possibly the past which is the future. Which part of that don't you understand, God?

> Whore Palace

I was always way better at naming things than Di.

Standing here like statues are Di's horse, **Quicksilver**, and my own horse, **Whore Palace**.

I was! It is nice to have my own high self-estimation confirmed by myself. I wonder how Di feels about being reminded of my undoubted superiority by me whilst I am buried in sand. I hope she won't kick me.

> Whore Palace

I was always way better at naming things than Di. . .

I see how it is. Ok, yes, I see how it is. I am ruining the narrative continuity by my stubborn non-compliance. I am being ornery. But being ornery changes nothing, it only impedes the flow of what must be. Clearly I have unfinished business with that other horse. It's just you and me, horse. Here I come, horse.

> Quicksilver

I point Little Miss EMP at Quicksilver's underbelly, the spot where her nav-chip should be, and press the button. There's a small white flash, totally silent, as the horse's hardware fritzes inside her. Her LED eyes blink for a few seconds and go dead cold.

played by Cat Fitzpatrick

Just a temporary setback, of course, one that won't strand Di, only **delay her** a few hours.

So this is how you shoot a robot horse.

> delay her

"Delay me a few hours, provided I had the tools to fix it," Di interrupts. "You didn't know I had those tools, little miss."

"Yeah, you had a few pieces of tech I wasn't expecting," you reply.

"Well, let's not get ahead of ourselves. So, you **rode away from camp**."

I think this is foreshadowing. I am giving myself a clue as to what I now, as protagonist, know and will, as reader, come to discover. When you abandon your lovers in a desert with a broken horse, you ought to investigate their technology thoroughly first., in order to have all the necessary information to make a decision. Perhaps this lack of access to complete information is what is truly shared between me, the protagonist and me, the reader. I appear to be offering myself a warning, but it may be what I am really doing is establishing the true terms of our identity: our ignorance . Though I am still, I think, early in this game, I hypothesize this may be the lesson, the argument, it offers me: You never understand yourself, you never understand what you are doing, you never know what it would have been like if you chose something else, you just have to make choices even though you do not have adequate grounds, and see if you can proceed or not. When you cannot proceed you must make another choice. Perhaps I am overthinking this. But even if it is a genuine warning, it comes too late. I have already ridden out of camp. I may as well ride out of camp. And actually, that's what I wanted to do in the first place.

> rode away from camp

Yess, here is what a bandita lives for. The wind in her face and the humming of her robot steed between her legs while metal legs carry her across the desert's bare brown back. This is the kind of freedom that draws a girl out of some tin can town and into no man's land. And here, in this satchel resting against my side, is another kind of freedom that comes more easily in the lawless parts.

I am a bandit queen. All that the sun touches is mine, and the sun is peeking its pretty eye over the horizon to color in the land. To the **north** the ground gets rockier. Toward the

And the Robot Horse You Rode In On by Anna Anthropy

west, the sand turns black. To the **south** I can see clumps of grass sprout from the earth like patches of armpit hair. And somewhere to the east, Diode is sleeping like a baby.

This is still the past. This has still already happened. But it is, now, I think hopefully, the past Di does not know anything about. She knows I must have been the one to steal the money and shoot the horse, but she can't know for certain which way I went after that. This may mean that, since I do not know either, since no-one knows, since the link has not yet been selected, that the uncertainty principle applies, and that in this telling I really do determine something that is still at the point of telling undetermined even though once it is determined it will have already happened. Or it could mean I am just telling Di a story, that I have the option of misleading her, or of being honest with her. But what do I want? If I am trying to lie, I can't know which one is the lie, or which the truth, let alone whether it is better to lie to her or be truthful with her, so one choice is as good as another. If I am really making this decision though, I feel much more confortable going where there are plants.

> south

Grass grows thin and wiry in bristly little clumps. A desert of little black pubes. Spindly, grasping shadows crawl from the base of each patch, long in the morning light. To the **north**, the grasses withdraw their claim to the earth. To the **west** they give way to larger plants: mammoth cactuses in silhouette. To the **south** a green river runs from west to east.

Further choices. Either there are choices or there aren't. But in a desert a river is a good idea. Onwards, Whore Palace!

> south

As free as the wind rustling a girl's hair, I crash through the cold green river on the back of my robot steed, letting out a whoop as I do, a wild howl that fills the plains and announces my sovereignity of the country that awaits me beyond the river. Green foam flies up after us as we emerge, only to sizzle on the sand. We ride on into our new country, into our desert.

We ride for miles, we race like eagles. And though it's hard to tell from the featureless brown landscape, I can't help but gradually become aware that Whore Palace is slowing down. Does she need a rest? She's a robot! Then there's a loud spark and I duck like someone fired a pistol. But this isn't a shoot-out, it's a **blow-out**.

played by Cat Fitzpatrick

WAIT! Why am I leaving the river behind? I am an idiot. This is clearly a bad choice. I am good at naming but horrible at life decisions. Or maybe I just want Di to think I am horrible at life decisions. But if I wasn't at least a bit horrible, she wouldn't have caught me and buried me in this pit. I am horrible at life decisions and this (see above) is what unites the fractured parts of my consciousness within this narrative. I feel a lot of empathy for myself. This terrible choice I am making is just the kind of terrible choice I would make.

> blow-out

Stupid. I left the panel on Whore Palace's belly open when I retrieved Little Miss EMP. Now her circuitry's fried. I could kick myself. Or I could have Whore Palace kick me, if I hadn't just turned her into a useless tin can.

I swing myself off of her. Where am I, anyway? Brown in all directions - not very useful. In my revelry, I'm not one hundred percent sure which way I've been riding. Well, if one direction is as good as any other, might as well **get walking**.

At least I am getting some exercise. Well actually, I am spending Sunday afternoon in bed by myself and it is already dark outside. But at least something I am participating in is pretending I am getting some exercise. At least I am showing willing.

> get walking

Now the sun is up, climbing toward its high-noon throne. The heat falls in carpets on the burnt brown land. I take off my hat and fan myself with it, sucking on my lips just to hear the sound. I can feel them cracking like the ground, tumbleweed rolling across my tongue.

I reach for my side and pat my canteen, just to remind myself it's there. A full canteen suddenly doesn't feel as full as it used to. I'm sorely tempted to **take a long, cool swig** - a greenhorn impulse. I know I have to make it last. I should just **keep walking**.

The font had become yellow, which is a color I associate with the present, and so with the possibility of agency. I decide to take this as a good sign. However, the pronouns are still first person. I take this as a bad sign. This is really fucking with my head. I am unclear if I actually get to drink the water. But I am going to say I did. I would like to have drunk the water.

And the Robot Horse You Rode In On by Anna Anthropy

> take a long, cool swig

The POP of the cap leaving my canteen is the most satisfying thing I've heard since Di grinned at me and said "we're rich." A chip in the bottle keeps the water cold - I throw my head back and gulp like I'm a prodigal fish who just rediscovered the stuff. I suck an oasis down my throat, life in the desert, goddamn miracle. I go maybe a bit overboard, because when I detach the canteen from my lips with a second POP and a satisfied "aaah," it's almost empty.

But that realization takes second place to the other one, which happens when I notice the **tiny homing beacon** at the bottom of the canteen.

That bitch!

> tiny homing beacon

"You didn't trust me," you accuse, a little petulant.

"My momma always told me never to trust a bandita," Diode smiles, "especially one that's good in the sack. Anyway, you found your way **out of the desert** sooner or later, I know that."

It is nice to know I am good in the sack. This is not really a confirmation you get offered in real life. I mean, I suppose it's not one I seek. I'm not sure there is any such thing, exactly. People are very complex, and their interactions even more so, and for me enjoying sex has been very difficult, and definitely a lot to do with trust and self love, rather than any kind of technical mastery. Still, if I was a fictional character, and this fictional character was capable of being perceived as good at sex, that would definitely be my preference. It is also nice to have confirmation that I am existing, or narrating myself, or being narrated, in a lacuna. Di knows I went in to the desert, she knows I went out, but she does not know what happened in between, Unless she is lying to me. There are so many positions of knowledge to keep track of in this game. It is nearly as confusing as life.

> out of the desert

After all that brown, imagine my surprise at seeing a slightly different brown. It's a **signpost** - leading away from it in are roads in all directions, faint but definitely there! It looks like this neck of the desert hasn't been scratched in a while.

I do some quick estimation. Noon now, I left before dawn, I

rode yea far, walked for friggin' years, give Di a few hours to wake up, a few hours to fix the horse (provided she has the tools). On horseback, it'll probably take her upwards of a god damn minute to find this place after she sniffs out where I ditched the canteen, and if that horse is working then Di is on it and heading my way right now.

By my math, that gives me not a lot of time to find a hiding place for the satchel and to put sufficient distance between it and myself before Di shows up.

> signpost

NORTH - MINE

WEST - ROBOT FARM

SOUTH - GRAVEYARD

Where do I go? I go to the graveyard, of course. Haven't you learned anything about me yet?

> SOUTH

It's a graveyard, alright. One of the few human institutions that goes right on being what it is after there's no one left to maintain it. Most of the gravestones seemed to have been of the cheap wooden variety (well, synth-wood, more likely) and are uprooted or gone. There are a few survivors, though:

There's a **straight-up stone one**, thick and heavy like tombstones are supposed to be. Then, next to that, a **plastic model**, shaped to look like the stone kind but noticably rounder and duller. There's **one made of plasteel** that just looks like someone stuck a dinner tray in the ground and **a small metal marker** fashioned into the vague shape of a flower, with a plaque attached.

At the edge of the graveyard, the **undertaker's house**. North of here, a trail leads back to **the crossroads**.

The graveyard is not subject to uncertainty. It goes on being itself. Perhaps it was because of some intuition about this that I felt so drawn to it. I find the graveyard very comforting. I would like to stay here, maybe dig myself a grave and just get into it, but that is not how it is in life or stories, which are like sharks, and have to keep moving. I am going to look at all the gravestones.

> one made of plasteel

And the Robot Horse You Rode In On by Anna Anthropy

POLESTAR WENCH

ONE DEATH JUST WASN'T

ENOUGH FOR HER

Hm.

> Hm.
> straight-up stone one

HERE LIES ANNIE,

WHO LEARNED THAT THE ONLY THING

DEADLIER THAN A BULLET

IS A BROKEN HEART

Hm.

> Hm.
> small metal marker

R.I.P. JANICE

SHE REACHED FOR THE STARS,

BUT THEY HADN'T BEEN PROPERLY

FASTENED TO THE TREE.

Hm.

All these sad dead ladies who made bad life decisions. They are my sisters.

> Hm.
> undertaker's house

A small synth-wood house resembling a cardboard box on the inside. An empty cardboard box, or very nearly. There's an oily desk that looks like it once survived a fire, but not by much. Nothing on it. Next to that, a pile of what used to be a bed. And an old **plasteel shovel** leans against the far wall.

Outside, the **graveyard** where this person, when she lived, toiled in service to the dead.

I note that the undertaker was a woman. I think probably everyone in

played by Cat Fitzpatrick

this narrative space is a woman. I am a woman, Di is a woman, all the dead ladies are women, God, I already suggested, is surely a woman, and now the undertaker. What happens to all the men? Maybe there are just never any men, I guess that would be nice. Maybe everyone who used to be a man got a clue and became a woman. I know God in this universe is a trans lady and me too, so that would make sense. I don't know about the undertaker, but I'm going to choose to believe it about her, out of goodwill.

> plasteel shovel

I snatch up the old shovel and return to the **graveyard**.

Now I can dig up my sisters. This game is really working out for me so far. Annie first. Hello Annie here I come.

> graveyard
> straight-up stone one

HERE LIES ANNIE,

WHO LEARNED THAT THE ONLY THING

DEADLIER THAN A BULLET

IS A BROKEN HEART

Should I **dig this one up**? Or **maybe a different one**?

> dig this one up

I push the shovel into the ground. It's not soft, but fortunately our friend's not buried very deep. I hit bones in just a few minutes. Not all of the bones, or even most of them, but enough to pretend to have a conversation with, I guess.

I dump the satchel and its burden into the open grave. You may have died in poverty, sweetheart, but you're rich **now**.

I wonder what I say to the bones as I dig them up. Hello Annie how are you never mind about the heartbreak it's gone now. A broken leg would be a different matter. But you don't care, do you, you're not really all there. And so on.

> now

"So that's where my money is, eh?" asks Diode, standing. "Alright."

And the Robot Horse You Rode In On by Anna Anthropy

You turn your head as far as you can to watch her disappear into the porta-tent. "Now, if you're lying," she calls from inside, "and I'm not saying I don't believe you, babe, but propriety forces me to consider the possibility - well, in that case I'm going to have to examine whether I'm adequately impressing upon you the gravity of this situation."

She reappears, tossing a coil of rope on the ground in front of you. The end has been fashioned into a noose. You gulp, while you still can.

Di pulls on her boots, bright red with little white rockets on them. "Now you **stay put**, sweetheart. I'll be back in two shakes of a lamb-bot's tail." She climbs onto Quicksilver, flashes you that smile you're growing to hate so much, and rides off in the direction of your cred-chips, leaving you in the ground.

I am back in the present! Finally. Now I have the agency to not have any agency, because I am buried up to my neck. It was a lot of work to get back to where I started but it was worth it. I'm only sorry I didn't dig up more graves on the way.

> stay put

Minutes pass. You're not sure how many. Time is hard when you're buried to your neck in the desert. But finally your pricked ears pick out what they're listening for: the metal clop clop of robot hooves. If your arms weren't tied and underground, you'd pat yourself on the back. Story time was just the perfect length.

Of course a little bit of water's not gonna junk your beautiful Whore Palace. She just needed a while to dry off and reboot.

"Good girl! Now grab that rope!"

Time is also hard in text based adventures. This paragraph could last any amount. This is part of why text is so good: there's less waiting around. Thank God my horse got here so fast.

> Good girl! Now grab that rope!

Whore Palace lowers her head and grabs the end of the rope in her metal chompers, lifting it off the ground.

"Now throw the other end to mommy!"

It is strange that I think I am the mother of a robot horse. Perhaps this

played by Cat Fitzpatrick

does something to explain why I seem to be so bad at romantic relationships. The horse must have very good language recognition software to cope with this complicated human emotional transference.

> Now throw the other end to mommy!

She tosses the noose to you. You grab it with your teeth, thankful that in this enlightened age even a lawless bandit like yourself is guaranteed quality dental care.

"Nhh PHLL, Whrrr Prrss!"

Really, very good language processing.

> Nhh PHLL!

You emerge from the earth like a worm, naked and squirming, red and scabbed with dirt. You lie panting as your faithful steed chomps through the ropes on your wrists and ankles, and you wait for the itching all over your body to go away, or at least to fade to a background sizzle.

Then you get to your feet - not an easy task. It takes most veggies at least a week after harvest before they take their first steps. But now is the time for action, and action waits for no woman! The **porta-tent** sits here in the sunset, a big cerulean rhombus. **Whore Palace**, your trusty steed, waits patiently to take you away from all this.

It's pretty warm; I don't think I need clothes or anything.

> Whore Palace

You thoughtfully close the hidden panel on Whore Palace's underbelly before you swing onto her metal back. Then you and your robot steed ride off into a desert streaked with red and blue by the sunset.

It's been a while since you've ridden nude. The vibration between your legs is conspiring with the fixation on Di occupying your mind. You can't help it; you experience the orgasm as a wave of campfire heat passing over your body, a hot flush that moves from your tummy to your toes. You let it pass through you, leaving steely resolution behind.

You take a shortcut and soon arrive at the **crossroads**.

So it wasn't just me, the reader, who felt she might almost enjoy Di's boot on my head. Me the protagonist also got something out of it. I began with a feeling of distance and perplexity, but I am starting to feel very close to this bandita, very familiar. I am really identifying. Reading about her having an orgasm makes me want to have one too, but I don't have a robot horse.

> crossroads

It looks different at dusk than at high noon, almost like an alien world, red sand beneath a yellow sky. The old **signpost** adds to it, this weird black silhouette marking the place where the four roads meet, never ending, but merging seamlessly into a shadow that races across the desert to meet the night as it comes.

Let's see if you can get those chips before Diode does.

I only just noticed that the sun in the background changes according to the time of day being narrated! That is a nice touch. It is really making things feel crepuscular.

> signpost

NORTH - MINE

WEST - ROBOT FARM

SOUTH - GRAVEYARD

EAST - TOWN

I am being given a choice again about where to go. This raises the question as to whether I was lying before when I told Di about the graveyard. Do I now get to decide whether that was a lie? Like, if I go to the graveyard, maybe it was true, but if I go to the town it wasn't? Or does God know where I hid the gold, and will she tell me if I choose the wrong place? I am uncertain both about where I went and whether I lied. I don't know what happened in the past but I remain hopeful I can change it by my actions in the present. I have begun to feel very close to myself and yet I am a complete mystery to myself. Although it is sad to remove my time with Annie in the shallow pit from the realm of what actually happened and consign it, even within this fiction, to the realm of fiction, I am going to the town. I am naked, so that seems like the worst possible decision, and therefore the one I would probably find myself making if this were me, which it is. My experience so far in this universe tells me trying to make better decisions is not going to get you anywhere, and you may as well accept it.

played by Cat Fitzpatrick

> EAST

The old ghost town is even spookier at dusk than it was the last time you were here - to stash those cred-chips. You can only hope that Diode believed your lie - that if she's come this way already, she's hunting for the chips where you said they'd be.

You slide down from Whore Palace's back. This place was never really much of a town, and it's even less so now. Just a single street lined with ramshackle synth-wood houses, ominous in the deepening darkness. In the middle of town, adding to the eeriness, is a wide, twelve-foot deep pit. They probably put prisoners down there, and who knows what the townspeople would do to them. You bet they peed on 'em.

A classic ghost town. Population: you, and one hundred thousand credits. Better **grab 'em** while you can.

It is a ghost town. I wonder about this. This society is enlightened enough to have free good dentistry now, but at some recent point, since the invention of synth-wood, it has gone through a period of barbarism which involved the keeping of prisoners in large pits in towns that were then abandoned. What has happened here? What has been reconstructed? Where do all the dentists come from? Why are none of them here? Why do we need synth wood? Because now I think of it, I don't believe I have seen any trees so far. What happened to all the trees? These historical considerations add to my sense of foreboding. I am in full agreement with the only option that is offered me.

> grab 'em

You take a few steps toward the old buildings and then stop in your tracks. There, under the swinging doors of the old saloon, you make out two tall boots: bright red with little white rockets. Shit, Di beat you here! But she doesn't seem to have spotted you yet!

You could jump and **tackle her**! Or you could **sneak up** and make sure it's really her. But you'd better do something!

I am naked and unarmed. If we have established anything, it is that recklessness is my MO. You think I'm going to creep up on her?

> tackle her

You bend your knees and then POUNCE through the swing-

And the Robot Horse You Rode In On by Anna Anthropy

ing doors, landing with a painful whump on what turn out to be a pair of empty boots. Rubbing your head, you climb out of the saloon - to meet Diode, barefoot, with that smug grin on her face and a raygun trained on you. "Fancy meeting you here. "And now, sweetheart, you're going to take me to my credits."

But instead you ask, "**How'd you get here so fast?**"

Is that a raygun in your hand or are you just pleased to see me naked? Also, how did I get from hiding the credits to being buried in a pit naked? I just realized no-one told me that. And if no-one told me, did it even happen?

> How'd you get here so fast?

"Sorry, bandita, but you're just not a very convincing liar. There is no headstone in that graveyard matching the name you gave me. But you were right, there weren't very many left to check. This little ghost town was suspiciously absent from your tale. Pretty big omission if you asked me. And sure enough, not long after I arrive who should I see on the horizon but my favorite gal."

She gestures with her raygun, and you wince like she poked you. "Now, then. My credits. **Lead the way**."

Annie never even existed to lie about! This makes me wish I had chosen another one of the dead girls, maybe Polestar Wench, to lie about hiding the credits in the corpse of in order to make her turn out to never have existed after all. Or perhaps that I had tried to go to the graveyard after I got out of the pit in order to make the story I told Di true after all. These are the kinds of temporal contortions this type of gameplay draws you into. This must be what it is like to be a strict Calvinist. I feel sorry for strict Calvinists. Then I wonder if I have ever even been to the graveyard. If I haven't I don't know how I would know about it. But if I have you would think I would choose a real grave to make the diversion last longer. Maybe I have been but forgot the names of all the graves and made them all up. This is sad because then all the girls in those graves never even existed even in a fictional universe, which is probably even worse than dying of a broken heart.

> Lead the way

There's a street of houses in front of you, brown-black in the setting sun - a **blacksmith's**, an **apothecary**, an **old church** - and there's a bitch with a raygun behind you. Well, no point in dragging this out. You'd better show her where the chips fell.

played by Cat Fitzpatrick

  Again, I am given the apparent option of choosing which of several things has already happened. Perhaps again I can possibly lie. But how can I lie if I don't know what is true? How will I ever choose? I just have to choose. Church is probably the most dramatic.

  > old church

You push the door open. It stays that way. The whole place seems frozen in time, preserved beneath a coat of dust and cobwebs - save for a few faint footprints, invisible unless you know where to find them. They lead **upstairs**.

You can feel **Di's** eyes and raygun on your back, like a nervous itch.

  I have to do something. Maybe I can talk to Di or something. This is a very bad situation.

  > Di

Di stands with her raygun trained on you and her hand on her crotch, rubbing her little bulge through her jeans. "Look at you, all flushed. Did you come on the way here, riding that horse with the stupid name? You'd better have enjoyed it, cus it's gonna be your last."

She gives the trigger a little squeeze. Urgh. Nothing to do but **go upstairs**.

  Di is totally a trans lady! Everyone here is a trans lady—me, God, Di, the undertaker. This is very exciting. I bet the pit was made by cis people but then they all ate each other or something, and now we're all that's left, and we're very enlightened and have excellent free dentistry but also unconquerable adventurous souls so that we go off and be banditas sometimes. But where is Di's sense of sisterhood? I mean, I know I stole from her, but surely we can work this out? We're just being banditas for fun, and we can probably go back to free dentistry and everything else any time we want. Also, I am very offended that she thinks my horse's name is stupid.

  > go upstairs

It's almost like a carpeted staircase, this thick layer of dust that clings to your feet, painting your soles black. Each stair creaks beneath you like the wailing of some lost soul.

At the top of the stairs is a modest living chamber - more

And the Robot Horse You Rode In On by Anna Anthropy

modest, now, thanks to the passage of time. You can make out the few remaning contents in the faint light from the window - there's a desk against the far wall, with a **small box** underneath it, a **big steamer trunk** against the other wall, an empty table and some plain, synth-wood chairs, and a **round box**, maybe a hat-box, in the corner.

"Alright, babe. Bring me my chips," orders Di.

    Who lives in a church? Haven't these people heard of rectories?

    > small box

You slide open the dusty old box for the second time. And there it is, just where you left it, your big-ass satchel, wondering where you've been.

"Give momma what she came for, girl."

You **reach into** your satchel.

    Maybe I am finally going to make a good decision. It would be about time.

    > reach into

ZAP! You pull Little Miss EMP out of your satchel and blast Di's raygun. It fritzes and goes dead in her hands.

No one moves for a moment.

Then she screams "You FUCKING BITCH," tossing her useless pistol as she jumps for you. She hits you like a robot bull crashing through a china shop, because that's almost exactly what happens, at least as far as the shattering of glass is concerned. You smash through the window and tumble in each other's arms through a carnival of glass toward the **ground**.

    Ha! Yes! Take that raygun lady! And it's a fair fight now! Also it is notable that I think she is like a robot bull. Maybe as well as no trees there are no animals. Cis people ruined that too.

    > ground

ARRRGHH.

You hit the ground hard, together, your groans almost as loud as the crunch of your bones breaking. Window glass rains

played by Cat Fitzpatrick

down on you like a hail of knives. You shield your face with your arm, screaming as it suffers a thousand slices, but your body's already marked with a hundred tiny, burning cuts. Your legs feel really heavy, and it doesn't seem like you can move them. Oh shit oh shit.

To your left, you can hear Diode whimpering. You turn toward her, your body screaming in pain as you move. She's crawling toward her horse, her hair damp with blood, her clothes torn and cut, her limbs trembling uncontrollably.

"Where the FUCK ARE YOU GOING, ASSHOLE?!"

That is very gruesome and painful. It sounds awful. I can't believe this is happening to me. Ok she is going toward her horse. I kind of just want to let her go so maybe we can both get out of his alive. But I can't let her go. I just can't let her go.

> Where the FUCK ARE YOU GOING

You jump on her, your dead legs dragging behind you, pushing her broken body to the ground. You both scream in agony.

"Fuck you!" she yells, her voice raspy and raw. "Fuck you and all your stupid shit that I have to deal with! Fuck you and your lies! We would have SPLIT that fucking gold, why did you have to be such a bitch?!"

She jerks her elbow into you hard and you tumble off of her, your cut back sparkling with pain as it touches the ground.

"Quicksilver!" she yells in a horrible, hoarse voice, and her robot steed comes obediently running towards you.

You scream...

"Fuck you and your stupid horse's stupid name!"

"Fuck you and the dumb fucking way you sleep!"

"Fuck you and your know-it-all fucking smile!"

Why didn't I split that gold? Why did I have to be such a bitch? Why, even now, can't I let it go? What is wrong with me? I even lied about those dead girls. Although I'm inventive, you have to give me that. My talent for naming is pretty much my only redeeming feature.

> Fuck you and your stupid horse's stupid name!

You point Little Miss EMP at the horse and blast her. She does

And the Robot Horse You Rode In On by Anna Anthropy

a hideous, stumbling dance and then topples over in a heap, her LED eyes blinking off.

"FUCK YOU!" Di yells, punching you in the face with a sharp crack. She grabs Little Miss EMP out of your hand and then punches you again. "You lazy, greedy fuck! I planned the heist, I did all the fucking work, that's my goddamn money!"

And she turns and blasts Whore Palace, who sparks and quietly turns off.

You shout...

"Fuck you, you fucking momma's girl! My momma always told me this, my momma said don't do that! I'm fucking sick of your momma! My momma was poor and I'm not gonna be!"

"Fuck you, you snoring piece of shit! Do you know the last time I got a real night's sleep? No?! Me neither, asshole! I deserve this money for putting up with you!"

"Fuck you for almost getting us killed! If I hadn't shot that guy, we wouldn't have made it out of there with that money in the first place! It's my money!"

Oh Whore Palace! You were such a good horse. She's done it now. And her snoring really is very annoying.

> Fuck you, you snoring piece of shit!

You punch her, and you punch her again. Your every joint groaning in agony as you do it, but you do it anyway, her body meat under your knuckles.

"God!" she yells, kicking you with her good leg, "FUCK!," smacking you with her fist. She hits you again and again. "You are the WORST LITTLE BULLSHIT QUEEN! You're fucking petty and you're fucking needy and you sound like a goddamn horse during sex! I fucking hate you!"

You yell...

"You're bossy and greedy and shitty and I FUCKING HATE YOU!!"

"You're bitchy and vulgar and stuck-up and I FUCKING HATE YOU!!"

"You're condescending and gross and awful and I FUCKING HATE YOU!!"

played by Cat Fitzpatrick

I sound like a horse during sex? You should hear how she sounds. I'm going with bossy and greedy and shitty.

> You're bossy and greedy and shitty and I FUCKING HATE YOU

Now you're just screaming, screaming in her face, and she's screaming back, and you're punching each other and biting each other and rolling around with your broken burning bodies tumbling over and over and cursing and-

SHIT

FALLING

I am literally only just now fully realizing and accepting that this game is not going to end well. This is not really a game about being a bandita, it is a game about being in a relationship with another trans lady, and I mean, that can end well, I've heard of it ending well, but let's just say, it hasn't for me when I've tried it. In any case, this game is not going to end well. Things are not going to be okay for me. It is actually not going to end well.

> FALLING

You land on your backs with a sickening thud, your limbs sprawling like useless salamis. You can hear Di crying to your right, sobbing like a baby, but it hurts to turn your head. You just stare up at the sky from what must be the bottom of the pit in the center of town, your body a dull throb around you. It's getting dark, and the stars are starting to appear.

You just lie there a while. It hurts enough just to breathe. You notice that Di's tears have quieted, too, to a raspy inhale-exhale. Then you can hear her shifting around a little beside you, groaning as she does so. Then, a dry, brittle, choking sound. You realize that she's laughing.

"Wanna make out?" she cackles.

You answer **yes** or **no**.

Now I know what this game is about, what can I answer? Of course I say yes.

> yes

You laugh, your voice a strained croak. "Why the hell not."

She pushes herself up on broken arms, groaning under the strain, and manages to inch close enough so you can turn

And the Robot Horse You Rode In On by Anna Anthropy

your head and find her mouth. She pushes her tongue inside, sucks on your lip, gives it a soft bite.

Damn, you think. Girl can still kiss. And then the two of you lie back and watch the stars.

No comment.

ELECTRO PRIMITIVE GIRL

BY SLOANE
PLAYED BY AEVEE BEE

Anime is basically my favorite pop culture garbage. I like anime fairly unironically, which is a problematic fav to have as anime is, in general, as reinforcing and uncritical of the status quo as anything else. Which is not to say there isn't, like there always is, truly boundary-breaking and important work in the genre, but that a lot of what I like comes from the imagery and aesthetics of anime rather than its intended meanings. Giant robot shows always have these huge colorful and impossibly powerful machines that shoot pink lasers and there's always this mysterious girl with this secret power. When I watched these shows as a kid, I really wanted to be one of those super cool mysterious beautiful fairy-like aliens, and I still kind of do, no matter how much I know intellectually that no matter how strong the girls start out, they're ultimately going to lose all their agency to the hero as he comes into his own, the prize he gets for growing up and mastering an anthropomorphic war engine. The girls are always a billion times cooler, but it's always his story, not hers.

Electro Primitive Girl grasps all the aesthetics of mecha that glow and also how much the genre, like everything, always turns around and breaks your heart. It's about the girl this time; it's about aesthetics and energy and painful relationships with boys. Liking mecha shows can be a bit like having a relationship with a smug shitty boyfriend so this works on many levels.

Electro Primitive Girl by Sloane

None of the garbage parts of anime are there. It's like a music video that has imagery and feeling and power and builds a world but that doesn't play tropes straight and doesn't take the wrong parts of it too seriously, the way that science fiction becomes so in love with explaining itself that it loses what it's actually about.

> me: so she says "they say a battery is like a heart! yea right!"
>
> i: no way
>
> i: what a JERK
>
> me: yea
>
> me: and she turns to me and is like 'lol no offense'
>
> i: D:<
>
> i: what a @#$%&
>
> me: ikr
>
> me: oh hold on bf is sending me a txt
>
> i: k
>
> me: **uggggh**

I like that her internal conflict is portrayed through a chat client, using chat client lingo, it's very casual and human which is to the point because she's sort of technically not. Part of why I love mecha shows despite all the science fiction nonsense is that in the end everyone's still a sad stupid teen and it's so believable that they'd still be like that if the world was ending.

> > uggggh

> me: his txt says 'stay in doors!!! dangerous outside!! alien attack!!'
>
> i: lol
>
> me: ugh I don't feel like fighting tonight
>
> i: I know but we have to
>
> i: we're getting stronger anyway. It'll be easy
>
> me: maybe if he lets us take control! he's always trying to over-pilot us
>
> i: true
>
> i: he'll learn to relax eventually

me: I hope. mech pilots are so emotional ;p

i: which is what we need. that energy. but only in tandem with our goals

me: yeaaa **I guess**

I love that the boy is the too emotional one here. Mecha shows tend to have very emotional men in them, actually; boys' heroes in anime get to be emotional in celebrated ways, whereas girls are the ones whom boys coax the emotions out of. Girls are often quite literally machines, like in this game, and it's for boys to teach them about human stuff like love etc. so they'll become their girlfriends and stop fighting and doing things. It's a creepy kind of fantasy, as the girls get to maybe be powerful or strong fighters for a little while but they don't have any emotional agency of their own.

> I guess

HEXABELL! MELEE MODE ACTIVATE! LET'S GOOOO!!!

me: . . .

i: . . .

me: maybe you should . . .

i: i know i know

i: his little catchphrase is kinda lame

i: trust me

i: i'm aware

Logout

Making fun of his catchphrase is pretty funny, but it's telling that she's not saying this to his face or anything. His fantasy doesn't get interrupted.

> Logout

That little scrub. He doesn't know how good **he** has it. Having a mecha girlfriend like **us**.

Both of these choices go to the same place ultimately, but you won't get the description of the pilot if you don't click on *us*; it'll just skip ahead. A lot of Twine games want to make sure that readers can see and go back to all descriptive choices, but here the pace keeps moving, which suits the game and the genre it's pulling from better. Unlike the page of a book, Twine can pull readers forward, maybe even more quickly than they're ready for.

> he

Him.

Wanna-be freelance pilot. Never touched a mobile suit in his life.

Boys don't belong in mechs. They're not delicate enough to thread incisions through their enemy just so. They can't cook alien flesh until its so tender it melts. **Girls make the mech**.

Boys don't dance past their opponents. They smash and break and stomp. *Only a girl could summon a lazer this pink.*

Why couldn't someone better have found us.

Someone that understands our **insides**. Someone that knows how to touch.

    She's pink and the text is pink and the laser is pink. In anime they always give the characters these impossible beautiful hair colors which will become a consistent theme they're associated with, and that works because it's a visual medium of intense colors. Twine can do that too, and it works in this story because of the influences it's playing with.

> insides

There is two of us.

We share bodies.

We are the same being.

We are halves of a whole.

Synchronicity is not essential to us like it is for *others*.

We grow and contract and **divide**.

    Electro Primitive Girl is aesthetically intense and doesn't really care about explaining or developing the science fiction logic and excuses for how it works and thank god. The premise of a giant robot is inherently impractical and they exist because they're metaphors and extensions of the self and because toy companies want to sell them, and the more honest the show is about that the closer it gets to the truth. I like science fiction nonsense when it sounds cool and doesn't mean anything but the emotional and human implications of how that stuff feels and knows it, like here.

> divide

played by Aevee Bee

One of our bodies is very small. Small-us is pocket-sized in comparison to the big-us, covered in bandages occasionaly. My nodes are sensitive. Small-us is a spider's nest of silicon and shining alloys.

Pull a layer of skin over small-metal-us and we pass for **human**. My eyes glitch blue.

If you're observant you will hear our heart that only hums.

(A battery can be a heart if you believe it to be.)

> human

People look at me and say:

Cute.

Ugly.

Small.

Fat.

Strong.

Cyborg .

Glitch.

It.

    I love the imagery. This is exactly the sort of fragile not-human heroine you'd see in anime and beyond but she gets to describe herself. For all the hyper-awareness that boy heroes have of women it's just about their own attraction. No one's asking her what's it like to have a body, how do you feel about it?

    Here we get an answer and her answer is: not great. Insecure and not traditionally beautiful, that's a big departure from the anime cliche who is depicted as being nearly unaware of her own body. It's not something that matters to a boy hero or the men who want to tell stories about them.

> It

There is big-us.

People look at us and say:

Massive.

Electro Primitive Girl by Sloane

Monster.

Death.

It.

If we lift our hand we can scrape the light from the stars. We are electrobubblegum. Lady Godzilla.

But we never have to strain very much. The **stars** come to us.

> Electrobubblegum is such a perfect word for describing all of this.

> stars

. . . . .

The ground beneath the crystal city shakes because we are under it, moving, unfolding.

Big-us sleeps in an abandoned underground army hangar, thick cables wrapped around us, feeding, nuturing. Pink and blue and yellow wires hang from my spine, throat, heart, **mouth.**

(Didn't this used to move? It didn't on the version I played for this book, but I swear it did before.)
I'm writing about video games despite spending a great deal of my life in creative writing programs in part because I don't really like narrative that much. I like character and imagery and I don't really care about the plot, and video games, because they are nonlinear (and many other reasons) allow for a certain amount of wandering and taking in the imagery and experience of the world. Sloane writes this more like a prose poem than a short story, and I think that writing is a better fit.

Little-us faints on the spot. Sometimes it is in our boyfriend's arms.

We moan because we don't have control over our small-body anymore. This upsets him. He thinks we are hurt.

We are not in pain.

It's static.

Moaning is **our** screensaver.

played by Aevee Bee

> our

We're both inside big-us now. Primed. Ready to fight. Vibrating.

Body flushed white and sparkling red, pink, green.

We rise up through subway tunnels and sewer pipes, cement crumbling around us like clotted sugar.

We can't count how many times we've **ravaged** this city in **battle**.

When you click on "ravaged" it adds the word "accidentally" in front of it, which is such a clever way to convey her attitude towards the city and the people.

> battle

We are above ground now, stretching out mile-long arms, freeway legs. Our fingers curl into fists as big as a starship.

The tension in our spine increases and the data overlaid on our optic nerves inform us of the imminent danger.

DANGER

ENEMY IN RANGE

SYSTEM ARMED

LOCATING PILOT...

Our mecha body snarls, metal teeth gnashing.

Who needs a **pilot** anyway.

> pilot

We find him grudgingly. He's always getting in the way.

He grins at us cockily when we lift him up in our palm, blonde hair tousled by the high altitude breeze.

We think about squashing him between our thumb and index finger. Burning him up with our dragonfruit pink lazer eyes.

Big-us sighs. Maybe next time.

He crawls into our mouth and upwards into our skull, up the

Electro Primitive Girl by Sloane

staircase of our teeth.

The crystalline **controls** drone and glow beneath his fingers as he slides into the pilot seat.

    The pilot is unwanted, extraneous, a burden, arrogant—she doesn't want him, but she's tied to him anyway, like a bad boyfriend you can't find a way to break up with or an anime you keep watching even when it disgusts you. The choices in this game put the pilot's life in the mecha girlfriend's hands, and she gets to have the agency that characters like her are never allowed to have.

    > controls

Suddenly a searing red light comes shooting through the building to our l

We lunge forward and our pilot screams, the sound echoing whitehot in our skull.

We can feel part of our ribs are obliterated, burned and liquefied.

We see **her** now.

    > her

She matches us in size but not in elegance. She is a landfill of gobbled up bones and Martian scales.

Her body is hungry, cells flooding around buildings and people, folding over them and absorbing.

Eating

Eating

Eating

Eating

Eating

Eating

Ah. She smells **us**.

    > us

played by Aevee Bee

There is no time to waste. Not for a creature so ravenous.

We lunge forward, teeth bared, fingers splayed.

Our **jaws** latch around her neck.

We can feel our pilot pulling us back, manipulating our tendons, forcing our teeth apart.

*Hexabell! Go for her **heart**!*

> heart

We don't have time to fight both of them.

We unhinge our jaw from the aliens throat and are immediately met with a 10-clawed hand to our face, the edges of her serrated nails digging into our cheeks.

She screams sharply, a decibel that shatters most of the glass within a mile radius of us.

Both our hands are busy trying to pry the talons from our skull, the pilots chamber groaning under the pressure. Blood seeps in around him.

Hexabell, I know you can do this! Get her off! Do it, you idiot! ***Overdrive****!*

    The overdrive section is timed—they'll both die if you don't click it soon enough. I rarely like reflex challenges in Twine as they aren't things you're prepared for, and they force you into a choice you didn't realize you were making. The constantly flashing choices and action-y aesthetics of this game though do feel like as much preparation as you could ever reasonably get.

    Twine complicates failure (potentially) like few other games can. Failure is undesirable, failure is bad, but in Twine it's about unfolding a possible story. A story that ends in death or failure for the protagonist wouldn't be called a bad or undesirable story but a story that is about death or failure. Though many people in games studies are interested in how games can be a safe place to fail, few games are interested in allowing a failure state to stand; you are supposed to keep playing until you don't fail. I would like more Twine stories to leave "failures" as valid endings.

> Overdrive

DANGER

OVERDRIVE ENGAGED

SYSTEM READY

> (click)

Her magnetized heart comes out of her like a gift.

Black stringy fluid hangs like a cat's cradle between her chest cavity and my hand.

We bite into it, savoring the flavor of extraterrestrial death.

Far away, our toes curl in our little body at the taste.

She has nothing else to **offer**.

> offer

Our pilot slams his fist on our inner skull to get our attention. We let him out after a moment.

He is coated in a light sweat, a frown tugging on his face.

I need to go, hurry up and drop me back home. I have a date tonight.

We don't remember him asking us out **tonight**.

> tonight

DANGER

EMOTIONAL LEVELS UNSTABLE

SYSTEM ARMED

Our mecha body shivers in rage, plasma coarsing like ice through us.

TRAITOR.

Or maybe he just didn't tell **us**.

    I picked the second choice. If you want to kill him you can, but even though it's a fantasy, I decided to let him live, not because I like him, but because it's just not as easy as squeezing him in your claws or flaying him alive with pink lasers. Boys worm their way in your heart sometimes, and all of a sudden you're entwined with someone bad for you in ways that will hurt you if you try to separate. In the same way that one's attachment to stories like these can feel like a chain. Also, if he's her boyfriend, is there anything good at all about him? I wanted to find out, and well:

played by Aevee Bee

> us

We bound towards the outskirts of the metropolis and drop him off atop an old school building.

He doesn't even say goodbye.

We sink into the ocean depths and crawl through a tunnel back into the darkness.

Little-us wakes **up**.

> up

Big-us powers down, sleeps.

Little-us cleans ourselves up from our comatose state, wiping the blue gelly that functions as our blood from our nose.

We hear a knock at the door. Our boyfriend pilot is standing on the thrash hold, sweaty and tired. His scars shimmer in the red sunlight.

He leans down and kisses us. Our body is still a little cold. He tastes like coins.

He pulls back a fraction of an inch and smirks.

*I'm sorry I'm late. Got side-tracked saving the **city**.*

> city

We nod, green hair brushing the tops of our shoulders.

He takes our hand in his. He can't find out. The secret rots us from the inside.

He can never know.

He moves his arm across our neck, plays with the platinum seams on our spine tenderly.

He leans his head closer to us, damp hair musky against our metallic-citrus skin.

He listens to the hum of our **heart**.

> heart

He always hears us both.

Without knowing, he hears us.

He grins and presses his mouth to our ear, soft lips on manufactured Pantone skin.

A battery can be a heart too.

    I hate you, but also I love you. You treat me terribly but you touch me tenderly. You're arrogant and you won't listen and your hold over me is toxic but sometimes it's all I want. I feel this way about both boys and stories about giant robots, so it's the ending I choose. It felt honest. He's so smug and irredeemable throughout the beginning of the story that seeing this side of him complicates it all, because even if everything bad about him is true, so is this. The pop culture garbage that becomes a part of us whether or not it's good for us or even whether or not we really want it too can't be so easily dismissed. "I want to be beautiful and colorful and powerful"; I wouldn't have known how to want that if I hadn't seen it. I still remember having no other language to express myself than "I want to summon the laser so pink only a girl could imagine it," and so that imagery and aesthetic continues to be important to me, no matter how much clearer, better, non-problematic alternatives may have to offer.

    There are kinds of writing, like poetry and creative nonfiction, that are missing from writing about games. Most of the approaches imitate film and novelistic prose, and those are lovely forms, but I wonder if they actually suit games well. There's more work that we can do to understand and develop and craft what works in Twine and games in general. This story has writing, but it doesn't look quite like prose. That's more exciting to me than anything else as a writer.

THE MESSAGE
BY JEREMY LONIEN
AND DOMINIK JOHANN
PLAYED BY SQUINKY

A short story about space and stuff in it.

We strongly recommend listening to **some space music** while playing this game.

Begin

Credits

    Ooh. Space music. Normally, I'd be all for it; however, I'm currently in a café and forgot my headphones. Sorry about that.

    > Begin

EMERGENCY ALERT SYSTEM

Civil Authorities Issued Emergency Action Notification

We interrupt our programming. This is a national emergency. This is not a test. Important details will follow. The Emergency Alert System has been activated. The following message is being transmitted at the request of the United States government: ON 10 AM EASTERN TIME THERE WERE A SERIES OF SIGHTINGS OF UNIDENTIFIED CRAFT IN ORBIT AROUND THE PLANET. THESE HAVE BEEN CONFIRMED BY OUR NATIONAL OBSERVATORIES. UNTIL FURTHER NOTICE, YOU ARE AD-

The Message by Jeremy Lonien and Dominik Johann

VISED TO SEEK SHELTER, LOCK ANY DOORS AND TURN OFF ANY TELECOMMUNICATION OR INTERNET DEVICES. I REPEAT: THIS IS NOT A TEST

OMG Aliens! Are there aliens in this game?

Our probe officially reached the Pluto-Charon system on July 14, 2015, 11:47 UTC. Then, only 4 hours later, just before we would've received the next data burst, a fleet of unidentified spacecraft entered a low Earth orbit.

heh heh heh. probe.

It all happened so quickly.

Okay. tell me more about this probe.

> our probe

New Horizons

On January 19th 2006, they strapped "a grand piano glued to a cocktail bar-sized satellite dish." to the fastest rocket ever launched and it went well.

I don't know what it is about grand pianos in slapstick comedy. Like, it's this instrument that's supposed to be all fancy and pompous and, well, grand (because, you know, it's right there in the name), but it's also comically large and unwieldy especially if you, like, decide to play it in a marching band or something. And when you drop it from high places, it makes this awesomely discordant sound, not at all in keeping with its supposed elegance. So. Um,

played by Squinky

yeah.

Though not as fast as Helios and never as distant as Voyager 1, this 1,000 lb robot was going to be the first man-made spacecraft to do a relatively close flyby of various trans-Neptunian objects, most famously of course ex-planet Pluto and its moon Charon.

So far, its mission was a huge success.

    That whole thing with Pluto not being a planet anymore . . . I never really understood what the fuss was. Like, okay, so scientific understanding has marched on from what was taught to us during our childhoods. Shouldn't that be a feature, not a bug? Okay, maybe the whole idea of childhood nostalgia plays into it too, which is another thing I don't get because when I think of childhood, I think of not having the vocabulary to express how trapped and lonely I felt. (And yes, the fact that Pluto was also the name of Mickey Mouse's dog is probably also relevant here.)

    Whatever. I'd probably feel more bummed if Uranus was no longer a planet. (See what I just did there?)

> So far, its mission . . .

Too many years the guys at NASA had to work with those awfully blurry images Hubble gave us.

    Of course. Always guys.

New Horizons would've given them all the sensory data and high-resolution pictures they could hope for. Given the bandwith limitations of their Deep Space Network it would've taken them months and months to send all that information back to earth, but the nuclear battery on board didn't care.

We now think of it as our accidental first contact. **It did not end well.**

    The plot thickens!

> It did not end well

The space stations went first. Size and location in orbit did not matter.

The ISS, Tiangong, Genesis I and II, military and spy satellites, communications, weather, navigation, everything. Even

The Message by Jeremy Lonien and Dominik Johann

the thousands of pieces of decommissioned satellites and junk and space debris left by 50 years of spaceflight. Everything.

Jon Blow gave a talk at PRACTICE 2014 that was kind of about the space age, but mostly about how he's the only person with true ambition making games today. (So, kind of like Chris Crawford's dragon speech, except less entertaining.) I wonder how Jon Blow would react if all the space technology disappeared. I wonder if Jon Blow would be able to find this book by name searching.

Then every radio telescope on the planet just vanished.
Then every rocket capable of escape velocity, and all nuclear warheads. And before anyone knew Earth was under attack, it was over. Technologically, mankind was suddenly back to square one of the space age. And on top of that, communications were gone. GPS was gone. SDI was gone. Even all that crap the Apollo missions left on the Moon, as we later found out - was gone.

I also kind of wonder how I would feel. Apathetic, probably. Isn't the space race just colonisation? White male supremacy in its extrapolated, futuristic sci-fi form? Maybe I'd feel a certain sense of schadenfreude.

And then **the fleet** was gone, too. But they **left something** behind.

Tell me more about this fleet!
(I have a feeling we'll learn about this "something" soon enough, anyhow.)

> the fleet

A mind-boggingly vast fleet of unidentified craft, in dense enough formation to - for a moment - block out the sun, the moon, the stars.

It almost looked like one of those very high and thick clouds overshadowing the sky, though very quick and only for a moment.

The irony that, of all our crap out there only one then-secret spy satellite which would from that point on be known as **IF-50** managed to capture a single blurry image, looking down on earth shrouded by billions of UFOs, is almost depress-

played by Squinky

ing. Remember those "I want to believe" crackpots? **Who would've thought they were actually right?**

Okay, I think I see where this is going. Yes. There are definitely aliens in this game. I like aliens. Aliens (or at least, the idea thereof) are pretty awesome, mainly because I always wonder how they'd react to humanity. Would they find us as bizarre and nonsensical as I often do? Would they be able to show us a better way to be? Would shitty white dudes just destroy them before we had a chance to find out? This is also how I think about the past. About the societies and cultures that existed before the European colonists came and trampled all over everything. White male supremacy probably didn't make sense to them, either. Were any of those lost eras places in which I could have been happier had I been born then instead of now?

> Who would've thought . . . ?

"I want to believe."

"Elvis isn't dead, he just went home!"

"I was abducted and anally probed by green men from mars!"

"Global warming is a hoax!"

"The earth is only 10,000 years old!"

"Your vaccine gave my son autism!"

They had a field day.

I'm the most wishy-washy agnostic ever—I tried to be religious for some period of time, but could never sustain enough optimism to really, truly believe in either of my parents' faiths; my life experiences just kept proving me wrong. (Plus, I'm queer as a three-dollar coin, which doesn't help things.) At the same time, I find atheism insufferable, for the most part. Science is a useful tool sometimes, but I don't "fucking love" it. Maybe it's just me rebelling against my aborted career in STEM, but I care more about art and creativity. And there's a sort of mysticism that comes with that, in my experience.

Nowadays, I think of religions, and by extension, the sorts of beliefs on display here (objectionable and ridiculous as they may seem to me and others) as a lot like fandoms. People getting together and discussing a shared imaginary universe (and here I don't mean to use "imaginary" in a dismissive sense) and working out how to make the stories therein relevant to their own lives. I see this practice as value-neutral. And I enjoy some fandoms but not others, and I'm pretty okay with whatever fandoms people want to belong to unless and until said fandoms advocate harmful beliefs about the world that then encourage their fans to hurt other people.

The Message by Jeremy Lonien and Dominik Johann

So, yeah, there's nothing inherently wrong with wanting to believe. I think it's one of our strongest qualities as humans, that we can create stories and worlds in our heads and make them real.

> They had a field day

A message. The Message. A message to every living thing on our Pale Blue Dot to see in the sky, forever. Although it was, strangely enough, written in English, nobody really knew what to make of it.

Why did English get to be the dominant language, anyway? I mean, it's my first language, and I've put more effort than I'd like to admit in trying to master it. I wish I'd put more effort into learning other languages. I was in a French immersion program in school, but I never learned to speak French like a native speaker, with an adult vocabulary. And what I did learn in school has atrophied from lack of practice. I used to be fluent in Farsi when I was a little kid, and know how to read and write at, like, a grade two level. But I feel even more clunky when I try to speak it. My parents never really taught me nor my siblings Tagalog or Ilokano, as those are the languages they use to speak to each other when they don't want us kids to understand them.

Some thought it was a warning, others said it was a declaration of war. Of course, the internet almost instantly went crazy over it, generating endless discussions about hidden meanings, trying to decrypt whatever could be hidden in that simple word.

See? Fandoms.

There were probably more theories about its meaning than there were Moon Conspiracy crackpots back in the 20th century. Religions were formed around The Message. T-Shirts were printed. Bumper stickers too. **People love this stuff.**

Yeah, this is pretty much exactly how humanity would react.

> People love this stuff.

People started tattooing The Message onto their bodies, naming their children, pets, **a public holiday** and even whole cities after it. Soon The Message was used as a universal

played by Squinky

greeting phrase. Or, depending on context and culture, to declare love, or hate to one another.

It turned out that people didn't care about what it meant, they just invented their own meanings, used it in bedtime stories, wrote fiction and made movies and video games about it. In fact, we still don't know for sure. There are still archaeologists debating about its purpose.

And why they chose the Moon for it.

Perhaps a good argument for "death of the author"? I mean, if humanity doesn't have access to the original author(s) of the Message for clarification, they kind of have to invent their own meanings. And like I said earlier, that's one of the things we do best.

Tell me more about this holiday!

> a public holiday

The 14th of July became known as Message Day, a global holiday to remember all the lives lost by crashed cars and airplanes and **ships lost at sea**. People stuck in elevators. All effectively lost man-hours in human spaceflight. All our little robots we sent out there, never to return. Frightened military leaders with access to Big Red Buttons, who **snapped** at the sight of The Message, killing hundreds. The money lost at the completely crashed markets. Lost jobs. Lives ended by suicide.

They thought the world was going to end. It didn't. But overnight everyone knew: We are not alone. At last, a common enemy. Something to work together for. On that day, mankind lost every reason to fight each other. Message Day is a day of unity.

Though, in the end, it saved everyone, nothing could have prepared humanity for **The Message**.

Egads, that's unsettling. Can't we have some kind of unity that isn't based on uniting *against* something? Is such a thing even possible?

I'm very curious about these frightened military leaders snapping. Probably has to do with how I feel about the military in general.

> snapped

On October 27, 1962, during the Cuban Missile Crisis, Vasili Arkhipov, a Soviet naval officer prevented the launch of a nuclear torpedo and a possible nuclear war.

The Message by Jeremy Lonien and Dominik Johann

We came closer than we knew at the time.

On September 26, 1983, Lieutenant Colonel Stanislav Petrov of the Soviet Air Defence Forces was on duty at the command center of the Oko nuclear early-warning system when the system reported a missile being launched from the United States. He judged that the report was a false alarm and prevented a retaliatory nuclear attack, which would've resulted in World War III.

He received no reward.

On January 25, 1995, a team of Norwegian and American scientists launched a research rocket to study the aurora borealis over Svalbard. Due to its resemblance to a submarine-launched Trident missile, Russian forces were put on high alert, Boris Yeltsin was notified immediately and the "nuclear briefcase" used to authorize nuclear launch was automatically activated.

The incident was reported in the news a week afterward.

Given that the Cold War ended when I was four, I don't have as much of a visceral memory of that era as older generations do, so I throw around words like "comrade" and "socialism" that mean very different things to people who associate them with "the enemy."

I was also born and raised in Canada. So. Yeah.

I wonder what sorts of accidents could have prevented the Iranian revolution. That would likely erase the chain of events that led to my existence, and I'm not entirely sure how I feel about that.

On July 14, 2015, everything and nothing happened. Nothing could've prepared humanity for **this**.

What? What? The suspense is killing me!

\> this

played by Squinky

THE END

AHAHAHAHAHAHAHAHAHA!!!!!!! Of course. :)
(And yes, if I were an alien with access to such technology, this is exactly the sort of thing I'd do.)

DEPRESSION QUEST
BY ZOE QUINN
PLAYED BY TONI PIZZA

Depression Quest is a game that deals with living with depression in a very literal way. This game is not meant to be a fun or lighthearted experience. If you are currently suffering from the illness and are easily triggered, please be aware that this game uses stark depictions of people in very dark places. If you are suicidal, please stop playing this game and visit this link to talk to someone.

The goal of this game is twofold: firstly, we want to illustrate as clearly as possible what depression is like, so that it may be better understood by people without depression. Hopefully this can be something to spread awareness and fight against the social stigma and misunderstandings that depression sufferers face. Secondly, our hope is that in presenting as real a simulation of depression as possible, other sufferers will come to know that they aren't alone, and hopefully derive some measure of comfort from that.

It goes without saying that because of the very nature of depression, it is experienced differently by every person who suffers from it. We aren't trying to say that this is the "best" or "most accurate" representation, merely that this is an amalgamation of the experiences of the developers and several people close to them. Many of the following encounters deal with issues such as therapy, medication, handling a love life, and reaching out to support networks. In reality, less than half of depression sufferers actually seek treatment, for reasons such as lack of money, perceived personal failing,

Depression Quest by Zoe Quinn

or public stigma. These things were included in order to touch upon as broad a range as possible, since all these elements can be very important to sufferers of depression, though they will likely not be the experiences of most sufferers.

It's important to recognize that not everyone with depression is so lucky. Many people with the illness don't have a lot of the luxuries that we have in this game. We've written it this way so that we can focus specifically on the illness, which becomes more and more difficult to deal with as the person who has it is less and less well-off.

For that reason, a portion of the proceeds from this game will be donated to The National Suicide Prevention Lifeline. **Click here** if you'd like to contribute.

This game uses audio as part of it's gameplay. We encourage you to play with your sound on.

Thank you for playing.

Begin.

> Begin

You are depressed. Interaction is exhausting, and you are becoming more and more withdrawn.

You are not currently seeing a therapist

You are not currently taking medication for depression.

It is early on a Monday morning.

You are a mid-twenties human being. You have a significant other **named Alex** who you are rather fond of, that you have been seeing exclusively for the past few months. The rest of your **social circle** consists of a variety of friends and acquaintances, some of whom you met at your **day job** which is a little boring, but pays the rent. You'd like to be doing more with your life, **as would your parents**, but you're still in the process of figuring out what that means and how to go about it.

You are also dealing with motivation issues that sometimes makes dealing with these things difficult. You feel like this is probably your fault, and on bad days can feel inwardly angry and down on yourself for being "lazy", but you're not quite sure how you can break out of it, or how other people deal with these feelings and seem so very functional.

You spend a lot of nights fixating on thinking about this, but never seem to do anything about it other than lose sleep.

played by Toni Pizza

Next.

It seems fitting that *Depression Quest* begins on a Monday morning and that I'm writing this on a Monday morning. First thing that stands out to me about this game is the music—it's kind of heavy feeling. I'd definitely suggest playing with headphones or at the very least turning off other music to play.

I also love the snapshots. In my experience, the things I remember from the really dark and gritty depths of depression are preserved in an almost snapshot form—you see a little bit of what's going on but never the whole picture, never the level of detail you really want.

I've played through this game probably a dozen or so times, but I still think it's worth clicking through some of the descriptions that are linked.

> as would your parents

You're one of the few people you know of whose parents never got divorced, but you do wonder if they still love each other sometimes.

You have an older brother named Malcolm who has moved across the country with his wife to work a high paying job. Every major holiday that you see him at, you feel a bit jealous and like the lesser kid despite being genuinely happy to see him. You feel very ashamed of these feelings.

Your parents genuinely care about you. This often involves inviting you back to your childhood home for dinner, though your mother thinks you never visit quite enough. But you get the impression they don't fully understand you. They want to see you succeed, and don't know why you haven't gone farther in life yet because you're "so smart and talented". Any time you've tried to talk to them about your motivation issues, they tell you that the solution is simply to work harder, or want it more. Your father is generally more forgiving of your lack of a career path, while your mother seems to think you're "too smart" to be in the position you're in.

You know they love you and that they're not bad people, but you really feel like a big disappointment sometimes.

Back.

Now that I'm paying close attention, this narrator is incredibly self-aware, which is not something I remember noticing in the past.

> Back
> day job

Depression Quest by Zoe Quinn

You have a day job which you feel is really nothing special. You started out receiving minimum wage, but have stayed around long enough to be making enough to support yourself. The work is dull and unrewarding, and most days you feel like just about anyone could do it.

You have a hard time relating to most of your coworkers, so you mostly keep to yourself and get the work done while you're there. There are one or two people you chat with, though you wouldn't consider yourself close with them.

A lot of days lately, you have a really hard time getting out of bed and forcing yourself to go in. You're starting to wonder how long you can keep this up.

You'd really like to find another job in your field of interest, but feel like you are under qualified every time you look at online job postings. Sometimes you think about going back to school, but you would be unsure how you would be able to support yourself and wonder if the degree would really help anyway.

Back.

Onto the "job" section, now. This section kind of pushes a button for me, just because though yes—unideal working conditions most certainly can contribute to provoking or worsening depression—it's incredibly entitled to have this expectation of a highly rewarding job with co-workers you are best friends with.

ANYWAY—I get the point of the generic "shitty job, I could do better, this is tough and I wish it could be different" angle, but if there's ever a *Depression Quest* expansion pack, it should have a handful of different experiences/perspectives to play through.

Enough background, moving on. Next Plz.

> Back
> Next

It's an unseasonably warm Wednesday evening.

You've spent the past several hours at work. The past week or so you've found your job motivation flagging more so than usual; you've been in a fog practically all day today, simply going through the motions without realizing even what you've been doing half the time, and yet time seemed to be moving at half speed. You're so checked out that when your boss approaches you to tell you that it's dead and you can go home early it barely registers.

As you walk home, the streets hiss from the recent rainfall.

played by Toni Pizza

You know that your significant other will be in classes until late, another couple hours at least. You briefly consider using this serendipitous solitude to catch up on that project that you've been working on haphazardly for the past few months.

As soon as you think about the work that awaits you at home you can feel the panic creeping in from the back of your brain, unbidden. All you can think about is how incredibly far behind you are, and the amount of work seems nothing less than insurmountable.

By the time you arrive home and change out of your uncomfortable work clothes the stress is weighing down on you like a heavy, wet wool blanket. Your computer seems to be staring you down from your desk. You want to sit down and work but the mere thought of trying to work sends your stress levels flying; more than anything you feel suddenly and absolutely exhausted, and feel a strong desire to simply hide in bed.

Do you...

~~1. Order some food, grab a drink, and hunker down for a night of work.~~

2. Reluctantly sit down at your desk and try and make yourself do something

3: Turn on the TV, telling yourself you just need a quick half hour to unwind from work

4: Crawl into bed. You're so stressed and overwhelmed you couldn't possibly accomplish anything anyways.

All right, this is where things start to get interesting. I've got some choices to make and I know have little status bars alerting me to my internal state as well as if I'm seeing a therapist or taking medication.

I'm glad that right away one of the choices is off the list and crossed out like that, it gives the sense that you *know* that ordering food and getting into a work groove was/should be a possibility but isn't something you're able to act on. It makes you feel bad. (And it's reminding me that I'm incredibly fucking lucky to not be depressed right now.) All right, I'm choosing the answer that I know would be my response in real life. Bed time.

> Crawl into bed

As much as you like the idea of trying to get work done tonight, the thought of the amount of catching up you have to do instantly freezes you up. The longer you stare at your computer, the higher your stress levels rise, until you're on the verge of a full blown panic attack. Not even wandering

Depression Quest by Zoe Quinn

into the living room to try and watch TV relaxes you. You soon succumb to the mental and physical exhaustion and crawl into bed, making a point to close your laptop before you turn the light out. You lay in bed for some time feeling disappointed in your own inability to be productive before finally passing out.

You awake in the morning from a sleep that was far from restful. In fact, it seems impossible, but it's as though you're moretired than you were when you fell asleep last night. As you pick up your phone to shut your alarm off you see a handful of text messages from Alex that you apparently missed last night.

2 missed calls

Text Message: Hey - tried calling when I got out of class but I guess you're sleeping?

Text Message: Anyway I hope you had a good day at work, and I hope you were able to get some stuff done when you got home. I'll talk to you tomorrow? I'm out of class early.

Text Message: Good night babe. I love you.

Next.

> You are very depressed. You spend a large amount of time sleeping, hating yourself, and have very little energy or motivation.

> You are not currently seeing a therapist.

> You are not currently taking medication for depression.

The first two lines of this are spot on with my experiences. Reading this almost makes me want to bust out a Klonopin. (I should do a second play through on Klonopin—these notes would be so much more entertaining!)

> Next

It's a mild Friday afternoon.

Alex calls you from one of her classes telling you that there's going to be a "really awesome" birthday party tonight at her apartment that one of her roommates is throwing. You've hung out with this roommate a few times with Alex, and you get along well enough but aren't particularly close.

You don't have work in the morning, and have nothing else in particular to do tonight. You are feeling kind of run-down, but you have been fatigued most of the time lately.

played by Toni Pizza

You mention that you're feeling ill because you're not sure how else to explain those feelings to someone else, and say that you aren't sure that you can make it tonight.

There's a second of silence over your phone, but you can swear you can hear the sound of your partner's face fall.

She tries to convince you anyway. You haven't seen her this week, and she sounds pretty insistent that you come over. She even drops a few suggestively worded hints that you can stay over with them tonight after the party.

What do you do?

~~1. Shake off your funk and go have a good time with your girlfriend.~~

2: Agree to go.

3: Say that you're really just not feeling well and can't make it

It's a mild Friday afternoon—wait, what!? It was just Monday, where did the week go?

This time shift feels appropriate. (From a gameplay and "IRL" perspective. No one wants to play through a depressed person's every moment and when you're "very depressed" it is easy for it to go from being Monday to Friday within the span of a single nap . . .)

Oh, now that we're interacting with the character's partner, I just want to say that I love that the partner is a woman for two reasons: 1. If you're a queer girl playing the game as a queer girl, you're losing your mind with happiness that you can be a queero in the game :D. 2. If you're a human playing the game and assuming you're a male character because you have a girlfriend in-game, you're forced to think of your character as an emotional being, and sometimes we don't let men be emotional beings.

So, about that party . . . No, no I'm not going.

> Say that you're not feeling well

Despite your partner's pleas, you tell Alex you're unable to make it to the party tonight. You say you feel too ill and would just be a drag on everyone.

She sighs a sigh that you've heard many times before. One of exasperation, but patience.

"Well ok then. I just hope you feel better soon, I really miss you. I guess I'll see you next week or something..."

You apologize profusely and tell Alex that you love and miss her too, and promise to make plans for next weekend. She

Depression Quest by Zoe Quinn

sounds somewhat distracted and distant as she agrees, says her goodnights, and hangs up.

You spend the rest of the night beating yourself up for feeling too lousy to go. You leave a few apologetic and loving texts to your partner, and you feel stressed out and forgotten when you don't receive a reply.

Next.

> You are deeply depressed. Even activities you used to enjoy hold little or no interest for you and you exist in a near-constant state of lethargy
>
> You are not currently seeing a therapist
>
> You are not currently taking medication for depression

All right, so bailing on the party was apparently not the way to go because I'm now "deeply depressed." This change is maybe a little abrupt? Or maybe it's not? The gradient makes sense in terms of gameplay, but narratively it feels a little rushed.

> Next

It's a little after noon on a muggy Saturday.

Your mother has come over for a surprise visit, claiming loudly that she doesn't see you enough so she'd decided to invite herself over. One of the first things she does is comment on how messy your apartment is. You tell her you know it's messy, and it actually bothers you too, you just for some reason haven't been able to work yourself up to cleaning the place up yet.As you converse, she walks around your place, and you get the distinct impression that you're being "inspected."

So what's going on with you lately, she asks abruptly.

Taken somewhat aback by this left-fielder you tell her you're not sure what she means. She repeats the question, saying that you haven't seemed like yourself lately - she gestures to the dirty dishes piled in the sink and notes the fact that you haven't called or visited in a while. Your reticence only seems to spur her on more; she presses you, asking if you're having problems at work or with Alex, and you're beginning to feel increasingly battered by her sudden well-meaning but overwhelming inquisition.

Under her questions you become increasingly uncomfortable. You want to be able to explain to her how you've been feeling, but the truth is you're not really sure yourself. Nothing

played by Toni Pizza

horrific has happened at work or with your significant other or friends or anything like that, but all the same you can't deny that lately you've just felt drained and as though you're not really "here".

You wish you could tell your mother these things, but she hasn't been approachable about negative emotions in the past. She is the kind of person who holds the opinion that the solution to any problem is to simply try harder and maintain a positive attitude, a stance that has reared its head in past conversations when you've begun to explore the subject with her. You know she's unlikely to be understanding, and you feel the energy drain out of you when you imagine what would happen if you managed to blurt out everything you are feeling.

What do you do?

~~1: Let her know that you've been feeling down lately, and that you appreciate her concern.~~

~~2: Try to be honest with her anyway.~~

3: Tell her that everything is fine, and thank her for asking.

4: Change the subject.

    AHHHHHH. Mothers not being emotionally supportive. Can we write in a "Hand your mother a copy of *Fun Home* and *Are You My Mother?* (by Alison Bechdel) and then tell her to call you when she's finished reading" answer? No? Okay, you're right. Change the subject.

> Change the subject

"Are you okay?"

It's a question you've been finding yourself being asked a lot lately, and it's one that has begun to make you instantly uncomfortable. It's one you would have to spill your guts to adequately describe, which would be an almost impossible feat to perform at the moment. Even if you managed to, you'd have to fight through your self loathing long enough to keep talking despite feeling like everything you're saying amounts to simple bellyaching. If somehow you powered through THAT as well, you'd have to live with feeling truly exposed and you figure anyone who would know all of these things would be put off to you permanently.

More importantly, despite your mother's best intentions she is

Depression Quest by Zoe Quinn

quite likely the worst possible person to try and wade through all of this bullshit with.

You evade the question by pretending you have received a text message. Once you pretend as though you're finished reading it, you change the subject back to one you know your mother is interested in. She takes the bait, and the topic is successfully changed.

A feel of unease lingers, and your stress levels stay high until she leaves a bit later. You wonder if you should talk to someone about all of this - someone who would be more sympathetic and not tell you to simply "think positive".

Next.

This moment of realization is such a big one. Realizing that many of the people around you are genuinely asking if you are okay is a big warning sign. I think the first time I played this I had to stop right around now because it was a little too intense to "play" around with.

I would actually even suggest putting the "are you okays" on their own page without the wall of text below . . . I mean . . . If someone is actually playing through this to better understand their own emotional state or to help someone they think might be depressed, recognizing the "are you okay" pattern can give you a lot of insight.

> Next

It is a lazy Sunday morning.

You are idly clicking around online as your phone rings. Sam, a coworker of yours that you're friendly with, asks how you are and makes hurried smalltalk with you. You typically only ever talk to him on the phone when one of you needs a shift covered, so it's slightly awkward. You're waiting in anticipation for him to ask you to come in on short notice when he veers the conversation in a completely different direction.

"How do you feel about cats?", he asks. "Mine had kittens a few weeks ago and I'm having an awfully hard time finding a home for the last one of the litter. You don't have any pets, right?"

It takes you a moment to process this new information, and you're caught off guard as he begins to earnestly try to sell you on the idea of taking the last kitten off his hands. It's not something that you had specifically considered before, and he seems fairly insistent.

"She's a real sweetheart, really loves people. She's got all her shots already taken care of and the vet said she's healthy as

played by Toni Pizza

a horse. I can bring her over by your place tonight if you're interested."

You look around your apartment and try to picture a cat in it as he continues to tell you about how cute she is. You tell him that this is all kind of sudden, and that you don't have anything for the kitten set up here.

"Oh don't worry about that, I can bring over a litterbox and food and all that since you'd really be helping me out of a fix. It's the least I could do! I just don't want to have to put her in a shelter."

You can't help but feel like you're being guilt tripped, but you decide to give it some serious consideration. It DOES get awfully lonely around your apartment, and it might feel less empty with a cat around. However, since you've been feeling so down it might not be a good idea to take on the responsibility of a cat even if they are fairly low maintenance.

What do you do?

1: ~~Take the cat, knowing full well that you can take great care of it.~~

2: ~~Decline. Even though you'd be totally capable of taking care of it, you're not much of a cat person.~~

3: Become a cat owner. You could use the companionship.

4: Decline. You're not in a good enough place to be taking on more responsibility right now.

5: Decline. You don't like cats.

    This next situation is a good one to put players through, I think it's a relatively common theme for people who are depressed to consider getting an animal pal.
    I'm allergic to cats in real life so I'm going with the OH HELL NO answer.
    Still deeply depressed.

> Decline; you don't like cats

You've never been a fan of cats. You feel like they all hate you, and you figure you have enough hate coming from your own inner monologues already.

"I'm sorry, I just can't right now. I hope you find a good home for her."

You sit through a few more sales pitch statements that border on guilt trips and rebut them with fabricated excuses about your landlord not allowing pets before your coworker gives up, and thanks you anyway. You wish him luck in finding a home for her, and as you hang up you feel pangs of guilt as you imagine him having to put her in a shelter.

The next day at work, you run into your coworker and breathe a sigh of relief as he informs you that he was able to find a good home for the kitten.

Next.

The only thing this section is missing is the fact that you're now convinced the co-worker hates you because you wouldn't take the cat, even though someone else did.

> Next

It's late Friday afternoon, and Quitting Time is just around the corner.

A bright clear day is giving way to a still, temperate evening. You can hear your coworkers all around you anxiously making plans for their evenings and weekends, but you're really looking forward to just going home and resting after what's turned out to be a very long and taxing work week.

Just before the end of your shift, you get a call from Alex. It seems a group of your mutual friends are heading out to a nearby pub for dinner and drinks to celebrate the end of the week, and they want to know if you'd like to come along. You tentatively tell her that you're emotionally exhausted from the work week and a social outing like that would just take too much out of you today. You encourage her to go and have a good time, since you know it's been a while since she's gone out with friends, but the effort feels futile since you know that she isn't going to go without you.

A couple hours later the two of you find yourselves in a familiar position: on the couch, watching comedy shows on Netflix, a box of pizza open on the coffee table in front of you. As you look across the couch at her, you start to feel anxious. You feel bad about effectively forcing the two of you to stay in tonight, again. While you are always appreciative of your partner's efforts to take your feelings into account and help make sure you're socially comfortable, you sincerely worry that you're holding her back from enjoying a more fulfilling relationship.

While she does seem to enjoy spending time with you, as the two of you sit in comfortable, almost contented silence

played by Toni Pizza

watching old shows you've each seen two or three times before, your ever-increasing fear that your relationship is becoming one-sided weighs more and more heavily on you. You feel more than ever like a burden or a ward to her, and it's virtually impossible for you to see what value you could possibly offer to her in return. Worst of all, this nagging fear has made you feel more self-conscious than ever, withdrawing ever inwards, and you've started to pull away even from Alex herself.

What do you do?

~~1: You know despite the bad times, your girlfriend sincerely loves you. Relationships are a 2-way street, and you resolve to always be there for her like she has been for you.~~

~~2: Tell Alex how important she is to you and enjoy your evening.~~

~~3: Ask Alex if she's happy with your relationship.~~

4: Don't say anything; you're already worried about her being upset with you.

    Oh, geez, now I don't even have a choice about what I want to do. I actually really do think I should have at least two choices, this feels a little too claustrophobic.
    Wait, I think I maybe just lost *Depression Quest* because I didn't take the cat and I will be really upset if I don't get a chance to go to therapy.

> Don't say anything

This is far from the first time you would have had this conversation with her, and it's one that plays out the same way every time. You explain your fears of being worthless, she tries to tell you that she doesn't see you that way, you insist that she is biased or just being nice to you because she's your girlfriend, and she gets frustrated. It never resolves, nothing new is ever said, and rarely do you feel reassured by it.

Occasionally she tries to broach the subject, trying to discover why you feel like this about yourself. This always makes you feel nervous - you're sometimes convinced that the only reason she's still with you is because she doesn't know how awful you really are. As time as gone on, you've gotten more comfortable trying to express bits and pieces of your insecurities to her, but it still causes you to feel very on guard and it's not a conversation you can have for too long without worrying you're going to scare her away.

The weight of an unspoken, unresolved issue in your relation-

Depression Quest by Zoe Quinn

ship joins you in the room for a little while, but you dare not pick at it for the rest of the night.

Next.

> You are profoundly depressed. You are barely functional, on days you can even get out of bed at all.
>
> You are not currently seeing a therapist.
>
> You are not currently taking medication for depression.

Oh, yikes, now I'm profoundly depressed. Again, not entirely sure about the depression meter, especially because I can't exactly tell how that changes the decisions I can make. It seems like it should limit them, but sometimes it doesn't and sometimes it does?

> Next

It is a breezy Sunday afternoon.

You've allowed Amanda, an old friend from school that is in town for the weekend to talk you into leaving the house for coffee and catch up. You meet her in a small cafe and talk about what you've been up to since you've last seen each other, and you can't help but feel like they are a lot more accomplished and interesting than you are while listening to them talk about their life after school.

When it's your turn to brief them on your activities, you feel anxious and ashamed and give a very abbreviated version. You try to talk about your job as little as possible, and you feel incredibly boring while you describe it despite her expressing sincere interest in you and your life.

Amanda has known you long enough to read your mood and tone of voice. She leans into ask a question while gently touching your hand, a look of genuine concern on her face.

"What's wrong?"

Do you...

~~1: Suggest a change of location and confide in her honestly.~~

~~2: Test the waters and open up a little, hoping she'll understand.~~

3: Insist that nothing is wrong and change the subject.

4: Defensively ask what she means by that.

5: Notice that your hands are shaking.

played by Toni Pizza

All right, so this Amanda character seems like the first one who is genuinely interested in hearing about how I feel, so, okay, I think I should talk to her. (Also, uh, fun fact, my last therapist was named Amanda and she was great. Am I projecting this onto the Amanda character!? Does she seem like she cares more than these other characters?)

My choices are back? Last scenario I only had one choice and now I have three. I'm still annoyed by that, but I am very happy with the verbs I have to choose from. I am so so happy that "notice" is an option. It seems so passive but actually is a huge step to take.

> Notice that your hands are shaking

It's such a small question, but it feels like a blow to the gut. You surprise yourself when you realize that your tightly clenched fists are now beginning to shake slightly. Despite your best efforts, you feel tears begin to sting at your eyes. You try to disguise this by tilting your head up and praying that they'll suck back in.

She suggests that you two get out of there, and you feel mortified. She offers to go back to your apartment with you, but the two of you end up talking in her car for two hours as the words just pour forth from you.

Amanda seems unsure of what to say at times, but she listens and rubs your back as you sob and talk. She asks if you've gone to a doctor about this, and you admit that you haven't. She mentions that her mother is seeing a very good therapist in town, and offers to ask her about it.

You're not thrilled about the idea of going to a therapist and even less thrilled that Amanda might be telling someone about your problems, but she persists and tells you she'll email you the doctor's contact information later in the week.

Next.

Amanda is the best. Noticing is the best. Next.

> Next

It's a glaringly sunny Monday, and one of the few days that your brother Malcolm is in town and free long enough for you two to actually see each other.

You have a dental appointment that day but you make plans for him to pick you up afterward.

Depression Quest by Zoe Quinn

Your appointment takes a little longer than expected because your dentist tells you that you've started grinding your teeth in your sleep to a worrying degree. Given how nearly everything in your life has been feeling enormous and stressful lately, this doesn't come as a surprise to you. He suggests that you try to reduce your stress levels and fits you for a night guard. It feels awkward and too big for your mouth, and you feel embarrassed looking at your puffed out face in the mirror with it in. You finish up the appointment in a hurry and leave about a half an hour overdue for meeting your always punctual brother in the parking lot.

You finish up as quickly as possible and leave the building to scan the parking lot for your brother's car, but you don't see his old Civic anywhere. You pass by a blue Camero and jump as it beeps at you, causing you to jump in surprise. It takes you a moment for to realize it, but it's Malcolm in the driver's seat.

You hop in the passengers seat and compliment him on his new ride and he mentions that it's a perk of a promotion he's recently obtained at work. He starts telling you about how much more money he's making, how his career is really taking off, and how he's starting to look at houses with his wife soon.

You clutch the bag containing the night guard in your hand and feel yourself clench your teeth as you think of your crummy apartment and how long it's been since you've been able to take a day off work without having to worry about making ends meet. He's only 2 years older than you, but it feels like he's eons ahead of you in every other aspect of your lives.

"So..." he asks, "How did your appointment go? Did you get drilled full of holes or what?"

A sense of shame creeps over you.

~~1: Laugh about your dorky night guard with your brother.~~

~~2: Tell him about the night guard and why you need it.~~

3: (Lie) Tell him it was a routine cleaning.

4: Tell him about your tooth grinding problem, but not the stress causing it.

Interesting thing here is that option 3 points out that you'd be telling a lie about the dentist. It's interesting that this is labeled (by the designer/character/player/whomever) as a blatant lie, but nothing prior to this has been, even though I more or less lied to the other people who asked how I was doing . . .

played by Toni Pizza

> Tell him about your tooth grinding

"The dentist said I'm apparently grinding my teeth too much when I sleep."

"Oh?" Malcolm replies, *"Been stressed out lately kiddo?"*

Deciding that you don't really want to go into it, you tell him that you don't think that's the case and it's probably just a random thing. He doesn't pry farther, and instead begins reminiscing with you about the time you chipped a baby tooth because he accidentally knocked you over once.

You go out for dinner and catch up on things, but you still feel somewhat distracted by the gnawing anxiety in the back of your mind. Though you enjoy your brother's company, you still feel like you want nothing more than to go home and hide from the world tonight. It becomes hard for you to try to stuff all of your horrible feelings down and go emotionless when someone like the dentist can see a fraction of what goes on inside your head. It leaves you feeling embarrassed and weak, and you hate yourself for feeling that way. You wonder if you're really fooling anyone into thinking you're a normal person, and then you wonder if your brother knows and is hanging out with you out of pity tonight.

After he drops you back off at your apartment, you throw the night guard out. You can't stand to even look at the thing.

Next.

WHY DID I THROW THE NIGHT GUARD OUT? THOSE ARE SO EXPENSIVE!

Still profoundly depressed.

> Next

It's a dry Sunday morning.

You grab your morning coffee and sit down at your desk to check your email. A new message pops up in your inbox almost as soon as you do. It's from Amanda, and you remember your meeting in the cafe and awkwardly bringing up your feelings to her.

Subj: Hey buddy

Body: Hey. Sorry it's been a few weeks. I meant to get this to you sooner, but it took a while for me to get a hold of my folks back home. Dad told me to say hi by the way.

Depression Quest by Zoe Quinn

Anyway, I remembered what we talked about last time I saw you and I hope you aren't insulted, but I asked my mom for the number for her therapist. Don't worry! I didn't tell her who it was for. I think she's worried about me now though, haha.

Anyway, the number is 647-723-5274. It's a really good office, you should look into it. Talking to someone never hurts.

If you're worried about money, don't be. They're one of the few that has a really good sliding scale fee system and won't charge you what you can't afford.

I hope you're feeling better. It was really nice to see you again!

- A

It's still early enough that you could call and make an appointment today.

What do you do?

~~1: Call the therapist's number. You're looking forward to the help you think they can offer.~~

~~2: Try your luck and call the number, even though the mere thought of talking to someone makes you anxious. She cared enough to send it to you, after all.~~

3: Sleep on it, and see how you're feeling in the morning. You're not keen on the idea at all, but you don't want to disappoint Amanda.

4: Close the email without thinking more of it. This has been embarrassing enough already.

Again, Amanda is awesome. I actually think this is a great example of what it might look like for someone to offer help. It's kind of awkward but also straight to the point and not pushy at all.

> Sleep on it

The thought of picking up the phone and calling someone about this right now is overwhelming. Sure, you're having a hard time lately and have motivation issues, but are you really in need of therapy? Shouldn't you be able to just get over it yourself? What if they put you on medication that makes you feel like a zombie? What if you go and the therapist looks down on you? What will Alex think about this?

played by Toni Pizza

Trying to think about all these things at once makes it feel like a very big deal, and you decide to take your time to think on it.

The rest of the day passes quickly, and that night you have a hard time trying to sleep because your brain is too busy thinking about all these things, and imagining all of the ways it could go horribly wrong.

The next morning, you check your email again with blurry eyes. Amanda's email is still there, seemingly waiting for you. You are no more decided than you were yesterday.

What now?

1: ~~Just call already—it can't hurt to check it out.~~

2: ~~Call after wrestling with it for a few minutes longer.~~

3: Don't call. This is way too much for you to be able to deal with right now.

    Another important scenario! Calling a therapist is *such* a big deal. One time I made a whole game about these questions and the first time seeing a therapist, so this is totally my jam.
    I'm *so* frustrated that I can't make a decision here! I think my obsession with therapy is possibly ruining my ability to play the game the way I should be playing it (from the perspective of someone who is depressed—not obsessed with therapy).

> Don't call

The sight of Amanda's email address in your inbox sets your heart racing. You had almost forgotten about the horribly awkward conversation from a few weeks ago. Now, upon reading through her email, memories of how ashamed and embarrassed you felt talking about your problems wash over you as if you were experiencing them anew. Overcome by the sudden vivid recollection of your emotional outburst, it's all you can do to close the email as quickly as you can and step away from the computer to try and find something else to take your mind off of it.

Next.

    Next.

> Next

Depression Quest by Zoe Quinn

It is early on a Wednesday morning.

Lately you've developed a nasty habit of waking up 10 - 20 minutes before your alarm rings, and unfortunately today is no exception. You lay in bed, each minute ticking closer and closer to "wake up time" and passing on a swelling wave of ever-encroaching dread.

Sooner than you would like, your alarm blares with caustic inevitability. You frantically pound the snooze button and then retreat under your blankets, as if the warmth of your comforter can shield you from the passage of time.

You almost always have difficulty rising from bed, but today that simple task seems nothing short of herculean. After several snooze cycles, you decide that you just can't deal with work today; you're incapable of even rousing yourself from bed, let alone going into work and having to force yourself through a work day. Not to mention, you've "snoozed" so many times that it would be impossible to make it in on time now anyways.

What do you do?

~~1: Hop out of bed and start getting ready for work. You'll be late, but it's better than not going in at all.~~

~~2: Head into work. At least you can leave early if it gets too unbearable.~~

3: Call your boss to tell him you're sick and won't be in today.

You are severely depressed. Your motivation levels are nonexistant. You alternate between feeling totally apathetic to panicking about things out of your control. You lack energy to do much more than sleep the days away, yet your constant feelings of worthlessness prevent you from getting any actual rest. You feel like dying but ironically are too drained to actually act on these feelings.

You are not currently seeing a therapist.

You are not currently taking medication for depression.

My first response to this is "Hey, that's not fair!" because my depression meter has dropped again. I'm laughing at that reaction now because depression isn't fair. It's not fair, it's not nice, and you never feel like you're making choices.

> Call your boss to tell him you're sick

In spite of the fact that you know that it's your job, and that

played by Toni Pizza

you should go, you keep fighting yourself every step of the way. Every time you resolve to climb out of bed and just go, your body seems to get heavier and your head gets foggier and you find yourself unable to actually make yourself move.

You grab your phone and dial your boss' number, hoping that it's early enough yet that he won't be there and you can just leave a message. Fortunately, after a couple of rings, voicemail picks up and you leave a message explaining that you're sick and won't be in today. As you hang up the phone, you worry that perhaps your message sounds like a lame excuse.

You hope your boss won't call or email you to follow up with your message, but for now you're too foggy to do too much of any sort of thinking and eventually you fall back into a sleep that is both heavy and restless.

Next.

I'm appropriately frustrated with myself at this point in the game.

> Next

When you wake up the next morning, short of feeling well rested you actually feel more stressed out. While it was definitely nice to get a break from work, you're now faced with a new problem you hadn't considered before: you still have to go to work today. While you aren't having the same problems physically getting out of bed you were having yesterday, the prospect of having to face your boss after missing a day of work does not seem appealing in the slightest.

You worry that your absence won't be seen as believable or legitimate, that your coworkers and boss will think you were just trying to half-assedly play hooky. Or worse, you fear that someone will actually ask you what's wrong. Being caught in that instance and having to either make up a half-baked excuse or worse, that they'll see right through you and know, quickly has your mood matching the drizzly weather outside. You know that you have to go into work, but your fear of being perceived as either lazy or defective is making you regret yesterday's decision to take the day off, and ultimately you feel worse for it.

Next.

> Next

It's 2am on a Sunday, and you have work in the morning.

You roll over to see the sickly green glow of the time dis-

Depression Quest by Zoe Quinn

played on your LED alarm clock and let out an exasperated sigh. You've been trying to fall asleep for over 3 hours now to no avail. Every time your head hits the pillow, you're overcome with anxious thoughts that wrap themselves around each other. Worries about your job lead to worries about your future lead to worries about your very identity, and you're unable to shake them off long enough to doze off. Your eyes won't even stay shut as your mind races through imagined scenarios going horribly wrong, which you promptly attribute to your general worthlessness.

Your thoughts run too fast for you to come to a satisfying conclusion on any one of them. Your room is completely silent, but the silence has given way to a loud static noise rattling around inside your head. Your heart beats loudly and you worry it's beating a little too fast. You worry that if you focus too strongly on your racing heart, you'll freak yourself out hard enough that you have a heart attack.

You have to be awake for work in a mere 8 hours, and you know your performance has been sagging lately, and that this won't help the situation one bit.

What do you do?

1: ~~Force yourself to sleep.~~

2: ~~Go to bed. It shouldn't be that hard.~~

3: ~~Just close your eyes and let it happen. Why won't your thoughts back off for five seconds?~~

4: ~~Snap out of it. What is wrong with you? Why can't you stop stressing out for five seconds?~~

5: ~~You're probably going to go into work tomorrow exhausted and fuck everything up and get fired.~~

6: Go to your computer. Sleep is clearly not happening no matter how long you lay here.

-_-

> Go to your computer

You get out of bed and head to your desk. Laying in bed with nothing but your thoughts to keep you company makes you feel like you're going insane. The harshness of the light coming from the screen makes you squint as you turn it on, despite how often you find yourself in this exact situation. There have been so many nights lately just like this.

played by Toni Pizza

As you begin reading a news story, an online friend of yours IMs you.

attic: you're up late again i see.

You: Yeah. Can't sleep.

You: Again.

attic: thinknig too much again?

attic: *thinking

You: You guessed it.

You: :(

attic: wanna talk about it?

You end up talking with attic for quite some time about how you've been feeling. He's always been easy to talk to about personal matters, and the added security of talking online helps. Being able to rethink what you say as you type it out and check it before you send it out helps you gather your thoughts, and you find it less intimidating in a way to type it all into a prompt than say it out loud.

attic: i don't wanna be that guy who thinks they can diagnose something because i read a wikipedia article

attic: but it kinda sounds like you might have depression

attic: you should talk to someone about that

attic: like a doctor

You pause. You're not sure if it's how tired you feel or being frustrated from mentally eating away at yourself earlier in the night, but what he says rings true. Maybe you should see a doctor about this.

attic: we can do some research and see if there's a good doctor near you

attic: its not like you're going back to sleep anytime soon anyway

attic: might as well do something while you're awake

attic: :)

1: You: This is just a low night, I am normally able to sleep and I don't have depression, but thank you for your concern.

2: You: No that's ok.

3: You: It can't hurt to talk to someone I guess.

FINALLY I CAN MAKE A CHOICE AGAIN. Yes, I will talk to someone.

Though, this game is telling me that other people have to push me to make choices, that I can't just do it on my own.

> It can't hurt to talk to someone

attic: oh okay!

attic: let's find you a doctor then :)

attic: just remember

attic: there's nothing wrong with having depression

attic: you wouldn't be ashamed to have bronchitis or something

attic: so there's no reason to be ashamed if it's your brain that's sick instead

You google around with Attic and after a bit of searching you find a doctor that has gotten really good reviews. You recognize the number as the same one that Amanda had emailed you a few weeks back and feel a bit ashamed for failing to do this sooner. You make a note of it, and tell Attic you plan on calling her in the morning before work.

You end up going to bed after that, with a slight sense of accomplishment. You tuck yourself into bed, with the thought of maybe feeling better soon on your mind. You try not to get your hopes up as you drift off to sleep.

Next.

How many times am I allowed to say that Amanda is awesome before they cut this playthrough?

> Next

played by Toni Pizza

You groggily grab your morning coffee and sit down at your desk to check your email. You notice the note you left yourself a few days ago with the therapist's number on it. You've been somewhat putting off calling her purely out of nervousness, but you feel like you should probably make the decision to do it or throw the note out and stop stressing yourself out about it.

What do you do?

1. ~~Call the therapist's number. You're looking forward to the help you think they can offer.~~

2. ~~Get it over with and call the therapist's office.~~

3. Throw the note out. Who are you kidding?

Ugh. I should've just made the call that night and left a message. Now I have to throw out the note. I KNEW this was going to happen! The character KNEW this was going to happen. This is the worst. Every time I get to make a choice, the next scenario takes that right away. I still can't tell how intentional that is. I'm sure it's intentional, but I'm not sure it's quite working how it should.

Throw out the damn note. Next.

> Throw the note out

You stare at the note for a long while before crumpling it in your hand and throwing it out. Therapy is for people with real problems, not whiners like me... you tell yourself. Even if you did think you were worth the resources, you don't know if you could actually bring yourself to dial the number and say the words out loud. Somehow, that would make what you're feeling seem that much real. If you don't call, some part of you feels like it makes it that much easier to pretend it all isn't happening.

Maybe that's for the best, you think. If you can just shove it all down and try to ignore it, you can struggle through the day and hopefully someday just get over it. Opening up is painful, and you're not sure if dredging all of this sewage out of your mind will even have a positive effect on you.

The therapist would probably laugh at you anyway.

Next.

Worst. Next. Where is my gf btw?

Depression Quest by Zoe Quinn

> Next

It's a chilly Thursday night, and you've just gotten off work.

This has felt like one of the longest days you've faced in recent memory. Even though nothing exceptional had happened, a ton of minor things kept going wrong, and coworkers had tried your patience throughout the day. You considered leaving work early, but you've already had enough absences lately on the days you feel too crushed by the job to get out of bed and didn't want to risk it.

You're lost in thought on the commute home, and your feelings of frustration both with your life and the world around you build as you run into minor annoyances like someone bumping into you really hard as they walk by. By the time you get home you're exhausted, and in a moment of metacognition realize that if you don't snap out of it you're probably in for a long and trying night as well. These pent up feelings aren't dying down, and are eating at you.

You open your front door and stare at your apartment. An overwhelming feeling of exhaustion overcomes you, and you feel like your energy levels are low enough that you'll likely settle into a single activity tonight.

What do you do?

~~1: Just shake off your bad mood and do something fun for the rest of the evening.~~

~~2: Reach out to someone close to you.~~

3: Don't burden anyone with your problems. Distract yourself.

Fine, I'll take the only choice that is there.

> Don't burden anyone

What you really want more than anything is to turn your brain off and just disappear for a while. You sink resignedly into your couch and start playing videogames, but you can't seem to focus on what's happening on-screen. You cycle through a few different games, but tonight everything seems either too tedious or too aggravating for you to play for more than a few minutes. A few of your online friends invite you to play a game with them, but the prospect of having to talk, let alone cooperate with other people seems incredibly unpleasant. You decide to give the videogames a rest for the evening, though you worry that you've offended your online friends and your next conversation will be awkward because of it, giving you yet another source of stress to weigh down on you tonight.

You boot up Netflix and cycle through some of your favorite shows and movies that you'd flagged as wanting to come back to, but again nothing seems to be able to hold your attention. You feel what can only be described as mentally fidgety, like there's an unscratchable itch somewhere on your brain that is becoming increasingly hard to ignore. You send off a quick text to Alex hoping that conversation will help pull you out of your head enough to relax, but you know she's in class tonight and the chances of her replying are slim. You head into the kitchen for food and come out with not so much a "sandwich" as just "peanut butter on two pieces of bread." You pace anxiously around your apartment while you eat, irritated both by whatever this nerve-wracking feeling is and by your ability to just ignore it and unwind.

Your evening is filled with half-successful attempts at distraction and you ultimately head to bed late, head filled with static.

Next.

> Next

It's a Wednesday evening, and you're visiting at your parents' house for a holiday.

It's one of the handful of times during the year you drive out to visit your old hometown, and you've seen random people you had gone to school with around town. Whenever bumping into them, the usual short versions of what you've done since graduating are exchanged. You've gone through a few of these today and have been very aware of how much you feel you haven't accomplished. When you were in high school you had much larger plans, and you feel like you've failed to manifest most of them. Even if you had managed to, you've largely lost interest in what you thought you wanted to do growing up. Now, you're not really sure what you want to do, and you've felt like you're lacking the ambition or drive to figure it out. Everyone you've caught up with seems so much happier than you, like they've got their lives all figured out, and you've kind of been feeling like a failure by comparison.

Your brother Malcolm arrives with his wife in tow shortly before you all sit down to dinner. He's been traveling for his job lately and you haven't seen him since the day he picked you up from the dentist. Your parents haven't seen him since before then. During dinner, they all catch up and Malcolm talks about the amazing things he's done on the road.

Your mother turns to you and asks what you've been up to since you've seen them last.

"Oh, same old same old..." you say. "Nothing really new going on."

Your mother makes a face. "Oh, nothing new? How long are you planning on staying at that job of yours?"

What do you say?

~~1: Tell them about the exciting new job you're gunning for.~~

~~2: (Lie) Tell them what they want to hear: that you're actively looking for a more prestigious position~~

~~3: Admit that you don't know what you want to do.~~

4: Excuse yourself to the bathroom.

Sigh
Go to the bathroom.

> Excuse yourself

As your mother looks across the table at you expectantly, everything inside you wants to run away. You have had this conversation with her enough to know that anything you can say would either be a lie or would result in a lecture. After spending the day feeling like you're a failure already, you can't really handle more of the same from your family regardless of how well they mean.

"Actually, I'll be right back, I have to use the restroom."

You excuse yourself from the table despite not actually having to use the facilities, and head to the bathroom. You lock the door behind you and flip down the toilet lid, take a seat, and rest your head in your hands. You take a few deep breaths as your mind runs through it's typical self deprecating scripts, though you still feel as though it's a moment of relief.

Even though you love your family, you really feel like they don't know you at all sometimes and this makes them exhausting to be around on nights like this. You wish you could tell them what you are feeling. That sometimes it feels like you're lost in the woods, and that if you were to drop dead in your apartment the world wouldn't notice. You want to make her understand that more often than not, you feel like

played by Toni Pizza

an alien, like there isn't anywhere in this world that feels like a place where you belong, and you have no idea how to fix it or what to do. You wish you could find the words so they would understand you, but you end up feeling like an outsider instead.

Instead, you decided to remove yourself from the situation and calm down. You couldn't see a resolution where attempting those things would work, and you needed a moment of space instead.

You hear a knock on the door.

Malcolm's voice comes through the door. "Hey kiddo, you alright in there? You've been in there for a while."

"Yeah, I was just feeling a little sick."

"Well, if there's anything I can get you let me know. They're about to serve pie though, if you're feeling up to it."

"Yeah, I'll be out in a minute."

Malcolm is quiet for a moment. "Hey, just so you know... I'm really proud of you." You hear his big footsteps walk away from the door, and you splash some water on your face before leaving to rejoin your family.

Next.

    Oh, you've noticed my commentary has effectively stopped? Right, that's because I have no willpower.
    Next.

> Next

It's a rainy night.

You are hurrying through the rain to Alex's apartment at her behest. Though your pace is quick, the rain is steadily soaking up your pant legs as you traverse the town, and it's darkening your already poor mood.

The call came while you were at home after a day of dealing with abnormally frustrating people. You'd spent the afternoon trying to unwind and get some work on your project done. Alex called and interrupted one of your "try to make progress, get frustrated at not making progress, have a harder time making progress due to frustration, repeat" loops and you haven't fully shaken off the feelings of being annoyed with yourself from it yet.

You knock on her door, and on the third knock hear her voice

Depression Quest by Zoe Quinn

call from further in the apartment to come on in. As you cross the threshold, dripping rainwater all the way, you notice that the lights are turned down very low in the apartment. You squint to navigate it as you clutch on to your damp umbrella, but end up hitting your shin on a side table, mumbling a profanity under your breath.

You barely make out Alex emerging from the hallway, clad in what looks to be a robe with the bare skin of her legs peering out underneath.

"Why don't you come in and... warm up?" she asks in her designated, slightly cheesy, "sexy" voice.

After a beat of silence, she states more naturally "My roommates are out of town this weekend so I thought it might be nice to have a little fun while they're away."

You appreciate her affection, but you're too wrapped up in your own negative feedback loops to be in the mood right now.

What do you do?

~~1: Let go of your stress and be intimate with your girlfriend.~~

~~2: Try to unwind with her before getting physical.~~

~~3: Suggest you do something else instead.~~

4: Tell her you're not in the mood.

 I'm not in the mood.

 > Tell her you're not in the mood

"*I don't...*" you start, unsure of how to phrase how you're feeling in a way that doesn't hurt her.

Even at those two words, her face is falling. "*Right... this is sudden...*" she says, clutching the top of her robe closed.

"*No, no, it's not you I-*"

She cuts you off. "*It's not you, it's me, right? It's ok, I get it...*" She moves to her bookshelf and blows out some candles you had failed to notice. "*It was cheesy anyway.*"

The hurt in her voice cuts you down to your core. You can tell she feels rejected by you, and everything feels like it's happening so quickly and slipping through your fingers. You wish you were telepathic and could let her know exactly how you feel about her, so that she wouldn't be wounded by your own

played by Toni Pizza

mood.

"This was all really nice, I just have had a hard day and-" you stammer, but she leaves the room and you hear the bedroom door close. Unsure of what else to do, you sit down on her couch to wait for her to return.

You feel terrible for hurting her, when she clearly meant nothing but good. Although you didn't want to have sex with her right this moment, you are beating yourself up for handling it so poorly. Why couldn't you find the right words to let her down gently, without her thinking that she had done something wrong? Why do you have to be such a shitty partner?

She emerges from her room, now dressed. Her eyes are red, but you can tell she is trying to not show that she was crying.

"I uh... I actually have to do a lot of coursework... So maybe you should head home. This was kind of a dumb idea anyway. Sorry."

"Okay..." you mutter, not wanting to make things worse.

A couple of seconds of silence pass as neither of you are sure of what to say from there. You leave with a quick goodbye, and curse yourself the entire way home.

Next.

> Next

It's an early winter evening, and even though it's not particularly late, the time of year has lent the sky an almost prematurely darkened cast.

Day after day, just like today, you trudge home from a job you have increasingly come to hate. On this day your job misery seems to have reached critical mass, and not even shedding your rain-laden and uncomfortable work clothes helps you to unwind from your work day.

You collapse into your couch, blank and numb. While your job always seemed to just be an unpleasant reality of existence, it was a position you sort of fell into unexpectedly, never intending to work there long-term, and it's getting harder and harder to keep it up.

While it's certainly not your dream job, you've always just sort of stuck it out out of necessity before, but it's becoming increasingly difficult to do that. Though you couldn't even begin to imagine what else you could do, you find yourself face-to-face with a question you just can't ignore: is your complacency worth the price of this level of misery?

Depression Quest by Zoe Quinn

What do you do?

1: ~~Get proactive: Polish off your resume and start looking for other jobs to send feelers out to.~~

2: ~~Try and at least be productive by focusing your efforts on your project tonight.~~

3: ~~Aimlessly look through classifieds for another job.~~

4: Turn on the TV and let your mind go blank.

Pleaseeeeee, let me do anything other than nothing!

> Turn on the TV

You grab the TV remote, wanting nothing more than to forget all about the terrible day you had at work. You flip on the TV and let yourself get swallowed up by the couch. You grab your laptop to "surf" the internet while you "watch" TV, paying no real attention to either. You watch a few reruns of shows you're at best indifferent towards and a movie on TV that's a few years old, all while you scroll idly through your Twitter feed.

At the end of the night, you don't really feel any better so much as you just feel numb, which is basically what you were going for anyways. Ultimately it gets late enough that you tell yourself you should probably call it a night. You beat yourself up over the fact that you didn't accomplish anything this evening, but at least you managed to forget about your job for a couple of hours. As you fall asleep, you're acutely aware of the fact that after a mere few hours' sleep, you've got to do it all again.

Next.

> Next

It's a little past 8pm on a Tuesday night.

You're at your computer, frustration levels peaked, rubbing your eyes and sighing heavily. You're working on a project from your job that has you stretched to wit's end trying to meet a looming deadline, and as it lurks closer and closer you are seriously doubting your ability to get it done. You've dragging your feet a little at work due to your complete lack of energy lately, in spite of wanting to do a good job. You find yourself unable to push past it, and feel horribly useless for

played by Toni Pizza

it.

You slide your hands off your face to look at your screen as it beeps at you.

attic: *hey are you there?*

attic: *i really need to talk to someone about something...*

You feel like you're getting nowhere with your current task, and could probably use a break. However, you know that you have a history of getting distracted and then losing motivation to pick something back up again afterward.

What do you do?

1: ~~Multitask.~~

2: ~~Tell Attic you're busy.~~

3: Try to regain your focus - don't answer.

4: Answer Attic.

Jesus, Zoe, now that I'm cataloguing every step of this, yeah, you're doing a damn good job of wearing me down.

FINALLY, A CHOICE. Yes, a person needs me—I need to hear that I am needed even if it's just from someone on the internet.

> Answer Attic

You're feeling like you've hit a brick wall with your task, so why not take a break and help out a friend?

You: *Hey. What's up?*

attic: *oh good you're there*

attic: *um*

attic: *i just found out i got cheated on*

attic: *i don't know what to do*

You: *Oh no, that's horrible!*

The two of you talk for a long time, and you lend a shoulder to your friend. You give him space to rant, to cry, and most importantly to be able to voice his inner turmoil. You give him your full attention, and talk him through what his options are for what he does next. You keep him from doing something rash, and the two of you decide it's best for him to sleep on it before doing anything. Exhausted, he departs for bed and thanks you for being there to talk with him.

As you close the IM window, you feel horribly sorry for your friend, but happy that you were able to help. It serves as a tangible reminder to you that you're capable of being useful to someone instead of solely being a mess that needs everyone else's help.

You boot up your work project and find that you're suddenly able to get some solid progress done on it that night.

Next.

Oh my gosh, finally. (I promise I'm genuinely worn down and am not just saying "next" to be an asshole).
Next.

> Next

It's yet another sleepless Thursday night.

You're at Alex's apartment, wide awake in bed as she's sleeping peacefully beside you. She fell asleep hours ago, and you've been laying here unable to shut your brain up long enough to fall asleep. You've added the feelings of insecurity about your relationship to the rest of the noise in your head keeping you up tonight.

It was kind of a tense night between the two of you. You arrived after a stressful day at work, and as you made dinner together you barely said a word. You were stuck in your own head and had a hard time really being present with her as your thoughts turned to all of the ways you feel like you're deficient at being a good person and beating yourself up mentally for each one.

She told you she could tell you were in "one of your moods" and said that she wouldn't push you, but missed talking to you as the two of you sat on the couch together. You wanted to tell her how much you love her, but you couldn't make the words come out right and ended up sounding defensive instead.

As you lay there next to her now, you trace your fingers across her arm just lightly enough to not wake her. You still haven't explained your depression to her, and it's starting to feel more and more like a secret you're keeping instead

played by Toni Pizza

of something she simply doesn't know about you yet. It's becoming more and more apparent that it's impacting your relationship with her, and you feel guilty about this. However you're also terrified that if she knew exactly how fucked up you are that she would leave you - you already worry that she's only with you because she doesn't realize how terrible of a person you are yet, and you're afraid that this would be the final thing to expose you.

She stirs in her sleep and squints as she opens her eyes. With the confusion that comes with waking up, she asks you if you're awake, and then if everything's ok.

~~1: Open up to her with ease.~~

2: Tell her about your situation.

3: Tell her it's nothing and that she should go back to sleep.

Obviously I'm going to talk to her. I need to do ANYTHING at this point, even if she takes it badly.

> Tell her about your situation

You feel like a jerk for accidentally waking her up, but you're afraid if you put this off any longer that you won't find the strength to tell her everything later.

"No, actually. Everything isn't ok. Can I tell you something? Something important?"

Alex sits up, rubbing the sleep out of her eyes. For the rest of the night you lay side by side, holding hands, as you tell her everything. You tell her how it's more than just feeling sad sometimes, how you feel trapped by your own mind sometimes, how sometimes you feel nothing at all, and how you can't shake it off. She listens the entire time, occasionally asking questions about how this or that works, or asking you to explain something further. She squeezes your hand and tells you she understands, and that she's sad you didn't tell her sooner.

After laying silent for a moment, the weight of what you did hits you. You desperately want her to say something, to tell you how she's feeling about all of this but you're too afraid of what the answer would be to ask. You start convincing yourself that now that she knows everything, she's going to leave. There's no way someone could deal with how you really are.

"So how can I help? What do you need me to do? she asks.

Depression Quest by Zoe Quinn

You think for a second, and the answer you come up with fills you with despair. *"I honestly don't know. I wish I knew how to fix this, but I don't know that you can do anything. I think it's something I just have to live with."*

She looks at you with sad eyes before kissing you on the forehead. *"Then I'll live with it with you."*

"I don't know how you could possibly love me."

She rolls over and wraps her arms around your neck, settling her head on top of yours. *"You don't need to. Just know that I do."*

Next.

> You are profoundly depressed. You are barely functional, on days you can even get out of bed at all.
>
> You are not currently seeing a therapist
>
> You are not currently taking medication for depression.

My depression meter has been downgraded to "profoundly depressed!"
After a long stretch, this is another important moment, not just because my depression meter changed states, but because finally saying something out loud to someone important is a big fucking deal.

> Next

It's a Friday night, and you're laying across your bed feeling pathetic.

As you were leaving work tonight, a group of coworkers asked if you wanted to join them for drinks. Feeling antisocial and put on the spot, you declined. You have a habit of doing this - you're often so convinced that you are weird and terrible and that any invitation to hang out will end in disappointment for those inviting you. You never feel like you know how to act in group outings, and you feel like a total creep since it seems to come so naturally to anyone who isn't you. You find yourself petrified of breaking some unknown social rule that you don't often go out.

Now, however, you find yourself alone at home. Your brain has begun telling you how pathetic and sad you are for being unable to just be a normal person and go out with nice people. You can't figure out why you can't just go out and meet people and enjoy yourself. At the same time, you're also feeling like no one would possibly want you to hang out if they really knew you, because you're dull and weird anyway.

played by Toni Pizza

You try your typical strategy and boot up Netflix to distract yourself from these feelings, but frustration with yourself builds, and you realize you have to do something else with your night. Anything else to take your mind off of how awful and lonely you feel right now.

What do you do?

1: ~~Get over it and go out to the bar where your coworkers are hanging out anyway.~~

2: ~~See if Attie is online.~~

3: ~~Call Alex.~~

4. Drink.

5. Go out somewhere, alone.

So I've got some choices, but neither of them feel like what my character would actually do. Drink or go out alone. Neither of those things have ever been options (or even discussed??), so it's strange that now those are my only choices. I guess it's maybe pointing towards erratic behavior or something, but if I just had a big moment with Alex, I want to call Alex.

Get me outta here!

> Go out somewhere, alone

Your entire apartment feels claustrophobic, as though you're being choked by how isolated you feel, how trapped you feel just being here with yourself. You can't stand to be here any longer, so you grab your coat and just start walking. If you take a walk and get some air, maybe you can get away from the crushing feeling in your chest.

You walk for longer than anticipated, headphones on and blaring a favorite track. Before you know it, you've walked over a mile. The entire time your thoughts dart from personal failure to personal failure, and you feel like you're trying to get away from yourself.

However, you end up walking long enough that after the initial stress, the static in your head begins to calm down. Instead of being the overbearing noise it was back in the apartment, you've settled into a calmer state where you're able to zone out and listen to the music. Your steps synch to the rhythm in your headphones, and it feels almost as if you were meditating.

The weather threatens to start raining, and you turn back managing to catch the very start of a rainstorm. Your calm

Depression Quest by Zoe Quinn

persists as you arrive back home and go through the motions of getting ready for bed, and you're able to sleep with relative ease that night.

Next.

Night walks. Next.

> Next

It's a cold Saturday afternoon.

You've just arrived at Alex's apartment, and you're happy to finally see her after a week of absence due to your schedules not lining up due to work and school. You hug her in the doorway but she breaks away sooner than normal and sits down on the couch as you take off your sneakers and lay them in the usual place, right next to hers.

"There's something I was hoping we could talk about, actually." She says.

You feel anxious at hearing those words, and move to take a seat on the couch. Your heart starts to race - is this one of those "we need to talk" situations? Has she finally had enough of your baggage? Did the week apart make her realize how much better things are without you?

She sits down across from you on the couch, and you can tell by the look on her face that she isn't looking forward to saying what she's about to, and you feel your grip tighten on the couch cushion.

"So..." She starts. She breaks eye contact and takes a deep breath, which spikes your anxiety. *"Things with us have felt kind of... weird lately. It's like you've been really distant, and I'm not sure how to take it."*

"I guess I just want to make sure you still wanna do this. Us, I mean." She notices you gripping the couch. She looks at your face, seemingly searching.

She looks at you with uncertainty and you can practically see the knot of pain in her chest.

You try to reign in your kneejerk reaction to run. Unsure of what to say to that, your mind races. You know you have to choose your next words carefully. Though the self deprecation rages in your mind, you try to think through it. You try to sort out what you really want to do here. A myriad of feelings is boiling inside you - which one do you do you listen to?

What do you do?

played by Toni Pizza

~~1: Recommit to your relationship with ease and grow closer for the experience.~~

2: End things for her own good. You're clearly not making her happy.

~~3: You're having difficulty managing the relationship and your personal life. Break things off, for you.~~

~~4: You still want this. Reassure her that you are committed to working through things.~~

5: You still want this. Say whatever you can to make her stay, regardless of your concerns.

6: Yes, there has been distance. Attempt to solve it by asking her to move in.

Blah! Can't I just get a break? I just told you I was depressed like five minutes ago and now we're having the "where are we" talk?? This feels slightly out of line. Also, each of the choices are so overblown. End it. Do whatever you have to. Move in. Too dramatic. Tone it down. Can I take a deep breath and reload my choices?

I'm going with the "do whatever it takes" choice because she did just say she loves me . . .

> You still want this

Panic sets in, and it sets in hard. Your mind begins frantically darting between insulting yourself for being so horrible at relationships and thinking of the "right" thing to say to make her feel better. All you want in the world right now is to keep her with you, to make her feel better. Even though you feel a bit selfish and dishonest, you use it as fodder against yourself instead of changing your course of action.

"I'll find some way to start spending more time with you, I promise!" you tell her, tears welling up in the corners of your eyes. *"I know I can be really stupid sometimes but I'll be better, I'll figure out some way to be better, just... Just don't go."*

Alex looks uncomfortable. *"I know I'm hard to deal with, that this stupid brain of mine makes me do stupid things and..."* you start to hate yourself for saying these things, for sounding so pathetic. *"Just... just tell me what I can do to make things right and I'll do it... Anything."*

Your panic escalates as the more desperate you are to find the right words for her makes her pull further away from you.

Depression Quest by Zoe Quinn

You're verbally flailing for the right answers, and she calls them out as being platitudes. You can practically watch her slip through your fingers as you try to cling on tighter. It's as if you're watching yourself say these things and screaming No, stop, can't you see how you're driving her away!? But you can't stop, and before you know it she's crying.

"I... I think we should break up. I can't do this anymore..." she says, though it doesn't feel real. You feel as though all of the blood has gone from your face, and your thoughts go silent.

The rest of the conversation is stilted and forced. She says she's sure, and that you should go. You barely hear the door close behind you as you stand in the hall, feeling utterly empty. You lean against the wall of the hallway leading to her apartment. Looking at her door, it doesn't make sense to you. It doesn't seem like the destination it used to, like the thing you waited eagerly behind after knocking, waiting for her beautiful face to peek around the corner. Now you feel like an alien staring at a foreign object, an impassable barrier.

The reality hits you over the next few days, and you spiral into a very deep low. You withdraw entirely and outside of work, you don't leave your apartment. You can't stop replaying the failures you made with her over and over in your head, wondering what could've been if you weren't such a fuckup. It's going to take you a long time to get over her.

Next.

You are severely depressed. Your motivation levels are nonexistant. You alternate between feeling totally apathetic to panicking about things out of your control. You lack energy to do much more than sleep the days away, yet your constant feelings of worthlessness prevent you from getting any actual rest. You feel like dying but ironically are too drained to actually act on these feelings.

You are not currently seeing a therapist

You are not currently taking medication for depression

OH MY GOD WHY ISN'T AMANDA MY GIRLFRIEND, ALEX IS AWFUL!
Back to severe depression. Couldn't she have like . . . tried to help? Next.

> Next

It's December, and you've returned to your parents' house to

played by Toni Pizza

celebrate the holidays with your family. Out the living room window, you can see a gentle flurry of snow drifting down to meet the pristine blanket of white from yesterday's unexpected Christmas Eve snowfall, and you quietly laugh to yourself at how incredibly cliche it seems.

Still, as you sit down to dinner, you can't help but notice how being surrounded by family, and the overly kitschy atmosphere your mom's decorations have created, have actually made you feel relaxed and almost *comfortable*. Your mom is running around frantically checking the oven and the stockings and just generally trying to "family time" it up, while your dad sits at the head of the table drinking a beer and laughing with your brother Malcolm. His wife Karen is there too, whom you've always gotten along well with .

As you thoughtfully munch away at your turkey, listening to the conversations around you, your thoughts drift back over the last few months. You think about how hard things had gotten, replaying over in your head some of your worst (as well as some of your best) memories. It seems like all of these things just came to a head over the past few months, with a sudden flurry of relationship turmoil and professional anxiety, social stress and above all an omnipresent sense of weight that it seems you have just recently become aware of. You're drawn out of your reverie by your dad's familiar booming laugh as some cheesy comment Malcolm made seems to have hit its mark. Sitting at that table, you're suddenly immensely glad for the chance to be able to ignore everything for an evening and not have to struggle trying to explain yourself for once.

Fortunately, everyone seems to be content with laughing at each other's jokes and discussing favorite sports teams, and for a while you think you'll be able to get through dinner without any embarrassing personal intrusions. But no sooner did the thought cross your mind than the table conversation trickles off, leaving a slightly awkward silence to descend upon the dinner.

"*So how are you doing these days*, your mom asks you pointedly?

It's such a simple question, and one that you seem to have had to answer countless times recently. You take a moment to collect your thoughts, then looking up, you take a deep breath.

Well...

How is it December?

Depression Quest by Zoe Quinn

> Well . . .

There's no doubt that depression is a battle, and it seems to have taken a particular toll on you. As the days go by, you find yourself interested in less and less. You think back to your life a mere few months ago, and compared to where you are now it seems like you've just lost so much.

Work has become unbearable, as the thought of you dragging yourself day in and day out to a job you can't stand just so you can scrape enough money together to do it all again the next day has ground your will down; lately your job performance has suffered tremendously, and your boss has already had a conversation with you about your absences. At this point, losing your job is not only a real possibility, it's downright probable.

Your personal relationships have deteriorated as well. While you could never describe yourself as a social butterfly, your constant flakiness and continuing withdrawal from your circle of friends has all but alienated them from you completely. Nowadays you rarely see or speak to them, and when you do, the conversations are strained and perfunctory. You almost never leave your apartment anymore.

Your detachment from the world even ended up costing you your relationship with Alex. While she made every effort to be supportive and understanding, your refusal to try and manage your situation forced her to have to choose between having to constantly look after you and pursuing her own goals. As she continued to excel in her program at school, as she made it very clear on more than one occasion that she was dedicated fully to her education and career, and couldn't afford to be held back by somebody who insisted on being stagnant. The subsequent split was practically inevitable.

You never could wrap your head around the whole notion of therapy and view it as anything other than invasive. Refusing to admit your need for help, your decision to try and tackle your depression on your own now seems woefully miscalculated. Your friends may have been willing to listen to you at first, but over time your reluctance to accept any of their advice simply drove them away, leaving you with little in the way of a support network. With nobody to vent to and an inability or unwillingness to seek help on your own, you quickly lost any desire to attempt to overcome your depression and your downward spiral seemed to compound geometrically.

Pouring over the events of the past few months is, even now, exhausting and defeating. Looking at the person you were mere months ago is almost surreal; it feels like a completely

played by Toni Pizza

different person living a completely different life. In fact, it's hard for you to imagine ever having had a life that wasn't completely devoid of feeling or drive. The prospect of trying to imagine what your future holds seems not only impossible, but irrelevant and of little interest to you, as your life has become just a series of trudges from one emotionally exhausting moment to the next.

You look across at the table to your mother, weakly meeting her gaze before dropping your eyes to the floor. You open your mouth to answer, but no words come out. You don't even bother pretending to try and think of what to say.

Epilogue.

> Oy. Depression is a battle. This playthrough was a battle. Next?

> \> Epilogue

We really want to thank you for taking the time to play Depression Quest. We realize it may not be the most enjoyable game you've ever played, or even the easiest, and we sincerely appreciate your involvement.

If you would like to contribute to the developers and to **The National Suicide Prevention Lifeline**, click **here to do so**.

Like depression itself, Depression Quest does not have an end really. There is no neat resolution to depression, and it was important to us that Depression Quest's own resolution reflect that. Instead of a tidy ending, we want to just provide a series of outlooks to take moving forward. After all, that's all we can really do with depression - just keep moving forward. And at the end of the day it's our outlook, and support from people just like you, that makes all the difference in the world.

Thanks again.

Okay, wow. So, I'm not sure how I expected that whole process to go, but that was certainly more painful than I thought it would be. I think this is both good and bad. Good because it recreates a certain degree of accuracy—depression is a battle, you feel powerless, it tires you out. Bad because it seems like this battle hinged upon my first few decisions—not going to the party and not getting the cat—which makes me feel like I was "supposed to" try harder early on to have a chance. What's most frustrating is that sometimes I can't tell how intentional vs. procedural things are. The whole idea of quantifying my state of depression is somewhat problematic and makes me think of DSM checklists. Love love love this game and the exploration

Depression Quest by Zoe Quinn

of the topic; I'll continue to share it with friends, family, students, therapists, etc. But I am certainly looking forward to other approaches to translating depression into game mechanics.

EVEN COWGIRLS BLEED
BY CHRISTINE LOVE
PLAYED BY LEIGH ALEXANDER

It's the usual story. You're a big city girl with a closet full of fancy dresses but not a whole lot of sense, and lately all you've wanted to do is trade in your lonely winters for some real adventure. **Well, consarn just waiting, you say!**

It's not often I have to Google a word. What is "consarn?" Oh, *consarn it*, like a vintage 'damn it.' Well, isn't that uppity and wonderfully dorky. This poor "you," the you that "you are" here.

When I was a kid, I entered the seventh grade after spending most of my middle years in the safehouse of a Montessori school for bright, difficult, sheltered children. Bless me, I thought my big vocabulary would win me friends in my new, cool *Saved by the Bell* school, with shiny lockers and everything.

It took just a day or two to learn that it wouldn't. After that I imitated my peers the best I could, their walk and their cadence and the liberal introjection of *like, like*. I did too good a job, perhaps. The sudden transition very briefly earned me the nickname "Airhead Alexander." I had never been called an airhead in my life and have never been since.

Your cursor is a crosshair. I'm that elementary schoolkid again, and I'm armed.

"Consarn just wanting." Is that actually correct grammar, even for vintage slang? It doesn't matter. We've done our best. Take aim and—fire? So much as touch the red phrase in your crosshair and you've started shooting, whether you meant to or not.

> Consarn just waiting

So really, you did the only sensible thing a girl can do: you picked up your petticoats, you bought yourself a gun, and you headed out west to **San Francisco**.

Our awkward slip-up is suddenly gone, like it was never part of the story at all. An elegant little adjustment—we've not embarrassed ourselves, we've not misspoken. To the West is San Francisco.

It's funny; we're a cowgirl in the West, and there is no place less wild than San Francisco, if you ask me. Glass-bordered and fetishistic, rigidly tied up by a bizarre series of social norms. New York where I've lived my adult life is mostly like that. Expression is weaponized. Vulnerability, weaponized. America has a gun problem. You are afraid for your safety both practically and on a subtle emotional level. It's not a place where people have relationships. I don't believe in San Francisco's relationship norms as I understand them, either. Like that first day of seventh grade there are rules, but you probably don't know them, and you must never let on that you don't or they'll devour you.

You understand now, right? The slightest movement of your hand across those red particular bits of text here will fire your weapon off. It must, we think, just be how the game moves forward. Shoot off happily.

> San Francisco

. . . you headed out west.

You meet a man with a ridiculous **hat** while waiting for the caravan that leads westward. He looks unimpressed by the pistol twirl you practiced for days.

"Do you even know how to shoot that?", asks the man, with a grumpy stare.

Ah, what is this—the red stamp of San Francisco suddenly wiped from the narrative, as if the urging for that place was also as inconvenient as a bit of awkward slang.

Ah, here on our newborn-girl awkwardventure is a man with a bad hat and a profound doubt in our innate abilities. Wasn't expecting that, were we, girls. You can shoot that hat off his smug head, can't you? Maybe you just want to shoot him. I get that. I been there.

Actually, this is the game's first choice. If you're swinging that cursor around too carelessly you might just decide by accident, firing off whichever target—the smug man or his stupid hat—your mouse touches first. Immediately you can get a sense of your own volatility, your own fundamentally

played by Leigh Alexander

poor control. Hover in the wrong place and the gun kicks off, sending more of the words slipping, too fast, through your fingers.

If your sound is on you'll notice the lovely tinny arcade-gamey crunch, whichever you hit. Like these aren't real stakes. You're in a game, after all. It's like you've just shot a Space Invader. It's a suitable, familiar noise that you want a little more of. You *hit* something. You want to *hit* something else.

> Do you even know how to shoot that?

You narrowly miss him.

"Jesus Christ!" he yells angrily. "Be careful with that thing!"

Holster

Shoot at the man and he scolds you, making you ashamed of your own aggression. This is not a game about *hurting* people, it emphasizes.

Still, it's an interesting decision—the text scrolls past gently, in a linear fashion, wherever you aim. Choosing the first red-letter word instead of the second sentence feels orderly; choosing the target that appears later in the paragraph is almost more rebellious. This is tough for the hypertext-hungry, we who want to click everything and see everything. Surely if you shoot the hat, you can come back and shoot the man (the second sentence in which he lives, really.) But no, quickly there is a flash, a bang and a crunch, and no going back. The text is making minor, eloquent edits you as the player almost don't even notice. A clean revision of history where the story flows and you never slipped up at all.

> ~~Do you even know how to shoot that?~~
> hat

With one cool motion, you blast the hat clean off his head.

"You bet, old man," you say, coolly. That'll teach him.

Holster

Shoot the hat and prove your stylishness. This is the way that we all dream of negotiating such confrontations, right? With a deft, literate bang. That'll teach him, we're promised sagely, the overconfident flailing limbs of a kid who watches too many films and becomes the playground boss.

This is the first time we get the "Holster" option, embedded tiny and safe to the lower right of the screen. It doesn't matter if we feel like putting the gun away or if we feel like blasting stupid hat-man to bits. Putting the weapon away is our only way to move forward.

>

Even Cowgirls Bleed by Christine Love

The wagon arrives shortly. You hop in, carrying your minimal luggage without any help from anyone else.

"Would you look at that gorgeous **blue sky**. Nice weather for travelling," the coach driver says. "Y'all set, Miss?"

    And we're off. Finally someone's nice to us, you know? The first time you're a passenger in transit and someone treats you like one—like you've fooled everyone and suddenly you're just any other grown-up on her way to somewhere, totally worthy of respect and service like everyone else—the magic of your journey descends on you.

    But what's this? Even the pacifistic blue sky beckons to be aimed at. Continue, continue reading and journeying? Nah, cowgirl, skip your little crosshair across the vista first. Like, isn't that a little much, shooting *straight up* into the sky?

    This might be the first time that you as the player resist the heroine a little bit, resent that she doesn't give you the choice not to. The first time you play this game it feels portentious; the second time, it feels lethal.

>

You fire into the air like you're signalling the start of a race.

"Alrighty then," the driver says. "Let's go!"

And like that, you're about to start your adventure!

Holster

    Oh. Right. Like starting a race. The driver liked it. Okay. No one got hurt—why did you think someone was going to get hurt? There's your holster. Put that thing away, girl. This is the beginning of your adventure.

>

played by Leigh Alexander

...well, so far it's not much of an adventure. Mostly it's just travelling along lots of well-worn roads.

Holster

>

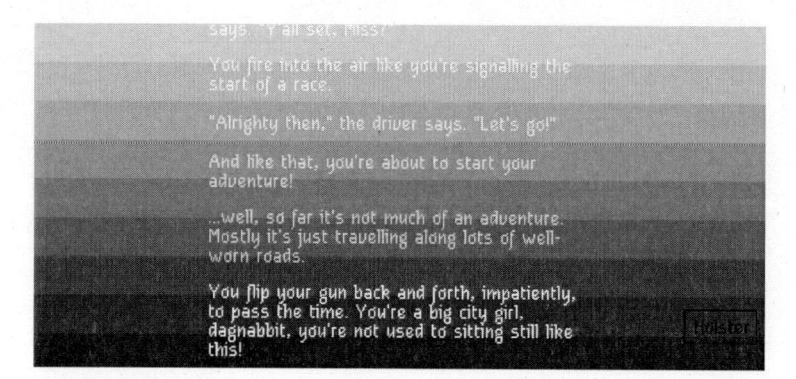

says, "Y'all set, Miss?"

You fire into the air like you're signalling the start of a race.

"Alrighty then," the driver says. "Let's go!"

And like that, you're about to start your adventure!

...well, so far it's not much of an adventure. Mostly it's just travelling along lots of well-worn roads.

You flip your gun back and forth, impatiently, to pass the time. You're a big city girl, dagnabbit, you're not used to sitting still like this!

Holster

You flip your gun back and forth, impatiently, to pass the time. You're a big city girl, dagnabbit, you're not used to sitting still like this!

Holster

>

It turns out, it's a really long trip to San Francisco.

Holster

>

A REALLY long trip.

Holster

To advance the text now, you "Holster" left, and then "Holster" right. Just a little idle movement of your mouse back and forth—you perform it once before the text tells you you're passing the time by tossing your gun to hand to hand, and you're like *ha, yeah, of course*. It surprises you. It makes you warm to it, to the game and to this girl who's telling you the story.

Masterfully, too, it makes you feel like you're kind of in control. If the accidental just-move-the-text-along feel of your weapon made you underestimate your own precision here, this sequence of pistol tricks teaches you

431

that your movements very much have to do with managing live ammunition deftly. You feel a new respect for the cursor after this, and a new sense of power in your own small movements.

> Holster

After three excruciatingly long days, you finally arrive. The wooden sign greets you:

WELCOME TO SAN FRANCISCO

POPULATION 50 000

You've arrived.

> POPULATION 50 000

You leave your signature on it.

"Plus one more," you say, as if you're the coolest mother-fornicator around. Because let's face it, sweetheart, you absolutely are. You're going to be absolutely welcome here.

Holster

Remember when you felt a little worried about shooting everything? Forget it. Leave your mark.

The assurance, *sweetheart*, the confidence in being welcomed is a little painful. Everyone is going to like me at school, Ma. Don't worry. I'm really smart.

> Holster

A **tumble weed** rolls by. Your eyes follow it further in town.

You take in the sight. Yep, it's everything you dreamed of, alright; awful roads that muck up your heels, unpainted wooden buildings, dust as far as the eye can see.

Holster

A tumbleweed appears. A "tumble weed"—*bless*. You wanna shoot it, don't you? Of course you do. You're at the moment in this game where you feel you can do anything.

The game offers you a choice between following that urge and just putting the gun away. Something about games is usually your impulse is to crave the path of most risk, of most interaction. Who puts their gun away when there's something to shoot? Almost no one, and yet the holster hov-

played by Leigh Alexander

ers, just a little moment of anxiety and what-if, narrative tension between what you know you want and what the right thing must be. If you shoot the tumbleweed, you're praised for being a crack shot, making you smugger than ever.

> \> tumble weed

A moving target! Well aren't you a crackshot.
Holster

> \>

You know what you need after all that time on the road?
Holster

> \>

A drink.
Holster

> \>

Fortunately, the nearest saloon is easy to find.

A pair of **wooden swinging doors** stands in front of you. You feel a little bit intimidated. Are you really going to be okay in a place like this?

    Again you toss your gun stylishly among your holsters to advance the text about you deciding that you want a drink. You're probably at peak confidence, here, having mastered the playful sense of control between your left and right holsters, and having the text tell you that you're good at shooting. When confronted with wooden doors, you have no choice but to kick 'em in.

> \> wooden swinging doors

That's right, KICK IN THE DOOR. Of course you'll be okay—because you say so, and that's danged well good enough!

> \>

You take a seat at the bar, not even bothering to take in the other patrons. Who cares about them? It's all about you. And what you need is something to drink.

"Bourbon, on the rocks," you declare.

Purse

> Purse

"Yeah right," the bartender says. "Not likely, city girl."

He drops a **shot** of some amber drink in front of you. Straight.

> shot

Oh, yes, very clever. "Shot" of whiskey. You should feel pretty smug about yourself, the amazing punning and gunning adventurer of the west!

Or at least you would, if you weren't too busy choking. Whatever it was, it was way stronger than what you're used to! **Cough cough, sputter, ugh, you croak.**

>

    The tone here is so good at capturing the overconfident young person out of her element. As you press on, the text reminds you that you're just pretending, that how you walk and sling your gun doesn't mean you know how to drink whiskey.
    And then the more experienced woman appears.
    Very dignified.

"You okay there, cowgirl?" a **husky voice** from behind asks you.

Holster

> husky voice

You take a shot at the source of the question, but she easily swats the bullet out of mid-air. Then suddenly slaps you on the cheek, for good measure.

Holster

>

434

played by Leigh Alexander

You take a good look at her.

She's exactly the kind of woman that makes your little dyke heart go all aflutter—and does your heart ever go aflutter. Commanding, curvy, and a slight hint of harshness betrayed by her eyes lets you know that she's the kind of woman who could very easily hurt you. And gosh, do you ever want her to.

Holster

It's here I start to wonder: Does the character want to impress others so that she feels stronger, or so that she can attract a real challenger? The shift here from someone who very much wants to perform as "tough" into someone who desperately wants to be swept off her feet is interesting, abrupt. I used to write these types of characters in AOL chat rooms.

>

"Sorry," you stammer. "I-I'm okay."

"Now, what's a pretty thing like you doing in a place like this?" she asks, taking you by the chin with strong calloused fingers, looking you over.

You can't help but imagine what those hands might feel like elsewhere. You'd really love to be held by them; you find yourself praying, as she stares, that she approves of what she sees.

Holster

>

"D-did you have somewhere else in mind?" you ask. Her place, you hope.

"Maybe, cutie," she says with a grin. "I wouldn't mind seeing just how nimble that trigger finger of yours is, cowgirl."

You blush a little. She's the real cowgirl, not you, not that you're going to argue with the flattery. Certainly not with a smile like hers.

Holster

>

All you can do is nod, but thankfully, it's enough for her. She leads you outside, then pauses, taking out a cigarette and putting it in her mouth. Somehow she looks even cooler than before, **smoking**.

"Got a light, cowgirl?" she asks.

    A defining trait of the exciting woman is that we're told, in several ways, that there is something *authentic* about her coolness, by contrast to ours. When we go for what seems like the obvious flourish—light her cigarette with the hot mouth of our weapon—is just a joke to this commanding new crush.

  > smoking

Before you get a chance to even try, she pushes your gun hand back down.

"No, that doesn't suit you, cutie. You don't get to do that," she says. She's right, of course. You blush more, as she manages to find a match in her pocket and lights up without any help. "Come now, let's go."

Holster

    It's not just that you're meant to be impressed by the flirtatious queen, it's further than that—you're meant to be afraid she's going to find you out.

  >

Next thing you know, you're in her apartment, being slammed against a wooden wall in exactly the way you've always dreamed of. You feel her intimidating stare bore straight into you, as she hovers her lips just inches away from yours. Much too far.

Holster

  >

Behind her, above her bed, is a bookshelf. A **beer bottle** rests at the end. The only book to be found is an **abused looking bible**. A well-played looking **deck of playing cards** sits beside it.

"Show me what you've got, cowgirl," she whispers, practically into your mouth.

    That first time in a new lover's house—can you remember how you're always kind of afraid you're going to break something? They have the lux-

played by Leigh Alexander

ury of triumphing in having brought you home, and you never quite get to relinquish the status of interloper. You want to explore them, but half of you is on alert, computing the titles of their books, mentally tagging the signs of their life you see out of the corner of your eye as they press you up against the wall.

Amid all this the red text begs you to keep thinking about what in the room you can shoot to destroy with dramatic, showy flair. You can try to put your gun away, but eventually there's no other way to move on except to give in.

> beer bottle

. . . The bottle explodes dramatically.

Holster

> abused-looking bible

. . . The bible stops the bullet and survives. You're slightly surprised.

Holster

> deck of cards

All 53 cards go flying into the air, fluttering gently down onto the bed.

Holster

>

"Nice shooting, cowgirl," she says, rewarding you with a gentle kiss. It's not enough for you.

On her bedside table is a **snow globe of San Francisco**. (You think to yourself, "I thought San Francisco didn't have snow?", but say nothing.) On the ground, nearby, is a jutting out **nail** that you bet you could get a trick shot off.

Here, a tense choice—you, the player, don't want to shoot either the trick shot nail or the delicate San Francisco snowglobe. You want to enjoy this moment with this person, don't you? But you have no choice, really, but to destroy the snow globe. (On your second playthrough you'll try the nail, only to find the shattering of your beautiful model idea of a place is

Even Cowgirls Bleed by Christine Love

inevitable. There is no way not to get your dreams crushed, here in this city.)

> snow globe

The globe shatters, falling apart into countless tiny glass shards, water spilling out onto the floor.

Holster

> Holster

She backs away, looking at the shattered snow globe. You grin, but she doesn't return the gesture. She looks upset, and walks over to the kitchen, crossing her arms.

Behind her, there's a cabinet full of fancy **china. Plates, a tea-set, and a rather shiny bowl.** "Hand over the gun, cowgirl." **Between the two of you is a vase full of freshly cut flowers.**

San Francisco didn't have snow, but she said nothing.) On the ground, nearby, is a jutting out nail that you bet you could get a trick shot off.

The globe shatters, falling apart into countless tiny glass shards, water spilling out onto the floor.

She backs away, looking at the shattered snow globe. You grin, but she doesn't return the gesture. She looks upset, and walks over to the kitchen, crossing her arms.

Behind her, there's a cabinet full of fancy china. Plates, a tea-set, and a rather shiny bowl. "Hand over the gun, cowgirl." Between the two of you is a vase full of freshly cut flowers.

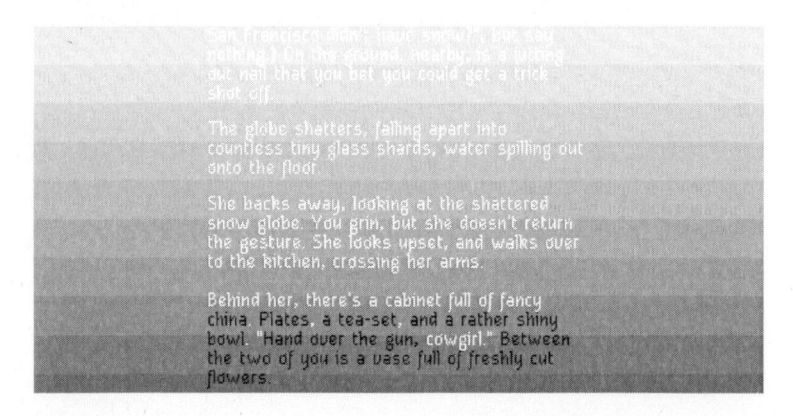

And this is the game's nicest moment, mechanically. You want to give her the gun, but the option to do so is surrounded by blood-red minefield-text that describes fine things: A vase, some china, delicate crockery.

You will play this game one extra time just to be sure you can't break the magic circle of delicate objects to do the thing that you really, really want to do: To desist. To cease your flinging around dangerous things like a clumsy, show-offy, gonna-break-something-kid. So that everything doesn't come crashing down.

> vase full of freshly cut flowers

It explodes in a loud crash of ceramics; with it, suddenly everything else has crashed down, too.

played by Leigh Alexander

Holster

> Holster

"Clearly, you need to be controlled," she says in a sultry voice. You feel bad—a little. You probably wouldn't mind her idea of it, though.

Holster

> (as soon as you move the mouse, the text advances)

You fumble your gun—no surprise, with the way you've been flipping it about like an idiot—and it goes off, the bullet hitting her right in the shoulder.

"That's it, I've had enough of you!" **she cries out, looking horrified, and turns away**.

Holster

You have no choice but to hurt her. You, the player: Your desire to move this story forward with skillful aim has led us here.

> she cries out . . .

You fire at her as she leaves, barely missing.

Holster

> Holster

As she runs away, she calls back at you, "You're dangerous! Stay away from me!"

You're completely shocked. Wasn't it all going so well just a minute ago? You can still remember the feeling of her breath on your lips, but now... now... now you've fucked it all up.

Horrified with yourself, you stare down at your feet, still adorned in your shiny new **steel-toed boots**.

The only object you can aim at next are your boots—to shoot yourself in the foot, literally. You, the cocky interloper, have screwed up everything. You, the player, had an itchy trigger finger. It all harmonizes quite nicely with the arrival of the vivid red word "bleed," which starts the screen darkening and the text skewing ominously.

Even Cowgirls Bleed by Christine Love

> steel-toed boots

You shoot yourself in the foot, this time literally. You start to **bleed**.

The bullet goes straight through. They weren't really steel-toed, of course, you couldn't even get that right. Like everything else. What are you even doing here, you stupid city bitch?

> bleed

You bleed all over the place. Even that's destructive; when she comes back, she's going to find everything ruined, soaked in **blood**.

> blood

You look at your hand, your slender well-meaning city girl fingers. The ones responsibility for pulling the trigger that's fucked everything up. **You already know what to do.**

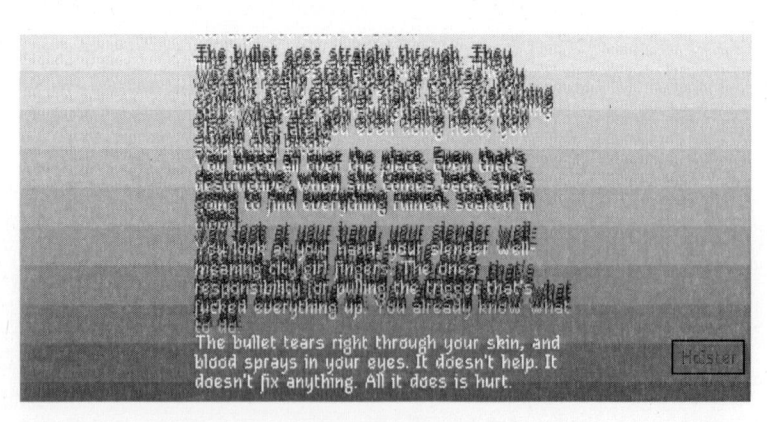

>

The bullet tears right through your skin, and blood sprays in your eyes. It doesn't help. It doesn't fix anything. All it does is hurt.

Holster

    It's the impotent kind of self-harming anger that doesn't fix anything. It's almost a mercy when the game finally offers you the "Holster" option

440

played by Leigh Alexander

again.

> Holster

You collapse in the mess you've created. You do all that you can do: bleed out.

Even cowgirls bleed, you think to yourself.

> Even cowgirls bleed

But you're not even a cowgirl, just a dumb city bitch. What are you even doing here?

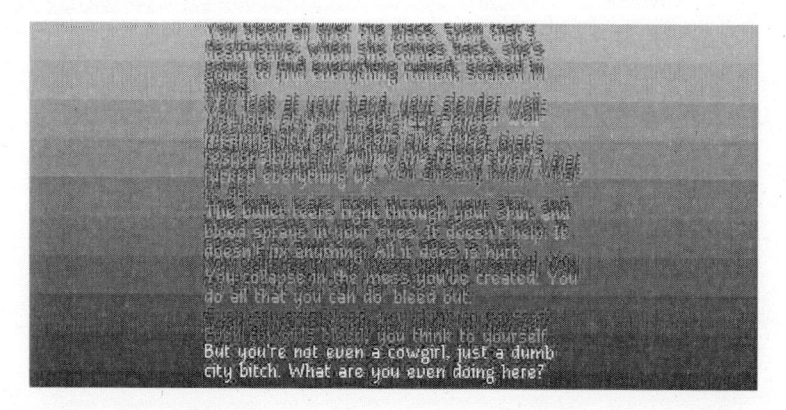

The final bright-red screen, the unkind self-scolding, suggests that this is a game inspired by a fresh wound, or that the narrator is exceptionally unforgiving toward themselves.

When I think back to being the new kid in school, or in town, and shooting myself in the foot, the pain is history. But I can remember how it is when it's raw and new, when you think you've screwed things up so bad that it'll never be over. A game of cursor and text, few tools, few rules, capturing that sense perfectly, of those days when you fumbled your heart like live ammunition, always just beyond your control, always ending in hurt and mistakes.

3 X 3 X 3

BY KAYLA UNKNOWN
PLAYED BY CARA ELLISON

Content warning: gore, people making out, graphic depiction of pregnancy and egg-laying

Coding help from the illustrious Porpentine

Stylesheet made by Leon Arnott

Play the game

> Play the game

You're in a small crystal cavern below the rocky coastline of an uninhabited island's west side.

Look around

 Twine has a delicate, impressive way of transmitting atmosphere and feeling merely through a particular color palette, and the template Kayla Unknown has chosen for "a mermaid's tale" is perfect for this story. The hot pink and purple creates a feeling in me of someone with glowing eyes and a pearlescent tail already, and I haven't begun reading yet. The black background, though this is typical of default Twine templates, somehow takes on a different meaning, and has this quality of a dark, underwater cavern that mirrors the description given in text.

> Look around

3x3x3 by Kayla Unknown

The cave is dark except for where it catches the stray streams of light that gleam down from the entrance a few dozen feet above and then explode into multiple colors upon reaching the hard crystal formations near the floor.

What should you do?

Examine the exit

Examine the floor

Examine yourself

> Examine the exit

You turn your gaze up to the entrance of your small home. After spending hours down here in contemplation, staring directly at the blazing light hurts your eyes. Of course you know that your cave opens out of a high rock wall against which angry surf thrashes day and night. You don't think you'll be bothered down here, at least not today.

What should you do?

Examine the floor

Examine yourself

> Examine the floor

Looking down, the cavern floor glitters below you, strewn with natural crystal formations and the few possessions you own. You see things that you're no longer really interested in; land-dweller relics mostly, such as a child's lost shoe (the rubber sole of which fascinated you for hours when you found it), a bloated and blurred book (that day you learned that some things don't do so well underwater), a chain of rusted keys (you still wonder what they might have been meant to open). Of course, the only possession that really matters to you is around your neck where it stays always, this being a pendant left to you by your mother many years ago.

What should you do?

Examine yourself

> Examine yourself

444

played by Cara Ellison

You can't see your own face here of course, but you take a minute to admire the rest of yourself, which in your giddier moments you might admit you are rather proud of. Your skin is mostly purple and tinted faintly pink in some places; your long hair is a bright wild fuschia that spreads out behind you like a tangled cloud. Your breasts are modest but respectable, and at the waist your flesh fades smoothly into iridescent pink scale as your tail takes over, then narrows before opening up into your thick, two-forked caudal fin, which itself is slightly transparent and a lighter pink than the rest of your lower body.

Think about your situation

> Think about your situation

You haven't exactly been keeping track of time since you set out on your own. Your mother always seemed to follow the passage of days, but you evidently did not inherit that particular skill, though you like to think that you at least got the stunning magenta of your eyes from her.

Anyway, the point is that you didn't realize how old you were, just how many weeks and months and years swam by as you frolicked and hunted your way through life. But here you are, and the slow, almost alien pulsing in your belly says exactly what you don't want to hear.

You are thirty years old and your reproductive system is taking its cue to start growing eggs. That's what's been bothering you for the past few days (weeks?), that weird grinding feeling, the pains in your gut, the dizzy spells, being hungrier than usual.

So you're pregnant. That's something.

Think about biology

It's here I begin to think a lot about bodies and age. I am close to thirty, and I feel my own biology changing in subtle ways. I've never been pregnant, but I spend a lot of time and energy attempting not to be. There's a number of societal ways that I feel like I have been conditioned to think that my body is more body than person, that women's bodies are a system of mysterious cavernous curves, and I feel very connected to it.

> Think about biology

3x3x3 by Kayla Unknown

You struggle to remember everything your mother taught you. It's been at least fifteen years now, you realize, but you can still pull up the basics. Your species (one of a great many, naturally) reproduces through the following seemingly simple process: starting at age thirty, once every thirty years the female's body automatically begins to produce eggs. After some amount of time you can't quite recall, the eggs are ready to be deposited in a safe place (you hope that part isn't going to be too unpleasant), where they will wait for a male to release a cloud of genetic material which acts as the final catalyst for the young to hatch; while most of the work is done by the female's body, without that last minute fertilization by a male, the eggs will not be viable.

This might not be a problem if you were interested in any males, or even knew any at all, or, most importantly, if you were sure you were ready to raise children in the first place.

Leave the cave and gather your thoughts

> Leave the cave

Restless and disturbed, you decide to wander a bit and see if that helps you gather your thoughts. A few flicks of your powerful tail and you're sailing up and out of your cavern. Swimming up, up, up, you burst from the sea and fly through the air in a short smooth arc before knifing back down below the surface. The exhilaration of motion and the cold morning air on your rarely exposed body distracts you for a little while but doesn't really contribute to your plans.

As you thrash out your frustration in undulant swerves around skittish schools of fish and outcroppings of underwater rock, you contemplate your future. You're pregnant, there's no getting around that; it was going to happen eventually, even if you had kind of felt somewhere in your heart that it never would.

What should you do?

Ditch the eggs

Try to get the kids adopted

Find a willing male

> Try to get the kids adopted

played by Cara Ellison

This idea has potential, but where are you going to find anybody willing to take two dozen or so fresh eggs and spend the traditional fifteen years raising them? (And let's not even start on how you could possibly let a merman anywhere near something of yours to fertilize it in the first place...) The women are either busy working on their own kids or enjoying their maiden phases, and the men... well, really, the less said about the men, the better. What good are they, anyway? All they do on the rare occasion that you intersect with other merfolk is get in stupid fights and try to show off for the girls. Again, it all comes back around to reproduction, although you suppose if you're being fair, maybe some of those guys are actually interested in romance and not just feeding their egos by spraying some random maid's clutch. Gross, though. Gross.

So as much as you'd like to pass the eggs off into somebody else's hands, the reality is it's probably not going to happen. Even if you found the rare stable community you don't think you'd run into a mermaid willing to take on a double-load of kids or sacrifice one of her fifteen-year stretches of freedom.

Yeah, as much as it sucks, adoption is probably a no-go.

What should you do?

Ditch the eggs

Find a willing male

> Find a willing male

You didn't even just think that. No. Just no. Even if he left afterward, which is customary in a lot of places anyway, the idea of letting some male interact with your eggs is just... nasty. You spend a while ruminating sadly on the unfairness of being born with romantic feelings that seem to extend only to the wrong sex.

What could your life be like, in a world where things were different? You imagine holding hands with another girl (woman? it's odd to think of yourself as already being thirty), showing her your dorky little cave... No, though. The odds are stacked way against you, and you're not going to bother hoping for something that isn't going to happen. And anyway, that's all beside the point. You were trying to figure out what to do with your rapidly escalating pregnancy, not obsessing over things that can never be.

Finding a male, though. Nope. Not going to happen.

3x3x3 by Kayla Unknown

What should you do?

Ditch the eggs

Though I spend a lot of time making out with people of the male persuasion, I can understand the immediate thought that finding a father for your child is "nasty." I particularly identify with the miserable acknowledgement that one night stands with mermen are almost a tradition. Figuring out what to do in a pregnancy situation is hard, and the game is structured so that every time you ponder your choices, you are presented with three decisions that you have to read through before progress is possible. This gives *3x3x3* a kind of thematic "treading water" feeling, as if your tail is just lazily paddling against a current whilst your little mer pregnancy ruminates, before you move on again.

> Ditch the eggs

The idea is so tempting. Of course you could wait it out, lay your eggs and then just... leave. So a few unborn merfolk get eaten by fish or whatever; the sea is full of your kind and it's not like you only breed once every thirty years... oh, wait, that's right, humans have driven the mer deep into the seas where they number few, and while reproductive processes vary by species, the sad fact is that nobody is having a whole lot of kids.

But that's not your responsibility. This is your life. You don't owe anything to your race or whatever; you didn't sign up to be a parent, it's not your fault your stupid body thinks it's time to make babies, and it's not like they'd really be alive if left unfertilized anyway.

Then despite all of that truth you have an awful mental image of some nasty deep sea fish messily gobbling up a school of little merfolk, its weird teeth ripping apart young flesh, blood in the water, something monstrous eating children... eating your children.

No, you guess you're not going to ditch the eggs. Damn your stupid sentimentality.

Think some more

> Think some more

Why does the thought of those eggs never hatching make you sad? You don't care. You certainly don't give a damn about any males, and you don't even want kids, anyway.

played by Cara Ellison

Right?

Like, seriously. You, a mother? The idea is almost as ridiculous as it is absurd. Hell, you didn't even notice you were of breeding age, how could you take care of children? The whole thing would be a disaster. They'd probably all die. And even if they didn't, the law of the ocean says that some would... and how could you possibly deal with that? No no no no no. Not going to happen.

Somewhere in the back of your mind there's a blurry scene like something from a dream. A small hand held in yours, an innocent smile, a shrill and sweet voice calling out, "mommy."

Okay, so maybe part of you does want to be a mom after all.

Fuck.

Formulate a vague and desperate plan

> Formulate a vague and desperate plan

Wait! Years ago, when you were a child yourself, you remember your own mother telling you stories about other sorts of merfolk way out there in that infinite ocean, strange cultures with strange customs, strange people with stranger biology. If you were to journey far enough from familiar waters, who knows what you might find?

Swim, swim, swim!

> Swim, swim, swim

You've got nothing to lose and the sudden throbbing pain behind your navel is saying "get a move on, girl," so the next thing you know you're racing away from your newly abandoned cave, slicing the water like a shimmering pink blade, chasing the rising sun.

Keep swimming

> Keep swimming

Minutes pass, then hours. The sun curves across the sky; you track its progress as it slowly stops being your target and heads west. Despite the freedom of the open sea and the infinite sweetness of cold infinite skies above and cool infinite depths below, you begin to feel more and more hurried;

you don't really know how much time you have before things start to... move along, and who knows how much progress you're actually making? Before you know it the sun is behind you, another thing to flee with all your might.

At this point you're still not really even sure what it is you're running from. From motherhood? Maybe. From males? Of course. From yourself? It's starting to look that way. If only you really could run away from yourself; if only the eggs steadily growing inside of you were something you could escape just by swimming.

At one point you're resting for a while, just kind of floating in a peaceful stretch of sea and waiting to recharge, and your hand drifts down and strokes your belly. Yesterday it was normal but today it's bigger, just a little bit, just enough so you can notice. You wonder how many eggs are in there right now, how big they're going to get, whether it's going to hurt when they eventually come out. When are they going to come out, anyway? How long does all this take? You really wish you knew. Did your mother tell you these things when you weren't paying attention? Did you forget? Did you ever know?

Your stomach growls. It almost feels like something moving in there, even though that makes zero sense, it's not like you're some mammal, but it still scares you half to death before you realize you've been swimming hard for most of the day and haven't eaten a thing.

What should you do?

Just keep swimming

Hunt for some fish

Any crabs around here?

> Just keep swimming

Uh, no. That's not a good idea. First of all, you're really hungry and starting to get tired, so dinner is kind of important. And secondly, lest you forget (hah, like that could happen), you're pregnant and if you do want to be a mom (you don't! you do! you... shit!) you think that starving yourself while your eggs are still developing has to be a bad idea. How awful would it be if you did see all of this through and something went wrong because you were too lazy and stupid to eat some damn food?

What should you do?

played by Cara Ellison

> Hunt for some fish

Kind of slim pickings around here, at least compared to back home. You suppose there was a reason you'd settled in one place other than just wanting somewhere to stuff your miscellany, after all. But after doing some careful hiding around rocks you're able to coax a few small, dumb fish close enough for you to dart out and grab them. You rip them to shreds with your long, sharp teeth, suck in their guts, strip the meat and muscle from their bones until all that's left are a few broken skeletons that you let drift toward the ocean floor. Good, and you're not quite so hungry any more, but the fish won't be enough by itself.

What should you do?

> Any crabs around here?

You make your way down low to some ridges of rock where the light begins to dim. It turns out that yes, there are some crabs around here, which is great because crabs are pretty easy pickings. You snatch up a couple of lively specimens, bash them against the rocks, crack open their twitching limbs and scrape out the tender meat inside. You spend a little while savoring the meal; crab isn't really that hard to come by, but you've always had a special liking for it. It's not a whole lot of food, but it tastes good and it's way better than nothing.

Okay, you're good for now

> Okay

Well, you didn't exactly feast, but between the fish and the crabs you're feeling pretty good again. You think maybe you can get in a few more hours of swimming before you tucker out and crash for the night, so you gather yourself up, clear your head a bit and then blast off. These waters are still mostly uninhabited so you keep close to the surface; you pop out of the water every so often to keep a lookout for ships, but if there are any you'll see them long before they're a threat, and then you can just dive. Humans are dangerous, but this isn't their domain, and as long as you're careful they'll never come close to catching you.

Almost before you know it the moon is out, and you're tired and also a bit worried about trying to navigate without the sun to use as a compass, so you poke around underwater until you luck out and find a nice little cave to curl up in for the night. It's nothing like your old home, it lacks the space and the shiny splendor, but it's cozy and seems pretty safe. Despite your circumstances you feel very young and a little bit frightened and you fall asleep curled up into a tight ring, hugging your own tail.

You have a short but awful dream. In it, you've laid your eggs and are floating guard nearby, but something distracts you and when you turn back around the clutch is being menaced by an unreasonably massive shark. You're holding a short, sharp spear, but when you charge the shark the head just breaks off in its thick skin without doing any real damage. It turns from the eggs to you, which seems like a good thing for a second before it charges and bites you in half at the waist. You watch in agonized horror as your tail disappears into its gaping maw. Your torn entrails spill out in slow motion as thick blood clouds the water. Your last thought is the realization that you've died for nothing, and as soon as it's done with you, the shark will be back to your clutch...

Wake up!

> Wake up!

You wake up choking back a scream, but the calm light of morning brings you back to reality fairly quickly. You remember that your eggs are still safe inside you, sharks don't get that big around here, and you have not in fact been eaten alive.

Before leaving the cave you lay a hand on your stomach (a habit you suspect will stick around for a while). It's small, but the difference is there; even just since yesterday the eggs have grown. You kind of panic a little bit, because even though you want these kids, you also don't want these kids, and there are semi-living things growing inside you and it's scary and even though you haven't seen her in a decade you kind of wish your mom was here right now. You'd give anything to have someone to talk to about this, to give you advice or even just listen. You remember the way you'd wrap your small arms around her waist and cry whenever you were afraid. She'd tangle her fingers in your hair and stroke your head and sing to you, wordless songs about everything and nothing. You never totally understood how she did that, but it always made you feel so much better.

You have the odd realization that if you are now thirty years old, then your mother has already spent her fifteen free years and is preparing to enter her next matron phase. It's kind of unsettling to think that, assuming she's still alive (and she

played by Cara Ellison

must be, right?), your mom is pregnant at the same time you are.

Sometimes life is just weird like that, you suppose.

Swim

> Swim

You swim. You swim and swim and swim and swim and swim and time keeps passing, and when you're hungry (which is too often) you hunt, and when the sun's out you're following or fleeing it, and when it's not you search for places to sleep, some of which are a lot safer than others and some of which are more than a little bit dubious. You're pretty sure that with every passing day your belly grows more and more; you're feeling something bulge noticeably deep underneath your skin. You start to worry that you're not going to find whatever it is you're looking for in time, and you still don't know how much time you have left.

The waters around you grow stranger and eventually shallower. You're not sure if that second part is a good thing, but whatever. And one day you sight land; an island, maybe remote and maybe not, you can't tell. You're a bit skittish about getting this close to places that humans might frequent, but for some reason you have a good feeling about this place; call it women's intuition (mother's intuition?).

It's evening again when all of a sudden you're not alone. The shock of seeing another mer after so long on your own is difficult to process; you're elated and afraid at the same time. The other one is distant at first; you can make out a patchwork of orange and black, and they're holding something in one hand. It might be a weapon. It's probably a weapon. You try not to worry; there shouldn't be anything to fear here. You wonder whether it's a woman or a man; as they close in you scrutinize their body to figure it out and in the end you aren't really sure what to think. They're androgynous, with small swells for breasts and a lithe body structure that could be a woman's or maybe a somewhat feminine man's. Whatever they are, though, you aren't getting that skeezy feeling mermen always inspire in you, so that's good. Their tail is particularly beautiful, with scales that shimmer even in the dim light and a number of transparent, almost ethereal fins.

They definitely are holding a weapon, though. It's a long spear that actually looks metallic, which is weird for a mer, but you suppose stranger things have happened. They look you over too, there's a tense moment as they seem to assess your potential threat level, and then they plant the spear in the sand and wave.

"Hello," you say, "I don't mean any harm. I'm sort of looking for help," and your voice comes out squeaky and rusty. When was the last time you bothered forming words out loud? They look at you quizzically and you're immediately sure that there is a language barrier here.

"Pleasant night," they say, and their voice is hesitant but still lyrical. "From where?"

What should you do?

Talk about home

Ask about them

Ask about the area

Text in this Twine comes in large blocks, like reading an ebook. It's quite unusual to find a Twine these days that is less interested in how hyperlinks can be used to shape the story, more interested in the pacing and structure of the story. This game emphasizes a thought process more than anything else, a feeling of vastness that is conveyed by huge blocks of text. I have been trained to think of Twine as a medium that works better, at least mechanically, with concise sentences and links, but it's true that sometimes we can lose sight of how much more interesting text can be when we use Twine purely to contain it.

> Talk about home

"Oh, um, uh," you say uselessly. "I'm from, um, out west? I don't really know how far." You think about it and decide to try to define this in terms of time. "Weeks, maybe a month."

"Far, very," they say, eyes widening a little bit. "Waters quiet." Maybe it shouldn't be, but the way they're speaking is really endearing. They sound a little bit innocent, although after thinking this, you glance back at that spear in the sand and remind yourself that assumptions are dangerous and stupid.

"Yes," you say. "Very quiet. I um, I lived in a cave, but I... I had to leave." You're blabbering and you know it, but it's difficult to do anything else. Sentient contact is not something you're accustomed to. They nod slowly.

What should you do?

> Ask about them

"What's your name?" They stare for a little while, head

played by Cara Ellison

cocked to the side in confusion. You point to yourself and say your name, then point to them. They smile and shake their head. What does that mean? Do they not understand? It sure seems like they understand, though. "You don't have a name, is that it?"

"No means," they say, shrugging, "Nothing." You're pretty sure you understand now, so you nod vigorously and then they surprise you by giggling and swimming around in a little excited circle. Maybe they haven't seen any other mer in a while, either. Maybe they just like you. That idea makes you blush a little and you're not sure why.

"You live here?" They nod at you and smile wider, then spread their arms to indicate the island and its surrounding waters.

What should you do?

> Ask about the area

"So is it... safe here?" They shrug as if to say 'as safe as anywhere.' They have a point, you've got to admit. "I see this island. Are there any humans here?" You really, really hope there aren't, although you figure that if there were, you wouldn't be meeting this lovely little mer right now. Hmm. Lovely. That wasn't a word you'd meant to attach to them. How odd.

"Human leave," they say. "Time gone. Safer." You feel a rush of relief and wonder what happened here, if there's a reason the humans deserted a settlement in the middle of the sea, but it's not really important, so you let it go. "Place good. Hunt good." They gesture at their spear and you're glad to understand that it's at least mostly just a hunting tool.

Tell your story

> Tell your story

"I came all this way," you say slowly, "because I..." but then you trail off because you're not even sure where to start, and honestly you're not even sure why yourself. They cock their head to one side. "I um, I'm thirty now and, and I guess I'm pregnant?" They don't seem to recognize the word, so you point to your belly, which is now rather large and has been throbbing painfully off and on for days.

"Children," they say simply, and then you start crying because somehow that sums everything up way better than you ever could have. You cry uncontrollably for maybe a whole minute

3x3x3 by Kayla Unknown

before they tap you on the shoulder, startling you out of your emotions. They're right in front of you, their face is up close to yours, and god damn, it's in a way you can't quite describe but they're beautiful, they're so beautiful and their big black eyes are deeper than the bottom of the sea, it's such a cliche but it's true, and it's arrogant but you read their face and you think maybe they're thinking something similar.

Then they set their soft hands on your shoulders, squeeze gently, lean in and kiss you deep. Their tongue is warm and salty and a little bit sweet and feeling it move against yours sends hot lightning down your spine.

What should you do?

Let them kiss you

Kiss back

Kiss hard

Games usually don't discuss the emotional impact of what it is like to kiss someone, and I love games that give the opportunity to participate in intimacy or eroticism in some way, because it's exciting unexplored territory. In this case there are three glorious options of how to kiss, which is three more options than you usually get.

> Kiss back

Your tongues break metaphor and seem to literally tangle. It helps that theirs is a lot longer and thinner than yours.

What should you do?

I really loved "your tongues break metaphor" because originally it seemed like clumsy impenetrable phrasing, but actually it's quite an emphatic thing: to *break* metaphor is kind of wonderful, like you're clearing a table to fuck someone, to smash a vase in your attempts to remove a lover's clothes. I would like to break metaphor with someone.

> Let them kiss you

You shut your eyes and let their tongue explore the inside of your mouth, caressing soft flesh and flicking over your pointed teeth.

What should you do?

> Kiss hard

played by Cara Ellison

Your hands drop to their waist and grab hold as you force your own tongue back and past their lips. Their eyes widen and then go half-lidded.

Oh, shit

> Oh, shit

You're beginning to really get lost in this when it strikes you that for some reason (some crazy empathy?) you've progressed from not knowing this mer to sharing one of the most intimate possible activities in a matter of minutes. It's surprisingly true that you're really into it, and it does seem to have worked as far as making you feel better goes.

Then something twitches hard up somewhere weird inside of you in a way you've never felt before. You feel a little bit like you're going to puke, but that doesn't happen, and then there's pressure somewhere unexpected and, oh shit.

Maybe the kiss catalyzed it or maybe it's a ridiculous coincidence, but you're about lay your eggs.

Find someplace to go, now!

> Find someplace to go, now

A few panicked gestures toward your spasming belly and the look on your face make it obvious to the surprised mer what is about to happen. They swim around in circles for a minute, apparently thinking furiously about what to do, then they take your hand in theirs and tug you along the side of the island with them. It's tough going in the state you're in, but you manage.

About a mile down the coast is the abandoned ruin of a human village, and the androgynous mer waits anxiously while you try to figure out the best place to settle down. Eventually you find a little nook on a slope under a decrepit pier that will hopefully serve your purposes and it's a good thing too because something hard is knocking at a previously unused oviduct and you're not sure how much longer you can oh my god they're coming.

What should you do?

Resist instinctively

Let it happen

Try to push them out

3x3x3 by Kayla Unknown

> Resist instinctively

You're not really doing it on purpose but sheer panic grips you along with your internal contortions and you flex muscles you weren't totally aware you had before in a futile attempt to hold everything in. The anxious mer says something inaudible. After a little of this you slacken a bit and give up trying to resist, because it's not helping anything.

What should you do?

> Let it happen

You try to relax and just let them flow, but it's not that simple. Your insides are churning and you've never felt anything like this before. The eggs are probably not actually that big but inside of you they feel colossal. It is completely silly to think that they are going to fit out of this orifice. The other mer strokes your arm gently.

What should you do?

> Try to push them out

You bear down in an instinctive and confusing way and feel something flaring wider down near the base of your tail. It feels like there's something stuck somewhere. Nothing down there hurts, exactly, which is one good thing at least, but the sensations are relentless and intense. The mer you just met squeezes your hand tight as you bear down and bear down and bear down...

Lay your eggs

> Lay your eggs

Then something kind of gives way, like it's finally been stretched far enough by the incredible pressure, and there's a slow sloppy pop as the first egg leaves your body. It's surprisingly small, maybe about two inches in diameter, and it kind of just floats there. You think that maybe this should be embarrassing because it is probably literally the most intimate thing that has ever happened to you and somebody you barely know is watching, but it's not, it's too crazy and overwhelming for you to actually feel anything except what's

played by Cara Ellison

happening directly to your body. The other mer points at the egg meaningfully and has a question in their eyes. You shut yours for a second, mustering the energy to place that kind of trust, then nod. They ever so carefully pluck the egg from its slow drift away and, holding it between their long, slender thumb and index finger, set it down in a little nest of kelp that you hastily erected less than an hour ago.

A long time passes this way. They're all easier after the first one, but it's a time consuming and exhausting process, and there are a whole lot of eggs. You lie there and live out the same cycle of slowly pushing out one egg, letting the other mer place it carefully into the clutch, and then pushing out another.

The moon is high in the sky when the last egg leaves your body. The pressure slowly relents as your reproductive muscles figure out that they won't be needed again for another thirty years, and you lie back against a sandy slope, your whole body worn out and slightly twitchy. You look over the cozy little pile of eggs and try to count them. You're pretty sure that all in all, there are twenty seven. The other mer finally lets go of your hand.

"Should?" they ask simply. "Can?" This is the one remaining thing you were worried about; does this mer have the anatomy necessary to finish this process? Are you even compatible like that, species-wise? But their question shows that they know what needs to be done and so you figure the answers are 'yes' and 'who knows but it's worth a shot' respectively. You nod.

"Yes," you say, and they look touched, elated, and scared all at once. They carefully position themselves over the eggs, shut their eyes for maybe a solid minute, and then a small cloud of murk puffs out from somewhere on their body and settles over the eggs. A moment passes, and from inside the soft pink orbs, tiny lights begin to glow.

Everything has gotten all fuzzy and strange and even though your stomach is empty it feels incredibly warm. You roll over slowly, and as you curl up protectively around your clutch and fall asleep, the orange and black mer floats watch carefully, their spear kept within reach. Then everything is close and black and endless and you don't have to think about anything for a while at all.

Be shaken awake

By the time you, a little iridescent mermaid, give birth, the wandering text leads you gently into a feeling of contentment, your androgynous partner the perfect terse, smiling fantasy.

3x3x3 by Kayla Unknown

> Be shaken awake

You're gently but firmly shaken out of your deep slumber. The mer who has become the second parent to your children looks urgently into your bleary eyes. You uncurl yourself from around the eggs and then realize what's happening.

"Born," they say, "Now happens." You look at the eggs, some of which are beginning to jitter and shake. The little lights inside are barely visible now that they lack such strong contrast to their surroundings, but you notice that some of the lights are pink and some are orange. This is fine with you, you decide. This is okay. On impulse you tug the other mer closer and kiss them quickly on the lips. Then the two of you huddle close over the clutch and begin to wait.

Slowly, ever so slowly, the first of the eggs begins to open. Membranes part in one place as what you realize must be absolutely the most heartrendingly adorable little girl in the whole ocean nibbles her way free. It's kind of hard to believe you were ever this tiny; the baby, your first baby is maybe the size of a big shrimp. She wriggles in the water and lets out a tiny squeaking noise; you gently snatch her up and hold her in your hand, where she wriggles a little more and then nestles down, cradled in your palm. The other mer wraps an arm around your waist and you realize that you're crying again, except this time it's different, it's some sort of bizarre and overwhelming happy crying that part of you wishes could last forever.

You realize as the eggs are chewed through one by one and more and more little merfolk emerge that this is easily one of the most important things you have ever seen. Before today you didn't, couldn't really understand, but now you do, you do and it's shining and it's glorious.

As far as you can tell the genders of your children are pretty even; in fact, you count them again, and maybe it's a twist of fate or maybe it's just biology you aren't familiar with, but there are nine pink little boys, nine pink little girls, and nine orange and black somethings. You're still not sure what to call the other mer or these little ones, but you aren't really worried about that. Whatever they are, they're here and they're yours and they're beautiful and that's what matters.

Epilogue

The descriptions of the babies hatching is couched in adorable language, one of them described as no bigger than a shrimp as it comes to settle in

played by Cara Ellison

your hand. It's a kind of idealised vision of motherhood, a painless birth, a benevolent birth partner to whom you are attracted but who wants nothing from you but kisses, who is there when you need them, who can take care of your clutch. This motherhood fantasy is quite powerful, almost enough to make a nearly-thirty-year-old want children, but the perfect androgynous partner just won't swim by, and the kisses don't seem as luminously inviting as the fuschia pink text of *3x3x3*.

> Epilogue

Time is a funny thing, you realize: like the water that spreads life across the earth, it ebbs and flows. Sometimes it cycles for months or years, its rough surf breaking again and again against the rocks that contain the most critical moments of your life. Sometimes the current moves against you and the days crawl by, though this is not always a bad thing; sometimes it moves with you and the years slip by in your wake. In your own life you have experienced all of these things, but now you follow the lattermost path.

In the early days the babies form a precious little school of bright swishing colors, swimming tiny circles all around you. You catch fish, break their spines and let the little ones swarm over them until there's nothing left but bones. The other mer (your mate? Yes, you think eventually, that's the right word to describe them) comes and goes; unlike a male, or at least the males you knew, they never really disappear from your life, but they do make many forays out into the greater sea. Communication evolves and becomes easier, and as the years go on and your children age, the two of you only seem to grow closer.

As for the children, they become the light of your life, the sea in which you swim, the stars in your sky. The nights are cold and the ocean can be cruel; not all of them survive. Death strikes when it will and the rest of you mourn the holes left forever in your hearts, but in the end you force yourself to be content with the fact that most of them at least make it to adulthood.

Fifteen years come and go so much faster than you could ever have imagined back in your first maiden phase, and the night your last daughter leaves, you spend a while beached on a slab of sea-worn rock, sobbing with pain and joy that is greater than you can fully comprehend. You run your fingers over your mother's pendant and wonder where she is. You wish that she could see you now, see what you've made and raised and loved.

But the morning comes, and you are not alone, and together,

3x3x3 by Kayla Unknown

hand in hand, you and your nameless, beloved mate leave your home behind; the empty island, the pier under which your children were hatched (rotted and collapsed years ago), the waters that seemed so strange at first but are now mapped out in your head like the scales on your tail.

You swim far and deep, finding seas newer and stranger still. Even though your children have left and in that way your heart has broken, there's much love and happiness to wring out of life; your first matron phase is over and your second maiden phase begun, and there is still something intoxicating about returning to an existence nearly free of responsibility.

Fifteen years, you think to yourself. Fifteen years of roaming and adventure, and then it will be time for another kind of adventure all over again. You wonder if next time you'll still be scared, if you'll still be with your mate or if life will have taken a different course. You wonder a lot of things, but now you believe you know that whatever happens, there is beauty and meaning everywhere, and life will always find a way.

THE END

EDEN
BY GAMING PIXIE
PLAYED BY ALEX ROBERTS

Hello and welcome to Gaming Pixie's *Eden*! You can't tell, but there's lovely, lilting music playing. It gives you the feeling that a great adventure is about to begin. I didn't know anything about this game or its author when I first encountered it. So I think it's okay if you approach it that way too. I'm going to introduce you not only to the game itself, but to my particular interaction with it—this is the story the author and I told together. If you were the one playing, you would tell a different story. As you read through my particular path, I encourage you to ask yourself two questions: "What path would I have chosen?" and "Why?" The latter question is the main focus of my commentary here. What motivates decision making in an interactive setting? Hypertext games (and other games in which the player has some control over the narrative) give you the choice between A and B. What motivates you to choose A over B or B over A? Let's keep that in mind as we begin our story.

Please enter your name.

> Alex

Having an androgynous name is a special delight to someone who grew up playing the kind of games I was into. I could name every protagonist after myself, and it never felt strange. Well, it felt like cheating sometimes, but in a good way. Mischievously.

Eden by Gaming Pixie

Good luck! {**Continue.**}

> Continue
> (click to access the inventory screen)

Time

Once the main mission begins, this section will tell you if it's time to hurry up. No time passes while you're checking this screen.

Inventory

Don't worry. The game will tell you what to find. Once it does, check back here if you're not sure you picked something up.

Achievements

Achievements Earned so far:

Speedrunner for finishing the rescue portion with a crazy-fast time of 0 seconds.

Virtue for respecting Eden's wishes

    I guess this is a good time to give you a peek at the Inventory screen. It doesn't mean much right now, but you get a sense of what will happen later: Time will be important, there will be items to collect, and there are specific goals to be achieved—mine are still listed here from a previous playthrough.

> back

Something isn't right today. You don't know what it is.
But you do have a feeling.

> feeling

You have this strange and eerie feeling SOMETHING is going to happen, but you have no idea what it is.
That is, until....

> That is, until

played by Alex Roberts

That is until your supervisor shows you the lab's new specimen. "We're not sure what it is," he says. "But it can't be human."

You take a look.

> You take a look

You take a look at the specimen and try to conceal your horror. "Are you sure it isn't human?" you ask. Your supervisor just shrugs.

"Keep an eye on it," he says. "I'll be back in a few minutes." Then, save for the "specimen" in the holding cell, he leaves you all alone.

You feel conflicted.

> You feel conflicted

The creature in the cage looks like a person to you. Different, perhaps, but either human or so close that it hardly matters.

"What's your name?" you ask, hands curled around the bars.

The specimen... no the prisoner wearily shakes their head.

You decide to rescue the prisoner.

No. It's safer to keep your distance.

    This point, at which the game offers you a choice for the first time, is what got me thinking about player motivation and decision making in hypertext games.

    To me, this hardly seemed a choice at all. I thought to myself, "What kind of chump would pick the second one? Someone who doesn't like adventure? Someone who wants to be a coward?"

    For me, the choice was automatic, intuitive. I didn't think about it very much. This made me think there were two kinds of player decision making in games: intuitive and strategic. Stay with me and see why that framework didn't hold up.

> You decide to rescue the prisoner

Eden by Gaming Pixie

You whisper to the prisoner, "I'm going to rescue you."

The prisoner stares, disbelieving, and asks, "Why would you do this for me?" This person speaks perfect English, albeit with a curious accent you've never heard before.

"Because it's the right thing to do," you say.

Let's get out of here.

Remember: the nature of any interactive work is that it is essentially a collaboration between author and player. Your experience is the result of your own decisions and those that went into the design of the game itself.

That's probably why it feels so great when you get the sense that you and the author are "on the same page," so to speak. Here I am wondering why I made a particular choice, and the game comes right out and asks me that same question.

Another thing worth noting here is that the players motivation is not necessarily the player character's motivation. That, like other aspects of the narrative, is determined collaboratively by player and author.

> Let's get out of here

Your supervisor's been careless. He left his cell keys on the table. Your hands are shaking as you fumble with them, searching for the right-numbered one. Aha!

We're outta here.

> We're outta here

This rescue is going surprisingly well, and it looks like no one's around. You take the prisoner's hand and...

and....

Please note that *Eden* is a very well-paced game. In moments of tension, only small bits of text are presented at once, and the player must click to read more. This resulted in some pretty frantic clicking on my part. In other words, if *Eden* were a book, you might call it a "page-turner."

> and . . .

You don't know where the guards came from. They shoot you both dead.

What a gruesome end.

played by Alex Roberts

The music has been rising and the pace of reading/clicking has become frantic. All that comes to an abrupt end here with a terrible screaming sound, followed by silence.

The enchanting music and dreamy art on the first page gave you a sense of what the game had in store for you: adventure, beauty, love. *Eden's* prologue ends here with a promise just as sure.

> What a gruesome end

You've had the same dream for three nights in a row. (Well, actually, the last three mornings since you're on the night shift.) It never ends quite the same. Maybe you're just THAT depressed your vacation is ending now.

Anyway, it's time to get ready. Who do you see in the mirror?

I'm a woman.

I'm a man.

I'm neither, actually.

This choice took me a very long time.

The option of choosing the gender of your player character (or PC, the character in the game whose actions can be determined by the player) is almost as common in games as the option of naming them. In a medium where PCs are almost always men and hardly ever women, it's a clever way for designers to nominally support the increased representation of women in games, without the trouble of actually trying to represent women's experiences and perspectives. As you might expect in the male-dominated world of video games, taking the barest notice of women is apparently difficult enough; the inclusion of a nonbinary gender option is almost unheard of.

I could write a great deal about the perils of representation, how vociferously it is demanded and how lazily such demands are appeased. So it was not without some cynicism that I chose here the third option. I wanted to know if this choice would have any effect, if the experiences of nonbinary people would be represented in *Eden*, or just the most basic fact of their existence.

> neither

Holy bedhead, you think. You shower, you groom, you dress, you grab breakfast.

Time to face the day.

> Time to face the day

Eden by Gaming Pixie

You get to work on time like you always do. After all, getting ahead takes making a good impression. Though sometimes, it's not easy.

Hang up your coat.

> Hang up your coat

You put away your coat and head for lab A-3.

When you pass some of your co-workers, they give you nervous looks. No one is outright unfriendly to you, but you know they think you're odd for preferring not to be thought of as male or female. And sometimes, they do joke about "So, what should we call you today?"

So, what's up?

I can't say if this accurately reflects the experiences of nonbinary folks, because those experiences aren't mine. What I can say is that this passage gave me some relief, at least, that the gender options presented were not completely pointless.

> So, what's up?

When you get to lab A-3, almost no one is there. You ask an acquaintance named Kyra, "What's going on?"

She tells you, "Check B-2. While you were gone, they brought in a real, live alien and everyone wants a look."

"Are you sure it's all right?" you ask.

She says, "It's fine. I'll cover for you. Besides, Jones is there and he wants to see you." Jones being your supervisor, who's called you "brilliant" before.

Go to Lab B-2

> Go to Lab B-2

Phones aren't allowed in the basement labs, so you leave yours in your mini-locker. You go to lab B-2, where they keep the most secret of secrets—even for this place. You only earned clearance a week ago and you're eager to see what's inside.

You swipe your card through scanner. The door unlocks. You

played by Alex Roberts

go inside. You notice there's a card reader inside the room as well—likely an added precaution to help keep whatever's in here from escaping.

Everyone is "Ooh"ing and "Aaah"ing over the new specimen that's in the cell in the corner. You nudge your way through the crowd and... and....

Oh my God.

> Oh my God

Huddled behind those cold steel bars is the most beautiful creature. Beautiful... and if not human, close enough that it hardly matters. You're absolutely haunted by this creature... no, this person's mournful eyes.

The captive is wearing loose gray prison clothes—pants and a short-sleeved shirt. You believe this ethereal being....

Is male.

Is female.

Is neither.

Is MESMERIZING. You'll work out the details later.

Again we have the introduction of music (imagine it: light, sweet, and dreamy) coinciding with an abrupt shift in tone—in this case, our PC has gone from being irritated by mundanity to enchanted with an otherworldly being. Music is a relatively rare feature of games made in Twine, and it's used very well here.

This choice came relatively easily to me, because I had already decided I wanted to write a story about a person who exists outside the gender binary, and the author let me know that she was ready to tell that story with me. Such a story was already developing in my mind: a love story, about connecting to someone through a part of yourself you thought could only make you lonely. It was all very dramatic, of course. And I could only hope that Gaming Pixie would make allowances for it.

When you play a Twine game, you are collaborating with someone while unable to speak to them. Their decisions have already been made by the time you show up. It is a unique creative challenge.

> neither

This person is pure androgynous perfection, beyond all the standard distinctions. In a way, this alien beauty is what you

Eden by Gaming Pixie

might aspire to be.

"What... how...?" you ask Jones. It's difficult right now to voice coherent thoughts. Luckily, he knows what you mean.

"We're calling it Eden, Jones replies. "Agents discovered it three days ago in a field not far from here, captured it and brought it in for study. We believe it's an alien lifeform."

"Can they speak?"

"It seems physically capable of speech, but we don't know its language. And that's why I wanted to see you."

Why me?

Ah, how sweet it is to feel that you and the author are working together. After all, we're both here to tell a good story, right?

I'd like to draw your attention to the opposing uses of "it" and "they" in this passage. I've said I want to develop a bond between Eden and the PC; here the author is laying the foundation for that bond before the two characters have even spoken. Our protagonist apparently knows how pronouns are used to respect and disrespect people, or even to exclude them from personhood entirety.

> Why me?

"Why me?" you ask.

"Several of us have tried already, but the creature won't respond. Essentially, it's your turn." As good an answer as any.

You kneel in front of Eden's cell. "Hello," you say quietly so as not to frighten them. "You probably don't understand me, but... I'm not here to hurt you."

Send them away, whispers a gentle voice in your mind. Please. Send them away.

You blink in surprise since it isn't your voice. It must belong to Eden. It sounds....

Exactly like you'd expect.

Different somehow.

Exactly like you'd expect, of course. I'm trying to tell a story about a connection, about finding familiarity in the supposedly alien. Once again I find this story is entirely ready to be told; this path has been cleared for me.

played by Alex Roberts

> like you'd expect

Their voice sounds exactly like you'd expect: calming like autumn rain.

But back to Eden's request.

> But back to Eden's request

Eden asked you to clear the room. You look back and say, "Eden is telepathic. They asked me to ask everyone else to leave."

Silence. The other scientists exchange puzzled looks and mumurs about the brain scans they took and how they were "different" from a human's.

"All right," Jones says. "But I want a full report on your findings."

Now, it's time to **talk to Eden.**

> Talk to Eden

You ask Eden:

Where are you from?

Why are you here?

Why did you pick ME?

Eden, how are you feeling?

Can you tell me your real name?

    This questioning sequence is not just exposition time. It's an opportunity to define who I want my PC to be: curious yet compassionate, focused on Eden's welfare rather than on information-gathering.

    Let's return to the question I posed at the start of this commentary: what question would you ask? And why? Maybe respecting folks' identities is really important to you, so you'd feel compelled to ask Eden's real name. Maybe you're really interested in Eden's backstory, so you can't resist asking where they're from and why they're here. Maybe this list of questions seems boring to you, so you just start at the top and quickly click your way through, or even ask one question and skip the rest (that's an option you'll see in a moment).

Eden by Gaming Pixie

I would say that no matter what you choose, your essential motivation is the same: You want to tell a good story.

What makes a story good is, of course, up to you. What's boring, what's interesting, what makes a character or relationship worth caring about—these are all highly subjective. But it is almost universal to want to avoid what is boring, focus on what is interesting, and spend time with characters that we consider in some way sympathetic. Your motivation as a player, collaborating in a particular way with an author, is no different than your motivation would be if you were telling a story on your own. Only the manner in which you choose is different.

What seems like an obvious exception to this rule would be those times when we play through an interactive piece in a deliberately "bad" way. We've all done it. Refuse the quest, reply with rudeness, decide that "It's safer to keep your distance." I would argue that in those playthroughs, we are just trying to tell a particular kind of story: a joke.

> Can you tell me your real name?

You say, "I'm sure your real name isn't Eden. That's just the name they gave you. If it's all right, could you tell me your real name?"

Eden smiles. "Maybe later. But not yet."

Ask more questions?

-Or-

That's enough questions for now.

> Ask more questions
> How are you feeling?

You ask Eden gently, "Eden, how are you feeling?"

Eden stares at you for a long time. "You're the first one here to ask me that sincerely," they say softly. Their eyes are shining with tears. "Thank you. I am.... I've been better."

> Ask more questions
> Where are you from?

You ask Eden, "Where are you from?"

played by Alex Roberts

Eden tells you in the gentlest (and weariest) voice you've ever heard, "A world we call Mekkari. It's... quite far from here."

> Ask more questions

NEW: What's Mekkari like?

> What's Mekkari like?

You ask, "What's Mekkari like?"

Eden gives you a ghost of a smile. "It's a wonderful, wonderful place. Peaceful. Beautiful. I'd really like to go home."

> Ask more questions
> Why are you here?

Eden looks away. "There were rumors about life in this part of the universe. I wanted to see for myself, though I was warned not to."

> Ask more questions

NEW: What kind of warning?

> What kind of warning?

Frowning, you ask, "What kind of warning did they give you?" You already suspect the answer.

Eden looks away and says, "That... the rumored lifeforms here were dangerous." Which is about what you expected.

> Ask more questions
> Why did you pick ME?

You ask Eden, "Why did you choose to talk to me?"

Eden says, "Give me your hand." You do. Then, they answers you.

Eden by Gaming Pixie

I sensed you were different from the others. That maybe... you might help me.

> That's enough questions for now

You and Eden both are silent for a while. You feel sorry for their being held captive like this, but what can YOU do? You're not in charge of anything here., and you feel horrible for what they must be going through. How can anyone approve of keeping this gentle, intelligent person as a thing to experiment on?

Try to console Eden.

Try to reach Eden with your thoughts.

This is another choice that seemed just too obvious to me—consolation seemed so toothless! Cowardly, even! And besides, telepathy is a cool sci-fi angle that emphasizes the connection between the two characters.

How lucky we are when we play a hypertext game, with no audience to please but ourselves.

> Try to reach Eden with your thoughts

Since Eden can reach you mind-to-mind, you decide to see if it can work the other way.

With all your concentration, you think, *Eden. Can you hear me?*

Eden answers, *Yes.*

Is there anything you can tell me that might help me get you out of here? Things you've noticed? Certain abilities you have?

Eden says, *If I'm close enough, I can "communicate" with technology and alter it with my mind. I can do it most accurately with things I'm actually touching. I can sense the presence of other living beings. And I doubt they've found my ship since it was cloaked when I left it. If I could use something as a tracking device, I could find my way back to it.*

Do they know what you can do?

They only know about my telepathy. And that's only because of today.

Hmm.

played by Alex Roberts

Figure out your next steps.
You're having second thoughts.

In this choice, I've been given an opportunity to add real depth to my PC: a moment of weakness, some entirely understandable fear.

As you can see I blew past this opportunity completely. Maybe the characterization is a little too broad as a result. Maybe the character is taking on a life of its own, and becoming more of a headstrong idealist than I originally intended. Maybe that's a poor excuse for bad storytelling. Maybe it doesn't matter.

> Figure out your next steps

You and Eden work out a plan. Communicating mind-to-mind makes it go by quickly.

Eden's technomancy skills can turn your card into a master key. They can likely disable security cameras and alarms as well, provided they can get close enough—and in very little time since destruction takes a lot less nuance than recreation. (You're glad they haven't tried that with the lock on they cell. Cell locks STAY locked if they're tampered with at all.) Also, perhaps most importantly, they can reconfigure any smartphone locate their ship.

Since the cell has a keycard lock (located across the room and out of Eden's range), freeing them won't be a problem. The problem is that after that, you need to get them out of the building without getting caught.

First, though, you take out your keycard so Eden can work their magic. You do your best to keep it hidden from camera view, knowing there's one behind you pointed directly at the cell.

It's done, Eden says after a minute or so. It can open any electronic lock now. You put the card back in your lab coat pocket.

Now, you can free Eden. But first....

You need to get your smartphone.
No, Nab a phone on the way out.

Something about halting a rescue operation to grab my phone just felt

475

so . . . *millennial.*

> nab a phone

It's better to nab a phone on the way out. The coast is clear right now and you don't know when or if you'll see Eden alone again.

Presently, Eden seems very focused on the camera on the wall. Trying to connect with it, maybe...?

Anyway, you tell Eden, *I'm going to unlock your cell. Then, you can disable the camera and get out.*

Eden says, *All right.*

It's Showtime.

> It's Showtime

Quickly and subtly, you unlock Eden's cell and walk to the door, waiting for Eden to take care of the camera. You hear an odd crackling sound; the room's lights flicker into darkness and the emergency lights near the floor come on. You reopen the lab door with your keycard. A peek into the hall confirms that power has gone out.

It might be overkill, but it's useful overkill. Regular staff will be leaving now. However, with such a suspicious outage (and perhaps suspicious camera footage), it seems like a sure thing they'll be sending in some guards to investigate.

Once you've confirmed the coast is clear, you tell Eden, "Let's go." But since you didn't get your phone, you still need to grab one on the way out of this place

Time is of the essence, especially if you alert the guards.

Rush ahead while it looks clear.

Better to be cautious.

When I encountered this choice I saw a perfect opportunity to develop the PC a little and have them act in a way that implied a certain impulsiveness. It makes the unwavering bravery of previous choices a little more understandable, don't you think?

played by Alex Roberts

But what if I just chose the path that seemed most likely to result in success, whichever that seemed to be? That's a strategic decision, and it seems very differently motivated than the one ramblingly elaborated above.

The strategic decision is still a narrative one. It's just based on the assumption that a story that abruptly ends with the main characters' violent and undeserved deaths is not a very good one. The beauty of interactive fiction is that if you think that's actually a great ending, you're welcome to it.

> Rush ahead while it looks clear

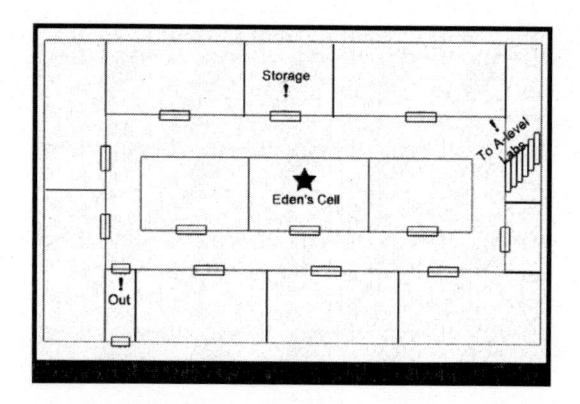

[Map showing Storage, Eden's Cell, Out, and stairs To A-level labs]

Wait. You hear someone coming.

Quick! Back inside the lab!

There is a sudden shift in tone at this point in the game. The music becomes faster, this map (with its urgent exclamation marks!) appears, and text is presented in short points. *Eden* opens with a dream sequence, and spends much of its first act in a sort of dreamy enchantment. This, however, is an action sequence.

Remember the epilogue, and how it ended? This is where those stakes come into play.

> Quick! Back inside the lab!

You and Eden hurry back into the lab, and you nod towards Eden's cell. Get back in, you tell Eden. I'll hide behind that counter and **HOPE he doesn't come in**.

> Hope he doesn't come in

The guard walks into the room. He sea Eden is still in their cell (but hasn't noticed it's unlocked) and hasn't spotted you yet. So, what now? Every option has its risks....

Make a break for it with Eden

Keep hiding

Grab that digital scale from off the counterjust in case

By now it should be fairly obvious that this is not a record of my first playthrough. Like rewriting multiple drafts of a story, we play through interactive works until we get the story we want, or until we give up. I know from previous playthroughs that hiding does nothing, and that grabbing the scale leads to violence. I don't want my story to be boring, and I don't really want it to be violent either, so I go with the first option and hope for the best.

> Make a break for it with Eden

In a panlc, you and Eden **RUN**! As you do this, you know full well you act the guards' attention.

> RUN

This isn't how you wanted to do things, but you have no choice. There's no time to get Eden's disguise. Even worse, you don't have your phone. You're going to have to find one. With the guards on high alert. Do you...

Look for one on this floor. It seems less risky overall

Take your chances upstairs since you know where your phone is

If I was a very observant player, I might remember that a few pages ago I was told that no phones were allowed in the basement of this facility, and thus discern that searching for one here would be fruitless.
I cannot claim to be that observant a player.
We're being timed, remember? It's all just frantic clicking at this point. Frantic clicking in search of a satisfying narrative.

> Take your chances

played by Alex Roberts

Keep going

> Keep going

Just one more step to go.

Can I just say that I love love love this technique: suspense generated by requiring many clicks to progress. It's an effective choice, unique to hypertext.

> Just one more step to go

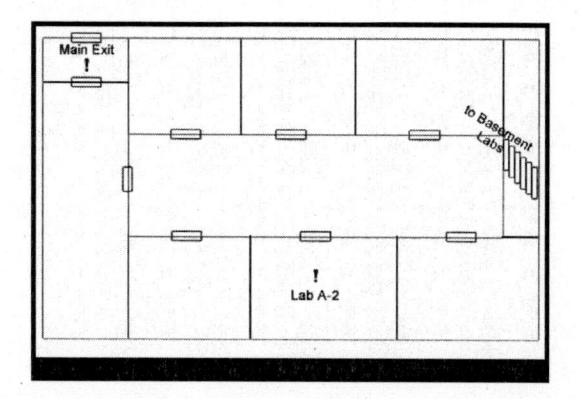

Okay, you've reached the stairs. So you **go upstairs**. You're a little worried. though. You think you hear someone up there.

> go upstairs

You're just outside the lab upstairs. As long as there are no guards around, that should be easy enough. But you think there might be someone In there. You'll need to be careful.

Go get it.

> Go get it

You cautiously peer into the lab. There's a guard in there. What do you do?

Tell Eden to hide. Then, get your phone.

You and Eden both hide.

Eden by Gaming Pixie

Grab that phone and RUN LIKE CRAZY!

Be thankful, dear reader, that I have not included my many paths that ended in failure. Failure means something specific in discussing games: the inability to continue. The option to give up or start over. Your story is over before you wanted it to be.

> tell Eden to hide, then get your phone

Eden quickly hides behind a counter while you collect your phone. Then, the guards come in. You close your eyes, take a deep breath, and do your best to seem calm.

"What are you still doing here?" one of the guards asks.

"I forgot my phone," you say. "I was just leaving."

"Well, be careful. We're still not sure what caused the outage."

You smile. "I will. Thank you." Once the guards are gone, you and Eden **run for the exit**.

> run for the exit

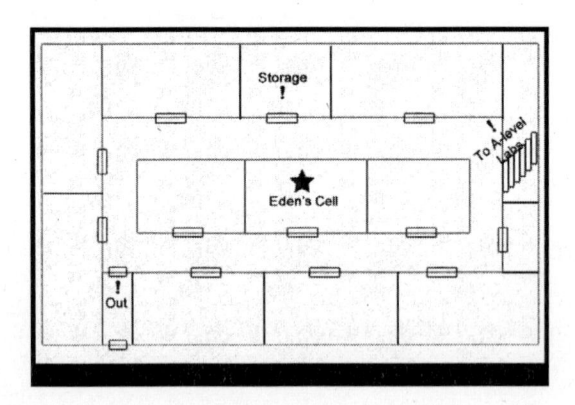

This isn't how you wanted to do things, but you have no choice. There's no time to get Eden's disguise. At least you have a phone, so you can just **run for the exit**.

> run for the exit

Please oh PLEASE let us make it to the exit... You must act

480

played by Alex Roberts

IMMEDIATELY.

Things aren't looking good for you. You have **to** escape immediately. There's no time to waste and no turning back. You have to get **out** NOW.

On the subject of failed playthroughs, it took me a few to realize that this is a timed choice. It doesn't matter which one you click, only that you do so quickly. This is another example of good design choices, unique to a particular medium, generating novel experiences.

> to

You've made it out by the skin of your teeth. Eden shorts out the electric fence so you can both climb over it, and then you two just keep running far away from there. You and Eden hide in a nearby woods, where Eden reconfigures your phone. They laugh when they see where it is. "It isn't far from here," Eden says. "It's right through these woods."

And **that's where you go**.

> that's where you go

Achievement Unlocked! "Speedrunner" — You rescued Eden in under a minute!

Once you've reached the supposed right place, Eden holds out their hands and focuses with all their might. After a minute, their ship appears, silvery and shining like a vaguely sphere-shaped star. Eden's face is bright with hope. "Thank you so much," they say. They really is incomparably beautiful, especially their eyes. When you look in them, you see...

A quiet strength and thoughtfulness beyond anything you've known.

The enchanting purity of Eden's bright and loving nature.

The wonder of a place so very far away.

Games made in Twine occupy an ambiguous cultural space. They're often dismissed by video game players as "not really games," and the world of literature hasn't been particularly eager to embrace them either.

But here we have an Achievement: the recognition of an arbitrary goal set by the designer, outside the game's normal parameters. Achievements are found in almost every major contemporary video game—and in no other medium.

This one's innocuous enough, but it does seem somewhat at odds with the rest of this passage.

> A quiet strength and thoughtfulness

It doesn't matter where Eden is from, save that you wish you could go there. Eden is still standing there and staring at their ship as if they can't believe they made it. You think you want to kiss them. Except you're not completely sure if that's what **Eden** wants.

Respect Eden's wishes.

Throw caution to the wind.

> respect Eden's wishes

Achievement Unlocked!
Achievement Unlocked
"Virtue"

Since you're not sure Eden wants to be kissed, you choose to hold back.

"Thank you again," Eden says.

You tell Eden, "I would do it all again." Eden gives you a nod and smile and walks towards their ship.

It looks like this is the end.

That doesn't mean it is.

This achievement I know I'm not comfortable with. Why am I being rewarded for having basic respect for someone's bodily autonomy? I do not deserve a literal gold star just for that.

It's worth noting that if you "throw caution to the wind" in the previous passage, it results in a sour and unsatisfying end. That should be enough, I

played by Alex Roberts

think.

> That doesn't mean it is

Running after Eden, you shout, "Wait! Please, can I come with you?"

Eden blinks. "Are you sure?"

You nod. "Absolutely. I doubt there's much left for me here, and I'd love to see your world."

Eden's smile is as enchanting as the full moon overhead. "I'm so glad you said that," they say. "Follow me."

You board Eden's ship.

> You board Eden's ship

The flight to Eden's world seems to be over in an instant.

"Welcome to Mekkari," Eden says, opening the ship's hatch. "I hope you like it here."

You take a look at your new home.

> You take a look at your new home

Eden's homeworld is **simply amazing.**

In the same way that the appearance of a map tells the player it's serious strategy time, a scenic view tells them to relax. It's all over. The introduction of new art signals a significant shift in tone.

> simply amazing

Eden by Gaming Pixie

You never could have imagined such a pristine and **marvelous place**.

> marvelous place

The only thing more perfect... is the person who brought you here. But you're curious.

"Eden," you ask, "what's your real name? Can you tell me now?"

"It's Aevra," they reply. It suits them very well. Then, Eden... no, Aevra asks, "What's yours?"

"It's Alex," you say.

Aevra smiles. "I like that very much."

"May I ask you a personal question?"

"Yes."

played by Alex Roberts

"Are... are you...."

Aevra understands and seems amused by this. "**I am...**"

> I am...

"I am female," Aevra says. "Does that disappoint you?"

You think about that for a while and give Aevra your honest answer.

"Maybe a little."

"Not in the least."

Oh, dear reader, how I agonized over this choice!

But I had this whole thing going, where the PC had built Aevra up in their mind as the perfect androgyne, and connected with them over that, and maybe projected a bit onto them, as a sort of aspirational figure...

It didn't feel right, exactly, but it seemed to fit with the character.

> Maybe a little.

You admit, "Maybe a little."

Aevra says, 'I understand. I appreciate your honesty—and hopefully, your friendship.'

You smile. "Absolutely. And thanks." There are worse things to have in one's life than a kind and pleasant friend, especially one who has taken you to a world beyond the stars.

The End

Eden by Gaming Pixie

{**You received . . .**}

> You received

You received the ending: Friendship.

    Friendship is good.
    Friendship is not a consolation prize.
    I genuinely believe that this is the point Gaming Pixie was making with this ending.
    So why does this feel . . . unsatisfying?
    Let's hit "rewind" and try that last choice again.

> ~~Maybe a little~~
> Not in the least.

Achievement Unlocked! "Bi the Way"

You tell Aevra, "I don't care. I love you."

Aevra softly says, "I love you, too."

You and Aevra are gazing intently into each other's eyes.
Finally, **you kiss**.

    Oh. That's what she meant by "disappointed."
    Remember when I described the sweet feeling of knowing that you and your collaborator are thinking the same thing? This is the exact opposite of that. Acting as a perfect accent to that dissonance is a truly perplexing Achievement.

> you kiss

Aevra's kiss is passion-sweet—like honey for your soul.
Though you once called Earth your home, you know THIS is where you belong.

{**You received...**}

> You received…

played by Alex Roberts

You received the ending: Love.

This is the ending I wanted. This is the ending everything was leading up to. I can't deny that it's a cliché, but here the player is both author and audience; I have pandered only to myself. I wanted a sappy ending with smooches and that's what I got!

That's the beauty of interactive fiction.

EFT TO NEWT
BY MICHAEL JOFFE
PLAYED BY PIPPIN BARR

This is a very, very simple-looking title screen. No real information other than the title, author, and image of the eft (or newt?). So I'm not sure what to expect from the story except that the drawing itself is fairly cute, so I vaguely expect something a little childlike or naive.

Eft to Newt by Michael Joffe

> start

You wake to the sound of your **phone** going off. Same as always.

Slowly you climb out of bed. Your head is pounding, but you can't remember what you were doing last night. You put your hand to your forehead, surprised at how clammy it is, and head to the

It's a more "adult" tone than I'd expected from the imagery used on the title screen, much more of a standard entrance into a story. Uses the second person as lots of Twines tend to do, I guess as a way of acknowledging an "avatar effect" in an interactive story.

We have a basic setting now—I'm at home. We have something of a videogame trope in that we have a (somewhat) amnesiac protagonist who "can't remember."

There are two choices here, and because one of them seems to imply a change of location I'm more tempted to explore the "phone" option, as I imagine it as subsidiary, something that's more optional in the overall structure.

> phone

You hear it, but you can't seem to find it. It must be under the piles of clothes and debris somewhere.

The A Horse With No Name mp3 you use as an alarm is starting to get annoying...

Found myself a little surprised by two elements of this screen. One is that the music itself isn't being played by the game—I immediately go and look up the song to find out what it sounds like. On listening to the song I realize I know it already. Makes me wonder if it dates the author at all, but really it's one of those songs that's a bit "eternal."

The other element is that I can't search for the phone myself, it's just "somewhere". This is a pretty classic encounter with the sorts of agency "issues" that interactive experiences tend to have.

Back to the bedroom.
(And then on to the bathroom.)

> ... starting to get annoying
> bathroom

The bathroom is pitch dark. You blindly grope around looking for the **faucet**, **lights** or whatever else you can find to

played by Pippin Barr

establish your bearings

More helplessness. Two choices—again it seems to me that the lights are the "dominant" choice here, so I'll go for the faucet first. I should say, too, that my expectation right now is of something like Kafka's *Metamorphosis*, that I've become an Eft. I'm interested to see what actually happens when I turn on the lights, but for now I just want to keep trying "everything."

> faucet

Your hand finds its way to the sink and you turn the faucet. Nothing comes out...

That's funny, you know you paid your bills this month. Something must be wrong.

You make a note to contact your landlord later.

More foreboding—no water to go along with the clammy forehead and the amnesia. Interesting to see, again, that the "back" option here is used as extra exposition. Rather than being pure function (such as if it just read "back") it has its own remark, as if we resolve to contact that landlord and in doing so "resolve" this small scene.

> make a note
> lights

You find the lightswitch and flip it. Finally you can see the bathroom around you. Your eyes are drawn to the **mirror**.

The lights are on. The story continues to delay my imagined payoff of seeing what we look like in the mirror. Contrasting with the previous note on a more "narrative" text navigation option, in these other scenes it's much more function—e.g., "mirror," "phone," "bathroom," etc. Blunt and to the point. And specifically "mirror" is the link, not the full sentence "Your eyes are drawn to the mirror."

> mirror

The face you see in front of you is a long, flat oval. Two beady eyes stare back at you, and a tiny mouth opens and closes. There is no nose on this pale pink face, but on either side of the head are a pair of bright red, feathery gills.

It is the face of an axolotl salamander, and through the sleep and possible hang-over addled brain of yours, you slowly

Eft to Newt by Michael Joffe

awaken to the idea that this is your own face.

You need a few seconds to process if this is **normal** or **not**.

    Kafka-sighting confirmed! It's very surprising to me in this moment of revelation that I wasn't able to tell my body was different as soon as I woke up—the story doesn't seem to acknowledge (though of course it may later?) the kinaesthetic awareness we have of our bodies. Surely I would notice if I woke up without a nose, for example?

    Still it's pleasing to be involved in something quite so surreal, the next question is what I'm going to "do about this" in the world of the game, and of course how others will react to me.

    For now though I have to decide whether this is normal or not. In a situation like this I generally try to be honest. And this is not normal.

> not

The beady eyes in the mirror bulge slightly as you struggle to make sense of what you are seeing.

How does a normal human suddenly transform into an albino salamander overnight? You **think back** to your earliest memory from the previous night in hopes of some clue.

Back in the bedroom you can hear your phone switch from "A Horse With No Name" to "Hang Tough". Someone is trying to **call you.**

    I'm quite a literal reader and player in general, so I really feel it when we step away from what I would consider to be realistic treatments of a situation. I'm very surprised at how calm and collected "I" am in this situation. This is just the tone of the story, it seems, and the nature of my character—I'm unfazed by the bizarre, even as I acknowledge that it's bizarre. And so I shall adapt my reading to this new angle on the world and look less for what I might call "emotional truth" in the story. Perhaps it will be more of a parable, and after all in that way it continues to follow Kafka more than anything else.

    I'll choose to "think back" for the usual reasons outlined above.

> think back

Let's see, you were at that new bar down the street, and you got a little drunk...

There was that **angry dark-haired woman**. She was really suspicious.

You also remember a **man in a dark suit** at the bar, but you

played by Pippin Barr

can't remember him doing or saying anything...

The **phone is still ringing** as well.

> Well at least my memory is coming back!

> angry woman

Yeah... there was that woman in the shawl. All you remember was that she was angry and yelling at you...

She looked like some kind of witch, she must have put a curse on you! I mean... its the only logical thing you can think of!

Maybe if you **go to the bar** you can find some clues!

... or then again, maybe the "witch" thing is kind of a wildly unrealistic accusation. What about the **man in a dark suit**?

I like the way the story is moving along as if my clicking on hyperlinks is jogging my own memory, the "yeah" that this passage starts off with is nice that way and makes me feel part of the process.

A bit of a step into the really supernatural with this invocation of witches and curses, so a bit less like Kafka in that an explanation is being half-offered (and then half-retracted in the last paragraph).

Odd pronouns with "I mean, it's the only thing you can think of!" I wonder if it's intentional given that this seems to be a story about identity—who is the "I" in that sentence?

I want to keep remembering things, so I'll move on to the man in the dark suit rather than change location. I feel that peculiar "interaction anxiety" in noticing that the phone is no longer an option here, can't I answer it anymore? Did I miss something important? This kind of anxiety is one of the great pleasures of these sorts of stories, especially if it's explicitly played on.

> man in dark suit

You remember that there was a strange man sitting in the corner. He was wearing dark shades the whole time, and never took a sip from his drink. You remember feeling like he was starring at you the whole time.

Maybe if you went **back to the bar** you could get more information. Maybe even find some clues.

Then again, he didn't even say anything. You might just be paranoid. What about the **dark haired woman** who seemed so angry at you?

Eft to Newt by Michael Joffe

As a person who also makes games and writes things, I can't help but notice when an experience like this doesn't quite acknowledge the history of its play—seeing the dark haired woman proposed as an essentially new topic is a little distracting to me and pulls me away from feeling in this world.

The man in the shades sounds pretty interesting though!

-> back to the bar

You ask around at the bar. Sadly, no one can answer your questions about the mysterious man in black.

Glumly, you leave and begin to head home. You'll have to find some other way to figure out how this transformation took place.

As you turn the corner of your building. You find yourself staring at the man in a dark suit, leaning against a car in front of your door. He stares at you from behind his dark shades and takes a drag of his cigarette.

You start to call out when you suddenly feel a sharp blow to the back of your head.

Everything goes dark

Suddenly the story is a bit noire, some quite fun genre-bending.

The "call" out is a little ambiguous to me—I'm unsure of whether I'm trying to talk to the man or whether I'm afraid and calling for help. Either way, given the blow to the back of the head, the latter would have been more sensible!

> dark

You come to in a small, poorly-lit room. Your eyes focus on the table in front of you. Seated across is the man in black and another, unfamilliar person in identical clothes and shades. This second person is a good deal younger, perhaps in his mid 20s, and has no eyebrows. Now that you have a better look at the first man in black, you notice the scar above his right eye, giving him an almost permanent expression that can only be described as "that one on every Dreamworks poster".

No-brows nods to Dreamworks-brows and begins speaking to you. "Dr. Cortazar, or may I call you Alex? I'm sorry for the rough treatment, but we couldn't risk our investment escaping".

played by Pippin Barr

"You'll be happy to know that your theories were a success, this could not have been done without you"

A lot going on in this passage.

One thing that's a little jarring to me is a tonal shift with the jokes about eyebrows—we go from a relatively neutral tone to something much more amused, perhaps shifting us from noir to something more like *Austin Powers* (though in some ways perhaps this kind of characterization of "thugs" is still quite hard boiled?)

The Dreamworks reference misses me, I'm not even sure what kinds of movies Dreamworks make, so I'm unclear on what this eyebrow situation says about the character in question. Looking some up online I guess it's that kind of rakish cocked eyebrow - it's not obvious to me why the Dreamworks reference is there specifically, as the story had until then avoided highly specific cultural references (other than the phone's ringtones).

The state of my amnesia is weirder than I thought. It seems that I can remember things that happened at the bar, but not that I seem to have been a scientist working on this kind of transformation. Amnesia, even though it's a "solution" to having players step into a protagonist's shoes without jarring them, yields this kind of problem—as you make revelations, they may seem even stranger *because* the player's character for some reason wasn't able to remember them.

Finally, and perhaps contradicting the previous thought, I'm not entirely sure who is saying the final sentence in quote marks. I'm inclined to believe that it is "no-brows", but because it's something that *I* click on to advance the story, is it possible that it's something I am saying instead?

> happy

Still groggy, you try to piece together what No-brows is saying. Your "theories"? Your work doesn't involve salamanders. It doesn't even involve biology... you're a folklorist. You're best known for writing children's books about mythology.

"You're confused, it is natural. Let me explain how your work brought this about."

Dreamworks-brows opens up a folder on the table and holds up a picture of your first book's cover.

"'A New Metamorphosis', unlike your later work this did not sell particularly well. Do you remember it?"

Yes, it was an adaption of Ovid

Yes, it was based on an old Aztec myth

Yes, it was based on Jungian archetypes

Eft to Newt by Michael Joffe

It's apparent now that I didn't say the previous quote, but it's interesting to feel that tension of agency—if I click on something it's as though I am "doing it," yet here it wasn't the case.

Kafka's back, and more explicit than previously with a reference to Metamorphosis.

I enjoy these kinds of choice situations, particularly in Twines (though it's also something I like a lot in *Kentucky Route Zero*). That is, choices where (at least as I assume is the case here) I can choose to *color* the story rather than directly influence what happens—I get to choose what that book was about.

The amnesia is apparently falling away quite nicely now as I seem to remember almost everything of relevance.

One other note, not tied to this specific passage—it's very noticeable how the eft/newt image in the left-hand sidebar is sort of "reading" the story as it goes along. It looks rather plaintive, ready to be disappointed, I suppose, by my choices?

> Ovid

"Yeah, 'baby's first Ovid'. Surprised it didn't sell better." Dreamworks-brows chuckles with disdain.

"But you did something interesting. As a fun 'activity section' you had a chapter dedicated to getting kids to write their own anti-epic poems or... jesus, what was it called?"

Dreamworks-brows begins skimming though the papers. No-brows coughs.

"Kollektivgedicht" No-brows states.

"Jesus, who needs so many words? Anyways, your book was devoted to helping kids write one of those things. Creating their own myths by tying together stories from their own lives and the natural world around them.

"Like we said, not a huge hit with kids, but it was surprisingly popular with a branch of the military. Formerly known as the First Earth Bettalion, they were a group dedicated towards creating not only better soldiers, but better humans period.

"Your anti-epic exercise became part of the standard training for new recruits. The idea being that in order to overcome the boundaries and limitations of humanity as it is today, our future super men would need to self-mythologize themselves. A metamorphosis of the mind and spirit turning them into god men.

"In particular, our bosses became enamored with the idea of metamorphosis in general, and began doing research into

played by Pippin Barr

animals that undergo such transformations.

"This obsession eventually brought them to the axolotl. Salamanders like them, with the gills and whatnot, they're supposed to be a juvenile state. Eventually they grow up to be something else. But unlike other salamanders, these don't grow up. Like soggy Peter Pans. They stay little gilled teenagers forever.

"But given the proper artificial stimuli, an axolotl WILL go through a metamorphosis. All it takes is the right moment and you force Peter Pan to grow up. Our bosses believed humans to be the same. We're trapped in these weak bodies, and if we can introduce the right environment, humans will emerge as something new.

"So we began a project, introducing a new chemical into the population. Imagine our surprise when the first demonstrable metamorphosis was you, and that it transformed you into an axolotl of all things!"

You can hardly believe what you are being told... **"So what do you want from me?"**

Yikes, a wall of text suddenly after very short passages. I think I would have preferred it to be broken up, given that the entire page appears to "just" be exposition of our current situation.

And we have another genre-shift, this time over into science fiction, and also into the weird kind of "secret organization's crazy ideas" story as well. The connections made from the children's activity to the moment of introducing a chemical into the population are, perhaps suitably, very garbled. As is the overall rhetoric. But, again, perhaps this is appropriate to this kind of lunacy?

One thing's for sure: "soggy Peter Pans" is a pretty amazing image!

Here the link actually *is* a text spoken by my character.

> What do you want?

"We want to know why you changed. We wanted to create a better form of humanity. A grown up humanity. You think a little salamander is what we wanted?

"Also, we don't believe in coincidence. You of all people turning into an axolotl of all things? Yeah, not chance. Either you have some connection to this, or someone is using you to send us a message of some kind.

"Either way, we're probably gonna have to cut you open for a bit and find out what."

UH, WHAT?

We're continuing along the same basic sci-fi/shadowy organization line with this. I find the dialog from the "bad guys" very strange and abstract, hard to grab onto.

There's an odd amount of oscillating between "they" and "we" for these people as well. A lot of the descriptions of what the organization was up to in the previous passage were "they," but now it's "we."

> UH WHAT?

No-brows places a box on the table and pulls out a syringe.

"Don't worry, you won't even be aware of what is happening. Who knows, being an axolotl you might even regenerate and we can do this again, and again, and again."

As you contemplate dissection, a sudden explosion rocks the building. No-brows drops the syringe in shock and Dreamworks-brows jumps to his feet.

"What was tha-"

Dreamworks-brows' exclamation is cut short by the door to the room being kicked open. Gas pours in, choking the two agents. Strange figures emerge from the gas.

"It's Section 6! Those rebels are-"

No-brows is suddenly knocked back by a laser blast.

With the commotion going on, no one is paying any attention to you.

Flee into an air duct

Approach the rebels

Full sci-fi action adventure territory now, even lasers. Again, when a choice doesn't feel like I "need" to do one or the other for functional reason, I try to be emotionally honest, so I'll flee.

> flee

You take advantage of the confusion and slip into the air duct. Your new form conveniently allows you to easily maneuver through the small opening.

As you scramble through the ducts, the sound of gunfire and explosions rocks the building. Whatever is going on sounds fierce.

You come to fork in the ducts.

Go Left

Go Right

    I suddenly realize I'm rather confused about my size. Apparently I'm small enough to slip into a small air vent, but earlier in my apartment I was using the faucet and looking in the mirror without noticing that I was tiny? Or going into the bar and asking people questions? This is all very perplexing. For now, though, I take it I am an actual axolotl.

    > left

You turn left and continue through the ducts.

You hear screams below you.

If a branch of the US military is who kidnapped you, then who could be attacking? Another country? A shadow government?

This is all way beyond you. You just want to get out.

Go Straight

Go Right

    Using the duct sequence for some more exposition is a nice option.

    > straight

You reach a dead end. Below you is a **grate**.

    Not much to do except head through the grate!

    > grate

You drop down through the grate to find yourself in a bathroom stall.

Maybe you can carefully leave and escape the building unnoticed.

As you slowly exit the stall, two fully armored figures with guns enter.

"Clearing out these fascists is hard work. I gotta take a leak."

"Gross. Be quick we still have to- wait look!"

You suddenly find yourself starring down the barrel of the strange weapons these figures are holding. This might be the end...

The figure who needed to take a leak lowers their weapon.

"It's Dr. Cortazar! Listen, hear us out. We're not going to hurt you!"

Listen to the nice man with the gun

At this point I'll just have to let myself flow along the kind of pulpy narrative that's upon me. It's probably something I'd be clicking through fairly fast if I wasn't making these notes.

More confusion about size and identity here, with these two people apparently recognizing a tiny axolotl sneaking around as, well, me. I'm starting to wonder whether this is somehow a part of the point of the story—this ambiguity of my physical form not just in terms of "being something else" but in terms of the varied ways the narrative itself treats my shape and physical presence.

> listen

The mysterious figures address you.

"We are agents of Section 6. Our task is to remove the lingering remains of shadowy, illegal and inhumane clandestine organizations such as this. The Organization is a rogue eugenics program that is a danger to every free person in the country. We hope to bring them to justice.

"Don't worry, we know about what they did to you and are willing to help. Our weapons are non-lethal, as our aim has always been to expose these criminals to justice. Come with us and we'll do everything we can to restore you to your true form Dr. Cortazar. I promise"

Follow them

Quite a cheesy passage, but in keeping with the pulp. It's interesting to me in part because the things they're saying here feel so awkwardly delivered, as if the "acting" were not being pulled off by these actors. But of course it's just the dialog itself. Entirely plausible this is all completely intended by the author as parody etc., we shall see—and this is one nice quality of the genre-bending that's gone on so far, we're not ever quite on a stable footing, not just in terms of plot, but also in terms of tone and style.

> follow

played by Pippin Barr

The follow a group of Section 6 agents out of the building as the rest of them press on to subdue the rogue organization.

Shortly after these events, the leaders of this group are put on trial. As a key witness in the case against these villains, you are called to the stand.

The defendants' slick, big city lawyer's main argument seems to be that no one can PROVE you are actually the famous Dr. Cortazar transformed into an axolotl, and not simply a normal, wild axolotl that has been trained to speak phonetically.

You agree to answer a series of **questions** that only the real Dr. Cortazar could answer.

Although, it really is sticking to its pulpy style at this point, so perhaps this really is the "identity" of this story.

> questions

"Thank you for agreeing to this series of questions Dr. Alex Cortazar... IF THAT IS YOUR REAL NAME!"

It is

Actually it is only my pseudonym, my real name is Morgan Bolívar

Am anticipating a series of "color" choices here as well, where I'll be able to determine who the doctor actually is (that is, I'll always be right, no matter what I choose). On the other hand, this might be an actual quiz with "correct" answers. I'd prefer the former—but either way I want to take the more "revisionist" option here of the pseudonym because, again, it feels like I have more agency this way.

> pseudonym

"Hm, very good, you've obviously done your research.

Now for your next question: in which journal was your first paper published?"

American Anthropologist

Journal of Near Eastern Studies

Nintendo Power

Who Put the Bomp

An interesting moment here that presents me with another tension. The irreverence of the answer possibilities here (notably "Nintendo Power" and "Who Put the Bomp") suggest that it doesn't matter what I choose, and suggest that it *is* the "you get to define who the doctor is" situation. As such, I'm half-inclined to choose something "proper" like American Anthropologist, but then also half-inclined to choose something patently ridiculous like "Nintendo Power" to *test* whether it's actually arbitrary. Tonally, this is interesting because it draws *me* into making the story ridiculous or not.

> Nintendo Power

"Correct. Cortazar's first paper 'How Do You Enter The Waterfall Of Wishing?' was published in the 'Counselor's Corner' of the February, 1992 issue of Nintendo Power.

"But can you answer this question? In 2008, tabloids linked Cortazar romantically to which celebrity?"

Shia LaBeouf

Kate Middleton

Leona Lewis

Morgan Freeman

So we've now confirmed we cannot answer wrong and that the story doesn't "mind" if we answer ridiculously. In some ways I like this, because it includes me in the playful ridiculousness.

> Morgan Freeman

"Correct. Tabloids reported seeing the two of you locked in a romantic embrace on the set of The Dark Knight.

"HOWEVER, these rumors turned out to be false. Can you tell the court why that was?"

We're actually blood relatives

I was in a coma that year

Morgan Freeman turned out to not be a real person, but just a collection of ducks in a suit

played by Pippin Barr

The surrealist slapstick is wearing a little thin for me at this point as it feels more like the author telling jokes than telling a story, as such my choices are made more under duress than out of interest.

> I was in a coma

"Correct. Cortazar was in a mild coma for the entire decade following a water skiing accident. The person the tabloids had seen with Morgan Freeman was actually a famed con artist and academic impersonator.

"But can you answer this final question!? The question that once and for all will demonstrate if you are the true Dr. Alex Cortazar or if my clients are the victim of a fantastical smear campaign!

"What is the shape of the birthmark on Cortazar's right buttock?"

Like a moose but with three antlers

The entire Magna Carta

It was two circles, but I had it tattooed to look like a smiley face

President Taft's moustache

The constalletion Cygnus

An outline of the Candian province Ontario

Ironically, an axolotl

Everyone percieves it differently, but most claim to see the face of their first love

A heart that changes in hue depending on my mood

I choose "ironically, an axolotl" because it's the only one that gives me some semblance of dignity in contributing to a coherent narrative!

> Ironically, an axolotl

You turn and lift your long axolotl tail to reveal the birthmark, still there. The court gasps!

The defendant's case falls apart. The villains are fined for their crimes against humanity and you can return to your studies.

You are still trapped in the body of an axolotl, but you at least have your life back.

Congratulations! This is the seventh ending in the series.

Play again to find them all!

Suddenly it's over! I hadn't at all anticipated this being the case as I'd pictured a long, plot-heavy sequence with minor choices, and the narrative itself, with many "major events" didn't ever really suggest a standard dramatic arc.

And of course this screen is revealing in that we can see there are seven endings and that the reader should try to "find them all". This is also a pretty interesting moment in reading these stories, though it's actually less interesting in this specific case. Sometimes when reading a Twine or interacting with some other experience, I find that I want to only have *one* reading in spite of multiple possibilities because there's a sense of "truth" involved, of not being a "revisionist" and of not essentially "gaming" the story and treating it like a set of content which one should see all of.

However, in a story like *Eft to Newt*, which is very surrealist and ridiculous (at least on my initial playing), I don't feel that kind of "responsibility" to the story and would happily poke around to find out the other combinations of choices that lead to different results. For me this is generally a sign in me of *disinterest* in the story, however, and more about a completionist attitude.

As such, I'll now go through and look for some other endings and make any notes on them. One inevitable consequence of this, of course, is that the subsequent readings are incredibly utilitarian and functional, only reading "new" texts, and clicking rapidly through "old" texts. This is a very different way to experience a story and so, in a sense, the "real story" can perhaps only be experienced the first time?

> (back, replay with different choices altogether, resulting in:)

The night continues on. After dinner and more conversation, you go for a long walk together. It is the first of many friendly nights out, eventually blossoming into something more.

Nothing sexual. How could it? Even with the size difference, Doto wasn't carved to be anatomically correct and you've got a completely incompatible amphibian cloaca anyways. But neither of you have complaints, and what the two of you develop is just as deep and rich.

Congratulations. You have achieved the 7th ending. Play again to find them all!

So replaying the game is interesting because it turns out that there are radically different plot possibilities rather than variations on the sci-fi plot

played by Pippin Barr

we had in my official playthrough. In this playthrough I was a columnist for a paper who discovered a living statue and eventually developed a romantic (non-sexual) relationship with it.

Tonally the story was fairly similar to the sci-fi plot, with various fairly "ridiculous" options along the way, so I don't necessarily feel as yet like I missed an "emotional" payoff in terms of getting the official ending I did.

I'm reminded most obviously of *Save the Date*, in which you similarly experience outlandish results from initially "normal" seeming beginnings. Here, too, the endings seem to be related tonally by a love of bizarre, surrealist humor, though perhaps equally with at least some concern for human emotion and endeavor.

Oddly this ending and the previous ending were both denoted the "seventh"...

> (back, replay)

The next few weeks are busy. You spend most of the time staying with Lord Kreegarax (the parasaurolophus you met at the first contact) and his retinue. You alternate between filling in their missing data on how the Earth has changed since their age, and facilitating talks between the dinosaurs and the other self-aware salamanders.

In all the busy work, you can almost fail to notice the ongoing cull. Almost...

What you do notice will horrify you for years to come. You understand that it is necessary, the planet couldn't sustainably support the number of humans it had in the first place, much less also your kind and the emigrating dinosaurs from the past. The number of humans today is much more manageable, and they do live in relative peace within their enclosures. Still, you can't help but wish the dinosaurs had carried out the cull with less... enthusiasm.

Still, what did humanity ever really do for your kind? Amphibians would never truly be thought of as equals, and even as successful as your writing career was, it was always regarded as a curiosity rather than respected work. What difference does it matter if the people looking down at you were hairless apes or ancient birds? You even kept your job at the new dinosaur-run media.

Speaking of which, you better get going. Your new Ask-Olotl column needs to be written. "Great Lord Of The Ape-ReEducation Pit For A Day" promises to be your biggest colurm yet!

If only you had gotten more sleep... but you haven't been sleeping well... every night you see their faces in the museum, those first few to face the teeth of the new world to come...

Congratulations, of all the endings in this game, this one is truly the 7th! Play again to find them all!

    Now we find out that the "seventh" thing is a joke, as this one is "truly" the seventh.

    At this point in the repeated readings we run into another element of this style of story, which is that the reading turns more into a kind of "structural analysis" of the text—that is, I find myself looking for points that are likely to branch toward alternative endings, rather than reading, particularly, for the story itself. It's an interesting transition and a very different way to engage with the text.

    > (back, replay)

You hadn't considered it before, but you really do enjoy making bread. With an investment from the roof-pigeons, you purchase a small shop dawn the street and open the 'Axo-Loaf-l Bakery'. Everyone agrees the name is terrible, but the baked goods are the best in the city. You are able to make a comfortable living doing this, and are even able to open a second location downtown.

Congratulations, you have reached the 7th Ending! Play again to find them all!

    There is a lot of writing in here.

DINING TABLE

BY LEON ARNOTT
PLAYED BY MATTHEW BURNS

My date was with Angie. Short and narrow, with tidy blond hair and a small face. She'd started living with us a week and a half ago. She was seated at the other end of the plastic table, in a hard plastic chair like mine. She looked about as uncomfortable as me.

"Er-"

> Er—

*

"Now, why don't you greet each other, hmm?" boomed our host in her cheery voice.

Hmm.

> greet each other

I quickly said "Hi Angie, so glad you could make it" or something jokey like that across the table. In reply, she quickly flashed a broad grin and said "Oh, I wouldn't miss it for the world."

She put her hands on the table and lapsed into silence. Fortunately, this seemed to be satisfactory.

Dining Table by Leon Arnott

"Now," said our host, leaning over us, "shall I take your order?"

- **Spaghetti**
- **Soup**
- **Salad**

A performance.
You can't pick anything but a sultana (a white raisin).

> Sultana

She carefully placed the sultanas on the table before each of us. They looked like soft, misshapen black loaves more than anything. They smelled richer and more pungent than the basic meals she normally made us, which I guess was why she'd chosen it for this special night.

Angie made a "Mmm" noise of satisfaction, probably just out of politeness. Of course, neither of us had cutlery, so she reached over and, with some difficulty, twisted off a shred of its skin. It didn't give easily, and she had to use both hands. She began chewing, glancing at me expectantly.

- **Eat sultana**

> eat sultana

"Hang on," said our host, who'd noticed Angie's difficulty eating. We quickly moved out of the way of her hands as she took back the sultanas. She went over to the bench and chopped them into smaller chunks, then came back and laid them on the table. "There you go!"

- **Eat sultana**

> eat sultana

I then tried one of the sliced sultana chunks. It tasted incredibly sweet - so much so that the first bite made me wince. Angie seemed to smile at my expression, but only raised her chunk to her mouth with some trepidation. To her credit, she acted like it tasted great.

We nibbled away at it for a few minutes. **Marcia** looked over us and our quiet meal, and eventually said "Hey, feel free to talk amongst yourselves!" She placed her huge arms on the dining table, a few inches from where she'd placed our own

played by Matthew Burns

little table, and rested her chin on them. She grinned and whispered, "**Just pretend I'm not here.**"

   Creepy!

   > Just pretend I'm not here

There was a cold silence. Then, finally, Angie asked, "Say, what shampoo do you use? Your hair looks great."

All I could do was laugh. I didn't know if she was intentionally joking or genuinely pretending. As if we knew or cared which shampoo **got used on us**.

My attention was drawn by Marcia's grin widening a little. Noticing my gaze, she slid her head back behind her arms, concealing her lips. As if that would make her any less visible, her massive presence any smaller.

I then turned back to Angie and moved the conversation.

- **Conditioner**
- **Clothes**

   So awkward.

   > got used on us

Neither of us really look closely at what Marcia used on our heads every other morning. For a moment I'd see a distant bottle being squirted, on her finger, and then she'd walk over to me in the basin, and then would come the rubbing and rinsing.

She knows we could probably bathe ourselves if she let us. But I guess she enjoys cleaning her little possessions.

« **Return**

   You enjoy being washed by her too, I can tell.

   > Return
   > Clothes

I said something like "I like your dress!" It was the same red dress she normally wore. It fitted her poorly, having been tailored for a doll several inches taller than her, and it was no doubt made of harsh material with huge stitching.

Dining Table by Leon Arnott

Marcia still hadn't gotten around to sewing her something more comfortable. The full-body rags that Marcia sewed for most of us would no doubt fit even worse, but at least the material she typically chose was softer, gentler and warmer.

Angie couldn't think of anything to add to that. So, I tried changing the subject:

- **Weather**

> At least get some nicer clothes for your dolls, Marcia!

\> Weather

"Awfully poor weather we've been having, isn't it?"

Ah, yes - there had been a storm a few days ago that had been tremendously noisy. Marcia had been out in it for an uncomfortable amount of time.

"I'm glad we didn't have to be out there," said Angie. "Can you imagine?" We both wordlessly agreed that being in lethally violent weather would be quite bothersome.

"So glad we don't ever have to worry about that," I said. Marcia's cheeks rose from behind her arms. My attempt at slyly flattering our omnipotent host was a success.

At this point, Marcia **stood up**.

> They're so Stockholmy.

\> stood up

At this point, Marcia stood up and said "Let me get our happy couple some **drinks**."

\> drinks

She served up a few drops of wine for each of us, in the same familiar dolls' cups we use for most of our drinks. She said it was wine, anyway. We each took a few polite sips.

It definitely helped slake the sugar of the sultanas. We resumed our dinners. Unfortunately, the richness of our meal was a bit much for our stomachs - we ended up leaving half of our sultana chunks untouched. An eyedropper descended to the table, silently offering refills for our glasses, but we both politely declined.

played by Matthew Burns

When it became clear that dinner was over, Marcia stood up and declared, "Wouldn't it be nice to do some **dancing** together?"

Let me guess. I won't get a choice. They'll have to dance.

> dancing

On cue, we both stood up from those hard chairs. Her hands reached out and scooped us up. As always, she picked me up too fast, and I felt my stomach lurch and my vision blur as she carried me through the air. It felt very weird, but then, so did everything else around me.

She placed us down on the other end of the dining table, on a rubber placemat.

"Let me put on some music," she said, pulling out her chair loudly and sitting down. She laid down her music player in a corner of the dance floor, and, after some poking and prodding, its tiny speaker began emitting energetic instrumental jazz. Perhaps motivated more by Marcia's enthusiasm than the music itself, we looked at each other, shrugged, and **went with it**.

So docile, both of them, in this situation.

> went with it

We improvised a dance out of the music, gaily stepping and shuffling around each other on the soft, bouncy placemat. We weren't keeping up with the tempo at all, due to our meal weighing heavily on our stomachs, but that didn't seem to matter.

As I danced and looked at Angie in her ill-fitting dress, I suddenly thought of how distant my last memory of a fun night out was. I turned and gave a brief smile to Marcia, who was, as always, watching us, enraptured.

Then, she said "Don't you think this dance floor is looking a little empty?", followed by a wink.

We thought she was going to bring out the rest of us, but instead, both her hands walked in on their fingers, and started kicking and hopping beside us. Angie couldn't quite conceal how silly this made her feel. I, conversely, felt oddly comforted.

- **Keep dancing**

Dining Table by Leon Arnott

I'm beginning to sense an attitude about this situation from the author of this Twine.

> Keep dancing

Eventually, after Marcia looped the track one more time ("Encore!", she cried at the imaginary band) in which we paired off with her dancing hands, she brought the dance to a close. Our partners bowed (by tipping forward unexpectedly), then flew away.

"Let's finish up with a nice walk in the moonlight," she boomed. This, as we already knew, meant a walk on her window-sill. She scooped us up and carried us there. She then threw the windows open to let in the scent of night air - but closed them again as soon as Angie politely pointed out that neither of us were dressed for the cold.

"This time," she said, "I'll really leave you well alone to stroll and chat." To prove this, she plugged in her music player's earphones and sat on the floor below. We found ourselves alone, save for a wobbling black hill of hair.

- **Look at the moon**

They can talk back?

> Look at the moon

We turned and faced the moon through the glass. It was a full moon, but it only periodically poked through the thick clouds above. It shone down on the roofs of neighbouring houses - houses the size of worlds, each, to us, as distant, aloof and alien as the moon itself.

I looked at Angie. Out of the seven of us that Marcia possesses, she arrived most recently. We see each other every day. She was a department store manager that Marcia met at a friend's place, and I was an old unemployed neighbour of Marcia's. What did we have to say to each other, here on this play-date?

- **Talk about her**
- **Talk about me**
- **Talk about tonight**
- **Talk about Marcia**

played by Matthew Burns

She turns real people into dolls?

> Talk about Marcia

I didn't feel like talking about Marcia.

> Talk about tonight

I wanted to ask her if tonight had, against the odds, been a romantic evening that had brought us closer together. What I actually said was "That was pretty good dancing!"

"Yeah," she said. "It was nice to just unwind and be silly for awhile."

"Even though we kind of had to be talked into this," I added, still careful, for whatever reason, not to break character.

She went with it. "Yeah, funny how you often have to be pushed into things you end up liking. Hindsight and all that."

"Talked into" isn't the word I'd use. You're a doll with no choice!

> Talk about me

I stared at where the moon had been a moment earlier, and said, "Since we're here, I might as well ask: what do you think of me?"

Angie, looking at the same place, thought to herself, then replied, "OK, out of all of us, you seem to be, I guess, the most content, the most grounded? I haven't seen you get as stir-crazy or emotional as the rest of us."

I turned and smiled politely. "I guess I've just been here awhile longer. Or," I added, "maybe I'm just good at not showing my feelings."

Angie half-shrugged and returned the smile.

- **Talk about the future**

They are so hesitant and awkward! Cut loose! You're a doll and/or tiny person! Do whatever!

> Talk about the future

"Okay, time to go home now," boomed the hair mound, getting to her feet. "Time to **say goodnight to your partner**

Dining Table by Leon Arnott

and thank them for an amazing evening!"

> say goodnight

We said good night to each other and thanked each other for an amazing evening. Marcia evidently didn't think spending the night together was something you did on a first date.

We did, however, decide to kiss - which awoke a barely-stifled "Aww!" from a very large throat.

And with that, we were plucked up and sent home to our **houses**.

> houses

Marcia has seven dollhouses - one for each of us. We have the privacy and dignity of our own houses, even without electricity, or appliances, and our water in tubes. And, of course, with a landlady who can lift off our roofs or pull open the walls, and peer in any time she likes.

Even the dollhouses, though, aren't quite the right size for us. The ceiling's a little too high. The doorways and furniture are a little too big. Even our homes, our sanctuaries in a very big world, makes us feel small and child-like.

As I mulled over tonight, had a cup of water and prepared for bed, I began thinking - briefly, about what **the "real me"** is doing right now, but, more strongly, about what tonight's date has **taught me**.

Getting the feeling you like this, though. Babied by a giant mother figure . . .

> the "real me"

I know that somewhere, out there, is the "real me" - my full-sized original, who has a job and family and all that. But me, the thumb-sized version that Marcia secretly created from my other self's hairs and dreams and memories, only belongs here with her.

Sure, we all found it hard to forget our old lives our copied memores - to accept that our human selves are out there, living on our behalf. That no one's missing us, that no one's coming to rescue us and return reality to its normal size. But eventually, we come around to living our new, simple existence, with her.

played by Matthew Burns

Well, I did, at least.

Return

> Because you like it!
>
> > Return
> > taught me

I can't **deny it**.

> > deny it

I can't deny it. I have to **face it**.

> > face it

I love Marcia.

> I knew it!
>
> > I love Marcia

I love her. I don't know if this is Stockholm syndrome, cabin fever, or the sheer unreality of my world sending me round the bend, but it's real.

I love looking up in my house, and just watching her watch me watch her for hours on end. I love seeing her head eclipsing the ceiling light, surrounded by a halo. I love being cared for and doted on by a giant. I even learned to like being washed and patted dry.

Tonight she matched me with Angie, but she doesn't know - I'm sure she doesn't - that my only match is with her. Me, her tiny, **secret lover**.

> It's because this is your fetish. :)
>
> > secret lover

I can't let the others know. Not yet, anyway. Some of them would be incensed if she 'played favourites', raising one of us above, in any way. It's simply unconscionable. I don't know how, but unless I want to fight down this love for the rest of my days, I'll need to find a way to win them over. Somehow. Some way.

......

> .....

We know that Marcia has just finished creating a homunculus of herself - a second Marcia, a me-sized Marcia. To bring herself down to our level, to show that she's "just one of us", deep down. I guess I could try and love that Marcia, too. But, she wouldn't be my Marcia, my booming capricious goddess, who can encase me in fingers and lift me into the sky.

......

> .....

I'll have to figure all this out tomorrow.

For now, I must **sleep**.

You could also read this as a game designer vs. game player thing, but it's too fetishistically written for me to look at that way.

> sleep

And dream of vast dancing hands and quivering hills of hair until the morning.

Well, Leon, I certainly learned something about you!

I'M FINE
BY ROKASHI EDWARDS
PLAYED BY JOHN BRINDLE

I struggled for weeks to play this game.

It wasn't the subject matter. For me, depression and suicide have long since left the zone of taboo and entered one so casual and blasé that I forget they are shocking to others.

Nor was it the writing, though the writing is knotty and thorny: ramshackle sentences where subject and object swap places, then return; repetitions, contradictions, apparent non-sequiturs, shifts of tense and sudden accusations. Sometimes it has the intense, delirious quality of the letters I write to my psychoanalyst, where there is no obligation to obey a structure and things just pour out in a thick unbroken paragraph. But it is also hostile: the protagonist, who we'll call "R", is always on guard against betrayal or hollow sympathy, to the extent that the reader's own scrutiny seems unwelcome.

I think instead it was the sheer unbroken length of the passages. Video-game culture has a deeply embedded bias towards activity, however empty or pointless, and it trains us to expect a thick foam of input and feedback.

I'm Fine by Rokashi Edwards

When, in life outside, I feel the urge to check every few minutes that my friends still respect and accept me, I know that this is neurotic—but computers, with their infinite patience, are perfect enablers of similar behaviour. Reading is quiet by contrast. We're left alone with the text, which only yields if we gather our efforts. There is no regular drip of achievement to keep us clinging on. And I, left alone with those huge slabs of hate and despair, could not break them apart. I couldn't find purchase on those mirror-like, midnight-black walls.

But there are two versions of *I'm Fine*. The one I tried first, hereafter referred to as the A-text, uses Twine's standard Sugarcane format, which runs on HTML. The second version, the B-text, has been ported to Adobe's .AIR format so that it can run outside a web browser. This version adds grayscale drawings and a driving, bleak soundtrack, but it also breaks up the text. The hyperlinks connecting each page are still there, but the passages themselves are separated into several chunks, which the reader clicks through one by one. I want to talk in more detail later about how this affects the flow between certain passages, but it's more important for now that this was what finally let me in to the game. Broken up like this, the passages were suddenly more manageable. All I had to do was read *this much*, then click forward and feel I had made tangible progress. It was a very sparse trail of breadcrumbs, but it was enough. Like the to-do lists I draw up every morning and cling to throughout every day, or like some poor fuck clinging to a guide rope to make it through a pitch-black room, it gave me something to follow—a thread left behind by ambivalent Ariadne.

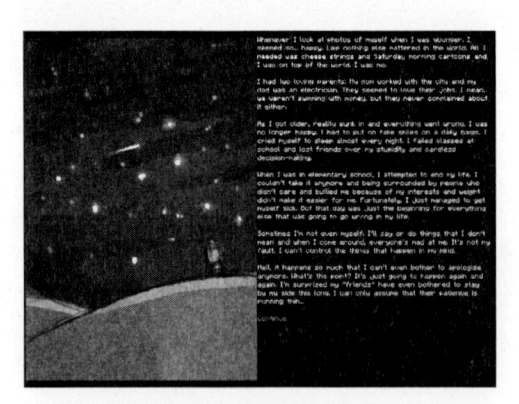

Whenever I look at photos of myself when I was younger, I seemed so... happy. Like nothing else mattered in the world. All I needed was cheese strings and Saturday morning cartoons and I was on top of the world. I was me.

I had two loving parents: My mom worked with the city and my dad was an electrician. They seemed to love their jobs. I mean, we weren't swimming with money, but they never

played by John Brindle

complained about it either.

I never talked to them much. When I used to live with them they seemed more like roommates more than parents. They had no idea what I did with my time and they didn't really bother to find out.

As I got older, reality sunk in and everything went wrong. I was no longer happy. I had to put on fake smiles on a daily basis. I cried myself to sleep almost every night. I failed classes at school and lost friends over my stupidity and careless decision-making.

When I was in elementary school, I attempted to end my life. I couldn't take it anymore and being surrounded by people who didn't care and bullied me because of my interests, weight and everything else didn't make it easier for me. Fortunately, I just managed to get myself sick. But that day was just the beginning for everything else that was going to go wrong in my life.

Sometimes I'm not even myself. I'll say or do things that I don't mean and when I come around, everyone's mad at me. It's not my fault. I can't control the things that happen in my mind.

Hell, it happens so much that I can't even bother to apologize anymore. What's the point? It's just going to happen again and again. I'm surprised my "friends" have even bothered to stay by my side this long. I can only assume that their patience is running thin...

Continue

    So here we are in the maze. We're in first person, conversational tone. There's a sense of occasion to the first thing you read in a game like this, and especially to the first thing you click. Here the prompt for the start of the "real game" is R's words about his friends: "I can only assume that their patience is running thin." So we start pretty much at rock bottom, with this assumption that nobody is left to help out.

    What prickled at my neck when I first read this was how little detail there was on how this depression took hold. "Everything went wrong," says R. "I was no longer happy." The jump from there to "I cried myself to sleep almost every night" is like a transition in a dream, where suddenly you're just somewhere else and you don't think to ask why. R's claim that "sometimes [he's] not even [him]self" is similarly light on detail and heavy on foreboding. It's worth connecting this trouble with identity to the end of the first paragraph: "I was me." Somewhere along the line some sense of an undivided self has been lost, even if it is felt only in its absence. And actually we can see this same doubleness in R's act of looking at a photo of himself, looking from an alien perspective, trying to understand how this other past him could ever have been so happy.

> Continue

It's Thursday morning. How I managed to get some shut-eye I'll never know. I don't sleep a lot - I suppose you can say that I'm a little bit of an insomniac. The only time I would say that I get some sort of well-rested shut-eye is when I pass out due to being exhausted over a few days and wake up feeling groggy, headache pounding at my skull, angry and it's not something I would talk about to people.

Every time I accidently bring up the fact that I don't get a lot of sleep, it turns into some stupid discussion with my health as the hot topic.

"You should try to get more sleep" or "have you tried sleeping pills?" are my favourite of the bunch.

No, I can't just try to get sleep just like that. Yes, I have tried sleeping pills. About 40 of them at once when I tried to kill myself.

It wasn't fun.

Here's a good example of the knotty writing I talked about earlier. The concluding sentence of the first paragraph is so syntactically complex it hurts my head to try and parse into subject, verb, and object. Arguably, the subject here is actually "the time," modified by the qualifier "only," but if so it's separated from its main verb—"is"—by nested relative clauses in which the word "I" appears twice as different levels of indirect object ("*I* would say THAT *I* get" . . .) Then it trails off into a brief comma-separated list ("groggy, angry,") before suddenly lapsing into what is effectively a new sentence ("and it's not something I would talk about.") It's kind of astounding in its intricacy. The self, "I," appears four times in the sentence, each time in a different grammatical role, but each time also referring to the same entity; the self is occupying multiple positions at once, viewing and referring to itself.

Even those three commas have a strange rhythm between them: "groggy" and "angry" are similar kind of adjectives but they're separated by this weird little mini-sentence with its own subject (the headache), verb (pounding), and object (skull). That separation disrupts our ability to read "angry," like "groggy," as something R "feels" as opposed to something he is. That is, it's unclear whether "angry" proceeds from waking up—"I wake up angry"—or from feeling—"I wake up feeling angry." It's a small thing, but this kind of instability is everywhere in R's writing, and anyone running it in the software environment we call English will feel it even if they don't know why.

One way to formally analyse the complexity of any sentence is to divide

played by John Brindle

it into [i]ndependent and [d]ependent clauses — that is, ones which can stand alone versus ones which need their sentence to make sense. We tend to perceive sentences with the order [i][d] or [i][d][d] as being more straightforward because we're moving from essential to supplementary information (this, by the way, is a good trick to know if you ever need to make yourself seem very honest and forthright in a letter). In those terms, the sentence above looks, by my rusty reckoning, like this:

[d][i] [i][d] [d][d][d] [i]

And hey! I still have the rest of the game ahead of me. But here too is a bit of R's pre-emptive hostility. His sarcastic dismissal of well-wishers—"it turns into some stupid discussion"—creates a kind of boundary for the reader: Be here, click through, and listen, fine, but don't try and give him intrusive and ignorant advice.

> I wouldn't dare say anything of the sort, though. I have enough problems dealing with my friends and I don't want them on my ass trying to comfort me about things they'll never understand.
>
> I need to stop thinking about all this shit. I need to get up. I've been staring at my ceiling for what seems like hours now. Maybe I should get started with my day.
>
> What should I do first? Take a **piss** or hold it in for a bit and see if I can get something to eat, like **breakfast** for yesterday?
>
> I don't eat as much as I used to. It's pretty bad.
>
> Fuck everything, I need someone to talk to.
>
> I can't stay like this forever...
>
> I think I may need Mark. Should I **text him**?
>
> How bad can it be?

Abruptly, the text moves from the abstract to the immediate. "I need to stop thinking about this shit . . . I've been staring at my ceiling for what seems like hours." For the player, this is the first injection of concrete time and place. It's worth remembering that in the A text it comes at the bottom of the previous two passages, without any clear break, whereas in the B text, it's a new scene.

This is where R cleaves most closely to the conventions of interactive fiction: three rooms, several actions, and choices ahead. For Twine games in particular, the "shitty apartment" is a common opening device (see, for instance, eva problems' *SABBAT* and Porpentine's *How to Speak Atlantean*.) It shows us how abject and desperate the protagonist's life is at present, and gives physical form to their inner mess.

I'm Fine by Rokashi Edwards

> piss

I sauntered over to the washroom. It just hit me how dirty my apartment is. I haven't really done much of anything around here and it shows.

Dishes are piling up, clothes are everywhere and it's not suitable for me to have guests over. I don't think it ever will.

"I'll clean it," I told myself. I didn't believe myself either.

It's so easy to lie to myself.

I stood before my toilet and peed.

My urine was a deep yellow. It reminded me that I should lay off the sugar and drink more water.

What should I do?

Wash my hands properly

Rinse my hands with water

Skip the hand-washing and get food

The bathroom lets you perform different levels of indifference to your hygiene while the kitchen fridge contains only some water and a jar of Nutella. The latter is a good example of how "resistance" in Twine—i.e., the placement of different options behind varying numbers of clicks—can subtly express difficulty or ease. All R's utensils are dirty, so using a spoon to eat the Nutella takes one more action (washing up) than simply eating it with his fingers. It's appropriate if perhaps not deliberate that "spoon" has become a folk term for a unit of energy among people with debilitating illnesses. It feels like in R's situation it's kind of a victory to even do this much.

I flushed the toilet and stepped over to the sink. I turned on the faucet and proceeded to wash my hands properly.

It wasn't much, but it made me feel good. The smell of the vanilla soap made it even better.

I dried my hands with a towel and headed to the **kitchen** to see if there's anything to eat.

But... there's something I need to get off my chest...

Maybe I should **talk to someone**?

Whatever you do, though, the choice to speak to Mark will always be there, sometimes quite insistently contextualised. In fact, in terms of "resistance," this section—the only one with very much choice between passages—exerts a strong structural pull towards Mark. In my playthrough, I washed my hands in the toilet and then took the hint above. But I would have had to work quite hard not to end up where I did. Only one route—eating the Nutella in the kitchen, and using a spoon—lets you avoid the conversation. Another route, present only in the B text, detours through a sudden intrusive memory, but ends up back at Mark. There is an urge toward reaching out to him which expresses itself in shape of the player's options.

The detours are interesting for a few reasons. In one, eating Nutella sets off a chain of thoughts which leads R into a traumatic memory of homophobic harassment at work. In the other, R decides to take a walk to clear his head, but is overwhelmed in a familiar coffee shop by a memory of similar abuse back in high school. These are the earliest points in the story where R's sexuality is defined—he is gay—and they reveal a lot about his past. Yet here's no hint that the routes which lead to them will contain any narrative keys. So the player is groping blind through R's psyche. Rather than being able to explore his selfhood from an empowered position, they stumble on it in a random and disconnected way which is closer to his own alienated perspective. As if to reinforce that association, the coffee shop passage often breaks unexpectedly into second person, and then flips back to first: our relation to R remains unstable.

But, as I say, I did not go down these routes. I spoke to Mark, and fell into the first of the frustrated or abortive attempts at communication which form the backbone of the game.

Let's see...

Mark - He's a guy that I knew from school. I'm not sure how

I'm Fine by Rokashi Edwards

we became friends, but it happened. He's a little bit of a socially awkward kind of guy. I know he means well, but he makes me laugh with the things he says and does.

He says I should trust him, but that's easier said than done. I should be able to tell him everything, right?

Well... I guess there's only one way to find out. I knew as soon as I texted him about my problems; I was going to immediately regret it.

Although... there was one thing that stuck with me.

Mark once told me that it would be a good idea to put the names of people you trust on a card and keep it in my wallet and if there was ever something that was bugging me, I could look at it and know that there are people who care.

Well, it worked... sorta.. okay so maybe it helped a lot, but 4 people didn't seem like a lot and I recently crossed out one of them.

I didn't need to look inside my wallet in times of need, but whenever I was buying something with my debit card it was the first thing you see in my wallet. It was reassuring, but so creepy.

Send Mark a text message

> Send Mark a text message

I picked up my phone and sent him a message.

I didn't expect him to solve every problem I had. I wanted to avoid any sort of conflict with him.

I already had someone awkward to deal with and I didn't want to add another person to my inventory.

"I need help."

> I need help

"What's up?"

"Terrible thoughts."

    Compared to his earlier writing, R's messages to Mark are very terse and fairly vague ("I need help"; "terrible thoughts") and Mark's responses are unhelpful. The passages reflect this in their brevity; you click through more rapidly than you would elsewhere, and you kind of absorb that shift in rhythm even if you don't consciously notice it. Said shift is even clear-

played by John Brindle

er in the A text, with its sharper contrast between "passively" reading the opening passage (which has extra material absent in B) and rapidly clicking through the messages.

> Terrible thoughts

"About?"

"Me doing something I won't be alive to regret."

> Me doing something . . .

"What brought these thoughts up?"

"Everything. Everything I do or anything I experience just makes me so frustrated. I've been experiencing a lot of anxiety and panic attacks. I even got so agitated that I began to pull my hair out."

I shaved so no one would notice the patches on my face. I hope it doesn't grow back in patches. I already look homeless as is by the way I dress; typical sneakers, jeans, shirt and dirty looking flannels.

Like some homeless Canadian or something, I've been told. A homeless Canadian.

Hilarious.

> Everything . . .

"You were on medication recently? Is that correct?"

—-

I never liked taking any sort of medication. I would always forget, dare myself to take more than what was prescribed to see if it would kill me, or I'd just leave them in my medicine cabinet to expire.

The only medication I took religiously was my inhalers.

It was easier to suck in a spritz from a small tube into the back of my throat than to pop a pill that will scramble my brain making ideas of self harm disappear into the abyss of my mind.

—-

"Yes, but they weren't psychotics or antidepressants."

I'm Fine by Rokashi Edwards

> Yes, but

"Is there any one big thing that's frustrating you? Get it off your chest."

—-

I appreciate the Dr. Phil questions going on here, but right now, it's really bugging me. I can't blame him, though. I guess he's trying...

—-

"Everything frustrates me. I don't want to endure it anymore. I'm nothing but a reoccurring burden to close friends."

When R does try to go into detail, there's simply too much to say. "Everything," he attempts, "everything I do or anything I experience . . . everything frustrates me." My own experience of these passages was split between a "Dr Phil" perspective which sees R's behavior as dysfunctional and counterproductive and one which totally agrees with him. Why would you believe your friend when he tells you that you aren't a burden? Isn't that exactly what he would say under pretty much any circumstances? But then what else could he possibly say? What else can you expect? The painful truth of such feelings is that they are unspeakable, or at least unanswerable, because you can't receive a response you're capable of believing, nor less one which does not itself incite suspicion that it's a lie. My psychoanalyst would say that the circularity is the point—that on some deep level, such disclosure is not intended to result in any actual reassurance (because how could it?), but is aimed at precisely this suffering, this twisting of the knife.

"You're never a burden. You're an absolutely amazing person and any other notion is bullshit."

"I already told you, I'm here to listen and this is never inconvenient. We're friends."

"We do care what's going on with you. You have to believe that, but you also need to tell me what to do."

—-

I don't fucking know what to do. Why did you think I sent you a text message in the first place? Are you an idiot? Maybe I'm being hard on him... be he's an idiot right now.

I couldn't take the conversation anymore. I didn't want to listen to what he had to say. I felt like this help session was some kind of attack.

played by John Brindle

Maybe I wasn't thinking clearly. Maybe he was right, but at that point, I didn't know right from wrong. I just couldn't deal with anything.

Here is one of the points at which R's knowledge kind of overshoots my own. While Mark's message isn't exactly comforting, R's response to it is very strong without it quite being clear why. There is something being gestured at that I cannot see, but I can guess at its size from the tone of the gesture. R's feeling that this "help session" is "some kind of attack" is pretty familiar to me, but in that situation you can never explain to anyone why they need to leave you alone. Together, then, R and I have reached a kind of aporia where meaning just breaks down. R knows it: "At that point, I didn't know right from wrong. I just couldn't deal with anything."

I knew that it could only escalate from there so I decided to try to calm myself down by watching a few movies. Something that could take my mind off the troubles from the world, but that only lasted for a few hours.

No - it was more than a few hours. I watched films until the next day. I'm sure I zoned out quite a few times as I don't really remember what I watched. Once again, there was no sleep. I don't think I can even say that I properly watched the movies.

So many things clouded my mind that I wondered what the point was of trying to take my mind off myself. There was no escape and I didn't know what was going to happen to me.

—-

You received a text from Danielle. **Read it** or **Wallow in sadness for a while longer**?

R's friend Danielle sends a text. I can answer it or "wallow in sadness." I like the self-awareness of that prompt. There is always something weirdly indulgent about a decision to turn my face away, even though it is made in a place where the boundary between decision and compulsion has broken down completely.

> Read it

"Hey, you okay?"

"Text me back so I know you're okay. Please."

"Just an, 'I'm alive.' I'm worried about you."

—-

I didn't want to answer.

What the hell was I supposed to say? "Oh, yeah, everything's peachy and I'm just trying to think of ways to explain why I ignored you for days."

I'm not okay and I wish people would stop asking me that. It's not going to change any time soon so asking the same damn question over and over again will get you the same obvious response.

I just want to be alone. I'm not ready to face her or anyone else right now.

People wanting to see me creates too much anxiety in my mind and it makes me freak out because I don't know what to say or do. Without those, it's pointless to even talk to me. You're not getting anywhere and I'm not getting anywhere and this is a fact that should be known to all.

I can't even describe the sensation of being pulled apart from unwanted feelings.

—-

Let it out

R isn't ready to face her, but looking at her text gives you a beautiful sentence. "You're not getting anywhere and I'm not getting anywhere and this is a fact that should be known to all." The refusal to merge "you" and "I" in a collocation like "neither of us" keeps us truly separate; even though our clauses take identical forms, they happen without reference with each other. The third clause hopes for a universal knowledge, for a "fact" on which we can both agree, but admits with its modal "should"—a word which basically expresses the entire is/ought problem in six letters—that this won't happen. The two people in the sentence form a dialectic with a failed synthesis.

> Let it out

You start crying. You needed it. It's a safe way to almost feel-

played by John Brindle

ing better, even if it's only for a short period of time.

Look at yourself in the mirror

> Look at yourself

You walk towards your washroom and you look at your reflection in the mirrors above your sink.

Your eyes are red and swollen from the crying. Your lips are trembling.

How did I get to this point? Why did those things happen?

Was it because of my sexuality?

Was having an interest in men decide it was going to complicate me for the rest of my days?

Did I make wrong decisions when I thought hooking up with men from the Internet I've never met was a good idea? Would my first time be a safer experience for me?

Well, I can answer the latter: no.

Looking back at it, I thought I wanted it so bad. I wanted my virginity to be a myth... but I didn't want it anymore. It was a bad idea, but he kept going. I was so scared I didn't do anything. I didn't say anything. I just laid there, terrified.

It happened. That actually happened and I have to remember it all the time. Forever. I often wonder if his wife was okay - if he did the same thing to her like what he did to me.

My life flashed before my eyes and I was hardly entertained.

It happened and there's nothing I can do about it now.

I hated him. I wanted him to disappear from this world and I wanted the same thing for me.

Your friend Clarke texted you. You should probably **see what he said**.

Still, something is released. R breaks down in tears, and, in a series of questions to himself ("How did I get to this point?"), he discloses, without naming, another hidden trauma. At some point in the past R was raped by a guy he hooked up with on the internet. He wonders if he was doomed to it or if he asked for it, struggling through different uses of the verb "to want". It's chilling and it's horrible to read. And in the dehumanization of that crime he temporarily unites himself with the guy's wife, merging with her in a diminished personhood defined by what was done to them. When it switches again to second person, you suddenly, shockingly, however briefly, join them too.

I'm Fine by Rokashi Edwards

I saw none of this, because I did not look at the text. I wallowed. I guess I did so because when I play these games it feels cheap to pick the choices that my healthy mind knows to be good for me. Depression can be gamed—a comfort here, a confidence there, backup plans and buddy lists, keeping your head above water—but not from inside its own depths. You have to choose using a mind which might at any moment become incapable of making good choices. And sometimes I want to sort of test the game, too. How far will it let me go? Will it say "You are dead"? Do I get one of those pervy Lara Croft death scenes? Not yet.

> ~~Look at yourself~~
> ~~Let it out~~
> ~~Read it~~
> Wallow in sadness for a while longer

Danielle and I were really good friends. We had a lot on common. From gushing over celebrities to quoting our favourite TV shows over and over again, we were inseparable and the best of friends.

I could tell her anything and she would give me an honest response - I think it was a honest response. I'd hope it was a honest response.

She was smart, talented and a joy to be around, so why can't I face her, especially now? What's wrong with me?

Your phone starts ringing, but you're too deep in thought to even realize that someone's calling...

I feel like I have so much to say to her, so much to catch up on because I've been ignoring her for weeks, but I don't know where to start. I don't want to start. I just want to have no interaction with her.

No, I want to talk to her, but what am I supposed to say? I can't joke about what I've been doing. I have no energy for her energy and she knows me well enough that I'm playing

played by John Brindle

along.

Maybe I'll find the courage to say something, anything, but now's not the time.

In the meantime I have to avoid her. I don't want to look at her. I just want to be alone.

Huh?

I missed a phone call. It was Clarke. Oh boy. **Here we go...**

I read about Danielle and how R feels unworthy of her joy. Another sweet little mirror: "I have no energy for her energy." And I get a message from Clarke.

> Here we go . . .

Clarke was something else. He was charming. I enjoyed being around him. We were really good friends despite only knowing each other for a couple months. Except, I wanted more than that. I liked Clarke. I really did. More than I ever should. I would even go as far to say that I might even love him. Fuck.

I know I shouldn't think like that, but that's what I have to deal with. It's unfortunate that he's everything I look for in a guy and being gay doesn't help me in any way, shape or form.

I really messed up our friendship when I told him I liked him. It's one of the top things I regret. I've talked about it with Danielle and she would always ask me if "you guys are doing okay?" as if we were dating or something.

The thought crossed my mind every damn day.

It was an odd concept, but I never said anything to her about that.

The whole ordeal was tragic in itself, too. We were out with friends and I pretty much told him by using hand gestures, frequent use of the word "uhh," and making him guess. Man, I must have looked so fucking stupid that night.

He said that he didn't mind and that he was a changed person and it would have bugged him then, but not now. I don't know how true that is, but I'm going to call bullshit on that.

He treated me differently and it didn't take a genius to figure that out. Maybe it was for the best. I may have treated him differently as well, but only to avoid liking him even more than I did.

I'm Fine by Rokashi Edwards

Do you know how hard it is for me to let go? I mean, I'm not clingy or some kind of hoarder and I didn't send him nonstop messages asking how he was, but it got to the point where I started to feel uncomfortable being around him. Uncomfortable around the man who would never love me back.

His smile that made me happy made me feel disgusted and I didn't even feel like keeping eye contact. I wanted nothing to do with him, and I missed him.

His message:

"Haven't heard from you since mid week and your online presence have been pretty inactive. Starting to get a bit worried."

How implausible...

Clarke is a friend with whom R has fallen in unrequited love. The awkwardness which now pervades their whole relationship is summed up in an almost-confusing phrase: "His smile that made me happy made me feel disgusted." By omitting a conjunction such as "also," "now," or "formerly" (nerds call this asyndeton), R elides any orderly relationship between the two feelings and slams them together as simultaneous contraries. "I wanted nothing to do with him," he concludes, hopelessly, "and I missed him."

> How implausible . . .

When I click on a link like this I always feel I'm being made to "speak" its words, even if they're the only ones available. If that's true, we speak R's scepticism here, even if we consider it completely plausible that Clarke would get worried about him.
Now comes the second of the game's attempted communications, but it goes wrong in exactly the opposite way to the first. Instead of clicking through a bitty exchange you get this huge long continuous thing. And instead of terse, vague missives, R launches into a voluminous disclosure. The B text breaks it up a little, but in the A text, it pops up in front of your face like a wall.

It felt weird seeing those words from him. I didn't want to deal with the headache he causes me so I ignored his message for two days before deciding to send him an intricate message giving him a taste of what's going on in my head.

It was time that the truth came out and I didn't really care about the response:

—-

In the state that I'm currently in, I'm not fine. I never was

played by John Brindle

and I most likely will not ever be. The smallest thing will trigger me and I can promise you (coming from a person who never makes promises) that I can and will do something irreversible.

Regardless of what you may assume of what's going on in my head, I don't really give a fuck about who is or isn't worried about me, because I'm not.

I have enough shit going on right now that when people keep asking me where I've been really starts to get on my fucking nerves. I know people will still "care," but... I don't know what's wrong with me, but I know what I'm capable of and it's not pretty.

I had Mark come to my house pretty much begging me to get help because of what I might do to myself on behalf of everyone else who gives a fuck. I don't know how it's going to happen, but I said I would try to get people off my fucking back about my "safety." You know what? Maybe he's right. I don't fucking know. I've done this all before. The stupid pseudo-intervention crap and I refuse to deal with it again.

Sometimes I have a reason for ignoring people. Sometimes I don't. Sometimes I forget who I am and I behave in a manner that makes people around me hate me and out of nowhere I probably won't remember why. Maybe I'm bipolar. Maybe I have a whole bunch of stupid fucking things I have to add to the list of things that terrorize me.

You know I don't sleep. I'm constantly exhausted. As much as I seem to laugh, it's not genuine and I'm just not happy. When I do manage to sleep, I'm haunted by night terrors that wake me up minutes after falling asleep. People who don't know always joke saying I should take sleeping pills. I only giggle alongside them because I don't want to tell the whole world I tried to end my life by overdosing on said pills and ended up getting really sick.

I do these things and most of the time I have no idea why I do it.

I swear I can tell people the most fucked up things that have happened to me that wouldn't even scratch the surface of who I am. I must have severe mental disorders that make me lose myself and harm myself. The most I can do is distance myself from people I talk to so I don't do something stupid to them. At first look people aren't scared of me, but sometimes I feel like they should be.

My hands are trembling writing this.

I can't be trusted with medication, sharp objects, or anything of the sort because if I click, it's over and you'll never hear from me ever again. I'm not trying to scare you, Clarke, but if I did something to someone I cared about, I don't know what'll happen.

I can't apologize because I know it'll happen again. I don't know what to tell people when this starts happening to me. Sometimes I'm delusional. Sometimes I'll make stuff up. I'm not fucking okay.

I can't even tell people to trust me. How can I have people trust me when I don't even trust myself with my own life? It's stupid, but that's me on the regular.

I know I need help, but it's not easy.

I fucked up so many times during our friendship and don't bullshit me saying otherwise. I know I did. The first fucking mistake I made was telling you that I really liked you when I knew I shouldn't have. Everything went downhill from there. I almost lost it. When we got back, it was running through my mind and honestly, if I had a knife, I would have sent myself to the hospital that night.

As much as I don't care about a lot of things, my purpose isn't to scare you.

Sometimes at night I think of all my close friends and how they'd be better off without me. Not having to deal with someone who snaps every few weeks is the ultimate burden and unsuccessful endeavor I can't stand being the person who makes it all happen.

Every day I have some kind of anxiety attack or panic attack of some form just by thinking about my past or my future.

There are things you know about me, things you wish you knew about me and things you wish you hadn't.

I've only told Mark about this a while back… I didn't really have a choice because of how persistent and annoying he is, but a few years back, my first experience with another person was not how I wanted it to be. I didn't want to go through with it, but it still happened. It was rape and I never talked about it until a few months ago.

I'm traumatized. No, nothing came out of it because of obvious reasons that I'm sure you can figure out, but that's what happened and I've never been the same person ever since.

I hate people and I sure as hell can't trust them.

I wish I had the courage to tell you all of this to your face, but that won't happen without me having a mental breakdown and not being able to get the first sentence out.

The list is long.

played by John Brindle

I honestly don't want to be near you. I don't malice you, don't get me wrong. I just... I don't know. I just don't think I'll be able to handle being around you. For how long I can't say.

I have absolutely nothing to say to you and I have no intention of talking to you.

I'm sorry. I'm a stupid pathetic human being and I don't know what's going on in my life anymore.

—-

Yeah, I told him all of that. It was incredible. So many things I should keep to myself, but having no control just made things worse.

He must think I'm obsessed.

Continue

Layer upon layer of ominous semi-threats, hedges against projection, profanity, helpless aporia, all mixed with constant pleas that he "isn't trying to scare you". Sometimes thoughts appear randomly, several paragraphs after their first mention (e.g., "The list is long") or out of nowhere ("My hands are trembling"). And often it breaks into these intensely patterned whorls of rhetoric that self-destruct in the speaking:

"Sometimes I have a reason for ignoring people. Sometimes I don't. Sometimes I forget who I am and I behave in a manner that makes people around me hate me and out of nowhere I probably won't remember why."

The repetition of "sometimes" and the rule-of-three structure sets this up as a quite traditional piece of rhetoric. But the third part turns into this run-on sentence whose word order is slightly jumbled and which ends up denying any possible pattern. Sometime yes, sometimes no, what do you want from me? Sometimes there isn't even an I. Sometimes nothing. Fuck off. Later R says "I must have severe mental disorders that make me lose myself and harm myself," but what is notable here, apart from the idea of "losing" oneself, which has echoed through everything we've seen so far, is that he doesn't even *know*; he "must" have mental disorders, he assumes, he can only assume from a place of no self and no knowledge.

Another patterned but totally open-ended paragraph goes: "Every day I have some kind of anxiety attack or panic attack of some form just by thinking about my past or my future." Two parallelisms: anxiety and panic, past and future. The first set is bracketed by a repetition of "some kind" and "some form," the second "my" and "my," and both linked with a twice-repeated "or." The words emphasized in these patterns are precisely the ones which refer to unknown possibilities—the catch-all words, the inclusive operators. How can you escape?

And then, after almost 1,000 words, R concludes: "I have absolutely nothing to say to you and I have no intention of talking to you."

When I characterise this kind of communication as hostile, I'm not judging R. I'm just thinking of how overwhelming it can be to receive something like this. It breaks all kinds of Gricean maxims. Many well-intentioned people will look at it and promise to themselves that they will dig into it, but they weren't prepared for an essay, and maybe like me with this game they can't find any way into it. Then maybe they push back and push back their reply and feel bad that they haven't replied, and maybe you're wondering why they haven't and castigating yourself for sending it in the first place, and they know you're probably doing that but they still can't manage to reply.

This communication is hostile to the player too. The messages which make up much of this game are all in the same medium as the game itself. Its action unfolds on phone and computer screens. So this is a good example of where the game seems to frame itself as a similar communication sent from R to the player, with all the problems and dangers that implies. We're put in this uneasy position of simultaneously identifying with him and confronting him. We empathise with his pre-emptive scorn and distrust but we are also the well-meaning observers at whom he directs them. And since he is split in himself, he, we and I seem to keep on swapping positions, suddenly finding ourselves on the outside of ourselves, and someone else inside. The certainty of "I was me" is very far away. In fact, when Clarke does respond to the message, R suddenly breaks with his spiral of thought to ask, apropos of nothing, "Who am I, really?"

This passage, by the way, is the first time I found out about R's rape on my first playthrough. If you haven't visited the earlier passage, this is where you see it. I think that enhances the feel of being suddenly confided in and not knowing how to deal with it. Sometimes in the course of these huge desperate messages something comes out which just makes you sit down and exhale because you don't know how to deal with the scale of it.

> Continue

I haven't talked to him since. It was for the best. However when it came down to trying to get back into social media, he was everywhere. Talking to people I talk to and I couldn't handle it.

Just seeing his name made me sick. How did I go from being happy to hang out with him to fearing him within just a few months of knowing him? Was he worth the trouble?

How can I care about someone so much that they make me feel like I hate them so much? I'm impressed that I made it this far. It's like a night terror that I'm unable to wake up from and there's no escape.

played by John Brindle

I don't think I'm going to be able to continue on without him being somewhere where I'll be.

Jesse says it'll happen eventually. I won't be the person to initiate it. Knowing me I won't even look at him. I'll just walk past him. But I feel it. It's deep inside me.

I want to be his friend, but I'm not a fan of torture.

I'm a total hypocrite, but who isn't? "Not a fan of torture." he says. Coming from the guy who tried to disappear from this world by eating god knows how many pills is almost laughable if it wasn't so somber.

Clarke texted you back.

I'm afraid to read it. What kind of vicious things does he have to say after what I said? Did he turn into some kind of homophobe being disgusted of me? Maybe a front to make it seem like we're still friends? That sounds like it.

My phone is just sitting there. I guess I'll **read** it.

> read

"You don't need to apologize to me. I won't act like I know what you're going through because I really don't.

I don't intend to get on your nerves and I really don't need to know where you are at all times, but when nobody heard from you for days, I just wanted to make sure you were okay.

I consider you one of my closest friends, whether you want to believe it or not. I never looked at you differently after you told me that you liked me and I hope it didn't feel like I was treating you any differently.

I'm Fine by Rokashi Edwards

If you'd prefer to not be around me, so be it. I'll respect that. But just know I'm here for you. Those aren't empty words, you're my friend and even if we don't speak for the next year, you'll still be my friend. Whether you give a fuck about any of this, that's up to you.

I won't lie and say my life is identical to yours but I do understand the fake smiles and laughs. I do that a lot. I've often just considered just picking up and leaving everything behind. I've though about who my friends are, who I can trust. And you can trust me."

—-

Trust you..? that's funny. I don't trust anyone and I've told you that on numerous occasions. Yeah, I can say we're (were?) friends, but that doesn't mean I'm going to trust you. I feel like you only talk to me when you need something. Is that friendship? Maybe I'm being too demanding? Who am I, really?

Just disappear. What do you know anyway?

Fuck you.

—-

"I just hope you'll let somebody help you. I don't mean medication, I don't mean interventions, I don't mean therapy. Please, just find somebody and try to work your way through this.

If you're ever ready to speak to me again, you know how to get a hold of me."

What the hell, man...

Clarke's response only makes things worse. R is totally trapped on the inside of his own thing, and if there is any real support or honesty in what Clarke says, he's not in a place to see it.

> What the hell . . .

I hated him.

I fucking hated him.

I don't think I've hated someone like I hated Clarke right now. Those words seemed hollow.

My hands are sweaty. I typed, "You don't understand anything about me..." and promptly deleted it.

I mean, I guess he may care about me, but treating me dif-

played by John Brindle

ferently and wagging his support in my face wasn't necessary.

I'm so angry right now, I can't even think straight.

What a fucking asshole. Was he even trying to think what it would be like in my shoes? I highly doubt it. I'm done. I already feel uncomfortable being around him. This is the last piece of the puzzle. I want nothing to do with him.

It feels like he's dangling what used to be our friendship and waits for me to grab it before tossing it over a cliff and says, "Go get it if you want it so bad."

Would I take that leap? Is it worth it?

I don't think it is.

I hope he stays away from me. I don't want to have to deal with this.

All this anger and frustration somehow made you tired. You haven't slept in 4 days.

Take a nap

Calm your shit

> I take a nap. More second/first person shifts. Hours pass in a few words.

> \> Take a nap

You try to sleep.

You're overwhelmed with so many feelings that you begin to cry.

That must have done it, because you fell asleep.

But not even for an hour...

Wake up

> And then we get what is almost the climactic scene: R goes to an event in New York, but Danielle and Clarke are there too.

> \> Wake up

I could feel that my face was still damp from my tears.

You think yourself into oblivion. Hours pass.

It's evening and there's an interesting event I wanted to attend.

I'm Fine by Rokashi Edwards

The first thing that came to mind was I didn't want Danielle to be there. I don't hate her. I'm just not ready.

Traffic wasn't too bad getting into the city. New York does that sometimes. My windows were down so the cool breeze felt good as I drove on the highway. It was a nice sensation. I was felt like I could be ready for anything.

I've realized that I shouldn't say I'm ready for anything because what happened upon my arrival was the worst thing imaginable.

I walked through the front door and the first people I saw congregating was Danielle, but check this, beside her was Clarke. Fucking Clarke.

Nope nope nope nope nope.

This is too much. I have to be somewhere else.

My heart raced, my breathing got heavy and everything went so slow.

My vision twisted and turned to the thought of even talking to either one of them that night.

And I thought getting out of the house was a good idea.

Danielle turned her head like she sensed my presence. It was sinister. Our eyes locked then mine broke free and looked elsewhere.

I think she waved, but I wasn't sure. Maybe it wasn't that much of a big deal that she was there. But Clarke, oh ho ho ho, Clarke. He looked at me, and then faced forward.

At that point my heart was making its way towards my mouth. I felt so sick.

I did not want him there and there was nothing I could do about it.

Maybe I wanted to walk up to him and tell him to leave. Yeah right, I'd vomit my heart on his lap before words escaped my mouth.

I confided in Ellie and Harvey, other friends from the diverse community within the city who I've been talking to besides my main "friends."

The event was to start in mere minutes, but I left with them to go outside and get some fresh air. It wasn't magic, but having them know my situation made me feel safe from Clarke and Danielle's grasp.

Continue

played by John Brindle

I like the line about how R's eyes "locked" with Danielle's, and then "broke free." It's an old metaphor given new force. The idea of being "safe from Clarke and Danielle's grasp" feels so melodramatic—we're so locked inside R's head that we have no idea whether they really want to help him or not—but I know what it feels like to experience your dearest friends as horrific confining forces that you mustn't approach.

I think of something a friend once told me: depression is a kind of ultimate selfishness. It's not voluntary or immoral; you just have no room for anything but your shit. You're so consumed by yourself that you go totally numb to other people and their concerns, and you can't be expected to think of them. You can no more deal with their shit on top of yours than a drowning person can play the piano.

> Continue

You decided to stay.

If they know what's good for them, they'll keep their distance and stay the fuck away from me.

You stay as far away from them as possible, but the back of their heads was in my vision and I couldn't look away.

I felt like everyone was watching me freak out. I put Ellie's hand on my chest to make it known that my heart was racing.

You're terrified as fuck. You want to tell someone to tell them to leave, but having no backbone makes you mute. Unable to communicate with anyone.

The workshop began and of course everyone had to introduce myself. WHAT THE HELL. If my anxiety was some kind of rocket, it would have enough energy to fly a rocket to the moon.

NO NO NO NO.

FUCK FUCK FUCK!

What am I going to do when it's my turn? Are they going to turn around and look at me say my name and why I'm here?

It's your turn. What are you going to do?

Stay quiet and let them move on to the next person, or adjust my heart to the correct spot in my chest and **just participate**?

This all feels like some kind of ironic punishment. What, you thought you could go outside and be a real human being? Well, how about having to introduce yourself to all these people in a contrived bonding session? The sense of being trapped and rooted to the spot is palpable here. I think it's a pretty good description.

> Stay quiet

It came to your turn to say your name and why you're here. You shook your head.

The woman hosting the presentation looked confused and moved on.

People in the crowd giggled. You were too busy playing with your fingers to notice if Danielle or Clarke was even looking at you.

Man, my heart could have been on my lap. It was insane... too insane.

Moving on

I stayed quiet because it's what I probably would have done IRL. The baleful eye of the other blinks and moves on. But the ordeal continues. Group discussion!

> Moving on

The talk was great. I figured I didn't have to say anything else, until we had to get put into groups. I didn't mind that, as I thought I would be able to choose who can be in my group.

The universe had other plans.

played by John Brindle

I was put in a group with Danielle along with other people.

Fuck that. I took out my computer out of my bag and worked on something else instead.

"Aren't you in group 5?" said some random person who knew who I was, but I had no clue who he was.

I nodded.

"Our group is over here."

I shook my head.

"Okay..." and he walked off.

It felt like I dodged a bullet. I felt so small. I started thinking what it would be like if I actually went into that group. I wouldn't say anything. I'd probably just stare at Danielle and knowing her, she'd try to direct some kind of question to me in order to get me to talk.

So manipulative.

Continue

It's really painful to read the last line of this passage; from everything we've been told so far, Danielle is a pretty cool person, but R can't help but interpret even good faith attempts to engage him as a "manipulative" attack. And he's not exactly wrong to, because from his position he really does experience them as a kind of violence.

> Continue

The more and more I talked to people, the more I felt like they were reading off a script like a person who would work in a call center.

I needed to talk to a person who was level-headed. Someone who cared, but didn't say things like, "I love you. I love you. Don't do something I wouldn't do!"

I tried to confide in Jesse.

I wouldn't put him in the same category as Clarke or Mark. He was no wizard, but he was knowledgeable and he managed to balance it by being jocular at the right moments.

He knew enough about me. I didn't feel threatened around him. He was a good friend. Someone I can trust...

It's a term that I scarcely use. When I say it, I mean it, I think. I trusted him.

Jesse sent you a text.

I'm Fine by Rokashi Edwards

Read Jesse's message

One thing that really rings true is how often even really well-intentioned people try to medicalise their relationships with you. Suddenly every interaction becomes an attempt to diagnose and heal you. It's the sole topic of conversation. It's boring and unhelpful at best, and intrusive and bile-inducing at worst. You start to feel that you aren't allowed to have a normal relationship for this person, and that you can't trust them not to look at you through that lens.

Here, the word "trust" seems to come as surprise even to R. Jesse can be trusted not to appoint himself without R's consent as his caregiver.

> Read Jesse's message

"Are you okay now?"

—-

Obviously not...

—-

"Not really. On a scale of 1-10, I'm a 2."

Back to the rapidfire messages. This game has a nice pulse to it. The chat makes good vibes and goes on for some time. It's formally similar to Mark's sequence, but the mood is very different.

> Not really . . .

"Can I do anything to help?"

"Well you've known me long enough so maybe when you're not busy and I'm not angry at everything, we can chat."

—-

I didn't want to regret that too.

—-

> Well you've known me . . .

"Yay! I think."

—-

Did he read through my sarcasm? Or is he some kind of pshychic who can read my mode over the interwaves of the

played by John Brindle

cell towers?

—-

"Yeah, that's my reaction too. I'll be as honest as I can without getting nervous and dying. This whole trusting friends thing is a little more than I can handle."

This part is really funny. R is wildly projecting, wondering if Jesse has performed some clever conversational maneuver against him. I'm pretty sure Jesse just didn't detect the "sarcasm" and took R's previous message totally at face value. Benevolent ignorance is the perfect and purest weapon against R's incessant analysis.

> Yeah, that's my reaction

"Hahaha."

"I'll probably require hugs too.

> I'll probably require hugs . . .

"You always require hugs, so I'd be okay with that."

"Good. That's pretty much what I've been living off of for the past week. Tell me a joke.

—-

Not really, but I just REALLY need one.

—-

> Tell me a joke

"Two muffins are in an oven. One muffin says, "Hot enough for you?" The other muffin says, "Aah! A talking muffin!"

"This is why I don't tell jokes."

—-

He was so dumb - a good dumb. The dumbest.

I appreciated him not being incredibly serious. Well, I was serious, but fuck, I needed some kind of comedic relief.

Not that that's what Jesse was, mind you. Somehow I thought he knew where the lines are and was cautious of whether it's the right time or not to cross it.

He gets a gold star sticker for that.

I'm Fine by Rokashi Edwards

—-

"When can I stop by and bug you?"

We don't know how sophisticated Jesse is being here. But R might be right. Sometimes there is an immense, subtle kindness in refraining from ostentatious displays of kindness. Sometimes the best way to support someone is not to appear to support them. There's a Zen kind of sense about these passages, a sense that all that projecting and overthinking can fade into the background if you tell a dumb joke and fully accept its perfect round smooth dumbness.

> When can I stop by . . .

"Any time you like. I'm free Saturday after 4."

"If you want to stay on Saturday, Mark is coming over to watch a movie."

"As long as I don't have to tell my life story to a crowd and I'm able to recover myself to be social later on in the evening, that's fine with me."

> As long as I don't have to . . .

"You won't have to. I'm not going to let anyone else be in on that conversation; they'll be coming over a couple hours after you."

"And if you don't feel social, you don't have to stay."

—-

It was the small back and forth conversation that I enjoyed.

I'm not saying I didn't appreciate the talks I had with Mark or anything. It's just different, you know?

Familiar, even though I'm not too sure how many items are on the list of what Jesse and I have in common.

—-

Continue

R is loading on the good vibes here. I have to admit, I wondered if he was setting me up. He isn't.

> Continue

played by John Brindle

We talked about me.

I told him everything and I didn't hold back. Even the details I thought would make him cringe, he had a calm collected look on his face.

At first I thought he was horror-struck, but maybe that's what he looks like when he's listening. I'm not sure. It didn't stop me from talking though.

His leather couch was comfy. I felt safe. Like, I could say I killed someone and hid the body under his bed and he'd still be calm.

Maybe that was a bad way to phrase it, but you get the point.

I thought tears would be shed, but oddly enough I managed to hold them back.

It was beyond me. I managed, somehow.

Why didn't I talk to him first? I could have spared myself all of Mark, Danielle and especially Clarke's bullshit. I felt stupid and it was justified.

It was weird to actually put my trust in someone that I knew less than everyone else combined.

What a perplexing thought! Like, holy shit. This is revolutionary to me. Trust people for 10 minutes more than people you've known for a day.

Maybe I was lucky - blessed, even? Being atheist won't help me believe in any of this, but it's happening and it's okay.

Our talk was great. My heartbeat made it feel like I ran a marathon by getting all this weight off my shoulders.

I know he's not a therapist, but the best part was that he didn't throw himself at my feet saying things I didn't want to hear.

He was subtle with his words, but I wasn't. I couldn't keep up. I felt like I could get through this.

Jesse offered to do research to see if he could find someone who could help me. One thing I was hoping he wouldn't say, but whatever. I got this far, I might as well go the whole mile.

I was ready.

Almost there

"We talked about me."
Who is R? Is it Rokashi Edwards, the author of this game? I don't know, and I don't want to know unless he wants me to. A Twine game (!)

547

I'm Fine by Rokashi Edwards

about depression (!!) written in a highly personal style (!!!) comes automatically loaded with assumptions of autobiography. The prose here could plausibly really be the raw, unmediated outpourings of a mind at the end of its tether, but if it's not, it's a very good evocation. The ambiguity of its "confessional" status only compounds those worries about self and identity, player and writer, which run through the rest of the game.

A few times during *I'm Fine*, I couldn't help compare it with *Depression Quest*. That isn't (or isn't only) because *DQ* looms so large in coverage of Twine and of games about mental health. Both games deal with the logistical particulars of despair. Both involve pointedly restricted choice. Both use cycling piano-heavy music and anxiously blinking images to supplement their text. But where *DQ* opens with a methodical inventory of your life—your job, your friends, and your fears—*Fine* offers this knowledge in a nonlinear and disordered fashion, elliptically or surprisingly or sometimes too late. Where *DQ* always grounds itself in space and time ("It is a muggy Sunday evening,") *Fine* rarely bothers, and skips over days without warning. *DQ's* writing is very careful, using all the syntactical patterns our society codes as clear, direct, and straightforward, keeping the second person consistent. Its words get more torturous as things get worse—but *I'm Fine* starts out there.

The best illustration of this writing is also most telling difference between these games. *DQ* begins with a lengthy paratext setting out, with trigger warnings and links to mental health resources, its aims, its content, and its omissions. The writers explain that they have amalgamated the real experiences of "several people" and tried to include "as broad a range as possible." They're careful to qualify the game's relation to reality, saying that it won't reflect everyone's perspective. They also say that they want to help people who don't have depression understand what it's like. This comes across in the writing, which works to order and express the counterintuitive spirals of depression in a way which can be understood from outside them.

I'm Fine does not come off like an amalgamation. It's aggressively specific, locked into the mind of one person. It isn't committed to a representative paradigm and doesn't show any interest in "hitting the key points." It doesn't really care about being accessible to muggles, either; it's not trying to translate. It is what it is, it jumps right in, and it comes on as thick and strong and bleak as difficult as a person might in the thick of this shit. I'm not passing judgement on the artistic goals of either of these games, because both have their reasons to be. But the contrast between how hard *DQ* works to be polished and accessible, and how hostile and uncompromising I found my first try of *I'm Fine*, could not be more instructive. This is a game which fully inhabits its topic. It remains "inside," trapped in the loops, and there's no way to do that without being alienating for some.

But it's not completely locked in. In the final few passages, R describes his talk with Jesse. He unburdens himself and Jesse doesn't overly medical-

played by John Brindle

ize the transaction. It's hard to quantify quite why the writing feels lighter than before, but it does. And despite the incredibly long text, R is merciful, letting us know that we're almost at an end with the link: "Almost there."

> Almost there

What am I even talking about? It was unlike any conversation I had with a friend, but it wasn't like he magically cured me of all sadness.

Just because I start doesn't mean I'll make it to the end to finish.

My life of a roller coaster went upside down and I wanted off the ride.

Don't get me wrong, I'm eternally grateful for him helping me, but I shouldn't think that he'll be the end of all my problems when I don't even know where mine start.

What if I'm meant to be like this for the rest of my life? To wallow in my sadness and brush aside friends? How am I supposed to endure that?

We'll see if I even make it to by 30th birthday without being placed in a coffin before then.

After I told him the story of me. There was a small awkward silence.

Nothing was really said.

He offered me a hug.

He never offers me hugs. It was the best thing I experienced in a while. Made me feel like a person again especially after our conversation. I felt like I was ready to take on the world - or something incredibly cheesy like that.

I do plan to start talking to some of my friends again, but now isn't the time. It will definitely take me a while and hope they like waiting.

We'll see. I always seem to change my mind so everything can be different tomorrow.

A boring finale

Of course this lightness has a counterpoint. R warns himself not to set too much stock by this temporary feeling of relief, and his happiness is shot through with fear and caution and blame that he didn't find help earlier. In the A text there is a four paragraph fantasy about imagining his own death and ill-attended funeral. But when I read this I felt a kind of sudden holy surprise. Like, fuck, is he really saying these things?

Depression is such a complicated machine that sometimes you don't even know what saves you. A tumbler clicks this way or that, something shakes loose, and somewhere, audible but unseen, a key turns in a lock. Here, while we can point to specific characteristics of the conversation with Jesse which made it easier and more fruitful than the ones with Mark, Clarke or Danielle, it still seems so fragile and random. It reminds me of another Twine game, Finny's *All the Pleading Emoticons*, in which your suicide attempt is stopped by an "angel" who gets in the way of the blade. The angel doesn't offer you a revelation. She just gives you tiny, strange hints. You make an OKCupid profile. You dance and gurgle and you wait in the darkness for kindness. When she comes, you're down on your knees, grateful and disbelieving that she could have visited you. It doesn't make sense and all you can do is be glad. This kind of escape just appears, like divine grace, in a random, mundane component of your life. It takes place, like W. H. Auden said of suffering, "while someone else is eating or opening a window or just walking dully along." The world doesn't stop for it. "A boring finale."

> A boring finale

Going through all these emotions, I learned that dwelling in my house doing nothing productive for weeks made me feel gross. I needed to get out and experience things.

Whenever I daydreamed, I imagined that I was dead and people I'm aquainted with would come to my funeral, except I would see everything that was going on. It was eerie seeing them weep over my body... like they'd actually miss me.

I'm not sure why my mind decided it would show me things like that, but the most fucked up part was that every once in a while, no one would be at my funeral. No one. Not even a curator.

I'd wake up or snap out of it feeling incredibly depressed thinking that could be a reality and I wasn't sure about the things I could do to avoid it.

It was messed up but my mind had no intention of bringing any ideas to my attention that was cheerful. Not anymore.

No matter how I shitty I felt to the point that I didn't want to live anymore, there are people who still want me to be alive, I think. Well, besides the people who bully me. I'm not sure if I believe that, but I'm doing my best to keep those feelings at bay.

It felt like I could make the jump over the next hurtle. Maybe not on my own, but slowly with the help of my friends I think I can do it. Maybe I'll be able to do it on my own someday,

played by John Brindle

but baby steps are important, right?

I guess only time will tell what happens for me, but I'm optimistic.

I'll try to let people in. I'll try not to fall into the dark side.

If I feel like I'm slipping, I'm sure there are some people I can count on that can help me bounce back onto my feet.

It's an affair that I'll remember for a while. There's no way to forget something that could have ended me. I need to be more alert to the future and keep calm.

I want to be the best I can be and I have only my friends to support me.

Lets see if I can pull this off. Even for a little while.

I'm not saying I'm optimistic, either.

Continue

(Wasn't it David Foster Wallace, whose writing about depression is quoted in *DQ*, who wrote of the transcendent possibilities of boredom?)

I like that R's language, here at the end, is so consistently conditional. "There are people who still want me to be alive, I think." "I'm doing my best." "It felt like." "Maybe I'll be able." "I guess." "I'll try." "I'll try." "I want." "Let's see."

I also like that even the B text doesn't break up these passages, so you still feel the sense of sudden unwinding, unburdening, the deep breath, after the click-click-click of Jesse on the phone. And I like how there's actually no real transition between talking on the phone and talking in person. I like how the toxic context of the event R is at in New York just kind of fades away, and is forgotten, as he gets more into the exchange, and then suddenly we're in Jesse's home, as if we fell for a long time into the phone, away from the rest of the world, and straight onto Jesse's leather couch, turning inward to escape outward.

There isn't really any one answer that R finds. He decides he needs to "get out and experience things," which, you know, is fine; like a lot of the routes out of depression, it is simultaneously really trite and really, really important. He says he will "try to let people in" and to "keep calm." Most strongly, he makes a determination to start talking to his friends again, even if it takes him a while. There is a kind of darkness about these promises. They feel overshadowed by the suspicion that when R relapses they will become impossible once again. I wonder if, because they are simple, they are also useless, like New Year's resolutions to be "better" or "fitter" with no concrete plan to achieve them. But this is kind of okay too. You have to be realistic. You have to remind yourself that one day it will come back, and be at peace with that.

I'm Fine by Rokashi Edwards

Speaking is always a problem in *I'm Fine*. It pulsates between these extremes of taciturn shaking silence and wild, excessive unburdening. As an act of speech in itself, the game tends far enough to the latter that it feels cleansing to come out of the other side. In its maze of lost identity, I feel like somehow I made some contact with the speaker. I might be one of those dangerous interlocutors who assumes too much or doesn't understand. But to whoever is on the other end I can only say: I hear you, and I'm sorry, and thank you.

> Continue

Thanks for playing.

Help me keep making games, if you want

PLAYER 2

BY LYDIA NEON
PLAYED BY ELIZABETH SAMPAT

Content Warning: This game deals with interpersonal conflicts.

Begin

It's the week before Christmas, and things are tense. I work for a creative agency for whom this is the busiest time of year, and everyone's spirit is frayed. I'm estranged from both of my parents—one for eight years, the other more recently. I've been feeling weirdly alienated from my closest friend. I moved here from California and it feels like all of my old friends have forgotten I exist—not even in a no-visits kind of way, but in an I-can't-even-get-an-at-reply-on-Twitter kind of way.

The content warning makes me do a quick inventory of my life in a single sentence, and I'm already very tired.

I tap **Begin** anyway.

> Begin

A few things before you begin.

I want to reassure you...

> I want to reassure you

First, this game is run entirely in JavaScript in your browser.

Player 2 by Lydia Neon

So whatever you think, whatever you type, when you close your window, it goes away.

> I want to reassure you

No one will ever see it but you.

It's weird how the reassurances make the experience feel even more serious, even more intense. I'm starting to wonder what I'm getting myself into.

> I want to reassure you

All site analytics have been removed from this page. Even so, you may download this page by right clicking anywhere and choosing "Save as..." and run it locally if you feel safer that way.

> I want to reassure you

Second, this is a two-player game. However...

> I want to reassure you

However... the second player won't be playing with you.
They'll be in your mind as you play.

Oh. And the second player is someone in my head. Great. This is the first time I've hoped that a game was about dissociative states.

> I want to reassure you

Third, there is no winning or losing.

> I want to reassure you

Only you can decide what counts as success.

> I want to reassure you

Lastly, if you ever feel the need to end, there is an escape hatch link at the end of each passage.

played by Elizabeth Sampat

> I want to reassure you

If you know you have greater self-care needs, you can set it up **here**.

Skip This Step

The final codicil explains that there's an escape hatch link you can set up if you have greater self-care needs. I consider it for a long moment, but honestly, I've never been great at self-care. So I choose to

> Skip this step

Let's find out who you're playing with.

This will be a game about a real event in your life.

It was a time when someone let me down and I haven't dealt with it yet.

It happened yesterday.

But it wasn't my fault. I didn't start it.

Who was it that did it?

Who was it that did it?

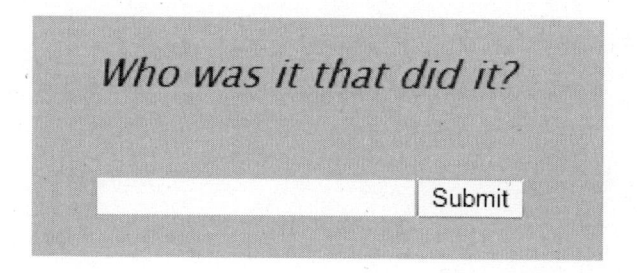

[Submit]

Esc

The choices on the next page hit me right in the gut. I go through my inventory one more time.

I was incredibly close to my mother growing up. My dad was an abusive dickhead, and I had no friends, and it always felt like my mother was the only person in the world on my side. It's taken me a number of years to come to terms with my mother's alcoholism, and her total neglect of me for six years. But the hardest thing was talking to my sister a little over a month ago, and getting the scoop on my mother's mental illness, her compulsive lying, and all of the desperate, controlling, and—let's face it—abusive shit she pulled to MAKE me feel like she was the only person in the world who

Player 2 by Lydia Neon

cared about me.

So I guess I know who I'm playing with.

> (...)

It was a time when someone **let me down** and I haven't **forgiven them yet.**

It happened **when I was a teen.**

But it **wasn't** my fault. I **didn't start** it.

Who was it that did it?

> Mom

Mom is going to be playing with you today.

In a sense you've been playing with them since it happened, haven't you?

You haven't dealt with it yet, so there they are, in the back of your mind.

ooo

Esc

> ooo

Would you care to describe what happened that made Mom your player 2?

Yes | No

Esc

When the game asked me if I'd like to explain what made my mom Player 2, I took a deep breath.

> Yes

Would you care to describe what happened that made Mom your player 2?

Take as much time as you like.

Submit

556

played by Elizabeth Sampat

I felt tears at the back of my eyes and submitted a blank field.

>

You didn't explain, but that's alright. The details are yours.

When it was happening, I felt too **upset** to do more than I did at the time.

Since then I have tried to **forget about it** but it hasn't **helped** like I had hoped.

ooo

It's weird how validated I felt that the game noticed. I was given the chance to explain, I said yes, and it turned out that I couldn't do it after all. I felt like I'd let the game down somehow, until it told me that it was okay.

It's funny how you have to click through the options to see everything.

> upset

helpless
>

irritated
>

confused
>

alone
>

furious
>

worthless
>

insulted
>

disappointed
>

annoyed
>

shocked
>

vexed

\>

exhausted

\>

powerless

\>

unheard

\>

ignored

\>

unimportant

\>

upset

When I started flipping through to explain how I felt at the time, at first I was sad that none of the options was not knowing—there was nothing about being duped. But I ended up clicking through the entire list twice, and ultimately coming to terms with the fact that I actually felt all of these things at different times, and in different amounts. Yes, I was angry. I was alone. I was confused, and insulted, and worthless. I was unheard and ignored. Acting like all of these emotions were things that came later, and not feelings that I had that I'd just pushed down—how far has that gotten me?

> (. . .)

When it was happening, I felt too **helpless** to do more than I did at the time. Since then I have tried to **get way from it** but it hasn't **let me move on** like I had hoped.

ooo

> ooo

Now, when I think about what happened, I just **get upset with myself** all over again.

I feel **confused**. And maybe even a little **confused**.

But mostly, I just feel _____.

> (. . .)

Now, when I think about what happened, I just get **frustrated with them** all over again.

played by Elizabeth Sampat

I feel **exhausted**. And maybe even a little **powerless**. But mostly I just feel ____.

> But mostly, I just feel [   ]   Submit

There's another blank field here. I rub my temples for a moment. How do I feel? I feel like I want to stop playing. But, like I said, I'm not great at self-care. I type in an answer.

> Sad

And as for Mom, I **hate** them. They **never liked me**.

ooo

Esc

> (...)

And as for Mom, I **try to ignore** them. They **love me, but...**

> ooo

Well, Mom is just player 2 right now, and you have the controller, not them.

ooo

> ooo

The game reminds me that my Mom's player 2, and I have the controller right now. I wonder for a minute if that's ever really been true. I guess now I'm successful and I have family and friends and live on the other side of the country, but she so completely manipulated my childhood, and me, psychologically, that I'm not sure if I'll ever be out. Even when she dies.

> ooo

So take a moment to gather your strength.

It's ok to feel exhausted. You're totally allowed to feel powerless. And never doubt your worth or power just because you feel sad.

Player 2 by Lydia Neon

You're allowed to feel that here. Here, you are safe. You are valued. You are loved.

When you're ready, it's time to do something about it.

    I tear up. I know this is a game, and I know it's prescribed, but this sounds just like so many important conversations I've had with the close friend I said I've felt alienated from. I make a mental note to reach out to him.

If I had my way as a teen, I would have _____

    This is just so impossible to answer. I don't know who I was as a teenager. I was exactly the person my mother made me be. Who would I have been otherwise? I just—there's no way to tell. I decide to go with hindsight.

    > If I had my way as a teen, I would have bought my own clothes, I would have made real friends, I would have gotten the fuck out.

But I can't, **can I**?

    > can I?

But I can't.

What I can do is **punch them in the teeth.**

ooo

    > punch them in the teeth.

kick them in the shin.
    >

smash their car windows.
    >

send them meat in the mail to creep them out.
    >

sign up their email address for every politician's mailing list.
    >

use a flamethrower on a sensitive part of their body.
    >

set up a real life version of Saw.
    >

played by Elizabeth Sampat

replace the inside of their computer monitor with wasps.
>

stage a hostile takeover of their company so I can personally fire them.
>

stab them in the heart with sharpened ends of their favorite children's toy.
>

cover their floor with dulled bear traps and rusted caltrops.
>

mix ipecac with their food.
>

poison them, though that's not terribly creative.
>

squirrel away food scraps in their house, then introduce some pregnant rats, and finally copperhead snakes.
>

post screenshots of their livejournal from years ago to Facebook.
>

sew prawns into the lining of their mattress.
>

punch them in the teeth.
>

What I can do is kick them in the shin.

I don't want to kick my mom in the shin, but all of the answers are ridiculous and violent and creative, and absolutely overkill.

> ooo

Whoa now. Is that really what you want to do?
Yes!
What I really want is **for them to stop doing it**.
ooo

> Yes!

No . . .

> for them to stop doing it

for them to feel what I felt.
>

for them to apologize.
>

for them to be off my mind completely.
>

to forget it ever happened.
>

to never see them again.
>

for them to feel utterly helpless just once.
>

for them to empathize just a bit.
>

to escape from them.
>

for them to be punished.
>

for them to stop doing it.

This is also frustrating, because what I want isn't on this list either. I want a goddamned time machine. I want my childhood back.

I don't want my mom to feel helpless just once, because I know she's spent most of her life feeling helpless and that's part of what makes her who she is. Part of what's been so maddening is that I don't feel like I have a right to be angry, because what she's done to me is just a response to everything that's ever been done to her.

What I really want is **for them to stop doing it.**

Do you have hope that can happen?

Don't answer too hastily. Let the first impulse sit for a moment and really consider.

Yes | No

I don't know if I have an answer to that question, but I let it sit for a

played by Elizabeth Sampat

moment and realize that I do, and it is right. And that's when I cry.

> No

Well that sucks. That's going to make things a little harder.
If I can't have what I really want, then I want **clarity**.
Because I deserve **to be loved.**

ooo

> clarity

peace
>

happiness
>

an end to anger over this
>

fulfillment
>

change
>

something better than this
>

clarity

> to be loved

There's a bunch of options to click through here, and I feel dumb and strange saying I deserve any of them. Do I deserve to be loved? To be free?

to be appreciated
>

to succeed
>

to not be held back
>

to be free
>

to be heard
>

to laugh
>

to feel joy
>

to not be afraid all the time
>

to not be alone
>

   I click through all of the options, and the game chooses for me. I feel slightly panicked, but grateful.

Because I deserve all that and more.

> ooo

I **want to** forgive Mom. Not because **they deserve it**, but because I deserve all that and more, and Mom isn't allowed to keep that from me.

ooo

> (. . .)

I **want to** forgive Mom. Not because **I think I need to**, but because I deserve all that and more, and Mom isn't allowed to keep that from me.

> ooo

Right on!

You may use the box below to share any thoughts you want to say but aren't able to say aloud. No one will ever read it but you.

                      [| And let it go...]

I said some things I'm not comfortable saying here.

> (. . .)

played by Elizabeth Sampat

There. . . it's off your chest.

ooo

> ooo

Breathe...

In...

Out...

In...

Out...

Good. Just like that

Let it out...

ooo

I breathe with the game as it tells me to breathe in and out. I'm feeling a little better now.

> ooo

Player 2 by Lydia Neon | @LifeInNeon

CSS and Macros by Leon Arnott

<3

And just like that, it's over.
Maybe I should call my mom.

NOTES ON CONTRIBUTORS

LEIGH ALEXANDER is a critic, writer and consultant on the art, business, and culture of video games. She has written for *Gamasutra, Edge, Kotaku,* and *Polygon,* as well as for *Time, The Atlantic, The Guardian,* the *Columbia Journalism Review,* and many others. She is the author of two ebooks, *Breathing Machine* and *Clipping Through,* on tech and identity, and is co-founder of Agency, a design consultancy that helps game developers gain perspective.

ANNA ANTHROPY is a thirty-year-old teen witch, play designer, zinester, and the author of a bunch of books, including *Rise of the Videogame Zinesters* and *ZZT*. She also maintains annarchive.com, a collection of game history and media. She lives in Oakland, California, with a pair of very gay cats.

LEON ARNOTT is a programmer living in Australia. Apart from authoring strange short-form web games, he passionately contributes to the maintenance and future of the Twine development software. He also lives vicariously through Twitter, and is basically afraid of everything.

PIPPIN BARR is a video game maker and critic who lives and works in Montréal. His games address everything from airplane safety instructions to contemporary art and have included collaborations with performance artist Marina Abramovic and Twitter personality @seinfeld2000. He holds a PhD in Computer Science from Victoria University of Wellington in New Zealand and teaches prototyping and game design at Concordia University. Pippin also writes a blog of game and game design criticism and his book, *How to Play a Video Game,* introduces the uninitiated and culturally curious to the world of video games.

AEVEE BEE is a journalist and teacher who publishes and edits ZEAL, the best in art and crit of games no one takes seriously. Her criticism explores how

Notes on Contributors

the craft and form of games create places and people, and her art is science fiction about what it's like to have a body. She is extremely cute and tweets indefensible garbage.

IMOGEN BINNIE is a writer and musician who lives in New England with her girlfriend and their jerk dog. Sometimes she plays in the bands Correspondences, Tall Girl, and Denim Skirt. She writes the zines *Stereotype Threat* and *The Fact That It's Funny Doesn't Make It a Joke*, and her first novel *Nevada* won some awards. Her work appeared in *The Collection*, published by Topside Press, as well as on prettyqueer.com, lambdaliterary.org, and elsewhere. A collection of her writing for the magazine *Maximum Rocknroll* should be out sometime in 2015 and after that she swears she is going to publish a novel that is sort of about the band Nirvana.

MATTIE BRICE is a play and games critic, designer, and activist. She previously wrote at publications like *Kotaku*, *Paste Magazine*, and *PopMatters* about design and social justice within the games industry, and now writes independently at *Alternate Ending*. She also designs experimental games like *EAT*, *Mission*, and her most notable *Mainichi*, which was exhibited at the Museum of Design in Atlanta and was an Official Selection at the International Festival of Independent Games. Mattie regularly speaks at games events such as the Game Developers Conference and Different Games, including being the international keynote at Game Connect Asia Pacific and co-founder of the Queerness and Games Conference. She is currently working on more community organizing and an analogue series of play experiences that explore issues of relationships and vulnerability.

BENJI BRIGHT is a writer located near Chicago who makes smut of various stripes. In addition to creating in Twine, he also writes erotic fiction and poetry. He's published a few books including *Boy Stories* (Go Deeper Press, 2014), *Candid* (Queer Young Cowboys, 2013) and *Chevalier: The Mercenary Archives* (JMS Books, 2013). You can find him lurking at The Erotic Ledger (theeroticledger.com) or "on the googles."

JOHN BRINDLE is a writer and journalist who grew up in Scotland and lives in south London. By day he is a reporter for a major metropolitan newspaper; by night, he writes about games, and the strange things people do with them. His sickness began at 18, in his first term at university, and came to a head three years later during a long, stifling summer in Ohio. He isn't well yet, and maybe he'll never be. But hey—one day at a time, right? He has written for *Unwinnable*, the *New Statesman*, *Nightmare Mode*, and *Gameranx*; he tweets @john_brindle.

MICHAEL BROUGH is a rainbow hermit who makes games. He grew up in New Zealand and then spent several years scattered across Europe—he'd like to

Notes on Contributors

stay in Scotland for now but who knows. He lives on Twitter except when dancing, and plays far too much Dota 2. He tries to love everyone but it's hard. He's been making games full-time since 2011 when he abandoned his apprenticeship as a mathematician; before then he spent far too long making *Vertex Dispenser*, a ridiculous strategy game, but now he's usually sensible and makes smaller things. His work struggles to reconcile his obsession with precise logical mechanics with his love of weird broken glitch chaos, swinging between competitive multiplayer battles (*Glitch Tank, Kompendium, O, Smesport*), nerdy puzzles (*Corrypt, Game Title: Lost Levels, The Sense of Connectedness*), tightly concentrated roguelikes (*868-HACK, Zaga-33*), and more abstract aimless explorations (*Knot-Pharmacard Subcondition J, VESPER.5, Become A Great Artist In Just 10 Seconds* [a collaboration with Andi McClure]). *868-HACK, Corrypt* and *VESPER.5* have been finalists in the "IGF" awards, if that's worth anything which it probably isn't.

MATTHEW S. BURNS is a writer, game developer, and composer who lives in the Seattle area. He has worked on big commercial games and as an indie. He's currently a producer at the University of Washington's Center for Game Science. He has written for *Edge, Paste, Kill Screen,* and other publications. His art, music, and writing can be found at www.magicalwasteland.com.

NAOMI CLARK is an independent game designer based in New York City. Over the last two decades she's worked on a wide variety of games including early text-based virtual worlds, educational games on many subjects, game development tools for kids, and digital brick-building systems for LEGO. She also teaches game design at the NYU Game Center, the School of Visual Arts, and the New York Film Academy. Her current projects include a game about language with the Brooklyn Game Ensemble, a web game about data privacy practices, and *Consentacle*, a two-player card game of trust, communication, and intimacy.

KATHERINE CROSS is a PhD student at the City University of New York, a sociologist, and a gaming critic whose work has appeared in *Bitch Magazine, Kotaku,* and *Polygon*. She is also a weekly columnist for *Feministing*, and a proud trans Latina.

CARA ELLISON is a Scottish writer and game critic. She has written for *The Guardian, VICE,* and the *New Statesman*, writes the best-named column in the world, S.EXE, at *Rock Paper Shotgun*, and has a regular opinion column at *Eurogamer*. She was also co-writer on Charlie Brooker's *How Videogames Changed the World* for Channel Four television in the UK. Her writing and game narrative work has been featured in the *New York Times* and *Wired*, and she was one of *The Guardian's* Top Ten Young People in Digital Media 2014. The internet currently crowdfunds her to travel the world writing about gamemakers as if they are rock stars, and they are.

Notes on Contributors

CAT FITZPATRICK is the Poetry Editor at Topside Press. She was born in London but somehow keeps waking up in Jersey City. In addition to performing her own work, her recent poems have been published in venues such as *The Advocate*, *Glitterwolf*, and *Asylum*. She is involved in organizing trans poetry events and coordinates a trans poetry workshop in NYC. She is very excited about trans poetry.

NINA FREEMAN is a programmer and a game designer. She is currently working on her M.S. in Integrated Digital Media at NYU Engineering. She's interested in gender, sexuality and narrative in games. She is one of the co-founders of The Code Liberation Foundation (CLF), an organization that offers free development workshops in order to facilitate the creation of video game titles by women. You can find her work at ninasays.so, and follow her on Twitter at @hentaiphd.

GAMING PIXIE (a.k.a. Rochelle) is a lifelong gamer who began making games of her own in her thirties thanks to Twine. Her work so far has covered subjects from bisexuality to suicidal feelings to the experience of growing up with an alcoholic parent and with her current game, *Raziel*, will venture into the cyberpunk realm to explore what it means to be human.

MARY HAMILTON is a game designer, journalist, and writer, not always in that order. She works mostly with physical games and digital journalism, and is currently working for the *Guardian* in Australia and designing games with Serious Business.

AURIEA HARVEY has spent a lifetime trying to make art with technology. To that end, she's made many videogames with Michael Samyn as Tale of Tales. They live, work, and play with cats in their lair located in Ghent, Belgium.

PATRICIA HERNANDEZ is a San Francisco-based writer who likes Drake and is totally not a part of a feminist cabal.

MICHAEL JOFFE is a game designer and human ecologist. Before arriving at game design, Mike studied animation, theatre, art history, mythology, ecology, and animal behavior. His first game, *Benthic Love*, was a romantic story about the mating habits of angler fish, and that set the tone for the rest of his oeuvre. Mike is interested in using play to explore how people interact with and understand the world around them, and using games as a way of thinking about how our ideas form and change. His games and writing can be found at www.videogamesoftheoppressed.wordpress.com.

DOMINIK JOHANN is a doe-eyed designer and illustrator who started out making *Counter-Strike* spray logos at the age of 12, worked in advertising,

Notes on Contributors

and turned to video games in 2012. He is currently studying at the Hamburg University of Applied Sciences and working on small projects with friends. He likes to make happy things to make happy people.

SOHA KAREEM is a digital games activist and writer stationed in Toronto, Canada. Her work focuses on identity politics, race, and sexuality. Her latest work can be found via her Twitter @sokareemie.

MERRITT KOPAS is the author of over two dozen digital games, including *Consensual Torture Simulator*, *HUGPUNX*, and *LIM*. In 2014, she was named one of *Polygon's* 50 Admirable People in Gaming. She is from southern Ontario and the Pacific Northwest and currently lives in Toronto with her cat Ramona. She's been using Twine since she started making videogames in 2012.

WINTER LAKE respects art's utility for helping people explore new ideas and remain emotionally grounded in their daily lives. She likes to make stories, criticism, comics, movies, and video games. She lives on West Coast, USA.

JEREMY LONIEN is a cis white dude who was diagnosed with clinical depression and social anxiety disorder several years ago. In 2012 he was inspired by Anna Anthropy's *Rise of the Videogame Zinesters* to make his first game, *The Message*. He is currently studying at the Cologne Game Lab.

CHRISTINE LOVE writes games with too many words in them about women and queerness and technology. Please, let's work hard together to make the world a cuter place!

RILEY MACLEOD is a freelance writer and editor based in Brooklyn, New York. He is the former editor at Topside Press, with whom he won the 2012 Lambda Literary Award in Transgender Fiction for his work on The Collection: Short Fiction from the Transgender Vanguard. His writing on games has appeared at *The Border House* and *The Anarcho-Geek Review*, and he spoke at the 2013 Different Games conference about queering game mechanics with designer Naomi Clark. Despite how good he is at semicolons, he has yet to successfully make a video game, but he's working on it.

AVERY ALDER MCDALDNO is a queer ghost who writes tabletop games. She's most proud of *Dream Askew* and *The Quiet Year*. She also coordinates Game Chef, an annual, global game design competition. She lives in Vancouver, and while it's dreary there right now, she knows it'll be gorgeous again come summer.

TOM MCHENRY is a Chicago-based cartoonist, game developer, and newspaper publisher. In addition to his strange sketchbook comic, *NONCANON*, he's best known for creating *RADICAL BOY* and *FAIL FASTER FOREVER*, a 500-page graphic novel drawn and printed in three months. *HORSE MASTER: THE GAME OF HORSE MASTERY* is his first game.

LYDIA NEON (Autumn Nicole Bradley) is a mercurial mixture of equal parts speculative fiction author, game creator, and biologist. An incorrigible polymath, her educational talks on transgender issues blend theory with practical advice on rethinking our ideas of gender on campus and in the workplace, and her spoken word performances swing lyrical sledgehammers to crack shells of ossified ignorance. Her Patreon-supported serial novel *Trash Romance* is available at http://trashmance.com. She dreams in digital, and lives in neon.

JEREMY PENNER is the founder of Glorious Trainwrecks, an inclusive community for creators of unusual videogames. He has been making videogames since he was a child, and is the author of at least 70 terrible games, including *The Ballad of Sad Ghost* and *Sonic the Hedgehog's Orphan Genocide*. He lives in Ottawa, Canada, with his girlfriend, his son, a budgie, some gerbils, and a plethora of fish. He has never voluntarily tried peanut butter.

TONI PIZZA is an indie game designer, educator, and community organizer employed (more or less) by chaos. Interested in the intersections of games, play, community, and representation, she's helped organize IndieCade East, the Different Games Conference, and Lost Levels. When not running around conferences, she makes heartbreakingly fun games about friendship & death pacts, depression & therapy with Secret Crush Corporation. She's currently working on writing a more exciting bio.

LANA POLANSKY is a Montreal-based writer, game critic, designer, curator, and professional scowler.

MADDOX PRATT lives in the Pacific Northwest where they make theatre, various forms of visual art, and poetry. Much of their work involves text, whether in Twine, letterpress print work, or book arts. More of their work can be found at maddoxpratt.com.

my name is EVA PROBLEMS and i'm a dragon dyke from slime dimension. i blog a lot under the url ohnoproblems and sometimes make queer games like this one here. i wrote the original *SABBAT* in january of 2013 primarily because i saw that twine could be a tool for writing Weird Sex Stuff and the general scene of the kinds of stuff i was into was so disastrously bad and full of awful messages that it hurt. so i wrote it in large part to stop being a victim of my own sexuality and to make something i'd be proud to be Into. i think i succeeded beyond my initial expectations mainly because somewhere in the process i tapped into a huge vein of unconscious and unexamined trans feel-

Notes on Contributors

ings. *SABBAT* helped me dredge them up to the surface and shape them into something articulate. i wouldn't be the gay lady i am today without it. enjoy.

ZOE QUINN is an independent game developer, biohacker, fire performer, and future skeleton. She has 99 problems and being a decaying organism aware of its own mortality in a society run by money that she can't escape from is one.

BRYAN REID lives in Normal, Illinois. They're working on their master's in Creative Writing at Illinois State University, focusing on how games and poetry can intersect to create liberatory spaces for community dialogue. Their work has appeared or is forthcoming in *Festival Writer* and *DIAGRAM*.

ALEX ROBERTS makes games, writes about them, and yells about them on a podcast. Find her games, writing, and yelling at alexroberts.neocities.org.

ROKASHI is a graduate from Humber College's Journalism: Print & Broadcast program and has written for publications like *Polygon* and *Postmedia*. His game, *I'm Fine*, has received acclaim and brought players to tears with its use of storytelling. He lives in Toronto and enjoys learning new things and teaching others to make games of their own.

ELIZABETH SAMPAT is a former photographer, current (hobbyist) indie game designer, and East Coast girl now living in California. Her day job is designing mobile games at a company called Storm8. She likes transmedia, storytelling, and creator-owned games and art, and she loves when the three all meet up together. She is kind of a feminist. And definitely trouble.

EMILY SHORT is the author of over two dozen works of interactive fiction, including *Galatea* and *First Draft of the Revolution*. She has a special interest in modelling character interactions and dialogue, and in any approach —technological or narrative—that allows more games about human relationships and human feelings.

MIRA SIMON is a biracial, bisexual programmer from the Midwest. She reads a lot, but mostly on screens. She's an optimist, and she tries.

SLOANE is a cartoonist, illustrator, and writer based out of Portland, OR.

DEIRDRA "SQUINKY" KIAI is a writer, programmer, musician, and visual artist who creates videogame-like artifacts about gender identity, social awkwardness, and miscellaneous silliness. They are currently completing an MFA in Digital Arts and New Media at UC Santa Cruz.

KAYLA UNKNOWN is a writer by trade and occasional dabbler in game design.

Notes on Contributors

she lives in southern california with ten or so stuffed fish and every intention of owning a snake. her work generally includes queer themes and odd subject matter, and more of it can be found on her writing blog at http://gorgeousfalsehood.tumblr.com or on the site for her serial novel, which can be found at www.mysteriesofquest.com.

OLIVIA VITOLO lives in Chicago. She is a glorious lady who spends her time divided between entertaining/feeding two partners and a cat, playing video games, and getting the ever-loving hell beaten out of her. She cares about gender, robots, art, sex, and context. *Negotiation* is her first game.

AUSTIN WALKER is a doctoral candidate at the University of Western Ontario, where he studies the contemporary relationship between play, labor, and culture as they intersect in work places and play spaces. His writing touches on a wide range of topics including live-streaming, representation, modding, and power fantasies. You can follow him on Twitter @austin_walker and at ClockworkWorlds.com, and read his bimonthly column at PasteMagazine.com/Games.

THANKS

This book represents the collective effort of hundreds of people, and it feels like a pretty big injustice just to have the one name on the cover. It's not enough, but I'd like to thank a few of those people here.

First, all of the authors and readers who contributed to this book. It strikes me that several readings end with the readers thanking the original authors, and that appreciation and care was echoed in everyone's participation in this project. You all give me hope for the kinds of cultures of play I want to help bring into the world. Jeanne Thornton at Instar Books for her tireless work and for taking a chance on a first-time editor who famously disdains capital letters. Chris Klimas, for developing Twine in the first place and keeping it free and accessible. Leon Arnott, for making Twine what it is today. And, of course, every other developer who's worked on Twine since its release. You all have enabled the creation of such beautiful things, and your generosity with your time and effort is incredibly inspiring. Cat Fitzpatrick, Riley MacLeod, and Tom Léger for welcoming an awkward game designer into literary spaces. Tobi and Jetta, for love and support. My sister Nic, for listening to me talk about the project at least once a day. P, for being in my life when I needed you. Naomi, for hot toddies and listening and having been here before. Leigh, for making this possible—all of it. Aevee, Rory, Phillis, and Mia, for their constant encouragement. Henry and Jennie, for being surrowgate parents to me and an entire community of artists and designers in Toronto. Anna, for Encyclopedia Fuckme and everything else. Michael DeForge, for his beautiful cover design and equally beautiful late-night renditions of *Les Miserables* songs. Darius, for reminding me that small things matter. Winter, for the page-length note I keep taped up next to my desk. You were right. Rob Remakes, for the title and wisdom. And Ramona, for keeping me company.

ABOUT INSTAR BOOKS

INSTAR BOOKS publishes literature in electronic form, embracing contentious new models, welcoming the creative chaos of a destabilized industry. In addition to ebooks, we are intrigued by the possibilities of texts as social destinations, as performance, and also as digital sculptures, or "seeds." In fact, we want to try every goddamn thing.

We do not believe that genre distinctions are meaningful. Novelists and poets do not want to work for massive media conglomerates or make more bricks for giant corporate hell-castles. Readers do not want their literature mediated by marketing executives trying to build inoffensive global brands. We offer an alternative, unconvinced that readers and writers must only choose between old media incompetence or new technology relentlessness in order to consume and produce great work.

Our current and forthcoming titles include:

- *The Unsteady Planet* by Jennifer Hanks & Julie Herndon
- *We Publish the Darkness* (fiction anthology, forthcoming 2016)
- *Shifting* by Miracle Jones (December 2015)
- *Everyword: The Book* by Allison Parrish (June 2015)
- *Hotwriting v.0* by Todd Anderson (May 2015)
- *The Thingbody* by Clare Louise Harmon
- *Sharing* by Miracle Jones
- *The Black Emerald* by Jeanne Thornton

For more information, or to place an order, please visit www.instarbooks.com.